MAINE IN THE WORLD

T0149592

MAINE IN THE WORLD

Stories of Some of Those from Here Who Went Away

Neil Rolde

Tilbury House  Publishers
Gardiner, Maine

Tilbury House, Publishers
103 Brunswick Avenue
Gardiner, Maine 04345
800-582-1899 • www.tilburyhouse.com

First paperback edition: October 2009
10 9 8 7 6 5 4 3 2 1

Library of Congress Cataloging-in-Publication Data
Rolde, Neil, 1931-
  Maine in the world : stories of some of those from here who went away /
Neil Rolde. -- 1st pbk. ed.
     p. cm.
  Includes bibliographical references and index.
  ISBN 978-0-88448-320-5 (pbk. : alk. paper)
  1. Maine--History--Anecdotes. 2. Maine--Biography. 3. Voyages and
travels--History--Anecdotes. 4. Travelers--Biography. 5. Adventure and
adventurers--Biography. I. Title.
  F19.6.R65 2009
  974.1--dc22
                                        2009014309

Jacket designed by Geraldine Millham, Westport, Massachusetts
Copydited by Genie Dailey, Fine Points Editorial Services, Jefferson, Maine
Printed and bound by Versa Press, East Peoria, Illinois

To the memory of my best friend, my father, the son of immigrants,
born in Bangor in November 1900.
His parents took him to Away when he was only two years old,
but his love of the outdoors, especially fishing,
brought him back to Maine time and time again.
The L. Robert Rolde Building at the Fields Pond Nature Center
of the Maine Audubon Society in Holden is a memorial to him,
close to his birthplace.

CONTENTS

Acknowledgments   *viii*

Introduction   *ix*

1   Gluskabe   *1*

2   The Five Kidnapped Indians   *13*

3   Sir William Phips   *29*

4   The Waldos   *47*

5   Commodore Edward Preble   *63*

6   Longfellow   *81*

7   Dorothea Dix   *99*

8   Artemus Ward   *115*

9   Oregon   *133*

10   Islands Way Out in the Pacific   *145*

11   Nathan Clifford, Democrat, and
James S. Pike, Republican   *159*

12   Madame Nordica   *181*

13   The *Saturday Evening Post*   *195*

14   Edna St. Vincent Millay   *213*

15   John Frank Stevens   *229*

16   Sangerville   *243*

17   John Ford   *261*

18   The Radicals   *275*

19   Samantha Smith   *293*

20   Sister Priscille Roy and Maine's Foreign Ties   *307*

Afterword   *320*

Annotated Bibliography   *322*

Index   *329*

ACKNOWLEDGMENTS

As always, leading the list are Jennifer Bunting, Tilbury House's incomparable editor and publisher, and Earle G. Shettleworth, Jr., "Mr. Maine History," the director of the Maine Historic Preservation Commission.

Nick Noyes at the Maine Historical Society Library was especially helpful in finding material there for me; lending assistance there, too, were Bill Barry and Dani Fazio. Elizabeth Trautman at the Maine Historical Preservation Commission was also helpful in providing photographic materials, as were Hannah Contino at the Coos Historical and Marine Museum in Coos Bay, Oregon, Marissa Harvey at the Niagara Parks Commission, E. Marilyn Sotialis at the Calais Free Library, and a number of persons whose names I didn't catch at the University of Maine's Folger Library Special Collections.

This latter institution held Reverend Benjamin Galen Snow's diary, and it was his missionary work on the Micronesian island of Kosrae that gave me the idea for this book. In that regard, I would like to thank Dr. Diane Ragone, senior scientist at the National Tropical Botanical Garden of Kalaheo, Island of Kauai, Hawaii, who organized our visit to that far-off place.

My thanks to Genie Daily for her copyediting, and to Geraldine Millham, who designed the cover.

On a personal family note, I need to thank my ever-encouring wife Carla for keeping my nose to the writing grindstone, and my "technical staff"—my sons-in-law Jeff Wilford and Craig Annis—who rescue me on an all-too-regular basis from the many perils of using a computer.

Finally, thanks to the whole hard-working gang at Tilbury House and, at Jennifer's suggestion, let me put in a plug for the Library of Congress's photography archives, a wonderful resource.

INTRODUCTION

Who in Maine has ever heard of the tiny Pacific island territory of Kosrae in Micronesia? Possibly a few geographers and coral reef enthusiasts. How many Mainers have literally set foot on Kosrae? If any in recent years, most likely they were adventurous divers, drawn to its crystal-clear waters. Nevertheless, in 2005 I spent an entire week at this obscure, far-off place, snorkeling and nature-watching with a group of ecologists from the Hawaii-based National Tropical Botanical Garden. During my trip there, I learned of historical connections, strange as it might seem, between Kosrae and the State of Maine.

The Sleeping Lady Awakens is the title of a volume, lovingly written for the Kosrae State Government's Tourist Division by a man named Harvey Gordon Segal, which serves as a guidebook for those venturesome enough to visit such a remote archipelago.[1] You are not on Kosrae very long before you physically see "the Sleeping Lady." She is Kosrae's "Old Man of the Mountain," but obviously of the opposite sex, a rock formation along a ridge that approximates (with a dose of imagination) a human form. With something of a leer, if the local person alerting you to *her* silhouette is a male, your guide will point out to you a dormant female lying on her back in profile, head, face, feet—and especially, upthrust breasts—in all the right anatomical locations. Expect to be shown the sight more than once; the sense of naughty humor usually involved reminds me somehow of my New England upbringing where tittering fun of this ilk exuded a touch of harmless rebellion against an all-pervasive Puritanism.

Here, then, is a preview of a part Maine played in Kosrae's past, begun through the exertions of a Congregationalist minister, the Reverend Benjamin Galen Snow, born in Orrington, raised in Brewer, and educated at our Bangor Theological Seminary. He was the first Protestant (and Calvinist) missionary sent to Kosrae, where he arrived in 1852. So well did he do his job of converting the hitherto-pagan natives that Kosrae is currently described as the most thoroughly religious island in the whole of the Pacific.

Learning about this dedicated Mainer, who did not return to his own native state until twenty-five years had passed—and then only to die—set me thinking about all the Down East citizens who left home and made careers elsewhere. The germ of a creative idea—a book title, *Maine in the World,* if nothing else—was born of my chance, utterly unexpected encounter with the late Reverend Doctor Snow. Moreover, it was compounded when I read on in Segal's tome and found another Maine man who had appeared in Kosrae's history but cut a far different figure. Harry Skillin, of a family still prominent (and respectable) in the Portland area, was by every account a rapscallion sailor who deserted his ship, fathered numerous illegitimate island children via various mothers, and, if legends about him are to be believed, was even a pirate, and a bloodthirsty one at that. Descendants bearing his surname still live on Kosrae, and several of these Micronesian kinfolk have actually traveled to a family reunion in Portland.

We will look into Harry Skillin abroad in much more detail later on, just as we will also examine Benjamin Snow's Micronesian career.

For good or ill, Maine people like these two men (and not a few women) went into the world, and because of them, our small state in the northeastern corner of the United States acquired a cosmopolitan tinge not often emphasized when we advertise our Down East homeyness.

There *is* a chronology and it begins well before there even was a Maine. Like Topsy, we "just growed" (to quote an immortal classic, *Uncle Tom's Cabin,* penned in Maine, incidentally), and along the way, those who inhabited our land, whether Paleo Indians, West Country of England adventurers, Puritans from Massachusetts, French Acadian peasants in the north, Germans, Finns, Slovaks, Swedes, Lebanese, etc., etc., were—and still are—in the process of "becoming" Mainers. Of course, some head for other places, too, taking their talents with them, and bits of Maine as well, to do amazing and interesting, if not always decorous (I'm thinking of Harry Skillin), deeds.

Some of the subjects of these stories, like Edna St. Vincent Millay or Henry Wadsworth Longfellow or Hollywood director John Ford, you will know by the mere mention of their names. Others are as obscure as Harry Skillin. Their experiences are as varied as their skills. They are poets and warriors, clever business people, adventurers, and humanitarians, an entertainer or two, a prize-winning engineer, politicians, and even a mythic hero through whom, in their tales about him, our earliest inhabitants, the Abenaki tribes, brought an entire worldview and culture into explained existence, the first in this state of ours.

Let us begin, then, with Gluskabe, the Abenaki hero-god (using the Penobscot pronunciation that sounds the *e* at the end). We can say he was from what is now Maine, but he was a prodigious traveler.

1. Harvey Gordon Segal, *The Sleeping Lady Awakens*. Kosrae State, Eastern Carolines, Federated States of Micronesia: Kosrae Print Shop, 1989.

Gluskabe turns a man into a cedar tree. From an etching on birchback by Tomah Joseph, reproduced in Charles G. Leland's Algonquin Legends of New England. *Boston: Houghton Mifflin, 1884.*

GLUSKABE

Maine, before it was the Maine we know today, had various iterations. The landmass encompassed by the state's present boundaries was always someplace. If the tectonic theorists are correct, "Down East" once stood five degrees from the equator. Their scenario then has us whirled over eons to a spot in Europe that broke off and drifted west, as the Atlantic, growing ever more oceanic, inched away from the Old World. Five hundred million years in the future, allegedly, Maine will end up where Minnesota is now.

Historically, when all of this geological bustle slowed enough to resemble a standstill, Maine was basically at its current location—yet a land we would hardly recognize, with volcanoes flaring away, stretched much farther out to sea, and periodically (that is, for thousands of years) buried a mile deep in ice. Even when the earth underneath emerged, it was tundra—low, bushy, marshy growth—no pines, no firs, and no maples to turn a gorgeous scarlet or flaming orange.

Probably around 12,000 years ago, the first humans arrived on our soil. Western-trained scientists call them Paleo Indians—*paleo* taken from the Greek word for "old." As for these *old Indians,* they had their own names for themselves—names quite often translated into English simply as "The People."

Ninnuock, with the exact same meaning, was one designation for the collective tribes formed in the northeast section bordering the Atlantic coast. Otherwise, they were also *Abenaki,* "People of the Dawn," because their homeland was the first area in North America touched by the rising sun.

They had place names, too—mostly descriptive, like "the rocks widen and open out," transliterated into *Penobscot* by the English after hearing the native *bahahwehbzek,* or, another example, "eel weir place," i.e., *Kenduskeag,* a rivulet near Bangor—and these constituted the first geography, albeit unwritten, bestowed upon Maine. Also, they forged a cosmogony—an explanation of the origins of their world—and as most peoples on this planet do, surrounded their genesis stories with religious awe.

In a sense, these Paleo Indians were monotheists. Or at least their descendants attribute the ultimate Intelligent Design of the Universe to an unnamed "Creator" or "Great Spirit" who had formulated the basic material setting for their existence. This Creator had helpers endowed with extraordinary powers, and Gluskabe, assigned to Down East, is the most noted hero-god of the tribes that still inhabit Maine. Each of them—the Penobscots, the Passamaquoddy, the Maliseets, and the Micmacs—has a different way of spelling his name (Glooscap, Koluskap, etc.), but the larger-than-life personage remains the same.

Can we call him a Mainer? Some might quibble, wanting to assign Gluskabe to the Maritime Provinces of Canada, where he is also celebrated. A counter argument might be offered via the oft-told tale that Gluskabe is permanently ensconced on Katahdin, holed up in a secret cave where he is busily manufacturing arrowheads for use in ultimately driving all white invaders from Maine (and presumably the Maritimes).

The Penobscot writer Joseph Nicolar, a pioneer who in 1893 published the first history ever of a Maine tribe, presents us with a Native's singular point of view of Gluskabe, influenced perhaps by biblical overtones derived from Catholic missionaries who had long before converted his people. Nicolar called Gluskabe "The Man from Nothing...the first person who came upon the earth," and he described this Penobscot Adam in the following poetic manner:

"When he [Gluskabe] opened his eyes, he was lying on his back in the dust.... His head was toward the rising sun and his feet toward the setting of the sun.... The right hand pointing to the north and his left hand to the south...he saw the land, the sea, the mountains, lakes, rivers and the motions of the waters.... In the dust, his flesh was without feeling.... A beautiful brightness came nearer and nearer...and a feeling came into his flesh, he felt the warmth of the approaching brightness.... Out of the brightness came the Great Spirit.... Strength came to Gluskabe.... 'Let us make man in our own image,' said the Great Spirit."[1]

Thus, we have Gluskabe in a human form—but more accurately, superhuman. A description of him as he prepares to go and chastise Oglabamu, the giant frog who sucked up all the fresh water in the

Northeast, is that of a colossal Indian warrior. Gluskabe has made himself twelve feet tall, and is decorated for combat, his body painted "red as blood," two huge clam shells hanging from his earlobes as earrings, a hundred black eagle feathers and a hundred white eagle feathers in his scalp lock, and his eyes ringed by yellow circles. He has fashioned a single knife out of a mountain of flint and he goes forth amid "thunder, lightning, and eagles soaring above him."

Tales of Gluskabe's exploits are variously—and not always consistently—embellished. They were told around many campfires and transmitted orally by people who had not yet perfected any writings except simple pictographs. For example, the most often cited weapon employed against that greedy, power-mad amphibian who had dried up the local lakes and rivers was a stone ax of considerable proportions, rather than an immense knife. A single whack with this ax broke Oglabamu's spine. Out gushed all of the liquid the frog had ingested—and the species also thereby acquired its perennial broken-back look. Furthermore, Gluskabe did to Oglabamu what he did to all naughty animals. He stroked and stroked the body until the creature was reduced to its present size.

So Oglabamu was soon just hopping about at Gluskabe's feet—and the land was running wet with rivers and shiny with lakes. At least one telling of the tale specifically mentions the Penobscot River forming from the frog's regurgitation.

Now, to backtrack a bit, we have to return to the arrival of Gluskabe on the Great Spirit's mission for him. Where did he, so to speak, alight? In Charles G. Leland's *The Algonquin Legends of New England* (1884), the following passage from a contemporary Abenaki spokesperson was cited:

> Glooskap [*sic*] came first of all into this
> Country, into Nova Scotia, Maine, Canada, into
> The land of the Wabanaki, next to sunrise.
> There were no Indians here then (only
> Wild Indians very far to the west.[2]

This statement, which is a prelude to the information that Gluskabe *created* the Northeast Indians, contains the germs of an academic dilemma. Until fairly recently, a truism of anthropology was that all North and South American Indians were descendants of Asians who migrated to Alaska over a temporary land bridge during a prolonged ice age. However, a new thesis has been proposed, drawing howls of protest from researchers with a vested interest in the previous conventional wisdom. *Newsweek* magazine in April 1999 ran a cover story challenging this Siberian–Alaskan orthodoxy by claiming new discoveries showed eastern American Indians more closely related to Europeans than to Asiatics and, moreover, that their culture exhibited traits related to early Caucasian life in France and Spain. In September 2007, *Smithsonian Magazine* included an article about Dennis Stanford, the head of archaeology at the National Museum of Natural History, postulating how the Clovis culture, hitherto ascribed to the Bering Sea crossing, really occurred "from a group that, roughly 18,000 years ago, left the [European] continent by boat to hunt along the ice shelf in the North Atlantic and then landed on the East Coast of North America"[3] before making their way west. "Speculative sensationalism"[4] was an immediate outcry from an anthropologist at the University of New Mexico, in which state the Clovis site is located.

On the other hand, if you speak to certain Native American intellectuals or scholars of their own beliefs, they will say "nonsense" to both scientific suppositions. A Native American "creationist" in Maine is the Penobscot elder Arnie Neptune, who believes his people began right where they are now, in the land to which Gluskabe was sent by the Creator to form them. How were The People born? Very simple. Gluskabe shot arrows into the trunks of ash trees and "out stepped men and women. They were strong and graceful people with light brown skin and shining black hair."

The above partial quote is taken from a description of a 1999 film shown at the Abbe Museum in Bar Harbor, Maine. Its title, *Koluscap and His People,* adds another complicating feature to the task of unraveling Indian origins geographically, since "Koluscap" is the Micmac name for the Algonquin hero-god we are discussing. The Eden that Koluscap naturally would be populating lay, in their eyes, in Micmacland, and except for a swath of Aroostook County, Maine, all Micmac territory was and still is in Canada. Of course, in these North American equivalents of biblical times, there was no

Maine, no Nova Scotia, no New Brunswick, etc.

Still, we find versions of the Gluskabe story that have him "swimming across from Nova Scotia to Maine" and "becoming lonely after many years of wandering in Maine" or "living at the mouth of the Oolostook at Menogwes" (St. John, New Brunswick) or in a "sea cave on the coast of Maine," or creating "Oktomkomkuk" (Newfoundland) and being at "Samgactihawk" (Saco) on the Saco River in Maine and near "Oonahgemessukweegeet" (around North Conway, New Hampshire) and at "Blomidon" on the Bay of Fundy. All this is the former wasteland that, through his efforts, becomes populated with humans who divide themselves into clans and tribes, are provisioned by him with animals and plants to feed everyone, and settle in a natural environment whose secrets he helps The People unlock. Some stories even depict Gluskabe going to the Ice Country, which we would have once called the land of the Eskimo, until we learned that these denizens of the frozen north now call themselves Inuit, "The People." Eskimo, by the way, is an insulting term—literally "cannibal"—of Algonquin derivation, foisted upon the igloo builders by their enemies.

Consequently, linguistically we learn that the Northeast Maritime Native American tribes had contacts beyond their immediate region in the dim prehistory of olden times. Did Gluskabe go south, too? Maybe under another name. The Wampanoags, another Algonquin people on Cape Cod and the islands, have a similar Gluskabe figure—only he is known as Moshup.

You will occasionally hear the Abenaki Gluskabe referred to as "Gluskabe the Liar." In effect, we find we are dealing with a creation story that is not as simple and straightforward as the seven days and Adam and Eve.

Here in North America we have Cain and Abel preceding, or at least accompanying, the fleshing out of Eden. Malsum is the former—Gluskabe's twin brother—the evil sibling. He doesn't last long, wherever he enters the narrative, but he is initially pictured as wantonly introducing wickedness and difficulty into the world, "anything to inconvenience the race of men," while Gluskabe happily provides that same human race with everything needed to give them comfort and the ability to live.

So why is Gluskabe the Good sometimes called Gluskabe the Liar?

Well, maybe *fib* is a better word to use here. For it is a fib that, in the end, actually saves us, the world, from the wiles of Malsum and the havoc he would wreak upon our planet.

One day, this nasty creature casually inquired of his brother, "Oh, mighty Gluskabe, what would it take to kill you?"

Being no fool, Gluskabe decided not to reveal any secret vulnerabilities he might really have. Instead, he thought quickly, cunningly, and replied, "There is only one way—if I'm hit on the head with a cattails."

Soon afterward, while Gluskabe was asleep at night, Malsum crept toward him holding a torn-off swamp plant he had acquired. With all his might, he brought the cattails down on Gluskabe's skull.

All this did was awaken the good brother. Again, nobody's fool, he had kept his stone ax with him in bed. A single smash was all he needed to kill Malsum—and presumably, after doing so, he just went back to sleep.

In any event, in the days and decades and centuries and millennia that followed, he carried on doing his good works, of which many tales are told.

Bits of Native American humor sometimes appear in these sagas. Our original inhabitants are too often pictured as grave, stiff, stone-faced—but they loved to laugh. Right from the start, in one of the Abenaki creation myths they told, there is reason to smile. Gluskabe, accompanied by two canine companions, a white wolf and a black wolf, is in the process of manufacturing human beings. There is a flash of blinding light. The wolves and other watching animals cover their eyes. All are afraid.

But when they next looked up, they all burst into laughter.

They saw human beings scattering north, south, east, and west.

"Look!" a bear shouted, "they walk on two feet!"

A wolf shouted: "Glooskap, you have a great sense of humor!"[5]

While Gluskabe's magic powers were generally extolled again and again—had there been tall buildings in those days, he could have leapt them in a single bound, and he had no need to outrun a speeding bullet; if it hit him, it would just bounce off—still, he did suffer from weaknesses. He could dispatch the giant sorcerer Win-pe with a mere tap from the butt of his bow, and he could conquer the Kewawkqui and the

Medeolin and the Great White Bear, but in Wasis, he more than met his match. Wasis, it turns out, was a baby. Gluskabe discovered the little tyke sitting and sucking on a piece of maple sugar. He beckoned, smiling and bidding the infant to crawl to his arms. However, the baby merely sat, ignoring the friendly superman. Then Gluskabe harshly ordered the child to come. Once more, no response. The hero-god tried magical tricks to force the baby to obey. Instead, he was greeted with cries and wails, but not even a budge. Wasis kept sucking his sugar until Gluskabe at last gave up all entreaties and went away defeated. "Goo-goo" was Wasis's final comment on the event.

In his human qualities, Gluskabe would sometimes be described as *weary*, even *bored*, with his task of helping the mortals he'd been set amongst. When he wanted to be off by himself, he'd hole up in a cave on the Maine coast. Soon, though, he'd be back in action.

For example, in the Maritimes' Bay of Fundy, he once came upon a group of Indians fearful of the Ice Giants who had descended from the Arctic, and he took care of this problem by fashioning a wooden ball from a tree bough, which magically turned into a hideous skull when the Ice Giants tried to play with it, thus scaring them away. Gluskabe was also seen as fond of lounging in the sand dunes and watching his Indian friends canoeing, admiring their skills as paddlers while they went far out to sea.

But restless soon again, he is pictured—with his wolves—going off to find a log house in the wilderness that had "a fire in the fireplace and a good meal on the table," a hideaway to which "there was no map."[6]

These stories weave into their narratives the accomplishments—birchbark canoes, wigwams, bows and arrows, log houses—perfected by The People themselves, but accredited to Gluskabe. Tobacco smoking was one more problematical invention they called his. Many years before cigarette advertising, they had Gluskabe telling the tribes: "Burn it and inhale the smoke and it will bring freshness to the mind and your heart will be contented while the smoke of it be in you." Today, the weed's sacredness is only sanctioned as "smudge" in ceremonies where a spiritual blessing is invoked.

Similarly, as the world modernized around them, the Abenakis' hero-god kept up with the times. The coming of strangers—the English and the French—into the lives of The People was reflected in Gluskabe's subsequent adventures. It is here that, in the thematic structure of this book—going out from Maine into the greater world—we can specifically fit Gluskabe. Previously, to be sure, he was traveling around an unmarked countryside in which Maine played a major, if not central, undelineated part. But as the sixteenth, seventeenth, and eighteenth centuries descended upon the original inhabitants of this coast and they absorbed the impact of contact, Gluskabe was described as deliberately voyaging eastward across the Atlantic, actually sailing on different journeys to England and to France.

Early on, it became evident to the Abenakis that the English were their most dangerous adversaries. Land settlement patterns were the tip-off. When the Natives "sold" their lands to the Anglo-Saxons, they—in their own minds—were only selling certain *rights,* like hunting and fishing or other temporary uses. Once the English fenced these acres, declared "this is mine," and punished trespassing, trouble arose. That it took until 1676, and King Philip's War, to roil New England in battle was perhaps a surprise, but the intensity and length (100 years) of the ensuing conflict was in no way diminished.

Around the campfires, then, the Gluskabe stories they related tried to compensate for the sense of victimhood The People felt. They had their hero-god show his face in the homeland of the *Yenghies.*

What's more, the timing was such that the Abenaki legends could proudly declare: *The white man did not DISCOVER America. Gluskabe discovered ENGLAND and told THEM about America.* Since that time, white men have come to America. But unlike Gluskabe, who returned home, the white man came to stay.

A bittersweet punch back, one might say, with a less than happy ending. Other details of Gluskabe's trip to Britain include rowing up the Thames in his stone canoe, drawing crowds of Londoners who gawk in awe, and the Indian's flat refusal to accept a large ship in a swap for his handmade craft.

On this round-trip voyage, Gluskabe was accompanied by "Grandmother," or Woodchuck, an enigmatic figure who logically seems to have had to antedate Gluskabe on earth and represents a female element in the Abenaki pantheon of semi-divines. She did not come from anybody's rib but, it was said, out of dew on rocks when they were heated by the sun. In another overseas story, she is introduced as

Gluskabe's mother. No foolish consistency here. The mother of both Malsum and Gluskabe was alleged to have died in childbirth once the evil Malsum insisted on exiting through her side rather than taking a vaginal route like his good brother.

At any rate, Grandmother Woodchuck is continually in evidence during Gluskabe's next transatlantic venture. Like so many Americans, Gluskabe decided he had to visit Paris, France. In the French and Indian Wars that convulsed the New World, the Indians always had Gallic allies. Their preference for the French over the English rested on several factors: 1) the French weren't as land-grabbing; 2) French Jesuit missionaries had won the confidence of the Indians and their souls for Catholicism; and 3) there were nowhere near as many French immigrants and they did not sneer at intermarrying.

Nonetheless, the French were still white men, and lingering distrust was never far from the surface, as Gluskabe's adventures in Paris were to reveal.

This time, Gluskabe and Grandmother sailed not in a stone canoe but on an island turned into a ship. It was heavily forested and populated by numerous squirrels who served as crew members.

A misunderstanding of sorts in Paris may have started all the problems that ensued. Having sailed up the Seine to the French capital, Gluskabe anchored his ship in the river close to the castle of the king of France. The next morning, seeing a large number of big trees suddenly nearby, the monarch gave orders for them to be felled and cut into lumber.

Accordingly, the royal army sent its troops forth and the soldiers began chopping away—in the process killing a number of the scampering squirrels. Gluskabe was furious and threatened to kill the soldiers but Grandmother said, "No, that wouldn't be polite," and instead had her grandson bundle the military personnel into boats, sending them back to tell the king, "Gluskabe and Grandmother are coming to see you."

The French king, too, was in a rage, since the soldiers had disobeyed him and stopped logging those trees.

"Who are you?" he demanded of Gluskabe and Grandmother when they came before him. "How dare you hinder my soldiers in their duty?"

"I am Gluskabe," announced the Abenaki hero-god. "This is my grandmother and the island is my boat, not a forest to be leveled."

"Shoot him!" the king ordered his men. They fired their rifles, but the bullets just bounced off Gluskabe. He smiled and smoked his pipe.

"*Eh bien,*" cried the angry king. "All right, stuff the two of them into a cannon and shoot it off."

The soldiers grabbed the Indian and Woodchuck and shoved both into the cannon's barrel, along with a great deal of gunpowder. A lighted match was touched to the fire hole. A huge explosion resulted and the air was filled with smoke and flames.

Amazingly, Gluskabe emerged, helped Grandmother Woodchuck to her feet, and re-lit his pipe. Around them lay the bodies of a thousand French soldiers, struck down by the blast.

The pair of North Americans—call them Mainers, if you like— walked back to their island, rounded up their crew, and headed home.

It has to be said that they were disgusted by this treatment at the hands even of white men purported to be their friends.

Therefore, this tale is the prelude for Gluskabe's final disappearance. Whether to a hideout on Katahdin in Maine or to an unknown spot elsewhere, he has assumed the role of a messiah whose advent is longed for as the signal for a world turnaround.

Gluskabe's trips abroad complete the literary evolution of the Abenakis. Out of 12,000 years of forging a life in this northeast corner of the continent, they had documented through creative genius a journey of their own, carrying them in legend past the brink of the life-altering collision with a different, more technically advanced culture.

And this Indian–European interaction was just beginning.

1. Joseph Nicolar, *The Life and Traditions of the Red Man*. Bangor, ME: C. H. Glass and Company, Printers, 1893—as presented in Peter Anastas, *Glooskap's Children: Encounters with the Penobscot Indians of Maine*. Boston: Beacon Press, 1973. Duke University Press issued a reprint edition of *The Life and Traditions of the Red Man* in 2007.

2. Charles G. Leland, *The Algonquin Legends of New England: Myths and Folklore of the Micmac, Passamaquoddy, and Penobscot Tribes*. Boston: Houghton Mifflin and Company, 1884, p. 17.

3. *Smithsonian Magazine*, September 2007, p. 40.

4. Ibid.

5. Howard Norman, *How Glooskap Outwits the Ice Giants and Other Tales of the Maritimes*. Boston: Little Brown, 1989.

6. Ibid.

A 1905 reenactment of the arrival in Maine of Captain George Waymouth and his crew from the ship Archangell, *in 1605.*
Collections of Maine Historical Society

2

THE FIVE KIDNAPPED INDIANS

Remember how Gluskabe liked to loll on the shores of the Bay of Fundy and watch his Indian friends handle their canoes on the open ocean? The three northeasternmost coastal tribes, the Micmacs, Maliseets, and Passamaquoddy, were intrepid seagoers. To this day, young Passamaquoddy will talk, as they did to me, about hunting marine mammals—porpoises and seals—and how they enjoy doing so like their ancestors did, with harpoons rather than high-powered rifles. In either case, they have to act clandestinely, since both in Canada and the United States the animals are protected.

Bones unearthed in local ancient middens reveal that sea mammals as large as whales were also taken by the Natives, as well as big fish the size of swordfish and full-grown sharks. These Down East folk were like-wise known to travel long distances and to raid other tribes farther south. They were the much-feared Tarratines who fell without warning on their fellow Abenakis and murderously ravaged summertime encampments and even more permanent inland villages.

Yet adept as they were offshore, nothing in their culture allowed them to build vessels large enough to traverse the Atlantic. Gluskabe's stone canoe or a squirrels-in-the-rigging floating island were works of imagination alone.

The Europeans, conversely, had the equipment and know-how to reach the New World by water and had been sailing across on an irreg-ular basis for several centuries, if not longer, before 1605.

When, in late May of that same year, a large vessel appeared under sail close to shore off midcoast Maine, chances are the Natives had seen something like it previously. By European standards, she wasn't a very big ship—probably a three-masted bark with a complement of no more than twenty-nine men—*Archangell*, under Captain George Waymouth, out of Plymouth, England. But the Indians who saw her, members of the Wawenoc subtribe, couldn't have known that.

In their dark Indian eyes, a certain trepidation must have surfaced.

The foreign is always initially disturbing. Yet there might simultaneously have been temporary relief in realizing the alien watercraft was not a host of dreaded Tarratine war canoes. Plus, the sophisticated among them had to grasp the fact that spacious sails, a high deck, and hairy white men meant *trade*—fascinating gew-gaws and useful tools for which they could exchange their furs.

The Maine site where Captain Waymouth finally anchored the *Archangell* on May 20, 1605 (or thereabouts), has been determined as just off Allen Island in a sheltered area marked on a present-day map as Georges Harbor, a short ride to and from Port Clyde at the tip of the St. George peninsula. Allen Island, entirely uninhabited, is now owned by Betsy Wyeth, wife of the late Andrew Wyeth, the world-famous painter. In the spring of 2005, Mr. Wyeth graciously allowed a visit to his private enclave by a group commemorating the 400th anniversary of Waymouth's arrival. They were led ashore by the lady Episcopal bishop of Maine for the purposes of speechmaking and laying a wreath in front of a stone cross marked WAYMOUTH 1605 erected a hundred years earlier. Another Wyeth donation to this three-day Waymouth birthday bash were illustrations to a symposium booklet of contemporary original papers about the 1605 event. These watercolors were the work, no less, of Andrew's illustrious father, N. C. Wyeth, and the equally talented Jamie Wyeth, Andrew's son.

Unlike many an anonymous transatlantic odyssey of the seventeenth century, the Waymouth adventure had its own scribe who left a play-by-play record of the proceedings. His name was James Rosier and he styled himself "a Gentleman." In *A True Relation of the most prosperous voyage made this present year 1605, by Captaine [sic] George Waymouth, in the Discovery of the land of Virginia*, a great deal of information is imparted or implied—political, historical, anthropological, environmental—but one looks in vain, if nautically minded, to learn the exact type and dimensions of the vessel that carried the Englishmen hither. We know only that the *Archangell* was big enough to carry a *pinnace* aboard, a small sailboat for exploring, later described as a "two-masted shallop"; but in pieces that could be assembled and dismantled.

A prologue to the *Relation*, not always printed, acknowledges Rosier's debt of gratitude to the sponsor of the expedition, who was Thomas Arundell, baron of Wardour. There is some mention that an

"Archduke and others" were involved; and thereby hangs a political-religious tale. The archduke was a Hapsburg and a devout Catholic; the original impulse behind sending Waymouth to the New World was to find a refuge for emigrating English Catholics. Although no longer ruthlessly persecuted as they had been by Queen Elizabeth, they understood that the new king, James I, crowned in 1603, was still overtly antipapist.

However, when Rosier goes on to write that "honorable gentlemen of good worth and quality" took up the idea of "transporting a colony," he is speaking about Protestant investors who had wrested command of the project from Lord Arundell. Two in particular are well known: Sir John Popham, chief justice of England, and Sir Ferdinando Gorges. They were both proponents of a concerted English effort to populate America with their Anglican Church of England co-believers. If, in his writing, Rosier shows a bit of paranoia about foreign spies trying to learn their purposes, this caution also revealed a need to keep one of their goals a hush-hush, top-level, highly classified secret.

So it was that only Captain Waymouth, Rosier, and first mate Thomas Cam knew that a major motive of this expedition was to shanghai a group of Indians back to England, where they could be interrogated and forced to help their captors ferret out appropriate intelligence essential for establishing Anglo-Saxon settlements.

Waymouth was no doubt chosen because he had been to the New World prior to 1605, when in 1602 he'd gone to search for the fabled Northwest Passage to the Orient. Dangerous ice floes off the Labrador coast had cut short his mission, but back home, he'd made a name for himself by publishing a book on navigation instruments called *The Jewell of Artes.*

Between 1602 and 1605, two other English ship captains also explored in the vicinity of Maine, and knowledge brought back by Bartholomew Gosnold and Martin Pring quite possibly had led to the route assigned for Waymouth's second voyage. Now he was not to go north to those frozen climes that had stymied him in 1602, but to a more temperate latitude.

Gosnold's voyage in 1602 also had originally been slated to find a path to China yet had ended up, as his logbook records, indisputably passing through a part of Maine—in the Cape Neddick section of the town of York. There, off a certain rock, he came upon a watercraft transporting eight Indians. Most notable about this incident is that the boat was of European design—"a Biscay shallop"—and some Natives were wearing articles of European clothing. The chief, for instance, had on "a waistcoat of black work, a pair of breeches, cloth stockings, shoes, hat and band" while others sported "pieces of Christian clothing" amid their deerskins and sealskins. One of these indigenes was able to use chalk to sketch an outline of the nearby coast and could name Placentia in Newfoundland and use a few "Christian words," perhaps French.

Gosnold's encounter in Cape Neddick may well have confirmed a suspicion in England that the French were making moves in North America, thereby increasing the need for Waymouth to go and bring back living sources of information. Thus, those Wawenoc who eventually gathered in the vicinity of Allen Island and made contact with *Archangell* and her crew hadn't the slightest inkling how some of them, albeit unwillingly, would soon be traveling overseas from Maine. Nor could anyone, English or Indian, predict that the effect of their removal to England might someday be expressed in the title of a 400th-anniversary essay: "When the Creation of America Began."[1]

Future repercussions were not in the minds of Captain Waymouth and his confidantes as they awaited the right moment to strike against the Wawenocs.

Archangell was almost two weeks at its anchor in Georges Harbor before this happened, and once it did, as if nothing untoward had occurred, Waymouth coolly hung around and actually traveled in the area with his captives hidden below deck.

At first, upon Waymouth's arrival, the Indians did not hurry to make contact with the intruders. The English merely tarried, going about their daily chores, both on board ship and on Allen Island. After exploring the latter, they dug a well and found clear water, and marveled at the incredible giant oak trees and the quality of the turpentine that oozed out of the firs. With swoops of a small net, they entrapped lobsters, so plentiful were the crustaceans that would become iconic to Maine; the use of nets for any kind of fishing was later to amaze the Indians, once they all became friendly. The first contact between the English sailors and the local inhabitants apparently transpired on May 30, when a canoe carrying three braves paddled out to the ship. It wasn't long before the two sides were meeting regularly, often aboard

Archangell, but even more commonly ashore—where the English, however, didn't always feel entirely safe.

Reflecting this sense of wariness, the Indians demanded that an English hostage remain with them if any tribal members spent the night aboard ship. The crewman invariably chosen was Owen Griffin, who had actually volunteered to stay behind in the New World, and he would appear in the morning to tell his shipmates about the strange and noisy "religious" ceremonies whose incessant drumming had kept him up most of the night.

The English had novelties to offer. There were culinary treats the Indians immediately liked, such as cooked pork, baked bread, and, most particularly, green peas, presumably derived from soaked dried peas. The English also had guns, whose firing frightened the Wawenocs. They showed them the use of a lodestone to magnetize a sword, and they had utensils the Indians already knew and appreciated, such as metal knives. There were also coveted items: decorative brooches and sugar and raisins. But one thing *not* appreciated was "firewater"—strong liquor—that the recipients tasted but refused to drink.

On the other side of the coin, the Natives impressed the Europeans with the quality of their home-manufactured bows, made out of witch hazel wood and birch, and their three-feathered arrows of ash, tipped by deer bone "made very sharp" and fanged like a harpoon. Their tobacco, too, demonstrated a superior expertise. Its quality was excellent, and an Indian pipe, made from the short claw of a lobster, could hold ten times as much as an English pipe. The Indians used the expression that they were "drinking tobacco."

Attempts were started to learn each other's languages. Rosier describes how he would point to things and write down the words he heard the Indians say, and that they continually would "of themselves fetch fishes and fruit bushes and stand by me to see me write their names."

Commerce began. On Saturday, June 1, Rosier reported, the English traded with twenty-eight tribal members, and for four to five shillings' worth of trade goods, they received "40 good beaver, otter, and sable furs." The Indians were quick to appreciate the concept of bargaining. They loved biscuits and traded goslings for them—two biscuits for four goslings—but not before they had countered, although in vain, with a bid of *four* biscuits for the quartet of baby geese.

One reason the English were being so chintzy was explained by Rosier: they were holding back on their trade commodities, he wrote, "to the end we might allow them still to frequent us."

Both sides were continuing to learn about each other. The English somehow discovered that these Wawenocs had politics of their own. They were one component—to put it in European terms—of an Abenaki empire or kingdom. The reigning monarch was called Bashebes, or this was his title, not his name. His headquarters was farther north, or at least the Indians pointed in that direction when they discussed him. Subsequent research shows the Bashebes's location to have been on the Penobscot River.

A rather puzzling incident is recorded next. Owen Griffin, the seaman left on shore, reported seeing 283 warriors armed with bows and arrows (which begs the question of how he could count so many so accurately, but the portent was disturbing), possibly signaling hostilities. Rosier used the rumor to justify Waymouth's decision to strike then and carry out the kidnappings, for fear the Natives would all flee if they thought the English had discovered their plotting.

A game of cat and mouse? Maybe. If so, the Anglo-Saxon feline pounced first, and porridges of peas played a major role.

Rosier's spin notwithstanding, the word had been spread among the English: *It's time to seize them.*

The first act took place alongside *Archangell.* A canoe carrying three Indians drew up alongside. A can of peas in porridge form was offered them, but they refused to come aboard for it. Relenting, the English let them have the treat anyway. In a reciprocal gesture of good faith, one of the braves did climb up and return the emptied can. Victim number one.

Numbers two and three were a pair of other Indians who paddled out and joined the can-returner belowdecks, warming themselves at a fire.

As Rosier described it, Captain Waymouth then manned the light horseman, a small rowing vessel, with seven or eight men and headed for a nearby beach with a box of merchandise prominently displayed in the prow and a platter of peas clearly visible, "which meat they love."

There were three Indians on the sand. One took off into the woods.

"The other two met us on the shore side to receive the peas." Rosier's classic words on the ensuing struggle have echoed down through the centuries, painting an epic picture of a very physical clash of cultures. "And it was as much as five or six of us could do to get them into the light horseman for they were strong and so naked as our best hold was by their long hair on their heads."

With their prey subdued and imprisoned below, Rosier could sum up: "Thus we shipped five Salvages, [plus] two canoes, with all their bows and arrows." The canoes, incidentally, were stowed on the orlop deck, the lowest deck of the ship, out of sight and carefully secured for the voyage home.

Some accounts depict the kidnap victims as bound and gagged. In her quasifictional work, *Five Kidnapped Indians*, children's book author Anne Molloy Howells uses that device by implication to justify the lack of open Native resistance while Waymouth was casually tootling around the Maine coast.

Much of the rest of *Archangell*'s American travel has come down to us in the form of a scholars' dispute over which river Waymouth and his crew next explored. Was it actually the Penobscot, as David Morey eloquently argues in his 2005 study, *The Voyage of Archangell*, or rather, as a number of Maine historians have maintained over the years, the St. George River, a much smaller waterway close by Allen Island.

But back to Rosier's *A True Relation*:

"The next day," he stated, "we made an end of getting our wood aboard and filled our empty casks with water." Then, "Thursday, the 6th of June, we spent in bestowing the canoes upon the orlop, safe from hurt, because they were safe from breakup, which our captain was careful to prevent."

On June 8 they weighed anchor and began coasting about the adjoining islands for five or six leagues, during which time they caught enough fish to feed "our whole company, though now augmented [by five Indians] for three days." Four days afterward, they commenced their upriver travel, and on various occasions went ashore, before finally leaving for England on June 16.

Rosier's remarks about the prisoners convey a number of different attitudes toward what the English had done.

He says of their initial captive, the youth who had brought back the empty container of peas porridge: "for he being young of a ready capacity and one we most desired to bring with us into England had received exceeding kind usage at our hands and was therefore much delighted in our company." His and the others' forcible apprehension by the Englishmen was explained away as "being a matter of great importance for the full accomplishment of our voyage." Rosier hastened to exculpate the abduction by claiming that kind treatment and assurance of no harm had changed the Natives' attitudes. "They have never since seemed discontented with us, but very traitable, loving and willing by their best means to satisfy us with anything we demand of them by words or signs for their understanding."

Nevertheless, during *Archangell's* further reconnaissance in Maine, when the English were invited to meet the Bashebes and his people, they demurred, "for we had no will to stay them long aboard, lest they should discover the other Salvages which we had stowed below."

That scary prospect ended when the ship was ultimately embarked for England—on a Sunday, because they had left England on a Sunday and made their initial landfall in America on a Sunday.

They had seen a good deal in the interim, and Rosier's observations included the sight of "notable high timber trees, masts for ships of 400 tons," schools of jumping salmon and flocks of great blue herons (he called them cranes), and how the Indians killed a 72-foot-long whale. The diarist was most impressed by how the sagamore divided the leviathan's meat among his people and, in general, the Indians' penchant, as displayed even by their prisoners, for sharing everything equitably.

On July 14, 1605, *Archangell* entered the English Channel. Contrary winds kept them from reaching the Scilly Islands until two days later, and not until the 18th were they able to put into Dartmouth Harbor, their momentous voyage at an end.

At the finish of his narrative, Rosier names the five Indians they had taken from Maine to England—and thereby created a lasting problem for historians. Here are the five captives, he named, along with each man's status:

Tahanedo, a sagamore or commander

Amoret, a gentleman

Skicoweros, a gentleman

Maneddo, a gentleman

Sassacomoit, a servant

The problem that subsequently developed was literally created by Sir Ferdinando Gorges, who along with Sir John Popham, received and maintained these Indians in their homes as guests. Sir Ferdinando named his three as "Manida, Sketwaroest, and Tisquantum."

It was the last-named who caused all the fuss, the first two corresponding, despite slight spelling changes, to those on Rosier's list. And *Tisquantum* constitutes a special case for us as Americans, since we know him from our history as Squanto, the Native who so signally greeted and befriended the Pilgrims in Massachusetts.

The inclusion of Squanto as one of the Indians taken from Maine has been challenged. Gorges's biographer in our state, the redoubtable James Phinney Baxter, added the caveat "if we accept his statement as correct" before reporting Sir Ferdinando's naming Tisquantum one of his houseguests—*castle* guests, rather. Although Sir Ferdinando owned a number of estates, it is most likely that his Indians were boarded at Plymouth, where he was the commander of an all-important fort.

Some knowledge of English geography will be useful now. The term "West Country," in which Plymouth is located, is applied in Great Britain to the country's *southwest* corner, where it borders the English Channel. Like similar designations in the United States such as "New England" or the "Deep South," the term denotes a special way of life and type of people. "West Countrymen" were known to be rough, good fighters, adventurers, feudalistic, devoted Royalists, and even more fanatic adherents to the established Anglican Church. The two men who took the captured Indians into their homes were natives of Somersetshire, one of the counties that makes up this unique region. Other noted sons of the West Country interested in English overseas expansion, besides Gorges and Popham, included Sir Francis Drake, Sir John Hawkins, Sir Walter Raleigh, and Raleigh's half-brother, Sir Humphrey Gilbert. Sir Ferdinando was a cousin of the latter two.

As a young man, he had made his name and achieved his knighthood fighting Spanish Catholics in the Netherlands. Then he almost lost his life for an act of treason. When his commanding officer, the earl of Essex, Queen Elizabeth's lover, turned against his monarch, Gorges was implicated in the foiled coup and jailed in the Tower of London. That he wasn't beheaded, like Essex, he may well have owed to the help of

Chief Justice Popham, whom Gorges had earlier saved from death at the hands of Essex's rebels.

It was in 1603, after the demise of Elizabeth and the accession of King James I that Gorges was freed from prison and reinstated in his Plymouth post.

He and Popham had both caught the imperialistic overseas bug, and they collaborated on the work of expanding English power to parts of the New World. The failure of Lord Arundell's scheme of transporting English Catholics to America gave them their chance to find backing for Waymouth's scouting effort. Gorges wrote about the trip's potential consequences that "this was an accident which must be acknowledged the means under God of putting on foot and giving life to all our plantations." The term "accident," however, reeks with irony. There seems nothing accidental about the kidnapping, and certainly Sir John Popham had a reputation for being totally unscrupulous in everything he did. As lord chief justice, he had condemned to death a number of illustrious persons, including Mary Queen of Scots, King James I's own mother, and Sir Walter Raleigh, Gorges's kinsman. It was said that in his younger days, Sir John, now England's top law official, had been a highwayman, robbing travelers at pistol point. His estates, in one of which he boarded his two Indians, were rumored to have been acquired through blackmail—acquitting defendants of murder if they turned their property over to him.

So why did Gorges team up with a man who had railroaded his cousin to a death sentence? Simple. Raleigh, in Queen Elizabeth's time, had been given a monopoly on the settlement in Virginia, which was the name given to the whole Atlantic coast of the New World. With Raleigh in the Tower, *North* Virginia—Maine, Massachusetts, New York, etc.—was granted by James I to these two aristocratic partners for their exclusive use.

Quickly, Popham and Gorges sent out two new voyages in 1606. Four of the five captive Indians—two to a ship—were included on them. The first, led by Captain Henry Challons, had Maneddo and Sassacomoit and left Plymouth on August 12, 1606. A few months later, Captain Martin Pring departed from Bristol, taking with him Tahanedo and Skicoweros. The fifth Indian, whoever he was—Tisquantum or Amoret—remained with Gorges in England.

Needless to say, there was never an *Indian* "relation" of their experiences overseas. We need to look to fiction for an insight. We find one in Anne Howells's children's book, where she pictures sagamore Tahanedo as worried while he prepares to return home. It was not so much the strangeness of the many English houses he saw, fixed in place, so unlike the mobile Indian dwellings. It was the sight of all the people around them and in the streets, "more numerous than leaves on a tree," that brought him nightmare visions. "Any day they might appear on his native shores and drive out his people from their long cultivated cornfields and the hunting lands they burned twice a year so that all might hunt and have food. [He] had seen the hedgerows and tightly-walled small plots of land of England. He knew that this overseas land was cut up in small pieces and used only by its owners."[2]

By chance, Captain Pring's vessel, although starting later, was first to reach Maine, where Tahanedo was restored to his people and reinstated as chief. His clan territory was centered on the Pemaquid peninsula, years later to be a major site of English settlement. Skicoweros, his cousin, who had come with him, was for some reason taken back to England by Pring and had to wait a full year to come home permanently. Most likely he was being kept to accompany an expedition planned for 1607.

Or was it truly by chance that Captain Pring had beaten Captain Challons to the New World? The pigheadedness of the latter had caused him to ignore his instructions and sail too far south, which resulted in his capture by Spaniards and a stay with his crew and Indian charges in a dungeon in Spain. It is reported that he escaped, along with Sassacomoit, and they eventually got back to England.

The next big news involving the kidnapped Maine Indians was of the 1607 Popham colony expedition. Actual settlement was starting.

Here was a major effort to cash in on the information gleaned from the captives and the contacts established with them by the entrepreneurs in England. In this singular year of 1607, the British transatlantic surge was launched in full panoply; one task force of emigrants headed out for South Virginia and founded Jamestown; the other went to Maine, where it jerry-rigged a short-lived community on a finger of land jutting into Casco Bay that is now called Popham Beach.

George Popham, Sir John's fifty-six-year-old nephew, was the commander or "president" of this two-ship fleet carrying potential pioneers to North Virginia. Second in command was a relative of Sir Ferdinando Gorges, Ralegh Gilbert, son of the late Sir Humphrey Gilbert. There were at least a hundred men on board the two craft, the *Gift of God* and the *Mary and John*, that anchored off the Maine coast. Ashore, they hustled to erect shelters for themselves in preparation for winter, and also conducted the earliest bit of non-native shipbuilding on the continent, constructing a 30-ton pinnace they named the *Virginia*.

Sir Ferdinando Gorges has left us his own *Briefe Narration* of this maiden venture of his and Sir John's Plymouth Company. It establishes that Skicoweros (Gorges calls him Skitwarres) did indeed come back to America again from England and served as a guide "for the thorough discovery of the rivers and habitations of the natives, by whom he [Captain Ralegh Gilbert] was brought to several of them, where he found civil entertainment and kind respects, far from brutish or savage natures, so as they suddenly became familiar friends."[3] Aiding the process, according to Gorges, was Chief Tahanedo (though Gorges calls him Dehanada).

There occurred an unsolved problem, however, that shadowed this budding relationship when the English were drawn into an intra-Indian conflict not of their making.

It was those fierce Tarratines in the north who were causing the grief. They had acquired firearms from the French, which made their raids all the more fearsome. On the defensive, the Wawenocs, led by another mid-Maine chieftain, Sasanoa, urged their putative English allies to go, as Gorges puts it, "to the Bashebes, who it seems is their king," and discuss a joint fight against the deadly marauders. Also, they asked for guns to arm themselves.

All of this was a nonstarter. President George Popham adamantly refused them weapons and also nixed Sasanoa's invite to parley with the Bashebes.

Various historians have sought to blame these souring English-Indian relations for the collapse of the colony after it survived a single winter of settlement. True, the two Indians they had counted on—their former "guests," sagamore Tahanedo and Skicoweros—had not taken on a Tonto role vis-à-vis the white men. True, too, that Ralegh Gilbert had a misunderstanding with an Indian chief named Sebanoa on the

Kennebec, which had momentarily led to cocked English muskets facing drawn Abenaki bows and arrows. And true, as well, that in a clash with the Tarratines, Sasanoa's son was killed by a musket ball the French-equipped northern Natives aimed at him, no doubt aggravating the Wawenocs' resentment over the English refusal to give them flintlocks. Nevertheless, none of these irritations constituted the major reason behind the Popham Beach venture's abrupt end.

Why did they give up? Lack of leadership, really. Only one of their number perished during the harsh winter, but this was George Popham, their commander. And, when relief ships appeared in the spring bringing supplies, they learned that Ralegh Gilbert had to go back home. His older brother had died, and he had inherited the family estate. Left rudderless, the others decided to decamp, as well.

Poor Sir Ferdinando bemoaned, "Thus were all our former hopes frozen to death."

Yet, although Gorges was now left by himself—Sir John Popham having expired suddenly, and mysteriously, not long after their expedition set sail—he did not abandon his involvement in America. In fact, he lived long enough to be known as the "Father of Maine."

One still-unresolved thread in the story of the five kidnapped Indians is Squanto's role, if any. Personally, I don't believe he was one of the five. For one thing, he was no Mainer. We can verify he was a Patuxet, one of the Cape Cod Wampanoags' subtribes. We are told that he was captured and sold into slavery by a dastardly English captain named Hunt, but this was in 1614, almost a decade after Waymouth's act of kidnapping. When Squanto appeared at Plymouth and greeted the Pilgrims in their own language, it was six years after that, with time in between for the adventures that brought him back to Massachusetts only to find that his people had been wiped out by a plague. Sometimes, too, Squanto is confused with Samoset, a true Maine Indian from Pemaquid, who also spoke to the Pilgrims in English.

Consequently, the mysterious fifth Indian must be conjectured as Amoret; taken to that Spanish dungeon with his companions who later escaped, he disappears from history, and admittedly from Maine, forever.

But for a final word on this whole 400-year-old historic incident, it is appropriate to listen to the words of a current-day Maine Indian leader, Donald Soctomah, as he expressed them at the anniversary symposium in Rockport in 2005. Donald, a Passamaquoddy, wondered aloud, "Would things have changed if the Waymouth voyage brought friendship and acceptance of the Native societies?" instead of, which he left unsaid, *kidnapping and later invasion and land-grabbing.* Then, having acknowledged "it is amazing the Wabanaki people still exists, surrounded by an alien culture and outnumbered 100,000 to one," Donald Soctomah pledged that "Native people will continue to adapt to the existing conditions," and again he left it unsaid: *the way the five kidnapped Indians still did after they'd been abroad and experienced all that had happened to them.*

1. Matthew Simmons, "When the Creation of America Began." Chapter 4 of *One Land—Two Worlds—Maine-Mawooshen, 1605–2005, The 400th Anniversary of George Waymouth's Voyage to New England.* Rockland, ME: Island Institute, 2005.

2. Anne Molloy Howells, *Five Kidnapped Indians.* New York: Hastings House Publishers, 1968, p. 67.

3. Sir Ferdinando Gorges, *A Briefe Narration of the Originall Undertakings of the Advancement of Plantations into the Parts of America.*

Sir William Phips and his crew being greeted.
Wood engraving, courtesy of the Library of Congress

3

SIR WILLIAM PHIPS

Our next traveler from Maine was neither a peripatetic hero-god nor an unwilling passenger to Europe. Like so many a young Maine person, he left his rural home to find adventure, fortune, and fame in reportedly greener pastures. But he did it in 1673.

Had Tahanedo lived for almost three-quarters of a century after he returned to Pemaquid, he still might have been worried about hordes of Englishmen invading his territory, although that really hadn't happened yet in Maine in the 1600s. To see the sorts of sights the kidnapee had seen in Plymouth, England, he would have had to go to distant Boston. To be sure, nearby Pemaquid had a rustic village of whites, and scattered farms were all around, carved out of the forest. The District of Maine existed as a component of the Commonwealth of Massachusetts Bay, named in part for an Indian chief. And here and there in the northern reaches towns were being formed, but in the 1670s, Nequasset (Woolwich) wasn't an exciting enough place to hold an ambitious young man like Billy Phips.

Because he became so famous later, some of the stories told about him were most likely apochryphal. One in particular—that he was the next to last of *twenty-six* children born into a family in this frontier area—has been questioned and doubted. The most noted of his biographers, the eminent Boston preacher, Reverend Cotton Mather, wrote in his *Life of Sir William Phips* that Phips had been born "at a despicable plantation on the river of Kennebeck [*sic*]"[1] and had spent time "keeping sheep in the wilderness until he was eighteen years old."[2] He has also been referred to as "an early example of America's self-made man" who came out of "the rigid background of the Maine woods and waterways."

In most respects, William Phips represents a *transitional* settler of Maine, a the descendant of one of the earliest men to arrive from England's West Country and stay—and own land—in the province that had been granted to Sir Ferdinando Gorges by the Stuart monarchy in recognition of his stubborn efforts to colonize North Virginia.

For Gorges hadn't in the slightest abandoned his colonizing ambitions after the fiasco of the Popham Beach project. In November 1620, an enlarged charter was given by the Crown to his Plymouth Company, which by then had already provided the Pilgrims with land in southern Massachusetts. Gorges had also procured a monopoly of all fishing rights for New England for himself and Sir Francis Popham, the son of his late partner, but it was later set aside by Parliament. Nevertheless, the West Country nobleman's ties to the monarchy were so strong that in 1622 he and a new partner, Captain John Mason, received another grant that stretched all the way from the Merrimac River to the Sagadahoc (or Penobscot) River. When they eventually split their demesne, Mason got the lower half, which became New Hampshire and ended at the Piscataqua River, and everything to the north became Sir Ferdinando's Maine. Further aid to him was yet another charter in 1639 from Charles I, containing unusual powers and privileges covering not only Maine up to the Penobscot but the northern Isles of Shoals and Martha's Vineyard and Nantucket. Gorges was acknowledged an "uncrowned monarch in a little kingdom of his own."

At some time during this acquisitive activity, James Phips, the father of the future Sir William, came to Pemaquid, that tongue of sea-girt land not far from the Waymouth landing site. A small English settlement had been slowly developing there since the early 1620s, using the West Country feudalistic pattern where an overlord like Sir Ferdinando Gorges, with a huge sub-grant of land from the king, would further sub-grant parcels to tenants who, in turn, would again sub-grant to lesser sub-tenants, and so forth.

Yet another way to acquire a possession of land in this New World was to buy a deed from the Indians.

No matter how they obtained it, British people wanted land. Many of the rural farmers in England had been chased off their holdings by rapacious landlords and wound up as vagrants and, before long, because of draconian laws, in prison, if not hanging from a gibbet. The word was soon out—from seamen as well as captive Indians—of the vastness of the territory in America and its apparent lack of owners who worked it. Many humble persons like James Phips, a gunsmith in the West Country port of Bristol, decided to emigrate.

He arrived in 1645 and subsequently made his way from Pemaquid to the Montsweag-Nequasset region of what is now Woolwich. Phips and a partner, John White, bought land in this newly opened area—500 acres each from an Edward Bateman who himself had purchased a larger piece from the reigning Indian chief of the district, a sagamore known to Maine history simply as Robinhood. The Phips farm has been variously located on Jeresquam Neck, or to the west of the most western branch of the Sheepscot River, somewhat north of Hockomock Bay. It should be noted that this territory lies within a complicated maze of waterways in midcoast Maine, where major rivers like the Kennebec, Androscoggin, and Sheepscot pass through a complex of islands, peninsulas, and tributaries to enter the Atlantic.

In this region, we are at the uppermost reaches of the initial British penetration into northeastern America in the seventeenth century. Beyond the site of Waymouth's landing was a strip of no-man's land between the Penobscot River, exclusively controlled by Indians, and beyond that, the French inroads in Canada that had been made since 1603. A story has been told that in 1605 the French explorer Samuel de Champlain was visiting Mount Desert Island and heard rumors that five Indians had been killed (not kidnapped) by English interlopers. Champlain thereupon had decided to confine a competing Gallic imperialism effort to Nova Scotia.

Europe was far away from these splotches of settlement in the vast Maine wilderness, and the protracted Franco-Anglo battle that set the world ablaze in the eighteenth century was still in the future. But events in the Old World did reach across the Atlantic and have an effect on ambitious Englishmen like James Phips who had cast their fortunes on a new life overseas.

There were religious troubles in England throughout the 1600s that grew out of and into political differences. It was no longer a question of just Protestant versus Catholic. The Anglican Church lost its monopoly on worship. Dissenting groups arose and from them came the "Separatist" *Pilgrims* and the "Reform from Within" *Puritans*. Together, in America, these two groups created the Massachusetts Bay Colony. Eventually, they cast their eyes to the north, to Maine, where small knots of Gorges-inspired Anglican and Royalist Englishmen had settled. Civil War in England temporarily led to the abolition of the Stuart monarchy. In 1652 the Puritan powers in Boston started a concerted drive to incorporate Maine within their boundaries—a move so successful that it sustained itself for more than 160 years.

Thus Billy Phips, growing up in Woolwich in the last half of the seventeenth century, found himself within an Anglo-Saxon culture that hadn't quite yet gelled. His father's West Country antecedents—and religious preference, if Anglican—probably didn't carry much weight, since James Phips died when the boy was six years old. His own churching in the wilderness may have been nonexistent. Phips wasn't even baptized until he was an adult.

Incidentally, life being what it was in Woolwich, Billy's widowed mother soon married his late father's real estate partner, John White, giving a bit of family stability to the rest of his childhood.

Having been a shepherd long enough, the boy then sought a livelihood. The only incipient industry in the region was shipbuilding, which was centered around the Clarke and Lake Trading Company, located on Arrowsic Island, just below Woolwich. Two enterprising Boston merchants, Thomas Clarke and Thomas Lake, had started their octopus-like operation, which also included land development, Indian trading, fishing, and other enterprises, and they hired young Phips on an indentured basis to become a ship's carpenter. Billy worked at the Clarke and Lake "mansion house" on Arrowsic for four years, through his late teens and early twenties, and was said to have learned to read and write there.

His indenture finished, he then took off for Boston.

What manner of young man was this twenty-two-year-old backwoods product? We know that he was a strapping fellow, good-looking, too, no doubt, and imposing. Once settled in this major city of the province, he lost no time in making an important conquest of a female heart—an event that shortcut, so to speak, what could have been a long tedious climb to fame and fortune.

So he was *smaht,* too, as Mainers would say it, as well as brawny. How he charmed Mary Spencer Hull into marrying him isn't known, nor are the traits of promise she saw in him, but the match took place not too long after the death of her husband, the respected and wealthy Boston merchant, John Hull. There is speculation that Maine was a tie between the two of them—Mary's father, Captain Roger Spencer, had lived in Saco and she considered herself a Mainer—but more than likely physical attraction and confidence in Billy's ambitions and talents led to the match. He made it plain, however, that he wasn't planning to live off her money. He soon had a shipbuilding project going back in Maine. It was on the Sheepscot River and when the vessel was finished, she would be loaded with lumber taken from the Phips family's own property. There was a ready market for cut wood in Boston. Young William was boasting that he would soon have his bride living in a "fair brick house" she had admired on fashionable Green Lane.

Before long, all was in readiness. The ship was launched, the cargo set to be stowed, and Phips returned home to Maine to supervise the sail to Boston.

But forces beyond his control turned this opportunity into a calamity. After decades of quiescent, smoldering resentment, the Native tribes of mid-Maine staged an uprising. It was swift, deadly, and utterly unexpected. News had probably traveled to Woolwich of the Indian troubles in southern Massachusetts that broke out in 1675 around Plymouth Plantation, but that was hundreds of miles away. Besides, the chief perpetrator, Metacom, whom the Pilgrims derisively called *King Philip*, the son of their great friend Massasoit, had been trapped and killed in the swamps of Rhode Island. But survivors of his band had straggled north, finding refuge with their Algonquian relatives in Maine and inciting them to avenge the many years of wrongs, real or imagined, from the ever-threatening white invaders. Arrowsic was attacked, the Clarke and Lake enterprise burned, and Thomas Lake was run down and slain.

Frantic settlers, 200 of them, hastened to the Sheepscot and the safety of William Phips's newly finished ship, which as soon as packed full, took off for Boston. Unfortunately, the lumber whose sale was to pay for the venture had to be left behind.

An admiring Cotton Mather later likened Phips to Noah, guiding his rescue ark through a tempest. The sober, hard-nosed Yankee businessmen of Boston had a different viewpoint. They wanted their investments paid back. One of them, Thomas Joles, won an award of eighty dollars, but Phips personally ripped the writ from Joles's attorney and threw it in a fire. Boston was soon to see more of the Mainer's forcefulness and temper. He openly used foul language and, if pushed too hard, his big fists. Yet, contradictorily, Phips's latter-day chroniclers, Emerson "Tad" Baker and John G. Reid, in their 1998 study of him, observed,

"Phips's environment was the port, where his peripheral origins and colorful language smoothed rather than hindered his path to acceptance."[3]

Cotton Mather described him during these years as physically "Tall beyond the common set of Men and Thick as well as Tall, and Strong as well as Thick. He was, in all respects, exceedingly Robust." The renowned cleric went on to add that "Difficulties of Diet and Travel," difficult enough to "kill most Men alive," Phips could easily overcome.[4]

One senses in these words a touch of hero worship from a high-strung Harvard intellectual, which Mather most certainly was, toward a man of action. It was a sign of Phips's absorption into the Boston community that he had formed such a friendly connection with the pastor of the city's prestigious North Church and with his even more influential father, Increase Mather. The two would eventually win him to their Congregational faith and baptize him in it at the tail end of a time when Anglican influence had returned to England with the restoration of a new Stuart monarch, Charles II, to the throne.

Charles II was still king when Phips made his first foray into the business—even riskier than lumbering in Indian country—of seeking sunken treasure in the Caribbean as the means of obtaining the fame and fortune he longed for.

In 1682 William Phips was thirty-one years old. He had now become a familiar figure on the Boston waterfront, which abounded in rumors of shipwrecked galleons on the Bahamas Banks, full of treasure awaiting discovery. Somehow, Phips arranged an expedition to find a source of this plunder, and succeeded in doing so. Massachusetts admiralty records show that the Commonwealth awarded Phips and his men shares of profit that amounted to fifty-four dollars each—and although Phips would have received the most shares, in his ambitious eyes, the money from this find was too modest to be anything more than a prelude.

To achieve any treasure-hunting on a grander scale, Phips needed to go to London. This he did in the spring of 1683, where he was able to win the backing of Admiral Sir John Narborough, one of the Royal Navy commissioners, who became his chief patron. Their target was a Spanish treasure ship, *Nuestra Señora de la Concepción*, lost in the waters north of today's Dominican Republic.

Through Narborough, Phips received the use of a royal warship, *Rose of Algiers*, a 163-ton, twenty-gun frigate, earlier captured from the

Barbary pirates. Phips sailed her first to Boston, where he created a commotion, throwing around his considerable weight as the commander of a king's vessel. When local fishing and merchant vessels neglected to strike their colors before *Rose of Algiers*, as they would to all Royal Navy ships, he fired a shot across their bows. Then Phips had the effrontery to send his crew members to those offenders and demand payment for the ammunition he'd expended. Hauled before Governor Simon Bradstreet, the ship's captain from Woolwich was admonished for his boorish behavior, but he continued it until he left for the south in January 1684.

If Robert Louis Stevenson had written an account of Phips's discovery and subsequent emptying of the *Nuestra Señora de la Concepción*, it would have undoubtedly commenced with a lurid scene in which he learned of the wreck's location from an aged Hispanic fisherman. This, allegedly, is what happened.

But only after considerable frustration, several years of false starts and false hopes, and even a back-and-forth trip to England for renewed support. Establishing himself at the northern Dominican coastal city of Puerto Plata in January 1687, Phips now had two different vessels, the *James and Mary* and the *Henry*, which brought him to the extensive offshore coral reef where his divers finally located the remains of what has been called the "Richest Ship that Ever Went out of the West Indies."[5]

There were mutters later on that Phips overworked his divers, who were all Natives, and often put them in danger. The scouting operation on the "Boilers," as the site was known because of its shallow depth and incessant spume, was in the charge of Francis Rogers, an ex-ship captain Phips had recruited, and it took the team only six days to find the first of the wreckage. None of the pieces was deeper than forty-two feet, a limit these free-divers could attain. The original discoverer, swimming in two to three feet over some coral heads, had spotted an interesting "sea feather" below that he wanted to examine. In the glassy water, he soon spied a far more arresting sight deeper down—"great guns"—strewn on the bottom. After a second dive, he came up with a real trophy—a "sow"—a lump of pure silver worth $200 to $300. Immediately, Captain Rogers had the spot strung with buoys.

During the next two days, Rogers and crew, who were in a "canoe" that Phips had built out of a giant cotton tree, raised eight bars of gold and 3,000 coins. But deteriorating weather made them return to Puerto Plata.

"Thanks be to God! We are made!" Cotton Mather quotes Phips as exclaiming upon being shown this initial cache of wealth that had been salvaged.

Of course, there was more—much more. In total, their trove was to comprise 68,511 troy pounds of silver and 25 troy pounds of gold, most of the silver in pieces of eight. The ultimate value of the entire treasure was pegged at more than $200,000 (Mather called it closer to $300,000). In the end, after the king took his share of a tenth, the crew members their share, the investors theirs, Phips netted $11,000, a princely fortune for one man. Mather also reported that "certain mean men" tried to convince the king to keep the whole find for the Crown but that although James II, who had replaced his deceased brother Charles in 1685, indisputably had tyrannical tendencies, he played fair with Phips. The duke of Albemarle, one of the major investors, also rewarded the Phips family by giving Mary Spencer Phips a golden cup worth $1,000, and on June 27, 1687, presented Captain Phips to His Majesty, who knighted the man from Maine—the first "American" from the original thirteen colonies ever to be so honored.

Some British historians, discussing the impact of Phips's contribution to the entire British economy, have been bold enough to argue that "it was sufficient to alter the course of England's financial history" [6] and even helped inspire the founding of the Bank of England. A knighthood, prestigious as this was, seemed the least that James II, embattled at the time in holding onto his throne, could do to reward the adventurer who had brought home so much loot.

One other tangible benefit of Phips's triumph was the brick home he had promised his wife in Boston. Mary herself went out and bought a place for them—Samuel Wakefield's showy house and grounds—and to explain the relationship of prices then to their $11,000-plus nest egg, she paid $350 for what had to be a prime piece of real estate.

In addition, there was another reward from the Stuart administration to the newly dubbed knight. The Crown appointed him to be provost marshal general for the Province of Massachusetts, or "high sheriff," to use the popular term.

This was a dicey time politically—in Massachusetts as in England. James II, an autocrat so different from his easygoing sibling, was deeply unpopular, particularly so since he was a not-so-closet Roman Catholic, suspected of wanting to resubject England to the papacy. Protestant New Englanders hated him, too, because he had taken away their traditional liberties and consolidated all territories from New Jersey to Maine into a single dominion under a tyrannical governor, Sir Edmund Andros. With Andros, who resided in Boston, was a pack of carpetbaggers, led by one Edward Randolph, who were intent on dissolving all land titles and taking the Puritans' property for themselves. The Mathers were resisting them fiercely, and Increase, who was president of Harvard, had to flee to England to avoid being arrested and jailed.

In this atmosphere, High Sheriff Sir William Phips did not remain long in his adopted city. He arrived on June 1, 1688, and departed for England on July 16. The report that he fled fearing assassination by Andros was deemed "a ludicrous exaggeration." Phips's beef was essentially with Edward Randolph, who controlled the governor's hand-picked council [the popularly elected assembly had been abolished by the Crown]. When the new sheriff wanted to install his own deputies, Randolph blocked him. Phips responded with unprintable language and a threat, which he carried out, to take the matter to London.

During his brief sojourn in Boston, however, Phips perhaps opportunistically cemented his relationship with the Mathers by attending the North Church. His political antennae may have attuned him to the way the governmental winds were blowing back in England.

It wasn't even a full year—December 1688, to be exact—before the "Glorious Revolution" deposed James II and substituted his impeccably Protestant daughter Mary and her Dutch husband William of Orange. It took until April of the following year for the news to reach Boston, and on April 19 (the same date as Paul Revere's ride eighty-six years later) the first American revolution might be said to have taken place. The Bostonians rioted, clapped Andros and Randolph in jail, and set about to restore their ancient form of self-government.

It wasn't that simple, though. Massachusetts had long been a thorn in the side of the royal bureaucracy, and during James II's reign, the Bay Colony had had its charter allowing an elected assembly and governor stripped away. There was no hurry at Whitehall, despite the intense lobbying of Increase Mather, for reinstating the rights of these feisty provincials.

Meanwhile, Sir William Phips made his move to return to Boston, no doubt encouraged by the Mathers, since Cotton quotes him as saying, "I have had great offers made to me in England, but the churches of New England were those that my heart was most set upon. I knew, that if God had a people anywhere, it was here and I resolved to rise and fall with them."

Religion was one thing. At the age of forty, he was baptized a Congregationalist. But left unsaid about this belated conversion was that in order to be a "Freeman" of Boston, he had to be a member of the established church. But why should Sir William Phips want such a title? He was already a "knight of the realm."

The answer was a new ambition he had—military command. The "revolutionary government" of Puritan fathers in Boston was looking for a general to undertake an attack on the French in Canada. The warfare that had driven Phips and his neighbors out of Woolwich and mid-Maine had waxed and waned since 1676. Behind this sporadic Indian hostility increasingly lurked the imperial goals of the king of France. In August 1689, the Yankee fort at Pemaquid had fallen to the combined Indian-French forces of Chief Madockawando of the Penobscots and his son-in-law, the Baron de Castin. A counterattack was called for and who better to lead it, despite his lack of martial experience, than Sir William Phips, who had shown his toughness and organizational ability in recovering the Spanish treasure.

Except that under Massachusetts law, he had to be a "Freeman" in order to be commissioned, so Phips promptly took care of this technical detail. The day after his baptism, Major General Sir William Phips attended his first meeting of the "Committee for setting out the forces in the expedition against the French in Nova Scotia and Lacady" (*L'Acadie*, or Acadia, the large swath of land the French claimed in eastern Canada and Maine).

The immediate intent was to capture Port Royal in Nova Scotia, the site where Samuel de Champlain had set up the first French headquarters in 1605. With a fleet of three warships and 500 colonial militia and perhaps beginner's luck, Phips accomplished the task easily. Port Royal surrendered without firing a shot. Phips's triumph was hailed in Boston as an astounding victory. Not only was plunder brought back—$740 in cash, cannons, three vessels, and other goods available for public sale—but much satisfaction in the heart of Puritanism that Commander Phips had allowed Port Royal's Roman Catholic church to be sacked and its holy altar desecrated.

Still, this was only the start for their hero. Next on the anti-French agenda was a much more monumental task—the conquest of what had become the center of their enemy's power in Canada—the mighty fortress of Quebec City.

Cotton Mather used classic language to describe the English strategy. *Delenda est Cartago*—the old Roman war cry, *Carthage is destroyed*, was suggested by him as a motto for Phips's operation. The erudite if sarcastic Mather also used a scornful Latin phrase to describe the American provincials' foe: *Calli in suo sterquilino*, or *Cocks crowing on their own dunghill.*

Only this time, the Gallic warriors were not the pushovers they had been at Port Royal. Their commander was the redoubtable Count Frontenac, and the 2,700 soldiers he had at Quebec more than matched in numbers the troops in the Yankee armada Phips was bringing from Massachusetts. The entire English complement was also supposed to include a mixture of 1,500 Connecticut and New York militia and Iroquois braves who would make a diversionary attack on Montreal, drawing Frontenac from Quebec to confront it.

The Reverend Mather, in accounting for the disaster that followed, had to invoke the inscrutability of the Almighty. "The Hand of Heaven," he declared, "dealt Phips...a very mortifying disappointment of a design, which his mind was, as much as ever, set upon."[7] As a spin doctor, the minister was a master, arguing that his and his father's protégé had saved New England from a French onslaught that winter and how the failure at Quebec was a blessing in disguise and—although Phips was a diver—these events were "too deep to dive into."

Reality reflected more the steadfastness of Frontenac's resistance. When called upon to surrender, he did not quail as his subordinate de Meneval had at Port Royal. He snapped that his answer "would be from the mouth of a cannon" and added, "Sir William Phips and those with him are heretics and traitors to their King and have taken up with that usurper, the Prince of Orange."[8]

Frontenac was at full military strength in Quebec, thanks to the failure of the English land army from the west to even reach Montreal. Phips bombarded the city to soften it up for an amphibious attack, but the French pounded back and damaged his fleet. There was talk in Phips's war council of a prolonged siege to starve out the defenders. The idea was to retire to the nearby Ile d'Orleans and blockade the St. Lawrence River. Except a violent storm hit. This was Mather's "Hand of Heaven." Camp fever and smallpox also decimated the New Englanders. So a consensus emerged that retreat was the only recourse.

New England was consequently left with a debt of $40,000 and "no means to pay it." The General Court of Massachusetts began printing *bills of credit* for currency. Cannily, Phips salvaged some of his popularity by taking the lead in exchanging "a considerable quantity of his ready money" for the promissory notes, thus giving them a value. Pundits might have thought, though, that the Quebec fiasco would have doomed the Maine man's career. Mather depicts him as "haunted by Canada." Yet we soon find Phips making his way across the Atlantic, determined to persevere. And his lucky star, it developed, would follow him once more.

All the while, the Reverend Increase Mather had remained in London. His single-minded objective was to obtain from the new English monarchs, William and Mary, the restoration of Massachusetts's old charter, which had given the Puritans such a free hand in the Bay Colony. Nor had the problems of the Stuart repression entirely gone away. Andros, freed from jail in Boston, was now back in England, busily seeking support and justification for his actions from prominent British politicians.

As soon as Phips reached the British capital on March 4, 1691, he joined Increase Mather in lobbying for the New England position. He also—unapologetically—pushed for another invasion of Canada, claiming the acquisition of the French territory "would be more important to Great Britain than all the territories in the West Indies." He harped on the danger that Jesuits would convert the Mohawks and other Iroquois, on Frontenac's plan to attack Boston, and how, with New York Indians added to the Count's Abenaki allies, all English colonies in the north would be lost.

Once the political difficulties of settling Massachusetts's status were concluded, there was yet another role for Sir William Phips. With the help of the influential Sir Henry Ashurst, both Increase Mather and Phips had been able to secure new charters for the pesky Calvinist colonies of Massachusetts and Connecticut. They would now be "provinces," instead of "colonies"; their legally resuscitated representative assemblies would have the same powers in New England as king and Parliament in England and enjoy full "English liberties"—most particularly, they could be "touched by no law, no tax, but of their own making." The Puritans would have full freedom to practice their religion and need not fear domination by the Church of England, plus—an extraordinarily big plus—every previous land title was confirmed. On the negative side of the bargain, however, the Crown would go on appointing their governors.

Once more, Sir William Phips was in the right place at the right time. As a bit of a silver lining, Increase Mather and Sir Henry Ashurst, enlisting the aid of the duke of Nottingham, induced the sovereigns to name Phips to the top executive post in Massachusetts, citing his "good service for the Crown, by enlarging your domains and reducing of Nova Scotia to your obedience."

A "commission under the King's Broad Seal" soon made Sir William Phips "Captain General and Governor in Chief over the Province of Massachusetts Bay in New England," and on January 3, 1692, Phips and Increase Mather kissed King William's hand upon receiving the document. Four months later they sailed home on the frigate *Nonsuch*, carrying the new charter. A grateful throng greeted them in Boston, the General Court ordered a "Day of Solemn Thanksgiving," and the people addressed "thanks to William and Mary and the chief ministers." Cotton Mather commented, "Why might they not look for halcyon days when they had such a 'King's Fisher' for the Governour?"9

As all office holders know, after election or appointment comes a raft of devilish problems. One was no surprise to Phips: the French menace in the north and the Indians' stubborn resistance to encroachment, exacerbated now since the new charter had given Massachusetts possession of much sparsely populated land conducive to settlement. The Bay Colony's northern border around Pemaquid badly needed strengthening.

A second, just as serious, public concern had been unimaginable, totally inconceivable, until it surfaced: the Salem witchcraft trials.

This was an especially ticklish matter for Phips since his good friend Cotton Mather was so heavily involved. The Boston divine cheered on the prosecution, which had begun acting upon accusations from young girls—several of them refugees from the fighting in Maine—of having been bewitched by certain fellow Salem townspeople. *Spectral evidence*—when the alleged victims claimed that unseen specters had tormented them—was heartily championed by Mather. Yet Phips knew he had to do something to curb this madness.

The third problem for the new chief executive was common enough: political rivals. His two most formidable were the lieutenant governor, William Stoughton, and Joseph Dudley, a onetime associate of Edward Randolph.

In no way daunted, Phips took charge of Massachusetts with his customary energy.

On the northern front, he sent veteran Indian fighter Colonel Benjamin Church to attack the tribes in the Kennebec region and establish an aggressive English presence there. He himself accompanied Church as far as Pemaquid, where the former stockade lay in ruins, and set in motion the creation of a replacement, this time built of stone, that he called Fort William Henry.

Concerning the Salem disturbances, the governor general moved cautiously. He began by establishing a special court to supersede the overwhelmed local court and put Lieutenant Governor Stoughton in charge. Under its auspices, twenty-six people were found guilty and nineteen executed, but there were still another 142 accused. With criticism of the trials mounting and people excited by the fact that one of the condemned, the Reverend George Burroughs, on the scaffold before his death had recited the Lord's Prayer perfectly (which was supposed to be an impossible feat for a witch), Phips acted to end this special "Court of Oyer and Terminer." In its place, he substituted the Superior Court of the Commonwealth, and within a few months, ordered a general pardon for all accused and the release of any remaining prisoners. It was uncharitably whispered by his enemies that Phips's abrupt behavior was due to fear that his own wife Mary was targeted for a witchcraft charge.

Little by little, though, Phips was establishing his grip on the Massachusetts governorship. In August 1693 he arranged a peace with the Wabanaki tribes led by Madockawando and Edgeremet, wherein those Maine Indians abjured their ties to the French and promised "hearty subjection and obedience unto the Crown of England." On the side, it should be added, Phips purchased a large tract of land from Madockawando—mostly the St. George River valley north of Pemaquid. Also worth noting is that the powerful chief's granddaughter—the child of his own daughter Pidianske and the Baron de Castin—was a servant in Phips's Boston household. Captured at Port Royal, she no doubt had been well cared for.

So here we see Billy Phips back in Maine, investing heavily in its future potential for land speculation. Concurrently, he had never given up his ownership of the Phips family's Nequasset property, and among the accusations thrown at him had been that he spent public money needlessly in order to increase the value of his own lands.

Dealing tactfully with opponents never seemed one of William Phips's specialties. In some instances, a brutal caning or battering with fists resulted, as with customs collector Jaheel Brenton and ship captain Richard Short. The politicians—like Stoughton and Dudley—were more subtle, as well as deadly.

To Cotton Mather, Phips's underminers were a "little party of men," out to get his hero; the cleric remarked that Massachusetts was "a Province very talkative and ingenious for vilifying its public servants."[10] Phips hurt himself with the General Court by pushing a bill to require representatives to live in their districts and to end the practice whereby towns could hire Bostonians to be their legislators. The machinations in the provincial house against the governor reached their climax with two votes to remove him from office. The first failed twenty-six to twenty-four and the second twenty-six to twenty. But in London, where such things counted most, a vote of the King's Privy Council was engineered, summoning Phips to appear before it and answer the complaints against him.

On November 17, 1694, Phips left Boston on his own yacht, reaching England the following New Year's Day. He proceeded to London, where he was promptly arrested on a charge of $20,000 in damages brought against him by Brenton and Dudley. Sir Henry Ashurst just as promptly bailed him out.

There was no sign that these events worried Phips. Apparently, he was at work on plans to involve the king in developing his Maine lands as a prime source of naval stores for the British admiralty. Eager to defend himself, too, he presented a request to the Privy Council for a trial, which took place on February 13, 1695.

Several days later, Sir William Phips caught a cold and it developed into a "malignant fever." Within a week, this giant of a man was dead at age forty-four.

His immediate heir was his wife, Lady Mary Spencer Phips, to whom his not-insignificant estate of more than $3,000 (one of the highest in Boston) was left. She, in turn, was to bequeath her worldly goods to Spencer Phips, the childless couple's adopted son, who was actually her nephew. Harvard-educated Spencer Phips went on to have a distinguished career in Massachusetts politics, advancing to the position of lieutenant governor, but has left a bad odor to posterity for a notorious document, signed by him and prominently posted throughout New England in 1755, offering large monetary rewards for Indian scalps and sparing neither women nor children.

Had Sir William Phips lived longer, would he, as Cotton Mather insisted, have developed New England in a much different fashion? The famous minister cited naval stores not exploited, mines not opened, treasures not found—in "poor New England, the chief loser" by his untimely death.

Joseph Dudley, the native Bostonian who had schemed so assiduously hoping to succeed Phips, was at first not successful. The new governor named turned out to be an Anglo-Irish aristocrat, the earl of Bellomont, someone far removed from his Maine-born predecessor. Of the latter, this self-made American, a grieving Mather gushingly wrote, "Few men in the world rising from so mean an original as he, would have acquitted themselves with a thousand part of his capacity or integrity."[11]

1. Cotton Mather, *The Life of Sir William Phips.* New York: Covici Friede, Inc., Publishers, 1929. First published 1697, reprint edited with a preface by Mark Van Doren, p. 14.

2. Ibid., p. 15.

3. Emerson W. Baker and John G. Reid, *The New England Knight, Sir William Phips, 1651–1695.* Toronto: University of Toronto Press, 1998, p. 25.

4. Mather, p. 341.

5. Baker and Reid, p. 48.

6. Ibid., p. 54.

7. Mather, p. 82

8. Ibid., p. 75.

9. Ibid., p. 123.

10. Ibid., p. 183.

11. Ibid., p. 193.

Samuel Waldo, 1695–1759, c. 1750.
Collections of Maine Historical Society, 20783.

THE WALDOS

In 1719, John Leverett, the president of Harvard College, bought from Spencer Phips the large tract of Maine land the latter had inherited from his uncle and adoptive father, the late Sir William Phips. It was basically the property sold to the hero of our previous chapter by Chief Madockawando and also, incidentally, encompassed the midcoast area around the St. George River from which the five Indians had been kidnapped and taken to England.

By 1719, much of Maine's history was beginning to focus on land development—and/or speculation in real estate—whenever lulls in the French and Indian fighting permitted.

In his purchase from Spencer Phips, President Leverett was adding abutting territory to about 1,000 square miles of Maine to which he had become heir four years earlier. This was the famous Muscongus (or Lincolnshire) Patent granted in part to one of his ancestors by the English Crown in 1629. Before that, it had been the property of the Pilgrims, and, in time, was to devolve entirely into the hands of John Leverett. With the Phips-Madockawando addition, it comprised most of today's Waldo and Knox Counties, plus a portion of Penobscot County.

Leverett needed help with such a huge management responsibility. He thus divided the land area into ten parcels and brought in ten investors who called themselves "proprietors," and they, in turn, invited twenty "associates" to join them in this speculative but hopeful venture. As long as the peace treaty arranged with the Indians during 1719 lasted, incoming settlement allowed for two towns in the region—Thomaston and Warren—to be started. More fighting intervened in 1722, but in 1726, peace was back again.

The subjects of this chapter, members of the Waldo family, entered the picture by being among the twenty associates supporting President Leverett.

Our principal actor will be Samuel Waldo, who as a relatively young man, went to England and accomplished an extraordinary act of political legerdemain that left its mark on Maine forever—namely, keeping the Muscongus Patent from falling into the hands of a group of highly placed British schemers. In his later life he was known to his contemporaries mainly by his military title, Brigadier General Waldo, or simply Brigadier Waldo. And he was *not* one of the twenty associates of the Muscongus Patent—those initial Waldo investors in the project were his father, Boston merchant Jonathan Waldo, and his cousin, Boston merchant Cornelius Waldo. The youthful Samuel was a budding Boston merchant, too, at the time.

There has been a bit of nonsense written about the origin of the family's rather un-English-sounding surname. One tale has it that their first forebear to reach England had been a Von Waldow, a minor nobleman transplanted from Hanover, Germany, with the court of King George I, the *Deutsch*-speaking princeling brought to England in 1714 to provide the British Crown with a needed Protestant heir.

A more credible story traces the Waldo heritage back to France and the noted *Pierre de Vaux,* or Peter Waldo, of Lyons, the twelfth-century founder of an heretical, anti-Catholic sect, the Waldenses, which both antedated and survived the Reformation. It seems a later descendant of Peter Waldo fled from the Spanish Inquisition in the Netherlands to England during Queen Elizabeth's reign and started the present line.

First in America was the original Cornelius Waldo, who is found at Salem, Massachusetts, in 1647 but later settled in Ipswich, one of the very earliest communities spun off from the basic Puritan settlements in greater Boston. He married an Ipswich girl, Hannah Cogswell, and they begat, in 1668, the Jonathan Waldo who subsequently, with Hannah Mason, begat Brigadier Samuel.

He was their second child, baptized (if not born) on December 22, 1695.

One of his biographers, Joseph Williamson, had this same Samuel Waldo born in England in 1696. That is clearly not true. However, that writer does acknowledge Brigadier Samuel's New England bonafides by associating him intimately with what was a distinct district in Massachusetts during Waldo's lifetime. "Although not a native of Maine," Williamson wrote, "[Samuel Waldo] was closely identified with its interests and [his] enlightened wisdom and personal efforts were largely instrumental in reclaiming from the wilderness what is now one of the most flourishing portions of our State."[1]

After 1719, the Muscongus Patent had been consolidated in the hands of some thirty Boston businessmen and was set to start cashing in on its potential. Lower Massachusetts was more than ever full of land-hungry Englishmen, eager to carve homes out of the endless forests in the "Eastern Parts," and every new settlement would increase the value of their investment. Even the very trees they cut down there had great value (as Sir William Phips had planned to show the king) for naval stores—turpentine, resin, pitch, and tar—for lumber, and most especially for the magnificent tall evergreens that could provide the best masts in the world to grace His Majesty's warships.

Yet all of these dreams of riches of the proprietors and their associates suddenly faced a terrible threat. Word had reached Boston that a conspiracy was forming in London to deprive them of their lands. Worse still, it was located in the highest echelons of the British government, instigated by men of wealth and enormous influence. The holders of the Muscongus Patent needed a champion in London's halls of power—and they had to act fast.

Near at home they found a clever, promising young entrepreneur, Jonathan Waldo's son, Samuel, whose credentials included a smooth manner (some would say *slick*), good business judgment, and experience in dealing with Maine real estate. With his brother Cornelius, he managed a store on downtown King Street, handling fish, naval stores, provisions, and lumber. He also shipped wood to the West Indies and Europe. His later lengthy career in the Massachusetts General Court (its legislature) argued that he had already acquired a veneer of political polish when he was tapped to go abroad and help defend the interests of his relatives and fellow New Englanders.

Samuel was promised that, if successful, he would be given half the land in the patent for his own.

En route across the Atlantic in 1730, the path of thirty-four-year-old Samuel Waldo intertwined, as it were, with another rising Bostonian of respectable family and important connections. Sailing back to Boston about the same time was Jonathan Belcher, who had just scored a political coup at the court of George I, where the king had appointed him the new governor of Massachusetts, his ministers having accepted the argument that filling the vacancy with a native of the colony might prove advantageous in ruling that unruly bunch of provincials. Belcher and Waldo, in the years to come, were to clash mightily.

But for the moment, in 1730, the England-bound Waldo was concentrating totally on his appointed task—rescuing the Muscongus Patent from the rapacious hands of what he may well have regarded as a gang of big-shot thieves.

This would-be land grab was ostensibly led by Thomas Coram, a rich philanthropist. But the real puller-of-strings behind the scenes was one of the most influential (if little known) Britons of that day—Colonel Martin Bladen, who ran the Board of Trade, the English governmental entity that controlled the colonies. Bladen, Coram, and company were operating on the specious premise that Muscongus no longer belonged to Leverett, Waldo, and company because a brief occupation of the area by the French had nullified all previous ownership titles. Moreover, they had dispatched an agent to enforce their claims, a pugnacious ex-British army colonel named David Dunbar, who immediately began starting settlements on these lands.

The adjective most commonly used to describe Dunbar was "choleric." He had a fierce Scots-Irish temper. Jonathan Belcher, with whom he also had a blistering relationship, scathingly labeled him "the bull frog from the Hibernian fens." Bull *dog* would have been just as apt. He commenced his career in Maine by establishing poor Scots-Irish Presbyterian immigrants on Muscongus Patent land at Pemaquid, while plotting to use his support in England to have the whole region declared a new province, separated from Massachusetts. It was to be called "Georgia," in honor of the king, and at Pemaquid he went ahead and unilaterally changed the fort's title from Phips's Fort William Henry to Fort Frederick, thus currying favor with the heir to the British throne, Frederick, Prince of Wales.

Dunbar had also raised a powerful political issue with his activities. Those giant mast trees in the Maine woods and elsewhere had been declared Crown property. You were forbidden to cut them down, even if they were on your own soil. As far as the Yankee proprietors were concerned, this was a law to be observed in the breach. Mast tree smuggling—the prices they could get in Europe were astronomical—was widespread. By promising to curb it, David Dunbar got himself appointed the surveyor general of the king's woods. He could now have his henchmen invade anyone's land and remove those incredibly valuable pines, and he could trumpet his fanatic regard for the king's "prerogative"—the sovereign rights of His Majesty, which in Maine and later New Hampshire, were anything Dunbar said they were.

All of this was going on in Muscongus country while Samuel Waldo was still sailing to England.

On a legal basis—that is, licensed by the Crown—Waldo had already likewise dabbled in the business of furnishing masts for the Royal Navy. He had done so in what is now Greater Portland and currently the city of Westbrook, then called *Saccarappa*. The eventual change of name honored Thomas Westbrook, a sawmill owner from New Hampshire, who early on became Waldo's partner. A contemporary author has written that it is "more than probable that Westbrook got his appointment [as royal mast agent] through Waldo's influence."[2]

No detailed analysis appears to exist of Waldo's influence and how he worked it on the British political scene. All major decisions, of course, were made in London. Lobbying was as fierce then as now in politics. Was money handed around? Almost certainly. To overcome Martin Bladen some masterly clout would have been needed. Waldo's most likely ally, in this case, had to have been Ralph Gulston, of Gulston Brothers, a commercial firm that succeeded in receiving a monopoly on supplying mast trees to the Crown and made Waldo its chief agent in Maine. This association was further cemented when the colonial entrepreneur named his youngest son Ralph Gulston Waldo.

Undoubtedly, at this point in time, too, Governor Belcher and the bulk of the establishment landed gentry in Massachusetts had no wish to see a large chunk of their commonwealth removed and made into an independent province by a lowly Irish interloper with a choleric temper like Dunbar. Consequently, various considerations militated among the powers that be in Whitehall against a northern "Georgia."

Waldo's efforts were soon to pay off.

On November 23, 1732, the House of Representatives in Boston received a letter from the Massachusetts agent in London and recorded it in its Journal. It contained an order issued on August 10, 1732, almost three months before, by "her most gracious majesty [Queen Mary] in Council." As stated, the Privy Council's communication, upon advice of the king's attorney general, directed David Dunbar, Esq., to quit the possession of "the lands therein mentioned," which were delineated as "lying between the Rivers Penobscot and St. Croix." In other words, Dunbar was to get out of Maine and stay out.

Thus ended the overseas threat to the Muscongus Patent. Thus, also, did Samuel Waldo, already prospering as a merchant and speculator, strike gold, so to speak, in acquiring 300,000 acres of Maine for himself.

His father had died while he was in England and he returned home to discover that he had inherited additional real estate holdings, but very little money with which to develop all this territory—a mere $5,000 in cash.

So now his problem was: how to go about profiting from his vast realm in the "Eastern Parts," adding value to a wilderness still always susceptible to the attacks of its Indian inhabitants, whenever angered.

Waldo at once gave his full and usual focused attention to the new domain. On both sides of the Medomak and St. George Rivers he had lots "set out in severalty"—made available for personal ownership. He built a lime kiln where settlers could burn lime for the Boston market. He had surveys conducted. He met with disgruntled Penobscot tribesmen and prospective home buyers and supervised the first permanent settlement on the St. George River. He erected a sawmill.

A domestic threat was next. Would there be room enough in Massachusetts for two highly ambitious native sons like Samuel Waldo and Jonathan Belcher? The latter, or so Waldo believed, had unleashed a plot against him. Those land titles in Maine were once again challenged and actually necessitated his publishing a pamphlet under the heading: *A Defense of the Title...to a Tract of Lands...commonly called Muscongus Lands.* In the end, Waldo held onto his property, but his enmity toward the governor was undying.

It was not until 1738 that Waldo managed to free himself from his local troubles and cross the Atlantic to settle accounts with Belcher by politicking at George II's court.

Moreover, he had a good issue. The Crown's original thought that a hometown boy like Belcher could best deal with his colonial compatriots, who were never humble enough nor obedient enough in the eyes of the British monarch's establishment, was on shaky ground. What Waldo set out to prove was how Belcher had been an abject failure, at least when it came to protecting His Majesty's mast trees. Of course, Waldo, as well, had his own pecuniary interest in the subject as the Gulston Brothers exclusive local contractor; it was money out of his own pocket if the valuable pines were illegally diverted.

By now he had already shown a distinctly combative side, exhibiting a quick readiness to sue when crossed and a pronounced independence in his ways. In 1738 he had split from his brother Cornelius and opened a shop of his own, importing luxury goods like "choice Irish duck [a type of cloth], fine Florence wine in chests, and good Irish butter," plus (it was right there in the advertisement) "a likely young Negro."

A year earlier, he had ended his arrangement with Thomas Westbrook, taken him to court, and won a judgment of more than $7,500. Westbrook complained to the legislature that the case had ended before he could testify and present his accounts, and he countersued for $13,000. Among his other beefs were that Waldo had kept false accounts and had charged *him*, Westbrook, for all supplies, although they were partners and the expenditures had benefited only Waldo. His former partner, he declared, wanted to "crush him while he was alive."

Whether Waldo's animus against Westbrook was as fierce as against Belcher was problematical. Once in London, he pulled out all stops to have his enemy removed from office.

Not only did he have the cogent argument that Belcher was "soft" on pine trees, but he had a viable replacement candidate to push. William Shirley, a second son of a minor noble (who wouldn't inherit the title and had to go to work), had come to Boston to practice law. Waldo, with his penchant for using the courts, became one of his clients. The two men plotted together to dump Belcher, and once Waldo was ensconced in London, Mrs. Frances Shirley, the barrister's attractive and well-connected wife, joined him there in the lobbying effort. From Boston, Shirley sent Waldo a steady stream of instructions on whom to lobby—top people like Sir Charles Wager and Lord of the Admiralty Winnington—and always for them to remind everyone "what an errant villain he [Belcher] has been to the King's interest in the woods."3

Back home, Belcher wasn't worried. His scornful nickname for Waldo was Trincalo—from a comic character in Shakespeare's *The*

Tempest—and in a letter to a supporter, the Massachusetts governor predicted that "Trincalo will return [from England] a sort of beheaded puppy, and if he should yelp, he'll not be able to bite...we have a squadron of deaths, writs, arrests, and judgments waiting to alight him." For Belcher, Waldo was "that restless, malicious mortal [who] had been under a fit of rheumatism and piles," and the writs against him "would make him clap his tail between his legs and leer like a dog."[4]

It was three years before English political factors swung in the anti-Belcher party's favor. In 1741, a Whig ministry took charge of the British government and it was led by the duke of Newcastle who, it happened, was William Shirley's patron. Belcher was out and so was David Dunbar as New Hampshire's lieutenant governor, when that colony was made a full-fledged province under Benning Wentworth, a mast-tree ally of Waldo's.

His triumphant coup notwithstanding, Waldo still faced a daunting task in exploiting his investment. The geopolitical situation in the north country was dicey at best. The Indians were always questionable, sometimes docile but just as liable to go on the warpath. The French, an imperial power since Louis XIV and intermittently at war worldwide against England, were always goading the tribes to stem the flow of settlers to Maine. Waldo's need, on the other hand, was to bring in more and more immigrants.

The flow up from Massachusetts of second- and third-generation colonials seeking homesites was steady, but insufficient. Consquently, Waldo turned to the Old World not just for outflanking his enemies but also to populate his domains. The people he sought had to be Protestants, but they didn't have to speak English.

Kurtze Beschreibung derer Landschaft Massachusetts Bay in New England was the title of a pamphlet distributed in the Palatine region of Germany in 1741. Translation: "Short Description of the District of Massachusetts Bay in New England." The rest of the come-on wording in the Teutonic tongue then announced that the Royal British official Samuel Waldo, the inheritor of the "unusual" (*absonderlich*) Broad Bay region, was seeking foreign Protestants as settlers. This broadside, issued from the Rhineland city of Speyer, was dated July 14, 1741, and signed by Samuel Waldo and Sebastian Zuberbuhler.

The latter gentleman with the mouthful of a surname was a Swiss-

German who had been in touch with the would-be American land baron since 1735. But their planned activities of transporting Germans to Maine had been deferred until the business with Belcher was settled. Starting early in 1741, Zuberbuhler installed himself at the Golden Lion Inn in Speyer and began recruiting. In 1742, having attracted a critical mass of volunteers from the area, he embarked with them for America, traveling first to Rotterdam, then to England, then to Massachusetts. Waldo and Governor Shirley greeted them in Marblehead, whence they went on to Maine, to Broad Bay at the mouth of the Medomak River "where...a few huts stood to mark the site of their new home."[5]

Culture shock certainly was in store for these transplanted Europeans. In the flyer he had circulated, Waldo, who styled himself the "Hereditary Lord of Broad Bay," had promised, among other things, "to build and complete at his own expense two houses for their [domiciles]—each house to be 35 feet square and two stories high and likewise a church," and the houses were to cost $100 apiece and the church $200. None of these constructions had even been started when the newcomers arrived. Jasper Jacob Stahl, the author of *History of Old Broad Bay and Waldoboro*,[6] has tried ex post facto to make excuses for Waldo, citing the expense of his effort to oust Belcher, which had left him having to borrow money from his cousin Cornelius and mortgage his home. Alleging that Waldo wasn't as bad as he's been painted, he depicts the hereditary lord assuring the survival of his German charges by supplying them, although they now had to build their own dwellings and church. The settlement at Broad Bay, one day to be named Waldoboro, was helped by Zuberbuhler's energy. Lots were handed out, log cabins were erected, and Waldo made sure they had food enough before winter approached. He showed up in person and assisted in straightening out some friction they'd had with Dunbar's Scots-Irish, living to the south of them around Newcastle and Damariscotta. Nevertheless, two German doctors named Kast and Kurz addressed a petition of complaint to the Massachusetts General Court that Governor Shirley tried in vain to have dismissed. Notwithstanding which, the house balked at appropriating money to get the Germans through the winter, claiming the Rhinelanders would have a full season to plant their crops.

It was a rough life for these German-speaking pioneers, yet in 1744, when England and France again went to war against each other, they joined up in large numbers to form part of a colonial expeditionary force, in a regiment led by Waldo, to attack the massive French fortress of Louisbourg on Cape Breton Island off the tip of Nova Scotia.

Here begins another facet of Samuel Waldo's career. He had already been a merchant, a landholder, a dabbler in emigration, and, apparently, also slavery; now he was entering military life—at one of the highest rungs—as a brigadier general. Under his command at Louisbourg were 270 men from Broad Bay and nearby St. George. Admittedly, many had flocked to his banner because they were having such "a hard time at home."7 Sebastian Zuberbuhler was commissioned a captain in the New England army, and several of the German enlistees took their families with them to participate in the successful siege of France's mightiest North American fortress.

This ambitious assault had been Governor Shirley's idea. Initially, he had hoped to lead it, but decided he'd better stay in Boston to keep an eye on his political enemies. Nor was he able to choose his close pal Waldo for the top command. This post went to a merchant from Kittery—arguably the richest man in New England—William Pepperrell. In time, he and Waldo made an effective team in an enterprise that, against all odds, proved astonishingly successful.

Fortress Louisbourg fell in 1745 when the French were defeating the British everywhere else in the world. Pepperrell was rewarded with a title of nobility—baronet—thus becoming Sir William. Waldo won no such honors. Still, he and Pepperrell remained close allies, even personal friends and near relatives of a sort. First, Waldo's step-brother, Nathaniel Sparhawk, married Pepperrell's daughter Betsy, and then Waldo's daughter Hannah was engaged to Pepperrell's son Andrew. These two great landowners also had a vested interest in timber management and protecting the mast trade, particularly so after Waldo gave a piece of his timber monopoly to the Kittery man's son-in-law.

At the battle of Louisbourg, the two nonmilitary ex-merchants worked well together. Each had his regiment (you could make money equipping and supplying your own troops), and Waldo's Mainers—Germans and others—acquitted themselves well. After an outlying French redoubt was captured, Waldo was put in charge of turning its cannon on the principal French stronghold. History records an interesting appeal he issued to Pepperrell: "We are in most extreme want of liquor; all the brandy and wine gone, even to a drop; beg you'll send the quantity of a hogshead in kegs...."[8] He then amended his order to French rum. His artillerymen were also instrumental in reducing French resistance on a small island in the harbor and allowing the entrance of British Royal Navy warships. Despite the collegiality between Waldo and Pepperrell, the latter did receive an anonymous warning that cautioned, "The expedition was calculated to establish Shirley and make his creature Waldo Governor of Cape Breton, which is to be a place of refuge to him from his creditors."[9]

As it turned out, Samuel Waldo did not stay in Cape Breton. The House Journal of the Massachusetts legislature, where both Pepperrell and Waldo served in the upper body, records on June 26, 1746, that Samuel Waldo, "Brigadier-General in the late Expedition against Cape Breton arrived from Louisbourg." A committee of distinguished citizens and military officers was formed to "congratulate him upon his safe return to his native country."[10]

Subsequent entries concerning Brigadier Waldo are found in this official publication throughout the 1740s and 1750s and even beyond his death in 1759. Mostly, they touch upon military matters, since the French threat did not end with their loss of Louisbourg; in fact, the British government gave the fort back to them in 1748, an act that infuriated the colonials. Waldo was ordered to prop up defenses in York County and, in "Brigadier Waldo's Representation," he asked to have "ten whole boats bought" and delivered to his forces, the money for them to be deducted from "the bounty granted on scalps and captives, if any should be taken."[11] As a member of the council (equivalent to a senate, but appointed, not elected), Waldo was frequently called upon to serve on a committee to investigate veterans' complaints and those of their families.

Reference is sometimes made in these entries to *Captain* Waldo. This was the Brigadier's *son*, Samuel Jr., one of his six children. His namesake had been with him at Louisbourg, and in 1753 father and son were together in Germany, lining up more settlers for Broad Bay. This final overseas trip for Samuel Sr. was said also to have been motivated by his anger over having been insufficiently rewarded for his service at Louisbourg. Allegedly, he went first to England to press a claim of $2,340 for expenses.

Their man in Germany was now Joseph Crellius, who spoke good English and had once lived in New England. He had previously sent to Maine a colony of Huguenots, escaped from Catholic France to Germany, who established themselves on Waldo land in what is now the town of Dresden. Crellius then lined up a shipload of his own country-men—the last of the brigadier's "German enterprise." While on the Continent with his son, Samuel Sr. had a chance to exercise his political skills at the Reichstag (the German legislative body) in Regensburg, in order to gain permission for his settlers to emigrate. Young Samuel remained nearby in Frankfurt until the autumn of 1753, supervising the project.

The home to which the younger man returned was in Falmouth (Portland) where he, too, entered politics, filling a seat in the Massachusetts House of Representatives for the "City by the Sea."

While Samuel Jr. had been at Harvard, one of his classmates—and a close friend—was Andrew Pepperrell, to whom he introduced his sis-ter Hannah. The decision of these two to marry was greeted happily by both families—a merging of dynasties. However, it was never to be and its failure to happen would play an intriguing future role in Maine and U.S. history.

Andrew, the only son of Sir William and Lady Pepperrell, turned out to be a quirky youth. Regarding his fiancée, he began to disappoint her by repeatedly postponing their wedding, until finally she angrily rejected him and soon found herself another husband. His name was Thomas Flucker and he was the able secretary of the Massachusetts Provincial Government. One of their daughters—Lucy, the only mem-ber of this Tory family to side with the American Revolution—married Henry Knox who, through her, was to inherit and/or buy all of the Waldo lands in Maine. Samuel Jr. himself fled to England.

In the last year of his life, 1759, Samuel Sr. was still playing an active role in Massachusetts and Maine public life. On January 25, 1759, he reported to the lawmakers in Boston that he had received word that "some papers of great importance relating the right of the English to Nova Scotia"[12] were possessed by a Frenchman at Cape Sable; a vessel they were sending to Seal Island should go to Cape Sable and obtain them.

The French, at this date, still were a force in Canada, centered in

Quebec, although the fortress at Louisbourg had been reconquered the year before.

On March 19, 1759, Brigadier Waldo was made part of a legislative group assigned "to establish the defenses of the Eastern and Western Frontiers."

No doubt it was in this connection that he joined an expedition scheduled to head north to Maine in the spring. The new governor in Massachusetts, replacing William Shirley, with whom Waldo had quarreled, was Thomas Pownall, the younger brother of an important London official. Pownall's intention was to head for the Penobscot River and firmly place its watershed under British control. At age sixty-three, Waldo went along as second in command with the idea of inspecting lands he owned in the area. By ship, the contingent moved to the mouth of the large water body, stopping at today's Stockton Springs, where they constructed a stockade on Cape Jellison to command the Penobscot's access and egress. From there, they ascended upriver. On the east side, approximately in modern-day Brewer, they came ashore at Waldo's urging. This was his land.

A dramatic scene occurred next. The brigadier was pointing out the limit of his property. "Here are my bounds," he announced to the assembled officers and men, following which he suddenly clutched his chest and promptly toppled to the ground. It was apoplexy, as they called it in those days—a fatal heart attack.

Governor Pownall described the incident as follows: "Brigadier Waldo, whose unremitted zeal for the service had prompted him at the age of sixty-three to attend our expedition, dropp'd down just above the Falls...and notwithstanding all the assistance that could be given him, expired in a few moments."[13]

His body was brought back to Fort Point (the stockade) and later transported to Boston for burial. This happened toward the end of May 1759. Shortly afterward, in early June at Kittery Point, Waldo's friend, comrade in arms, and fellow great landowner, Sir William Pepperrell, also passed away.

We last hear of Samuel Waldo, Sr., in March 1760, with two entries in the House Journal. On March 21, Samuel Waldo, Esq., representative from Falmouth (also known as Colonel Waldo), Francis Waldo, another son, and sons-in-law Isaac Winslow and Thomas Flucker—the four men acting as "Administrators of the Estate of the Honorable Brigadier Samuel Waldo, Esq.," requested action to have the superior court take up their relative's estate and court cases left pending when he died so suddenly twenty days before the sitting of His Majesty's Superior Court in York County. Four days later, these influential gentlemen received an order that their petitions had been accepted.

Two final postscripts on the Waldos:

The Ralph Gulston Waldo, who died young and was named for his father's employer, has left a bit of heritage in that name. Most Americans know *Ralph Waldo* Emerson. He was of the same family tree, and the famed philosopher-writer, although mainly connected with Concord, Massachusetts, did have Maine ties.

Next, the issue of slavery. There was that "likely young Negro" Samuel Waldo, Sr., had advertised for sale. Similarly, it's been discovered that he owned a slave ship. Under a Captain Samuel Rhodes, this 69-foot sloop, *Africa,* sailed to that continent and left Gambia with a cargo of 200 slaves, more than a ton of beeswax, and half a ton of ivory. This was in 1734. However, on the return trip to Boston, most of the slaves perished, and some 3,500 gallons of rum, used to help purchase them, was unaccounted for. Having already started his suing ways, Waldo took the captain to court.

In December 2005, a resident of Northport, Maine, which is in Waldo County, raised the question of whether Waldo's name should still grace this jurisdiction. Thomas Bamford thinks not, and presumably would change Waldoboro and the county of Waldo, as well. In January 2006 Bamford wrote: "Samuel Waldo's active participation in the slave trade makes him an unworthy namesake for our county, where hard work, independence, and self-reliance are so highly prized. He was a wealthy man, made even richer through his buying and selling of fellow humans, and it is time we held him responsible."[14]

Bamford added that he planned to present a formal request to the Waldo County commissioners to make the change to honor someone "more deserving."

That was several years ago. The name is still Waldo County.

1. Paper read to the Maine Historical Society, March 30, 1876. James Phinney Baxter, editor, *Documentary History of the State of Maine*, Volume 5. Portland, ME: 1897.
2. Leonard B. Chapman, article written for the *Portland Transcript*, 1883. In Stroudwater Scrapbook, p. 73.
3. Neil Rolde, *Sir William Pepperrell of Colonial New England.* Brunswick, ME: Harpswell Press, 1982, p. 44.
4. Ibid., p. 45
5. Roots Web Searches, "Sebastian Zouberbuhler." http//free pages.genealogy.rootsweb.ancestry.com, p. 2.
6. Jasper Jacob Stahl, *History of Old Broad Bay and Waldoboro*, two volumes. Portland, ME: Bond Wheelwright, 1956, p. 111
7. Roots Web Searches, "Sebastian Zouberbuhler." p. 3.
8. Rolde, p. 91.
9. Ibid., p. 103
10. *Journals of the House of Representatives of Massachusetts.* Boston: Massachusetts Historical Society, 1942.
11. Ibid., Volume 24, 1747–48, p. 147
12. Ibid., January 25, 1759.
13. Neil Rolde, *The Interrupted Forest.* Gardiner, ME: Tilbury House, Publishers, 2001, p. 181.
14. Thomas Bamford, news@villagesoup.com. Article in the *Citizen,* January 11, 2006.

Commodore Edward Preble, c. 1805.
Collections of Maine Historical Society, 17993.

5

COMMODORE EDWARD PREBLE

When Samuel Waldo died on the east bank of the Penobscot River in 1759, he was participating in one of the most strategic—and successful—English operations during the entire French and Indian Wars. The fort that Governor Thomas Pownall constructed commanding the mouth of the immense waterway was an unheralded event in and of itself. It was also one that in hindsight helped close off almost all Indian raids in Maine four years before the cataclysmic battle at Quebec ended the French presence in North America.

Put in charge of the newly built fort, originally known as Fort Pownall, was Jedediah Preble, a brigadier general of the militia, born in York but since moved to Falmouth (Portland). A veteran of the Louisbourg campaign, colonel of a regiment in battles against the French at Fort Ticonderoga, Preble was also, starting in 1753, a representative from his adopted town to the General Court in Boston, and by 1770 he was acknowledged to be among Portland's richest men. It has been documented that while he commanded Fort Pownall, he bought 2,700 acres of Penobscot land before being replaced in 1763. Twenty years later, once Massachusetts had become a state and was no longer a province of England, he served as a state senator from Cumberland County.

This distinguished citizen was twice wed, his first wife having died in 1753, the year he entered politics. The two ladies presented him with eleven children. His son Edward Preble, a man hailed as the founder of the U.S. Navy, was the fourth child of six from General Jedediah's second marriage.

The Preble home in Portland, in which Edward was born on August 15, 1761, fronted Casco Bay and the distant ocean. When the boy was fourteen years old, some eight months after Concord and Lexington, a Royal Navy fleet commanded by a particularly hard-nosed British officer, Henry Mowatt, sailed into the harbor and bombarded the community, burning and leveling many, if not most, of its buildings. Among these was the Preble home.

In later years, Mowatt, who had a grudge against Portland, where he'd briefly been imprisoned by revolutionaries, boasted he could claim responsibility for Edward Preble's going to sea.

Mowatt and the temporarily homeless teenager were to confront each other several more times. The haughty Englishman had won his freedom in Portland by giving his word of honor not to fight anymore, an oath he promptly violated. Assigned to sea duty along the upper New England coast, he was soon a constant thorn in the American patriots' side.

Meanwhile, a year after Mowatt's revenge raid, fifteen-year-old Edward Preble was off to private school, to the venerable Governor Dummer Academy, which still operates in Byfield, Massachusetts, as the Governor's Academy. Four years later, following a brief spell of farming in the Capisic section of Portland and still a teenager at nineteen, Edward entered the *State* Navy of Massachusetts in the spring of 1780 as a junior officer.

As such, young Preble would soon be facing Captain Mowatt.

It was a bit ironic that one of Mowatt's first actions in the Revolutionary War had been to dismantle Fort Pownall, where Edward's father had commanded, the ostensible reason being to keep it from falling into American hands. And everywhere Down East, Mowatt seemed perpetually active. He led an amphibious British attack on Machias that was beaten back by local patriots and their Passamaquoddy and Maliseet Indian allies. But more successful was Mowatt's assault on Castine, a key town at the mouth of the Penobscot opposite Fort Pownall. This vital place, the patriot leaders in Boston decided, could not be allowed to rest in British hands. They mounted a powerful armada of ships and troops to recapture the area, which the British were grooming to be both a refuge for Tories fleeing the Revolution and the springboard for an effort to detach northeastern coastal Maine and join it to Canada. The Yankee counterattack was a thorough disaster, called the worst defeat of an American naval fleet until Pearl Harbor. The hulks of the vessels sunk or scuttled in this foiled rescue attempt yet clutter the Penobscot's muddy bottom after a panicked retreat sent them fleeing upriver. Mowatt was prominent among the British victors.

The debacle occurred in 1779. The war was still raging the following April when Ensign Edward Preble boarded a Massachusetts warship,

Protector, with twenty-six guns, and headed north on her. At Portland, *Protector* stopped to disgorge the city's new military commander, another Portlander, General Peleg Wadsworth, with whom the Preble family would long be connected. Then it was on to British-held Castine, where Mowatt was in charge of the naval defense.

In his first taste of battle, Edward Preble helped capture an armed sloop Mowatt had sent out to fight them. When more British warships appeared, *Protector* escaped by retreating beyond Monhegan. Before long, she was ordered to American-held Machias for patrol duty and protection of Yankee ships and settlers from roving English privateers. One of those licensed pirates she ultimately sunk had outgunned her— the thirty-two-gun *Admiral Duff.* The range of *Protector* increased as she competed in this sort of guerrilla warfare at sea. Far from Maine, near Block Island in Long Island Sound, Preble's ship was overtaken by a superior British squadron and forced to surrender. Crew and officers, including Edward Preble, were thrown into prison.

Their confinement was aboard the notorious prison hulk *Jersey,* in which many Americans had died. Preble might have shared their fate but for a stroke of sheer good fortune. In New York City at the time was William Tyng, the former Portland sheriff, who had been a close friend of Preble's father, the general. The two of them had fought together at Louisbourg, and although Tyng was a Tory refugee, he used his influence to help the incarcerated young Mainer. Not only did he arrange for him to live ashore on parole and help nurse him through a serious illness, but within two months, facilitated his exchange for a British prisoner. The rest of Preble's shipmates were kept much longer.

Soon back on active duty, Preble was promoted to lieutenant and assigned to another Massachusetts warship, the *Winthrop,* with twelve guns. As one of his biographers wrote, "War went on, small and dirty, in Maine waters."[1] There is a romantic word picture of Preble, pistols in both hands, boarding a British privateer brig, the *Merriam,* on stormy waters Down East. Ultimately, the *Winthrop* was off to warmer climes, cruising the Caribbean. From headquarters at Antigua, the Yankees would raid enemy shipping and take their prizes to Montserrat and St. Kitts.

At the end of March 1783, all U.S. naval wartime activity was ordered to cease and the *Winthrop* was sold. But Preble continued his naval career by joining the civilian Massachusetts Merchant Marine, where he was employed on various vessels for the next fifteen years.

Throughout this decade and a half, until 1799, when he became a lieutenant commander in the fledgling United States Navy, Edward Preble was traveling the world. Had he had the literary talent of his son's boyhood friend Henry Wadsworth Longfellow, the commodore might have left us a mother lode of exciting tales of exotic places he visited, like the coast of Guinea in Africa, Tobago, St. Croix, Hispaniola, and Cuba in the West Indies, Lisbon in Portugal, Nova Scotia, even North Carolina in those antebellum days. Eventually, he achieved his first command, master of a sixty-ton schooner, the *Elizabeth*.

On his way home from Guadalupe, whose despotic governor he likened to an oriental potentate, Preble had to dodge the numerous French privateers in that part of the Caribbean. Yet his biggest trial was with one of his subordinates, a fellow Mainer from Gorham named Lamb. In the style of Sir William Phips, he pummeled this sailor so badly in a fight that he was arrested and it cost him a good deal to pay off the injured party.

That Edward Preble had the financial resources to do so was no doubt thanks to his well-fixed father. In 1792 he was also able to buy a house lot in Portland, but even more impressive was a later purchase of 800 acres of forestland on the west side of the Kennebec River.

It was on March 27, 1794, that President George Washington signed a bill signaling our country's intention to have a federal navy. Congress had passed the measure authorizing the construction of six frigates after several North African Barbary states had had their pirates seize eleven U.S. merchant vessels and literally enslave their crews.

At the time, Preble rushed to apply for a lieutenant's commission. "I believe I am the only person that has made application from the District of Maine,"[2] he declared, while seeking political support and approaching Secretary of War Henry Knox, who had large holdings in Maine. His own congressman, George Thacher of Biddeford, provided a strong letter of support. However, not until 1798 did Preble's commission come through, two weeks before a separate U.S. Department of the Navy was created apart from the jurisdiction of the secretary of war. Preble had been made a first lieutenant; furthermore, he was assigned to a just-built ship that was to become the all-time hallmark of the U.S. fleet: "Old

Ironsides," the USS *Constitution.*

Preble would later have command of her, too, as soon as he'd made his way up the ranks. His next berth was as a lieutenant commander in charge of the *Pickering,* a fourteen-gun brig, and he sailed her in the Caribbean, harassing those French privateers he'd once fled, and recapturing U.S. vessels they'd taken as prizes. All told, the *Pickering* snatched ten French prizes, including one much more heavily armed Gallic warship.

Preble was more than proving himself on the high seas. In order to keep such an energetic and now experienced officer, navy secretary Benjamin Stoddert offered the Mainer a captaincy, rather than see him go off to Japan on a merchant voyage. Captain Preble's next command, in 1799, was the *Essex,* built in Salem, Massachusetts, and if he regretted not seeing Japan, he was soon embarked on almost as epic a journey in the Pacific, heading to Batavia in the Dutch East Indies (today's Indonesia). Leaving frigid New England in January 1800, Preble reached Capetown, South Africa, in March and sighted Java at the beginning of May. His mission was to escort home four American merchantmen and protect them from French privateers—including the famed and much feared *Surcouf,* which he chased off after a spirited fight.

This undeclared naval war with France that had siphoned away American resources mercifully came to an end in 1801. The U.S. could turn its attention to other annoyances—British harassment, for one, but especially those North African states that were making the western Mediterranean unsafe. In the same month Lieutenant Commander Preble was being married in Portland, the sultan of Morocco, Moulay Sulaimen, announced he would join his Libyan Barbary neighbor Tripoli in declaring war on the United States.

The courtship of Edward Preble and Mary Deering had begun in 1799. Their families both lived on Middle Street—the Prebles actually in a house requisitioned from Tories to replace their dwelling destroyed by Mowatt. The navy man had been deeply smitten, but his duties as an officer kept interfering with his romance. In a missive to his intended's mother, the widow Dorcas Deering, he sounded more like a lovesick puppy than a hardened sea dog: "You have long known of my attachment to your lovely daughter and I feel truly sensible of the delicacy with which you have ever attended to my feeling whenever I have visited your house.... Could my lovely friend know how much I suffer from the thoughts of so long an absence from her, for whom alone I wish to live, I am sure she would pity me. Give my best love to her, and tell her the future happiness of my life rests with her and may the God of all goodness restore me to the joys of her loved society."[3]

It can be said the "God of all goodness" kept his end of the bargain since Preble won the fair lady's hand. It was a happy marriage despite his protracted absences. He and Mary built their own house on Middle Street before he was called back to duty, this time to be captain of the *Constitution*, newly down the ways at the Charlestown Navy Yard. On July 13, 1803, Preble received his orders to take charge of "Old Ironsides," and also in that capacity to replace Commodore Richard Morris as chief of the Mediterranean squadron—the front line of frigates and other battle wagons now lined up against the Barbary powers.

On board eventually with Preble was another Portland player in this drama, whose home was a few blocks from Middle Street, on today's Congress Street, now the city's main drag. Here, General Peleg Wadsworth had settled after the Revolution. His son, Henry Wadsworth, had chosen the navy for a career instead of his hero-father's army, and had himself reassigned to Preble's flagship for the North African campaign.

Midshipman Wadsworth, "a young man with literary ambitions," it was said, did pen a series of sketches he entitled "Letters written aboard the US Ship *Constitution*, Edward Preble, Esq., Commander and Commander of the American Squadron."[4]

During Preble's first confrontation with the Muslim enclaves (which were technically under Turkish rule but acted like independent nations) at Tangiers in Morocco, Wadsworth accompanied his superior ashore and left a description of the efforts at negotiation.

The ship's company in procession led the way, Wadsworth wrote, followed by "two mules, two Jews...carrying presents, which were several silver teapots, silks, muslins, linens..." plus more mundane items such as loaf sugar, tea, and coffee that Wadsworth thought "not such as an Emperor [which the sultan also styled himself] would be in want of...." Through the twisting Tangiers streets, they walked to the local potentate's castle and in the meeting room "on one side of us were drawn up in three or four crooked rows about fifty guards, dirty and languishing."[5] The *emperor* appeared; a cushion was put down on the step of a doorway. The sultan sat on it. Wadsworth was surprised the arrangement wasn't fancier. The parley proceeded. The Moroccan said he wanted peace with the United States. Preble responded by presenting the American conditions. They would release a Moroccan ship they'd captured and her crew if the sultan would formally ratify the treaty he'd made in 1786 and give up all U.S. prizes and prisoners in his possession. These terms the sultan accepted, and peace with Morocco meant Preble could continue his diplomatic efforts with the other two North African fiefdoms prior to focusing on the fourth and the toughest nut to crack, Tripoli.

So Algiers was next. Its sovereign was called the *dey*. To date, he had had friendly relations with the U.S. Also on this trip, the observant Wadsworth once more wielded his pen and started with the dey's gardens and stables and other surroundings, adding, "The horses about forty in number were the first of the Arabian breed, the most beautiful I ever saw." There were 700 house slaves on the premises, in this case Maltese sailors who had surrendered while under English colors. Wadsworth added a homey touch, too, inspired by his meeting with the wife of Tobias Lear, a close friend of George Washington's, who was the new American consul in Algiers. Mrs. Lear, herself a close relative of Washington's, had a "likeness," as Wadsworth put it, "to my much lamented sister Elizabeth." (By way of an explanatory digression, the Wadsworth-Longfellow connection enters here. Back home in Portland, there had been a tragic scene: Elizabeth Wadsworth dying; her sister Zilpah attending to her; her fiancé Stephen Longfellow holding her hand—but death followed by new life, Stephen Longfellow marrying Zilpah Wadsworth, and the couple having a son, Henry.)

At this stage of the North African expedition, Lieutenant Commander Preble did a little writing himself, at least home to wife Mary, describing Algiers as a city "as large as Philadelphia, neat and handsomely built," and the dey's gardens were "very extensive, cultivated with every vegetable, tree, and plant that is useful and ornamental."[6] The Algerians remained quiet, unbellicose.

The third of the quartet of Barbary powers was Tunis, the capital of today's Tunisia, located entirely on the Mediterranean. It was considered the most powerful of these privateer empires, but for the moment was at peace with the United States, so Preble didn't have to worry about the bey of Tunis, either.

His chief antagonist, therefore, was Yusuf Karamanli, the *bashaw* or *pasha* of Tripoli, which lies on the Libyan coast to the east of Tunis. Yusuf was a Turk, from the town of Karaman in central Anatolia, Turkey, who in 1795, helped by the bey of Tunis, seized the Tripolitan throne from his brother Hamet, whom he exiled. His own long, tyrannical reign lasted until 1832. Preble's struggle against Yusuf pitted him in a duel with a clever, tenacious, arrogant, and overweening opponent. Even before *Constitution* appeared off Tripoli in June 1804, the U.S. Navy had been sporadically yet vainly attacking the Tripolitans in their strongly fortified, rock-bound, and rather treacherous harbor.

Earlier, Midshipman Henry Wadsworth, aboard the frigate *New York*, had been involved in some of these actions. At Tripoli on May 22, 1803, his ship came under fire from shore batteries and took part, with another American frigate, *Enterprize*, in chasing a 25- to 30-ton enemy *felucca* until their quarry ran aground. In June, the young Mainer volunteered to help lead a sortie against Tripoli's land defenses. Two boats, holding ten men armed with cutlasses, muskets, and a pair of pistols each, landed on a large rock—and Wadsworth writes that he comically took possession of it in the name of the United States. During another sortie the next day, several Muslim horsemen were shot down. He had pictured the shore between Tripoli's two main forts covered by a thousand men "some on Arabian horses...riding full speed, flourishing guns over their heads, and cutting capers." Also, that July, Wadsworth was aboard *New York* when she towed a captured Tripolitan prize into the Bay of Naples, and he commented on how impressed the local Neapolitans were with the sight, "for in their wars with the Barbarians [*sic*], they have shown themselves such infamous cowards that a capture on their part seldom occurs."7

Once Preble arrived, Wadsworth managed to switch to his fellow Portlander's flagship. They sailed to Malta, which was a British colony, where we find Henry writing to his friend David Porter, later to be a major U.S. naval figure, about the kind of non-warlike adventures junior officers liked to tell each other: "Met a bouncing English girl at the masquerade last night. She said she was married, but I might cuckold her husband. Nice bit."[8]

Six months prior to Preble's arrival, an incident happened that set the stage for establishing the Maine man's name and reputation. Out of an American defeat would come heroics hailed by generations. *Philadelphia*, one of the U.S. Navy's major frigates, on duty in blockading Tripoli Harbor, floundered onto an inshore reef. Unable to dislodge herself at low tide, she was surrendered by chief officer William Bainbridge to the hordes of Tripolitans who had surrounded the stricken vessel; more than 300 Americans ended up as prisoners in Pasha Yusuf's dungeons.

Efforts to negotiate their release proved fruitless. Money had already led Yusuf to declare war on the U.S. in 1801 when his increased bribery demands had been rejected. Now his ransom requirements were huge, as high as $800,000. He met with Preble and exploded in outrage when offered a measly $40,000.

The war against Tripoli would continue, Preble knew. He foresaw that "the prestige of the United States, only recently raised by the settlement at Tangiers, would probably sink to new depths in the eyes of the Barbary regencies."[9] Far more disturbing was a rumor that Yusuf intended to swap the captured *Philadelphia* with his Tunisian neighbors for a bunch of smaller gunboats. Possessing such a dreadnaught, powerful Tunis would pose a greater danger than ever. And Preble knew the Tripolitans had already refloated the American vessel and were making her shipshape again.

An obsessive idea took hold of Preble: he would destroy *Philadelphia* where she lay, under guard in Tripoli Harbor. Writing to Secretary of the Navy Robert Smith, Preble declared this was what he had determined to do.

The plan he devised was daring enough. Preble's forces had taken a Muslim ketch and renamed her *Intrepid*. Disguised as a merchantman from Malta, she was the perfect small vessel for entering Tripoli Harbor, flying the English flag. Her complement of sixty officers and crew—all U.S. naval personnel—were equally well camouflaged.

Put in charge was Lieutenant Commander Stephen Decatur. Preble's orders to the future immortal U.S. naval hero included phrases like: "Board the Frigate *Philadelphia*, burn her, and make your retreat good with the *Intrepid* if possible." "The destruction of the *Philadelphia* is an object of great importance." "Be sure and set fire in the Gun Room berths, Cockpit Store rooms forward, and Berths on the Berth deck." "After the Ship is well on fire, point two of the 18 pounders shotted down the Main Hatch and blow the bottom out." "On boarding the Frigate it is probable you will meet with Resistance, it will be well in order to prevent alarm to carry all by the sword."

It was about 7:00 P.M. when the disguised *Intrepid* sailed up next to the docked *Philadelphia*. An Arabic-speaking Italian Decatur had brought with him asked if they could tie up alongside the captured American ship. But an alarm was given by a Tripolitan guard who noticed men with cutlasses. Decatur gave an order to board immediately and the Muslim guards were quickly overpowered.

Each boarder carried a three-inch length of sperm candle and, as lit torches, they served to turn the wooden warship into a blazing wreck.

Decatur's report back to Preble included the following information: "I immediately fired her in the Store Rooms, Gun Room Cockpit, and Berth Deck and remained on board until the flames had issued from the Spar Deck hatchways and Ports, and before I got from alongside, the fire had communicated to the rigging and tops.... The noise occasioned by the boarding and contending for possession [although no firearms were used] gave a general alarm on shore.... They commenced a fire on us from all their batteries on shore, but with no other effect than one shot passing through our Top Gallant Sail.... I can form no judgment as to the number of men that were on board of her; there were about 20 killed.... I boarded with 60 men and Officers...and it is with the greatest pleasure I inform you, I had not a man killed in this affair, and but one slightly wounded.... Permit me also, Sir, to speak of the brave fellows I have the honor to command, whose coolness and intrepidity was such as I trust will ever characterize the American Tars."

Decatur's commando raid was an unmitigated success and made his reputation and Preble's and that of the entire U.S. Navy, even though it entailed the destruction not of a Barbary boat, but of an American ship in enemy hands.

The impact of the *Philadelphia* escapade actually reached international proportions, at least in the Western world. Lord Horatio Nelson, the famed British admiral, called it the "most bold and daring act of this age." Even His Holiness, Pope Pius VII, chimed in: "The American commander with a small force in a short space of time has done more for the cause of Christianity than the most powerful nations of Christendom have done for ages."

Preble, though, remained unsuccessful in pressing Yusuf to accept reasonable terms. But throughout 1804, the American commander kept up relentless, aggressive action against the pasha's forces.

One memorable attack occurred when Preble launched six gunboats and two bomb ketches against Yusuf's fleet of two schooners, one brig, and two galleys, supplemented by 115 shore batteries. A strong wind was blowing, so wild that Preble lost a reefed foresail and close-reefed the main topsail. The Americans charged into the fight with "bayonet, spear, saber, and tomahawk,"[10] taking two prizes, killing thirty-three Tripolitans, and wounding and/or capturing twenty-seven more. Among the ten U.S. fatalities was James Decatur, Stephen's brother, shot in the head.

There is a story, often told and quite possibly apochryphal, of a distraught Lt. Commander Stephen Decatur, blinded by his grief as to the consequences of his impulse, punching out his commanding officer, Commodore Edward Preble. Yet instead of a court martial arrest on the spot, Preble ordered the younger man into his cabin, where the two of them proceeded to get roaring drunk.

There were still other tragic casualties to come. Although Yusuf brought his outrageous ransom demand down from $600,000 to $150,000, Preble disdainfully refused his offer. All through August 1804 and into September, Preble's ships bombarded Tripoli. A culmination was reached with Preble's scheme of "re-fitting" *Intrepid* as a fire ship, bringing her into the harbor carrying a hundred barrels of gunpowder, and setting her ablaze to blow a goodly portion of Yusuf's inshore navy to smithereens.

General Peleg Wadsworth, in Portland and now a Massachusetts congressman, had had a premonition. He had said of his son Henry, "His determination to earn a character and make himself gave me a great apprehension that I should see his face no more." Two months later, an unconfirmed report reached Maine that the fire ship had blown up prematurely, killing all the Americans aboard. General Wadsworth was heard to say, "Harry [what his family called him] no doubt has had his share in it."

Was the blast an accident? One school of thought declared that the officer in charge of the sortie, Richard Somers, had deliberately lit the fuse after 200 Tripolitans swarmed onto *Intrepid*. It was known that Somers, the scion of a well-to-do New Jersey family, had opted for a short fuse of hemp and cotton, allowing himself and his men only eleven minutes to escape after touching a match to the cord. Under him for this brave endeavor, Somers had assembled ten men and two junior officers, Henry Wadsworth and a Joseph Israel, eager volunteers, every one of them.

The thirteen victims were soon idolized in the U.S. The newspapers chose to accept the heroic version of a deliberate sacrifice, taking a large number of the enemy with them. A printed poem declaimed:

Twice fifty pirates bold
Sent shrieking in the air!
This tale wherever told
Shall make our foes despair.

And Somers was pictured thus:

Determined, cool, formed to command,
The match of death in his right hand,
Scorning a life of slavery.
And now behold! The match applied,
The mangled foe the welkin ride
Whirling aloft, brave Somers cried
"A glorious death or liberty!"

In his report on the tragedy, Preble echoed the theme of "death or liberty" and "scorning a life of slavery." White Americans held in slavery were a rebuke to Southerners who extolled the virtues of the "peculiar institution" when applied to blacks. For this reason, there was heavy pressure from Washington, D.C., to liberate these mistreated prisoners of war.

Whatever the source of the spark that blew up *Intrepid,* one thing was certain: Midshipman Henry Wadsworth was dead.

The world will never know what kind of writer he would have been.

At nine years old, a student at Portland's South School on Spring Street, he was deemed "a writer of poetry who exhibited the potential for becoming a very handsome speaker." After studying at Phillips Exeter Academy, "self-collected Henry" went into the navy and his chatty letters thereafter make for an interesting travelogue, whether it is New Year's morning in Italy and the sun "with unusual splendor" breaking on Mount Etna, "whose white sides were pouring columns of black smoke from the crater," or the narrative of the wife of Captain James Low giving birth to a son in the boatswain's storeroom, with the baby baptized in the midshipmen's storeroom by Midshipman Melancthon Taylor Woolsey and "Mrs. Hays, the Gunner's lady officiating." Wadsworth assures us: "All was conducted with due decorum and decency, no doubt to the great satisfaction of the parents," helping to "ameliorate the unhappy situation of the Lady who was so unfortunate as to conceive and bear on the Salt Sea." Then, eyes twinkling slyly perhaps, Wadsworth adds that the other ladies aboard—the boatswain's wife, the carpenter's lady, and the corporal's lady—"got drunk in their own quarters out of spite, not being invited to celebrate the christening of Melancthon Woolsey Low."

Henry's death took place on September 4, 1804. His illustrious nephew and namesake would be born on February 27, 1807, the son of Stephen and Zilpah Wadsworth Longfellow. The previous year, on February 22, 1806, Commodore Preble and his wife Mary had announced the birth of their only child, a son, whom they named Edward Deering Preble. By then they had built a magnificent home in Portland on the corner of today's Preble and Congress Streets, practically next door is the Longfellow House, where the poet was raised. He and Ned Preble, close in age, became boyhood friends, college classmates, and eventually even roommates overseas.

Edward Preble, Sr.'s return from North Africa had a touch of politics about it. Well before the *Intrepid* disaster, the commodore had received word that his command of the Mediterranean squadron had been given to a fellow commodore, but one junior to him, Samuel Barron, under whom he was to serve. The conventional wisdom about this downgrading was that Preble had been scapegoated for the original capture of *Philadelphia,* despite a letter signed by all of that ship's officers insisting he was in no way to blame.

However, there have been some intimations that Preble himself asked to be relieved of his overseas post on the grounds of illness.

He did have a history of serious bouts with sickness. Prior to leaving for North Africa, "a debility of the digestive organs" had laid him low, and at one point he felt so unwell that he submitted his resignation from the navy, only to have it turned down by Secretary Smith.

As it turned out, Commodore Barron appeared on the Tripoli scene five days after *Intrepid* exploded. Preble made it plain he wouldn't serve under him. Hitching a ride home aboard the U.S.-bound frigate *John Adams,* he reached New York on February 25, 1805. Quite possibly much to his own surprise—and the chagrin of those who had schemed to replace him—he was greeted as a national hero.

He was in Washington, D.C., a week later, on March 4, 1805, Inauguration Day for Thomas Jefferson's second term, and met with the president and dined at the White House. Congress decided to have a gold medal struck in commemoration of his attacks on Tripoli. The resolution to do so was approved just before he came to D.C. and he himself took part in its creation by supplying sketches of the Tripoli Harbor battle scenes. There was also a bit of a discussion about the size of the decoration: originally, it was slated to be four inches across; unfortunately, numismatic experts immediately reported that "medals for crowned heads never exceed three inches," and besides, one struck for George Washington was only three inches. In a letter sent from Portland in July 1805, Preble judiciously agreed that two and a half inches "is sufficiently large."

On his way home to Maine, the commodore was feted in Boston and toasted with the words, "Edward Preble! Our hero before Tripoli; may the laurels he has gained in the Old World belong to the pride of the New.... The whiskers of the Bashaw of Tripoli! May they have plenty of curling, twisting, and powdering!"

Ceremonial dinners were held for Preble in Philadelphia and Portland, as well as Boston, and on the Fourth of July a year later, he was honored in the Massachusetts capital by 400 to 500 fellow Federalists.

The commodore stayed in the navy, whose place in the national defense he continued doggedly to promote despite the Jefferson administration's penchant for fiscal austerity. He wanted a balanced fleet, including both ships of the line (big frigates like *Constitution*) and shallow-draft gunboats, which he had found so useful in North Africa. Assigned to "light duty" (possibly because of his health), he was given a contract to have nine gunboats built at Portland. These he subcontracted to Maine shipbuilders who followed a design provided by himself and a local naval architect, Jacob Coffin.

The unspecified gastrointestinal disorder that was to take Preble's life (could it have been stomach cancer?) had sent him south in the winter of 1807 in the hope that a change to a warmer climate might help. By late June, he was back in Portland. War against Great Britain seemed to be looming and he hurried to complete his gunboats, which would be turned over to the future hero of the War of 1812, James Lawrence.

Preble had planned another cruise to sunnier climes for his health, this time to the Portuguese island of Madeira, but he never made it. One last trip down the Maine coast in August 1807 was all he could endure and he died in Portland on the 25th of that same month.

Meanwhile in North Africa, Samuel Barron, also gravely ill, gave up his command to Preble's good friend, Commodore John Rodgers. Before doing so, Barron had authorized the going forward of an expedition against Yusuf Karamanli, led by William Eaton, the American consul in Tunis, whose strategy was to attack Tripoli from the land, across the desert rather than from the sea. The self-styled General Eaton pulled together a force in Egypt that included a handful of U.S. Marines (thus we have "to the shores of Tripoli" in the "Marines' Hymn"), and this ragtag army somehow captured the city of Derna, which was in Yusuf's territory. The tyrant of Tripoli, venal as he was, decided he'd better settle with the Americans and did so for a reasonable $60,000. The *Philadelphia* prisoners were released. Yusuf stayed on his throne for several more decades, but the bullying ways of the Barbary corsairs were significantly reduced and shipping was made safe for non-Muslim vessels off the coast of the Maghreb.

More than a century later, one of Maine's premier history writers, Kenneth Roberts, commented about Maine's role in this neglected but critically important episode in the development of our young country, indicating that people in our Pine Tree State should not be ignorant of it. He wrote in his autobiography, "Then, again, Maine captains and ships were constantly being annoyed by Barbary pirates and numbers of Maine people, headed by Wadsworths and Prebles, had spent years patrolling the Mediterranean.... Nobody in Kennebunkport or Portland knew anything whatever about the experiences of those Maine men in the Mediterranean, or what they'd seen, or done, or heard, or how they'd lived and acted...."[11]

Roberts had in mind a novel "to cover, generally speaking, the Prebles and Wadsworths in the Mediterranean, against a background of Eaton's expedition to Derna."[12] But after due consideration, he found he couldn't transpose the Preble/Wadsworth part into historical fiction.

1. Christopher McKee, *Edward Preble: A Naval Biography*. Annapolis, MD: Naval Institute Press, 1972, p. 20.

2. Ibid., p. 39.

3. Joyce Butler, "The Wadsworths: A Portland Family." *Maine Historical Society Quarterly*, Volume 27, Numbers 2-19, Spring 1988.

4. McKee, p. 164.

5. Ibid.

6. Ibid.

7. *Naval Documents Related to the United States Wars with the Barbary Powers*, Volume II. Washington, D.C.: U.S. Printing Office, 1940, under direction of Charles Edison, Secretary of the Navy. Reference *Wadsworth*, July 30, 1803.

8. McKee, p. 186

9. Ibid., p. 180

10. Francis Rennell Rodd, *General William Eaton: The Failure of an Idea*. New York: Minton, Balch and Company, 1932, p. 130.

11. Kenneth Roberts, *I Wanted to Write*. Garden City, NY: Doubleday and Company, Inc., 1949, p. 342.

12. Ibid., p. 343.

"Facsimile of a Pen Drawing by Mr. Longfellow, Göttingen, 1829"
Collections of Maine Historical Society, 12227

6

LONGFELLOW

The derring-do of Edward Preble and the martyrdom of Henry Wadsworth had appealed to Kenneth Roberts as the stuff of heroic fiction, although he never did sit down and write about either of them. It is fair to wonder why the poet Longfellow, so much closer to those real-life figures, and himself given to immortalizing historical personages, never chose Preble or Wadsworth for one of his odes. For that matter, his own grandfather's thrilling role in the Revolution escaped his pen, yet we were given Paul Revere's ride to admire.

There are some genuine ironies here. Both Paul Revere and Peleg Wadsworth took part in the catastrophic American defeat on the Penobscot River at Castine. Paul Revere, colonel of artillery, was court-martialed (but acquitted), while General Wadsworth was the sole officer commended for steadiness and bravery and rewarded with command of all American forces in Maine. Later kidnapped by British commandos and thrust into a Castine dungeon, he and a fellow prisoner engineered a daring escape full of hair-raising incidents, which could have been the source for any amount of epic poetry.

Nor could poet Longfellow plead ignorance of the deeds of his immediate ancestors. We are told of sessions at his grandfather's farm in Hiram, Maine, when General Peleg regaled his grandchildren with exciting tales of his wartime adventures. Henry Wadsworth's sacrifice was ever-present in HWL's own name, since he is not generally known as just plain Henry Longfellow. As for the Prebles, they were Portland neighbors, and although the commodore had died about the time of Henry's birth, there was son Edward Deering Preble—Henry's pal Ned—one of his dearest friends, and a sharer in some of his world travels.

Henry Wadsworth Longfellow did leave Maine and did go abroad, starting at the relatively young age of nineteen. He went overseas by himself to begin with, but at his very first stop—in the port of Le Havre in northern France—he wrote back to his older brother, Stephen, concerning something that reminded him of Ned Preble, adding, "If Ned only knew the one hundredth part of the laughable things which I have seen during one day's residence in Havre, he would lament long and loudly that he had not come to France with me."[1]

It would be more than two and a half years before the two Portland boys joined each other in Europe—in Germany—fellow students at Gottingen, rooming together again as they had at Bowdoin College.

Longfellow and the commodore's son had matriculated at the Brunswick college only one year after Maine had separated from Massachusetts in 1820. For political reasons, this was not a propitious moment for Maine's formerly dominant higher education institution. The triumphant Jeffersonian Democrats who had led the fight for statehood did not like Bowdoin, which was Federalist in party orientation and orthodox Congregationalist in religion. A request to the legislature for $13,000 to build a new chapel and establish a professorship in modern (i.e., foreign) languages was turned down cold.

But the Bowdoin classes of this period have been glorified in Maine history as the most distinguished the state has ever produced. Not only was there a poet of Longfellow's stature (and he *was* to become a professor of modern languages at Bowdoin and later Harvard), but also a prose writer of the caliber of Nathaniel Hawthorne—and a president of the United States, Franklin Pierce. Other notables in this period of Bowdoin's history included a promising congressman, Jonathan Cilley, who died young in a duel that ended the practice of dueling in Washington, D.C.; Horatio Bridge, Hawthorne's bosom friend, who became a major U.S. naval officer; William Pitt Fessenden, U.S. senator, secretary of the Treasury, and fiancé of Longfellow's sister Elizabeth before her untimely death; and Calvin Stowe, professor of religion, whose wife Harriet wrote *Uncle Tom's Cabin* in Brunswick, Maine. In fact, her writing was done in the same house where Longfellow, his brother Stephen, and Ned Preble boarded after their freshman year.

Well before Longfellow attended college, he had already been writing poetry and had even seen one of his pieces published—"The Battle of Lovewell's Pond," based on a true incident of Maine history during the French and Indian Wars, not far from Fryeburg and his grandfather's estate in Hiram. Published in the *Portland Gazette*, the work lacks his sympathetic interest in Native Americans shown in "Hiawatha," but his curiosity was piqued enough for him to read in his junior year

Heckwelder's Account of the History, Manners, and Customs of the Indian Natives of Pennsylvania and the Neighboring States. He summed up his reaction in a letter to his mother, stating of the Indians, "They are a race possessing magnanimity, generosity, benevolence, and pure religion without hypocrisy...and have been most barbarously maltreated by the Whites, both in word and deed." He had a further opportunity to express his feelings publicly during the Junior Exhibition at Bowdoin, when he and a classmate, James W. Bradbury (later a U.S. senator), conducted a "Dialogue between a North American Indian and a European." Longfellow played the role of King Philip, son of Massasoit, who rebelled against the Pilgrims, while Bradbury was Miles Standish. We also learn that, accompanied by Ned Preble, Longfellow journeyed to Fryeburg for the 100th anniversary of the fight at Lovewell's Pond and wrote an ode for the occasion that superseded his earlier juvenile effort.

American Indians were exotic—one might easily say *foreign* to the dominant culture—and fit well into the young Portlander's fascination with non-English cultures. It is said that his attraction to far-off geography had been sparked by his aunt, Lucia Wadsworth, who lived with his family and had created an atlas from which she taught her nephews about the outer world.

As his college days came to an end, Longfellow's plans for the future seemed vague enough. They were to include a year in Cambridge (England) studying history and literature, but also continuing to master the French language and taking on Italian, too. His father, a lawyer—and during this period a congressman—wanted him to be more practical—that is, to become a lawyer. Yet Stephen Longfellow, Sr., was not adamantly opposed to his son's wishes, and then, conceivably engineered by him, an amazing opportunity was put before the eighteen-year-old Bowdoin graduate.

At the college's 1825 commencement, the Bowdoin Board of Trustees (of which Stephen Longfellow, Sr., was a member) voted to establish a professorship of modern languages, thanks to a $1,000 donation from the widow of James Bowdoin given expressly for that purpose. Astonishingly, the post was offered to the newly graduated Henry Wadsworth Longfellow, allegedly at the insistence of Benjamin Orr, a leading trustee, who had been entranced by the boy's "elegant" translation of an ode by Horace. After that board meeting in Brunswick,

Stephen Sr. presented the boy with their proposal, which was to have him first visit Europe and prepare himself for the professorship, then assume it upon his return.

In this regard, the wide-eyed American teenager who arrived at Le Havre on June 15, 1826, was quite different from many of his compatriots visiting the Continent as part of a "grand tour." Henry Wadsworth Longfellow had left Maine not simply to broaden his horizons and add a cultural veneer, but with the highly practical object of preparing for a job that awaited him.

What immediately stuck in Henry's mind upon landing in a non-American setting was "the singular construction of the houses, all of which are old and dilapidated. No description can give you any conception of their quaint and peculiar style."[2] Possibly he was responding as a New Englander to the surprise of seeing uniformly all-stone houses, just as European visitors to the U.S. Northeast are amazed to see so many homes made of wood.

Catching his eye, too, he wrote his brother, was the "grand display from every upper window of blankets and bed clothes, old shirts and old sheets, flopping in the wind...."[3]

In a playful mood, he quoted a couplet from an unnamed poem:

Loose pantaloons and petticoats
Pendent on dyer's pole afloat

Those colorful scenes in the streets of Le Havre gave him "divers fits of laughter," and he continued his description of "*gens d'armes* with fierce whiskers and curling beards...women with wooden shoes full of feet and straw...the dames of Normandy with tall pyramidal caps of muslin reaching at least two feet above the head and adorned with long-ear lappets...."[4]

He also found it "amusing to see a Frenchman tuck his napkin under his chin and fall to...."[5]

By the time he got to Paris, though, the gloss of these alien sights had worn off to an extent and reality was intruding. Thus, to Longfellow, Paris was "a gloomy city, built all of yellow stone, streaked and defaced with smoke and dust, streets narrow and full of black mud, which comes up through the pavements," but redeemed by "the elegance of its public gardens, its boulevards, etc., etc."[6]

Like other generations of post-collegiate Americans, Longfellow found quarters on the Left Bank, in this case near St. Germain des Pres, at 49 Rue Monsieur le Prince, in a boardinghouse run by a Madame Potet. All seven boarders there were Americans, but they were fined if they spoke English. Nearby were the wonderful Luxembourg Gardens, the famed Boulevard St. Michel, the Sorbonne, and the Pantheon, where illustrious French citizens, including literary superstars, were and still are buried.

It was nose-to-the-grindstone time for Henry Wadsworth Longfellow. "I have not forgotten what I came to Paris for," he wrote his parents. And before long, he was even ready to leave the French capital and stay in a small village on the outskirts—Auteuil—where he bunked in at a *maison de sante*—a sort of nursing home. The place was extremely good for conversation, he reported, since "the French are always talking."

Next, more time was spent traveling throughout France during the summer of 1826, and included a meeting with General Lafayette, who had known Henry's father in America and sent Stephen Longfellow, Sr., his "affectionate regards." In the fall, Longfellow was still roaming the French countryside. He was much taken by the beautiful Chateau de Chambord, although it was in a "desolate state, unoccupied and falling to decay." He remembered Ned Preble had drawn excellent castles on "the covers of old writing books at school, with battlements and peaked roofs." Such romantic settings were to populate many of his poems.

Not for several more years would he meet up with his friend Preble in Germany. Apparently his original plan had been to leave France at the end of autumn and cross the Rhine, where he would spend the winter at a German institution of learning. Except his father was pushing him to go to Spain instead, and also to Italy, if possible. "Your ulterior object [the professorship] cannot be acknowledged unless you obtain an accurate knowledge of the French and Spanish languages," Stephen Sr. warned his son. U.S. relations with South America, he stressed, made knowing Spanish as important as knowing French. "If you neglect either of these, your whole object will be defeated."[7] German could come later and, if necessary, Italian could be sacrificed to it, should Henry find he couldn't handle four languages. As it turned out, the poet was not only eventually able to speak, write, and translate these top four, but could add others like Swedish, Danish, and Portuguese to his capabilities.

The trip to Spain, nevertheless, was taken with some trepidation. The Spanish countryside was rumored to be a haven for bandits. He found it "as quiet and peaceful as France, itself," yet with the implied threat of brigands always in mind, accented by frequent black crosses on the roadsides denoting sites of murders or other violent deaths, as well as the overwhelming impression of poverty in northern Spain. "The people have nothing left but rags and religion," he wrote. Still, he could also add jauntily, "Thus my journey [to Madrid] was by no means fruitful in adventures, I being neither robbed and pillaged nor having the honor of a little black cross by the roadside."[8]

In the Spanish capital, Longfellow soon fell in with the few Americans, most prominently his literary idol, Washington Irving, who was there writing a life of Columbus; Irving's brother Pierre; and Alexander Everett, the American minister to Spain. Washington Irving, whom Longfellow described as "one of those men who put you at ease with them in a moment," couldn't have been more accommodating. He gave the visitor from Maine letters of introduction to other literary lights he could meet on his voyages, such as Sir Walter Scott, and left the aspiring writer an example of his prodigious work ethic. One morning, Longfellow discovered him at his desk at 6:00 A.M. He also wrote that he "found the author whom I had loved, repeated in the man."

Longfellow took to Spain in a way he hadn't taken to France. He saw the Spaniards' warmth underneath their pride, and liked the sense of the past that remained in the present. This feeling even related to their strong religiosity. Catholicism, practically nonexistent in Maine, held a fascination for him. One of his letters home included an example of the reverence with which a procession of the "Host" to a dying person, complete with priests, church banners, and tinkling bells, was greeted by onlookers who dropped to their knees, and how, when this happened outside a theater, the whole play stopped, and actors, actresses, and audience all genuflected.

On May 15, 1827, Henry wrote his sister Elizabeth from Madrid: "It is just a year today since I said: 'My Native Land. Good Night.'"

Occasionally, perhaps inevitably, he was reminded of America. On a trip to Segovia, he saw a covered wagon, which gave him an image of

New Englanders, maybe from Maine, going off to Ohio.

His real fervent attraction to Spain probably did not generate until some four months later when he left Madrid for Andalusia. Most especially the Moorish heritage in the south affected him. He liked Cordoba, with its "multitude of columns, all of beautiful colored marbles and formerly 1,800 in number" and the old mosques that were "still preserved and are of the most costly workmanship." But it was really Granada and especially the Alhambra, the set of Moorish buildings immortalized by Washington Irving, that blew him away. "I was in Granada but five days," Longfellow explained. "But in those five, I lived almost a century. No portion of my life has been so much like a dream."

Throughout his travels, and here, too, even in southern Spain, he would connect with Americans who were around, like a Mr. Maynard at the house of the American consul in Cadiz, a man who had known Portland "in the olden times," and the consul in Malaga, George Barrell, who had been a midshipman with his Uncle Henry Wadsworth. But the loneliness of traveling alone so long in a foreign environment led him to lament in Granada, after gushing about the Alhambra's effect on him, "How much I wanted some early bosom friend to share these feelings with me."9 On November 15, 1827, Longfellow recorded: "I visited for the last time the Alhambra and took a last lingering look at those scenes of romance, which I thought I could gaze on forever."10

Although the poet took three subsequent trips to Europe, he never went back to Spain, his liking for the country notwithstanding. A poem, "Castles in Spain," was one means by which he expressed his appreciation.

With the arrival of the year 1828, Henry Wadsworth Longfellow was in Italy. En route, he partly filled in his companionship gap by meeting on shipboard an American about his age, George W. Greene, the grandson of the noted Revolutionary War general, Nathaniel Greene. These two descendants of famed senior officers of the War of Independence were to become lifelong friends. They parted in Genoa, where they both attended a midnight Christmas Eve Mass, and by New Year's Day, Longfellow was ensconced in Florence, ready to study.

Florence was not to keep him long. So far, he had little enthusiasm for Italy and was homesick for Spain. Rome turned out to be a better choice than Florence (Longfellow said he utterly disliked the

Florentines' Tuscan accents). In the Eternal City, he not only met up with his friend Greene again, but found living arrangements with a family where he could practice French, Italian, and Spanish at the same time.

A trip to Naples with Greene (they stayed three weeks) brought him even farther into the southern Italy he seemed to prefer to the north. Thirty-nine years later, Greene was to remind him of a moment during their trip that had had an important bearing on his own life plans. The two young men were staring out across the Bay of Naples at sunset, observing Ischia and Capri and Sorrento and even Vesuvius, and, as Greene goes on, "It was then you unfolded your plans of life and showed me from what 'deep cisterns' you had already learned to draw...." And the Rhode Islander, who had just sent his Maine friend a copy of the book *Life of General Greene*, added, "From that day, the office of literature took a new place in my thoughts."[11]

All of these European experiences had still not over-sophisticated the would-be poet out of Portland. In a letter from Naples to his brother Stephen, he demanded news of their native city, including the most trivial events. He stated he had recently received a "long letter" from fellow Bowdoin grad William Pitt Fessenden, who was courting their sister Elizabeth, and told Stephen, "I most heartily wish one of you Templars would come and spend with me the rest of my sojourn in Europe. You must make Ned Preble Charge d'affaires and Envoye extraordinaire to my court at Gottingen, whose venerable walls I hope yet to see."

This letter was sent on April 22, 1828. By February 27, 1829, his twenty-second birthday, Henry Wadsworth Longfellow was at last in Gottingen—and so was Ned Preble!

Writing to his father, Henry said he had been in Dresden earlier— "a little down-hearted"—and ready to return home. "But meeting here with an old and good friend has given a new elasticity to my spirits. I am contented and happy."

His low spirits undoubtedly could be traced to disappointing news he had received from Maine. The professorship at Bowdoin had been withdrawn by the college; all they were willing to offer him now was an instructor's post at a much reduced salary. It was a choice he indignantly said he would refuse. For the meanwhile, however, he would stay in Gottingen and learn German since, as he put it, "I am a little unwilling to give up what is now in my reach, as I shall never again be in Europe." His forecast, needless to say, was not accurate.

Preble had already reached Gottingen and taken quarters in the famed university city that had a special attraction for English-speaking students due to the institution's founding in 1737 by King George II in his dual role as monarch of Great Britain and the elector of Hanover. Arriving five days before his birthday, Longfellow hurried to the address Preble had given him, Judengasse 462 (or 462 "Jews Alley"). Preble, who did not know he was coming, was obviously overjoyed to see him. Henry thought the accommodations "splendid." The "sundry porcelain pipes with a tobacco pouch made of a bladder" that were in open view would soon be put to frequent use by the Portlanders, or at least they were depicted in a well-known drawing Henry made of the two of them, seated at a cluttered table, puffing away.

A publication they put out was called bilingually the *Old Dominion Zeitung* (German for newspaper), which they advertised as "published every Saturday evening at the corner of Rother and Weender Strasse—Gottingen." The contents, sophomorically satirical, had a few local features on German student life, but primarily served to bash Bowdoin College and its stuffy president, the Reverend William Allen. Longfellow's anger at what he felt was betrayal by his alma mater was a constant in every issue. As Charles Calhoun, in his *Longfellow: A Rediscovered Life*, writes, "The *Old Dominion Zeitung* could have cost Longfellow any opportunity to be employed at Bowdoin, had it fallen into the wrong hands."[12]

The pleasant interlude in Germany with Ned Preble did not last long. More disturbing news arrived from Portland. Elizabeth, who had tuberculosis, was alarmingly sick, and like her namesake aunt who had died so young affianced to Stephen Longfellow, this Elizabeth passed away at age twenty. By then she and "Pitt" Fessenden had become engaged and the future outstanding Maine politician was by her side when the end came. Brother Henry had not yet gotten home from Europe when this tragedy occurred in May 1829.

Despite his gloomy prognostications, Longfellow did get to Europe again—three more times. Each of these subsequent trips had its own flavor, its own timetable in his life, and its own sequence of events, some even tragic and potentially dramatic. But none could measure up to the impact of the adolescent impressions made on this relatively callow youth from Maine during his initial tramping about the Continent.

The exotic—whether French medieval, Italian Renaissance, Spanish Gothic, Teutonic legend, Anglo-Saxon folktale, and even Moorish, Sephardic, and Nordic elements—infused his poetic works, actually providing a framework for them at the start. His first collection was printed under the title of *Outre-Mer,* French for "Overseas." Yet he was resolutely American, too—close enough to his English forebears, fond of the literature produced in the British Isles, but no slavish imitator.

Henry and Ned were of a generation still trying to find itself. Their immediate ancestors were the heroic Americans who had fought Indians and French and their own British cousins to create not only their own country but a separate identity from anything European. Henry, the poet, the interpreter, perhaps unconsciously mixed these elements eclectically within the body of his work. For example, in one of his most popular collections of poems—*The Tales of a Wayside Inn*—whose structure is borrowed from Chaucer's *Canterbury Tales,* the setting is a Yankee tavern still extant in Sudbury, Massachusetts, and the stories the people there tell each other include Paul Revere's Ride, Baron Castin in Maine and France with his Penobscot Indian bride, plus different exotic legends from other settings around the world. Like another American author of the time—Washington Irving—Henry was becoming "cosmopolitan."

Upon his return to Maine, the youthful traveler received a surprise. At the Bowdoin commencement, the Board of the College met and—no doubt prompted by Stephen Sr. behind the scenes—chose "Mr. H. W. Longfellow" to be "Professor of Modern Languages" and established his salary at $800 annually, plus a one-year appointment as librarian for $100.

It was a compromise the young man accepted.

Whether he did it grudgingly or with alacrity isn't known. Yet it is safe to say he was never really happy teaching at Bowdoin. The facilities were meager. Needing a French grammar for his classes, he had to translate one himself. To his friend George Greene, who was back in Rhode Island, he described the prosaic view from his window of "the President's barn and the high road to Portland," and commented: "You see, I lead a very sober jog-trot kind of life."

Two years after he accepted the job, he was able in 1831 to take several significant steps toward his future: the first of his pieces was published in the prestigious *North American Review*, of which Alexander Everett, whom he'd met in Spain, had become editor; and he got married.

The bride was Mary Storer Potter, one of the beauteous daughters of his father's friend and Portland neighbor, Judge Barrett Potter. Professor Longfellow happily vacated his premises opposite the president's barn and moved with Mary into a cozy house on Brunswick's tonier Federal Street. Meanwhile, he continued his writing, producing more pieces for the *North American Review;* a pamphlet version of the travel sketches he called *Outre-Mer;* and what has been cited as his "first real published book," a ninety-page translation with introductory essay of *Las Coplas de Don Jorge Manrique,* which the Boston book company Allen and Ticknor brought out in 1833.

The entrance of publisher George Ticknor into his life was to lead Henry into his next trip abroad, as well as a new job. Ticknor had also been the Smith professor of Modern Languages at Harvard and when he resigned, he pushed hard for Longfellow to be his replacement. Harvard agreed but stipulated that the Bowdoin man first spend the next eighteen months in Europe perfecting his German.

It was an odd group that departed New York on April 10, 1835—a *ménage à quatre,* as Longfellow might have ironically dubbed it in French. In addition to the putative Harvard professor and his twenty-three-year-old wife came two of her female friends. They were Clara Crowninshield, actually the illegitimate but openly recognized daughter of the Salem, Massachusetts, ex-privateer and shipping magnate, George Crowninshield, and Mary Goddard, identified primarily as a very rich young woman. Clara, who knew Mary Storer Potter Longfellow from Miss Cushing's Finishing School, had enlisted the other Mary because she realized her former schoolmate would be more attentive on the trip to her husband than to herself and she would want companionship.

On the whole, the arrangements seemed to work out fine. The quartet started off in England, where Longfellow was able to connect with one of his literary heroes, Thomas Carlyle, and Carlyle's interesting wife, Jane, a German scholar. Carlyle himself had previously written a *Life of Schiller,* and after all, Longfellow's main reason for being in Europe was to pursue his German studies. His thought, too, was to acquire extra talents by loading up on Swedish, Danish, Icelandic, and Dutch literature and language.

So the Longfellow party, as soon as it left England, spent a summer in Stockholm. Sometime while there, Mary Longfellow let out the news that she was pregnant. Their travel plans until then would have had them stopping in Copenhagen, proceeding to Germany, and finally going to Heidelberg on the Rhine, where the professor would perfect his use of the Teutonic tongue.

A run of bad luck started in September when word reached them announcing that Mary Goddard's father had suddenly died. They were able to get her from Denmark to London, whence she caught a ship for home. The remaining trio next proceeded on the original intended course.

But they got only as far as Amsterdam. On October 5, Longfellow declared to Clara that his wife was very sick. Soon afterward, her pregnancy miscarried. Following two weeks of recuperation, the Americans moved to Rotterdam, where they arrived October 22. Five days later, Mary Longfellow took a decided turn for the worse. Before the end of November, the unthinkable happened: this sweet, lovely person, "most beautiful and most agreeable," was gone, as if in a flash, a little more than four years after wedding Henry.

With Clara to keep him company, Longfellow nonetheless went on to Heidelberg and remained there, buried in his studies and, of course, his grief.

Fate was to move him again—at the end of June 1836. This time, he was traveling alone and feeling his isolation, complaining in print, "Oh, what a solitary lonely being I am! Why do I travel? Every hour my heart aches." He passed through the Austrian Tyrol en route to Italy. Its evergreens and wooden houses reminded him of New England. But at the Italian border, there was a mix-up and he was denied entry. Thus it was that he entered Switzerland.

In Interlaken, he fell in with an extended American family—Boston Brahmins named Appleton. Nathan Appleton, the businessman father, was accompanied by his son Thomas, his daughters, Frances (Fanny) and Mary, and two youthful cousins, William Appleton and Isaac Jewett. Unfortunately, William was very ill, literally dying of tuberculosis, and Longfellow was to find his sad experience with Mary replicated in the hours he spent with the poor fellow, almost right up to the moment of his death, which occurred on July 24 in the Swiss town of Schaffhausen.

What thoughts were in his mind at that point about Fanny Appleton have remained his secret. We shall see that once back in Boston, she was to occupy a good deal of his emotional time.

Homeward bound from Heidelberg at the end of August 1836, the now thoroughly grounded German scholar roamed the Old World some more—through Alsace to Paris, and visiting some of his old haunts, like Auteuil.

His port of embarkation at last was Le Havre again, and as he waited for his ship to sail, he mused, "So we must idle our time always in this muddy place where everything looked so strange and new to me ten years ago, as I first set foot on this side of the ocean and where now all seems so stale and familiar."13

There is no reason to eke out any further suspense about the romance between Longfellow and Fanny Appleton. Everyone knows they were eventually married—in 1843, as it turned out. This was almost seven years after they had met. The interim was full of the quiet pathos of a one-way love affair; unrequited Longfellow, turned down but never giving up, taking long walks on the Boston Common, which the Appleton home at 39 Beacon Street faced, hoping for—if nothing else—just a glimpse of his enamorata. Then one day an invitation came from her. He walked, as quickly as possible, from Cambridge to Beacon Hill, over the bridge whose modern version bears his name. And for the next two decades, they were happy, had children—until her hideous, sudden death when her dress accidentally caught on fire.

In the interim Longfellow did go on yet another trip to Europe—in the spring of 1842. It can be called the "Dickens trip," although it started out as a health spa visit to imbibe the waters in Germany at Marienburg because of a bout of sickness he suffered while teaching at Harvard. The university gave him a six-month leave of absence. The last ten days he spent with his friend Charles Dickens, whom he had entertained in Massachusetts during the English novelist's controversial first tour around the United States. Rather, Dickens's book afterward about the U.S. had sparked the real controversy. He was hard on our country (except for New England) and totally scathing about slavery at a time when abolition was not a popular sentiment, even up north.

What did Longfellow do in this case? He not only defended Dickens's writings, but on his way home by ship, in a feverish burst of creative energy, wrote seven antislavery poems that he published in December 1842, knowing how much he might be abused for them.

The initial poem was addressed to the Reverend William Ellery Channing, a prominent Unitarian preacher and pastor of Boston's Arlington Church, who had begun to attack the idea of slavery. Unbenownst to Longfellow, as he was writing on the high seas, Channing had died that October in Vermont.

One stanza is particularly strong, although Channing was never an ardent abolitionist, only a pioneer. Still, Longfellow exhorts him poetically:

Go on until this land revokes
The old and chartered Lie
The feudal curse, whose whips and yoke
Insult humanity

An even stronger opponent of slavery in Boston who became an intimate friend of Longfellow's was Dr. Samuel Gridley Howe. He was the founder and director of the world-famous Perkins Institute for the Blind, the first such facility for the sightless ever created, and one praised by Dickens in his *American Notes,* after Longfellow arranged the visit for him. In the poet's correspondence is a letter he wrote to his friend Sam Ward, a relative of George Greene's, sent from Marienburg in 1842: "I am glad you like Howe. He is one of the noblest characters in the world." Incidentally, Dr. Howe was married to Julia Ward Howe, no mean poet herself, whose words became the lyrics of "The Battle Hymn of the Republic," while she served, too, as a fierce defender of Longfellow against detractors like the literary critic Margaret Fuller. And in his letter to Sam Ward, Longfellow also goes on to laud his intimate pals in the Boston area, who included antislavery U.S. Senator Charles Sumner, as well as Howe. "Are they not a glorious set of friends?"

Life in Cambridge was good for Longfellow. His stature in literature rose higher and higher, and his marriage gave him a contented family life.

Ned Preble had long since vanished from the scene. Returning to Portland from Gottingen, this companion of Longfellow's boyhood and adolescence lived out a life that could at best be called "unremarkable." It was, alas, also relatively short. Edward Deering Preble married a woman from Alexandria, Virginia, fathered three children, studied law but never practiced, was captain of the Portland Rifle Corps, was a municipal office holder, kept a private library, and was remembered as "a modest gentleman of great courtesy." The ubiquitous scourge of tuberculosis took his life in February 1846.

The horror of Fanny's death occurred in 1861. She left Henry with five children and a burnt face that required him to grow a beard, since he could not endure the physical pain of shaving. The internal pain of loss was consequently hidden behind an image of kindly, august benignity.

There was one more trip to Europe, accompanied by his surviving family, in 1868–69. This one had elements of a hero's triumphal parade. He received honorary degrees from Oxford and Cambridge, had an audience with Queen Victoria at Windsor Castle, breakfast with Prime Minister William Gladstone, dinner with Franz Liszt in Rome, and a two-day sojourn on the Isle of Wight, hosted by Alfred Lord Tennyson.

Occasionally, he went back to Maine. Summers he would leave Cambridge for his cottage by the sea in Nahant, with one-day side trips to Portland. Most famously, he came to Brunswick in 1875 for his fiftieth reunion at Bowdoin. The college's president, former general Joshua Chamberlain, had insistently invited him and he delivered—what else?—a class ode, "Morituri Salutamus," upon the occasion.

Henry Wadsworth Longfellow's ever-productive life came to a peaceful end seven years later. Although an anthology of Maine poets[14] includes only two poems by him—"My Lost Youth" and "Songo River"—as pertaining specifically to his native state, we claim him still for one of our most revered sons. While his work continues to be subjected to the vagaries of fashion in poetizing—inordinately praised or savagely attacked—it remains a cornerstone of American literature, but infused by a *worldview* of rich, magnificent imagination.

Postscript: *England's Homage to Longfellow* is a recent publication that tells how the Maine poet became the only non-Briton honored in England's national hall of fame at Westminster Abbey. The author is former Dartmouth College librarian Edward Connery Latham, and the book was released through the Maine Historical Society, which owns and maintains the Longfellow House on Portland's Congress Street.

The story begins only five months after Longfellow's death on March 24, 1882, when a minor English poet, William Cox Bennett, initiated the move, enlisting a fellow poet but also a businessman, Francis Bennoch, to serve as treasurer of the Longfellow Memorial Committee. A two-page circular they issued soon attracted a host of influential supporters, such as Earl Granville, the foreign minister; Joseph Chamberlain, member of Parliament and president of the Board of Trade; Alfred Lord Tennyson, the duke of Westminster; Lord William Napier; and the archbishops of York and Dublin. Soon the committee had 450 members, including thirty peers and thirty-six MPs. A spokesperson, Canon Roswell, summed up their sentiment that "the whole English-speaking voice was indebted to that great man for whom it was wished to secure a niche in Westminster Abbey."

But the attempt was not without its suspense. Not surprisingly, others spoke out in opposition. The *London Times* declared it was against "admitting monuments to strangers in Westminster Abbey" and that it "should remain a place of national memorial and not assume a cosmopolitan character."

A key decision had to be made by the dean of the abbey. Since the building was a religious one, under the control of the Anglican Church, he had to give his permission. This he eventually appeared to do, although hinting he'd personally like to see Washington Irving included, too.

Finally, a sculptor was chosen, Thomas Brook, of the Royal Academy, and a spot chosen between Chaucer and Dryden. The unveiling took place on March 1, 1883, with Longfellow's daughters in attendance and the American ambassador, James Russell Lowell, fellow poet and lifelong friend, delivering an oration. "Never have I known a more beautiful character," Russell declaimed.

On both sides of the Atlantic, controversy still flared, some English saying the Maine-born figure's bust shouldn't remain and some

Americans saying his family shouldn't have agreed to let him fill the niche in the first place.

However, there Longfellow stays—*outre-mer*—between Chaucer and Dryden. Not bad for a scribbler from Portland, Maine.

1. Samuel Longfellow, *Life of Henry Wadsworth Longfellow,* Volume 1. Boston: Ticknor and Company, 1886.
2. Ibid., p. 76.
3. I bid.
4. Ibid.
5. Ibid.
6. Ibid., p. 81.
7. Ibid., p. 89.
8. Ibid., p. 106.
9. Ibid., p. 133.
10. Ibid., p. 134.
11. Ibid., p. 146.
12. Charles Calhoun, *Longfellow: A Rediscovered Life.* Boston: Beacon Press, 2004, p. 65.
13. Samuel Longfellow, p. 237.
14. George Bancroft Griffith, *The Poets of Maine.* Portland, ME: Elwell, Pickard and Company, 1888.

Dorothea Lynde Dix, 1802–1887
Courtesy Library of Congress

DOROTHEA DIX

When Maine in the eighteenth century was still an integral part of Massachusetts, the only large amount of open land available for the Bay Colony's surplus population was in the north. Two types of settlement were at work throughout the District of Maine, as it was called: there were a few large-scale *proprietors* on the order of Samuel Waldo and his Muscongus Patent associates; and *township proprietors*, where communities in Massachusetts—whole towns—bought large tracts of Maine land and sold it to their inhabitants.

For example, Maine still has a town called New Gloucester, originally owned and populated by persons from the coastal port of Gloucester near Boston. Windham, Maine, similarly, was once New Marblehead. In 1789, residents of the town of Sutton, Massachusetts, south of Worcester, gathered at town meeting and voted to buy a section of Androscoggin Purchase #1 in Maine, where Webb's River enters the Androscoggin River in today's Oxford County.

This new municipality, however, did not become New Sutton. Because Colonel Jonathan Holman of Sutton had brokered the deal with the legislature in Boston, its initial name was Holmantown. Yet Holman would not keep his title for long. It turned out he was only the second largest landowner, the buyer of seven of the sixty lots into which the purchase had been divided. Number one on the list of owners was a Worcester medical doctor, Elijah Dix, who had paid the town of Sutton for fifteen lots. Also, the town voted to let Dr. Dix pick up much of the *undivided* land in the township in return for building a sawmill and a gristmill. Another deal this very wealthy man made was that, in return for his providing a library for the Suttonites, they would name the town for him.

Consequently, in 1803, in the Act of Incorporation passed in Boston, Holmantown legally became—and remains to this day—Dixfield.

Incidentally, Dr. Dix never maintained his end of the bargain.

When the Dixfield citizens pressed him for their library, he contented himself with sending a box of "musty old medical texts" written in German. As one local history complains indignantly, "This is all the town ever got for changing its name!"

In a paper written for the 14th Annual Washburn Humanities Seminar held at Norlands in Livermore, Maine, in June 2007, Peter Stowell, the editor of Dixfield's weekly newspaper, summed up Dr. Elijah Dix in one pithy capitalized sentence: "HE WAS A DIRTY NO GOOD SCOUNDREL."

Dix's speculations in Maine land were not solely in the Androscoggin River watershed. On some of his investments, he teamed up with another avaricious Massachusetts physician, Dr. Sylvester Gardiner, founder of Gardiner, Maine, on the Kennebec River, who, as a Tory, had to flee the country during the Revolution. Yet another Dix operation, this one close to the Penobscot River, resulted in the town of Dixmont, which he owned almost in its entirety.

Regarding Dixfield, Dr. Dix had his son John living there by 1800, while building the promised mills that were, in fact, delivered. Young Dix (he was nineteen) also built the first frame house in the community.

Another son was Joseph and he, too, migrated to Maine, ending in the Penobscot area that included Dixmont.

What is known for sure is that Dr. Elijah Dix died suddenly in 1809 and was buried in Dixmont. The conventional wisdom is that he was murdered.

Violence on the Maine frontier after the French and Indian Wars and the Revolution ended was always a possibility, mainly due to land disputes. Most often, it was initiated by "squatters," illegal settlers established on property claimed by "Great Proprietors" like Samuel Waldo, Henry Knox, Sylvester Gardiner, and, in this case, Elijah Dix. In parts of Maine, these interlopers would dress up as "White Indians" and terrorize surveying parties sent by the real owners, yet in only one instance was anyone known to have been killed. The sudden death of Dr. Dix, said Peter Stowell, was done in "cold blood," when he "was ambushed by mysterious cut-throats during one of his periodic visits to Dixmont."[1] This never-solved crime has been attributed by nineteenth-century Worcester historians to "squatters and fraudulent contractors and debtors."[2]

On the other hand, some writers have pooh-poohed the idea of a fatal shooting and blamed the mean man's demise to an onset of illness.

Either way, it seems incontrovertible that the person perhaps most affected by the unexpected loss was his seven-year-old granddaughter, Dorothea.

Her grandfather, nasty as he could be to his own immediate off-spring, "stood out as the one bright spot in her earliest memories,"[3] according to Francis Tiffany, one of Dorothea Dix's primary biographers. Dr. Dix treated her as his favorite grandchild, this oldest progeny of his quirky son Joseph, who, with his wife Mary, had settled temporarily on Dix-owned property in what is now Hampden, Maine. Their home has been described as a "one-room pine shack."

Joseph Dix was, to put it mildly, *a difficult man*. His own father had little use for him. In an incident recorded by Peter Stowell, the doctor arrived at Joseph's home and found him gone. Turning a "fiery, frightening red," the infuriated landowner raged before the absent Joseph's shivering wife, shouting, "My son—sent him here to do my business—sell lands, run this farm—and where is he when I need him most? Running around the country—preaching!?"[4]

But Joseph's religious fanaticism was only part of the problem. He had become a Methodist convert and self-styled itinerant minister, and possibly his father's ire had been increased by his sales of Dix lands to members of this new—and highly unpopular—sect in Maine. Still, and this was a total contradiction since Methodists preached against liquor, Joseph's bigger difficulty was his alcoholism. His father condemned him as "shiftless" and "a drunk."

It is generally acknowledged that Dorothea Dix's early upbringing in Maine was a nightmare. To the irregularity of her father's character was added the torture of a spare-the-rod/spoil-the-child philosophy. Corporal punishment in Joseph Dix's household started at the age of one. There was no outward love. All effort was spent on breaking Dorothea's spirit. Her mother, whether she wanted to or not, was unable to cope with her husband's rampages and abuse of the children. In 1815, when Dorothea was thirteen, the dysfunctional family returned to Worcester.

At the age of fourteen, Dorothea was apparently still in Worcester, now running "a school for little children," wearing long skirts and dresses with lengthened sleeves. It has been reported that as a hangover from her experiences in Maine, she did administer whippings to those she taught.

The question of her unhappy childhood has been relegated to a mere fuzzy background in her biographies. Obviously, there must be an almost total lack of material to fill out those hidden years, and her own silence about them completes the void. She is pictured as joylessly being forced to use her sewing talents to stitch bindings for the tracts her alcohol-tainted father spread among his "parishioners" in the wilderness settlements of Maine. We may well wonder if she considered Maine her native state, though the state today does recognize her as a native daughter. In Bangor, Maine's former Bangor Mental Health Institute has been re-named the Dorothea Dix Psychiatric Center.

BAMHI, which is what we called this operation when I was in the Maine State Legislature, had been opened in 1901 to receive the overflow from AMHI, the Augusta Mental Health Institute, the state's premier asylum. Bills to close BAMHI were perennials when I was in office (the 1970s and 1980s) and always encountered fierce opposition. In 2004, a complete revision of the state's handling of the mentally ill was instituted and thus the change that brought Dorothea Dix's name into play not far from her birthplace.

The Augusta mental hospital, started in a fortress-like granite building on the east side of the Kennebec River, was one of the earliest such facilities in the United States, completed in 1840. This was actually a year before Dorothea discovered her interest in helping victims of mental disease. But she was soon friendly with Augusta's superintendent, Dr. Isaac Ray, whom she convinced to remove to Providence, Rhode Island, and run the Butler Hospital, which she had refurbished with the support of a local "miserly millionaire," Charles Butler.

So how did the teenage female we had last seen teaching in Worcester, Massachusetts, at age fourteen, evolve into the social activist who could coax money—in this case $40,000, a princely sum at the time—from an old skinflint to help poor unfortunates whom society wished to see locked away out of sight?

Dorothea's unusual career path began quite unwittingly when she went to Boston to live with her grandmother, Dr. Elijah's widow. It was a natural transition, if for no other reason than to keep her grandmother company, since the elderly woman was all alone in the "Dix Mansion." It certainly provided a far more congenial atmosphere for Dorothea than her parental Worcester home, which was hardly less drear and emotionally chilly than had been the pine cabin in Hampden. There was even a garden on the Dix's Boston property producing a type of vegetable, "Dix's peas," that had become celebrated. More to the point for Dorothea's future, there was a room over the Dix Mansion stable where "poor and neglected children" were given shelter.

In 1823, when she was sixteen, Dorothea started a correspondence with Miss Anne Heath of nearby Brookline, Massachusetts, who became a lifelong friend. One letter survives and casts a light on Dorothea's inner emotional state, telling Annie rather enviously, "You have an almost angelic mother, you cannot but be both good and happy while she hovers over you ministering to your wants...your sisters, too, they can do for you. I have none [she had two younger brothers]."

Four years later, an important change took place in Dorothea's life. We have already met the Reverend William Ellery Channing, famous Unitarian preacher and Longfellow's antislavery idol. Suddenly the rather pinched world of the young female transplant from Maine vastly expanded when she accepted the position of tutor to Dr. Channing's children.

Summers, she stayed with the Channings at their "country seat" in Portsmouth, Rhode Island, on Narragansett Bay. Winters, she would either teach at the Fowle Monitorial School or seek a warmer climate because of respiratory problems she encountered in New England. In 1830 this routine changed when Channing took her as a governess with the rest of the family to St. Croix, then in the Danish Virgin Islands, on a tropical vacation.

Slavery existed in the Danish Virgins. Although William Ellery Channing was not to publish his controversial views on it for another five years in a book called *Slavery*, his disdain had to be evident to his children's governess. Dorothea had also become a devoted adherent of his Unitarian beliefs, which softened the Calvinism of the other two Protestant denominations to which she'd been exposed—Methodism and Congregationalism. In her letters from St. Croix, we see both her perspective of Dr. Channing as a sometimes teasing employer and also her exposure to blacks and slavery.

The torrid climate on St. Croix had induced an un-Yankee-like tendency toward "languor" in this daughter of New England. Often she lay abed, and she records the tongue-in-cheek, if not slightly sarcastic, tut-tutting of Dr. Channing, declaiming, "Where can Miss Dix be? But I need not ask—doubtless very busy, as usual. Pray, what is that I see on yonder sofa, some object shrouded in white? Oh, that is Miss Dix, after all.... How are the mighty fallen...."[5]

While she fought to "get over this vexatious *no-disease* that does nothing, thinks nothing, is nothing," Dorothea kept her eyes open, observing the West Indian scene of 1830. And she writes, "You have no idea how interesting the Negroes are here...." Unlike the blacks in the North, they have "no coarse features and clumsy gait and rough voices.... They are, in general, handsome, much above the generality of the White, with very fine figures and graceful beyond anything I have ever seen" and "in reality, cheerful and happy...and great dancers...." Still, she adds, "They are not *free agents*. Their managers, overseers, and too often their owners are very corrupt and the slaves are within and under their control." Added is a final coda that would one day become a mantra in the northern half of the U.S.: "No blessing, no good, can follow the path trodden by slavery."[6]

A daughter of Dr. Channing has pictured Dorothea Dix in St. Croix in the late spring of 1831. "She was tall and dignified but stooped somewhat, was very shy in her manner, and colored extremely when addressed."

A shrinking violet? Not exactly.

Dorothea was a strict disciplinarian with her pupils. She was very fond of nature and botany, and in the tropics collected specimens she later gave to science professors. She was also very religious, and close to Dr. Channing, absorbing his ideas about human nature's possibility of "endless spiritual development."

Back in Boston, Dorothea started a school for girls in the Dix Mansion, and it continued for the next five years. At the same time, she had to contend with her respiratory problems, which were eventually diagnosed as tuberculosis. As a result, in the spring of 1836, she closed her school. Her doctors had prescribed a sea voyage to England and a stay in southern France or Italy for a cure. Through Dr. Channing, she had received a letter of introduction to William Rathbone of Liverpool, a rich English merchant and prominent Unitarian who welcomed her into his household, where she remained for eighteen months. Arriving in Liverpool in April 1836, Dorothea had been too sick to travel any farther, hemorrhaging often, spitting blood, but slowly getting better. In September of the same year, she heard from Boston that her mother had died, followed not long afterward by news of her grandmother's death. The practical effect was that she inherited enough money to live a quasi-independent life, supplemented by teaching.

An epiphany of sorts in Dorothea's seemingly conventional spinster existence was to occur five years later in 1841. On March 28 of that year, she attended church in Boston, as was her wont, but leaving the building she overheard two men discussing the deplorable conditions for "prisoners and lunatics" at the East Cambridge jail. Miss Dix next formed a connection with a minister originally from Saco, Maine, the Reverend John T. G. Nichols, who was at a theological seminary in Cambridge and had been assigned to care for women in the East Cambridge lockup. Nichols soon arranged a visit for Dorothea—and others she brought—to come see the alleged *horrible* conditions for themselves.

Horrible they certainly were, with the insane kept among vicious criminals and treated as such. The place was freezing. There was no stove to supply any heat and the jailer told them it wasn't needed and would be dangerous. Dorothea went to court and was able to procure an order for the inmates to be kept warm.

One of the persons who had accompanied Dorothea to East Cambridge was the same Dr. Samuel Gridley Howe who had been such a good friend of Longfellow's. It was perhaps through him that another member of the Longfellow circle, U.S. Senator Charles Sumner, became involved. Since he, too, had seen the conditions at East Cambridge, he was asked to corroborate Dorothea's article describing them, which had appeared in the *Boston Advertiser* on September 8, 1841, and had been fiercely attacked as untrue by the powers that be. Sumner's letter to the editor in response stated bluntly, "It was a punishment by a cruel man in heathen days to tie the living to the dead; hardly less horrid was the scene in the prison at Cambridge."[7]

One can say Dorothea Dix at this point had found her calling. My own speculation is that her sensitivities to injustice, partially aroused by

Dr. Channing in his attitude toward slavery and her observations of it on St. Croix, gelled into a crusade much easier to deal with politically—ending the Calvinistic notion that the innocent insane were creatures of the devil and had to be treated accordingly.

Massachusetts no longer hanged or pressed to death those accused of witchcraft. But Dorothea Dix, after exposing East Cambridge, embarked on a two-year tour of the commonwealth's "jails and alms-houses" to see if East Cambridge constituted an exception. It didn't. Her findings were reported to the General Court in a "Memorial" that pulled no punches.

"The condition of human beings reduced to the extremist state of degradation and misery cannot be exhibited in softened language," she began, after an apology for the *roughness* of her report. And she proceeded to write of "insane persons confined within this Commonwealth in *cages, closets, cellars, stalls, pens, chained naked, beaten with rods*, and *lashed* into obedience."[8]

Individual instances were cited. A "respectable young woman" in Danvers who had become unhinged because of "trials and disappointments" was pictured "clinging to or beating upon the bars of her caged apartment, the contracted size of which afforded space only for increasing accumulations of filth," and the "foul spectacle" was intensified by descriptions of the stench, the inmate's "naked arms and disheveled hair," and the fact that she was "tearing off her skin by inches, her whole face, neck, and body disfigured."[9]

Another example was included from the town of Sandisfield in the Berkshires, but providing a different lesson. Here, a young mentally ill woman had been caged, chained, and whipped, then, like a slave, offered up for auction as other residents of poorhouses often were. Bought by a kindly old couple, their decent treatment of her soon stabilized her illness.

And there was the young man Dorothea had found in Groton with an iron collar around his neck.

Her "Memorial" containing all this material was sent to Beacon Hill in January 1843, and she asked the "Men of Massachusetts" to take action.

Not dissimilar from the torrent of abuse that followed Rachel Carson's publication of *Silent Spring,* the establishment met these accusations with howls of rage. "Sensational and slanderous lies!" they charged. But the frail Miss Dix, like the frail Miss Carson, had her vigorous defenders, too—in Dorothea's case, people like Dr. Samuel Gridley Howe, the Reverend William Ellery Channing, and the educator Horace Mann. The young man in Groton in the *band of iron* was identified as a James Gibson and transferred to McLean's Hospital, one of the earliest reformed asylums, which then had to fight off a demand from the town of Groton to send him back to be chained again because the selectmen resented paying three dollars a week for his care.

It so happened that Dr. Howe was the Massachusetts legislator who received Dorothea Dix's "Memorial." Happily, he was appointed chair of the committee to which it was referred. The result was a bill for relief of these disgraceful conditions, and it carried by a large margin. New facilities were created for handling the overflow of the mentally ill, and enlightened existing hospitals like McLean's expanded. Dr. Howe was praised for his role as "a man of humanity, energy, and abundant resources," while he wrote Dorothea he was only firing the cannon and she was the one "loading it with ammunition."

Once victorious in Massachusetts, Dorothea realized her work had just begun. Her gaze turned toward nearby Rhode Island.

We have already seen her coaxing $40,000 out of the miserly millionaire Cyrus Butler to expand and humanize an existing hospital in Providence. Afterwards, it was on to New Jersey, where she created a brand new institution "*de nova* and out of nothing," the Trenton Asylum. Dorothea called it her "first-born child."

As in Massachusetts, she had to work in New Jersey with the legislature, and stories are told of the amazing effectiveness of this always tastefully dressed, quiet woman with "rich, wavy, dark-brown hair" and a "wonderful voice." One redneck rural lawmaker in the Garden State, declaring "the wants of the insane in New Jersey are all humbug," went to confront Dorothea personally and left after ninety minutes, declaiming just as loudly, "I shall vote for the hospital!"

An effort to kill her bill in the Jersey Senate failed two to sixteen. Passage was subsequently voted eighteen to zero and the vote in the house was also unanimous. Meanwhile, a similar law Miss Dix had proposed next door in Pennsylvania was being debated in Harrisburg and succeeding just as well.

Her one-woman crusade was only beginning in 1845. For the next decade and a half, Dorothea Dix traveled the world over, not only spreading her message but working tirelessly to make sure actions were initiated to alleviate the plight of the mentally ill. She was no stranger to politics anywhere, whether in statehouses throughout the U.S., or in D.C. or the English Parliament, or the Vatican or the Ottoman Empire. And whether it was a recalcitrant congressman or an unfriendly Scottish sheriff—or even a highwayman in the wilds of Michigan trying to rob her at gunpoint—she always calmly stood her ground and triumphed in the end.

As the latter tale was told, Dorothea had been warned that a certain rural Michigan area she had to travel through might be dangerous. The driver of her carriage was accordingly armed. Yet before they left, she made him leave his pistols behind. Violence was not her thing. But on the road, a weapon-waving man dashed out, seized the bridle of their horse and demanded money. Instead of obeying, Dorothea lectured him about the work she was doing for the poor and insane. At once, the foot-pad recognized that unforgettable voice of hers. He told her he had heard it when he was in the Philadelphia Penitentiary. No, no, he could not rob Miss Dix. He would let her go on unscathed. Still, she lingered, using all of her persuasive talent to convince the man to take some money from her to tide him over until he could find "honest employment."

It was commented in a newspaper reporting this incident that Dorothea Dix's voice was "more powerful" than the pistols she had encountered.

In her work of enlarging or creating new asylums, she was success-ful in Indiana, Illinois, Kentucky, Tennessee, Missouri, Mississippi, Louisiana, Alabama, South Carolina, Nebraska, and Maryland—and also in Canada, in Halifax, Nova Scotia, and St. John, New Brunswick.

Writing to her friends the Rathbones in England, she said she had traveled 10,000 miles within the past three years.

A tougher nut to crack than these state and provincial governments, it turned out, was the federal system in the U.S. Thinking big, Dorothea "memorialized" Congress in 1848. What she asked for was what the law-makers had been giving to railroads—large chunks of the public domain in the West that could be turned into cash when they were sold. Miss Dix's first request was for five million acres, to be held in escrow as a "perpetual fund for the care of the indigent insane." Later, she would almost triple the amount she wanted—12,250,000 acres, an area one-third the size of England and Wales. One might gasp at her presumption, but also view it against the fact that Congress had already given away 134 million acres for education and internal improvements, which included the bounty for railroads.

Dorothea emphasized that she was not seeking help for just "one section" of the U.S. "I ask relief for the East and for the West, for the North and for the South," she said. Sectionalism was becoming more and more of a problem in these years before the Civil War, so this was smart political rhetoric.

Yet in D.C. she ran into various buzz saws of opposition. Northern Democrats declared themselves against "the free disposition of the public domain." Behind the scenes, land speculators and railroad executives fought any attempt to give away any land, except to themselves. Although Congress allowed Dorothea Dix to have a special office in an alcove of the Capitol library, her bill kept getting deferred and was allowed to lapse. Coming back in 1850 with her bigger request, she saw it pass the House of Representatives by a good majority only to have the Senate defer it to the next session. Dorothea, fearful of the Senate, told friends, "I dread Mr. Chase of Ohio" (presumably Salmon P. Chase, a future secretary of the Treasury and presidential aspirant), and still she won in the Senate, but had the House hold up the measure. Two years afterward, she won in both bodies, only to have President Franklin Pierce, the Bowdoin graduate, veto it. A pro-Southern New Hamp-shirite with a Maine education, Pierce defended slavery on the grounds of its constitutionality. His "strict constructionism" led him to assert that the Dix bill was unconstitutional.

Allegedly to recuperate from this strain and disappointment, Dorothea Dix headed for Europe in September 1854. First stop was Liverpool and a stay with her friends, the Rathbones. She rested, but given her Yankee nature, such idleness didn't last long. There was work to be done in Europe, as well.

She picked Scotland for her first target. The need there was the keenest in Great Britain, she'd learned, and so she ignored a warning from Mrs. Rathbone not to tangle with the Scots, who still considered all insane people bewitched and tainted by Satan.

Her testimony about the atrocities she found in Scotland culminated in having a "Royal Commission" (a government investigating committee) set up to examine conditions in the Scottish asylums. This caused Sir George Grey, the home secretary, to deplore sardonically on the floor of the Commons that to achieve such a reform move, it had taken the initiative of "a foreigner and that foreigner a woman and that woman a dissenter" (i.e., not a member of the Anglican Church of England).

Dorothea initially had gone north to York and enlisted the help of Dr. Daniel Hack Tuke, a psychiatrist (called "alienists" at the time). Then, bravely, she crossed into Scotland itself and reached Edinburgh.

She had an immediate clash with the sheriff of the Midlothian region who ran some of the asylums, and she determined she needed to go to London to seek an investigation through Sir George Grey. Consequently, there was a race by train to see who would get to the home secretary first, Dorothea or the Lord Provost of Edinburgh, who was set on preventing her from seeing Sir George.

Dorothea won!

The Royal Commission did not release its findings until 1857. But the preamble of its report minced no words. "It is obvious that an appalling amount of misery prevails throughout Scotland," it said, and condemned the "hard-hearted brutality" of many "overseers of pauper lunatics."

On August 25, 1857, Parliament passed legislation establishing "new and humanely administered asylums in Scotland."

Dr. Tuke, writing almost a decade later, was to tell Dorothea, "I think you might say to the Scotch: 'You are my joy, my crown,' for they have gone on wonderfully since 'The American Indian' aroused them from their lethargy."

Meanwhile, it was on to the Continent for Dorothea Dix, with a brief stop in the English-owned Channel Islands, where she caused a certain Mr. Pothicary to be arrested for forcing mentally ill people in his care to work for his own profit.

Hospitals were visited in France and Italy, and she found conditions so bad in the latter country, particularly in Rome, that she somehow managed, despite being a Protestant, to bring the problem to the pope himself. After her audience with Pius IX, who spoke with her in English, the pontiff visited local asylums unannounced and summoned

Dorothea back to admit how distressed he was by what he saw. Protestant Dix was likened to Saint Theresa and a new asylum was created by Pius IX.

In March 1856 this visiting American lady of mercy left Italy and made her way through Austria-Hungary and Greece and into Turkey. The Crimean War, involving Russia, Turkey, and England, had just ended, and Dorothea was disappointed in not being able to meet Florence Nightingale, the famous English nurse. But she did catch up with a Maine native, Dr. Cyrus Hamlin, president of Roberts College in Constantinople (and cousin of Hannibal Hamlin). He helped her get into Greek and Armenian hospitals in the Ottoman Empire, where she found conditions not to her liking. On the other hand, she was amazed at how well-run and humane the Muslim hospitals were, far better than anything she had seen so far in Europe.

Other hospitals that impressed her during further travels were in Russia, at Moscow and St. Petersburg.

In September of 1856, Dorothea headed back to the U.S.

Although the country was moving toward the cataclysm of the Civil War, she spent a good deal of the time traversing the South, and was warmly received in places like Texas, South Carolina, and Tennessee. As late as the winter of 1860, she still hadn't left Dixie. Politically astute to the needs of her own mission, Dorothea never breathed a word about slavery. Yet when the great conflict did break out, she remained steadfastly loyal to the North.

Right at the start, apparently, she was involved in a very dramatic incident that could have had dire consequences for the fate of the Union. Since Washington, D.C., was located so far to the south, it was extraordinarily vulnerable following Lincoln's election. There was a major question as to how the president-elect would ever get to the capital for his inaugural. It has been reported that Dorothea Dix, perhaps through her Southern contacts, received word of Confederate plans to cut off all communications to D.C. and prevent Lincoln from taking office. Baltimore was a choke point. Dix relayed this information to Samuel M. Felton, president of the Philadelphia and Baltimore Railroad, a Union supporter, and he worked to send the 6th and 8th Massachusetts regiments to beef up the D.C. defenses. Those soldiers, sent by Maine-born Massachusetts Governor John A. Andrew, had to fight their way through Baltimore. Felton was also able to smuggle Lincoln past the Rebel irregulars, and Dorothea herself caught the last train from New Jersey before the fighting broke out, in order to report for duty as a nurse to the surgeon general at the War Department.

The secretary of war, former Pennsylvania senator Simon Cameron, proceeded to appoint her the "Superintendent of Women Nurses."

Sixty years old and her health none too good, Dorothea took on this difficult job and stayed with it through all four years of the war.

The comment has been made: "She was very unpopular...with surgeons, nurses, and any others who failed to do their whole duty, and they disliked to see her appear, as she was sure to do if needed."[10] Behind her back, they called her "Dragon Dix." But Edwin Stanton, who succeeded Cameron as secretary of war, supported her completely. To this stern, no nonsense Ohioan, her unpopularity was "a commendation of fidelity, rather than a reproach."[11]

Once the war ended, one of her major efforts was erecting a monument at Fort Monroe, Hampton, Virginia. This southern federal outpost, unlike Fort Sumter, was never captured by the Confederates and contained the gravesites of "6,000 brave, loyal [Yankee] soldiers." Dorothea spearheaded the fundraising campaign and even returned to Maine seeking the right granite for a 75-foot-high obelisk that was eventually raised, bearing the inscription: "In Memory of Union Soldiers who Died to Maintain the Laws."

In time, Dorothea's feelings of anger toward the South softened and at one point she interceded in the running of a hospital in Charleston, South Carolina.

But her age and her physical condition, particularly lung problems and the effects of malaria, caught up with her. In 1881 she went to stay in quarters reserved for her at the Trenton, New Jersey, asylum, the first new hospital she'd inspired. This was her home until she died on July 17, 1887.

An epitaph of sorts might have been the words of President Millard Fillmore in a letter to her: "Accept my sincere thanks for the print of the Hospital for the Insane in Tennessee.... When I looked upon its turrets and recollected that this was the thirteenth monument you had caused to be erected by your philanthropy, I could not help thinking that wealth and power never reared such monuments to selfish pride as you have reared to the love of mankind...."[12]

Although a biographer has stated that "the childhood of Miss Dix [in Maine] has been seen as bleak, humiliating, and painful," and she does not seem to have devoted any of her attention to the mentally ill in the Pine Tree State, we Mainers in recent years have made a strong effort to claim her for one of our own."

In addition to renaming the Bangor mental health facility and a Dorothea Dix Park in her birthplace of Hampden, there has also been established a Dorothea Dix Award—created by state statute in 2005— to recognize exceptional contributions to Maine's mental health community.

The first one given out, in April 2007, went to Melissa Gattine of Cumberland Center, an employee of the Spring Harbor Hospital in Westbrook. In work that decidedly harked back to Dorothea Dix's experiences in the East Cambridge jail, Melissa Gattine was cited for training Maine law enforcement officers to deal with mental illness sufferers in crisis. She had helped set up Crisis Intervention Teams in more than twenty Maine communities and, most especially, in six county jails. Maine, it seems, is the only state that uses these police-centered teams in correctional centers.

No doubt this would bring a smile of encouragement to the normally serious mien of Miss Dix, albeit for the state she did not remember fondly, and a plea to continue this good work everywhere.

1. Presentation by Peter R. Stowell, 14th Annual Washburn Humanities Seminar, "Mysteries of Northern New England: A Killer Among Us," p. 4.
2. Ibid.
3. Joseph Tiffany, *Life of Dorothea Lynde Dix*. Boston: Houghton Mifflin, 1918. Reprint 1971, Ann Arbor, MI: Plutarch Press, p. 7.
4. Stowell, p. 4.
5. Tiffany, p. 29.
6. Ibid., p. 30.
7. Ibid., p. 75.
8. Ibid., p. 76.
9. Ibid., p. 77.
10. Ibid., p. 341.
11. Ibid.
12. Ibid., p. 382.

Artemus Ward
Courtesy Maine Historic Preservation Commission

ARTEMUS WARD

Waterford, Maine, is still a very pretty lakeside town. The central portion along the water has probably not changed considerably since the
first half of the nineteenth century, when its most famous citizen was
born there. He is not best known to history by his real name, Charles
Farrar Browne. Rather, it was under his nom de plume, "Artemus
Ward," that he became internationally famous and achieved the reputation of having been President Abraham Lincoln's favorite humorist.

Waterford can also claim other noteworthy citizens. Cyrus Hamlin,
the president of Roberts College in Turkey who assisted Dorothea Dix
during her trip to the Ottoman Empire, was born in Waterford. He and
Vice President Hannibal Hamlin shared the same grandfather, and
Artemus Ward, with his quirky sense of the absurd, must have loved
knowing some Hamlins had weird first names, like Africa, Asia, Europe,
and America. There was nothing funny about Elbridge Gerry, a
Waterford-born Maine congressman, descendant of the famed signer of
the Declaration of Independence, except perhaps that the surname has
given us "gerrymander." And finally, Mary Moody Emerson, the brilliant, eccentric aunt of Ralph *Waldo* Emerson, who often stayed at her
Waterford home.

One of Artemus Ward's admirers and biographers, the late John J.
Pullen, once speculated that his subject was not overly fond of Maine,
since he'd voluntarily left the state at an early age. But the humorist did
often return to his birthplace and praised it in his writings, even if perhaps a bit tongue-in-cheek, which was the way he always seemed to
express himself.

A Ward quote was: "The village [Waterford] from which I write you
is small. It does not contain over 400 houses, all told; but they are milk
white, with the greenest of blinds, and for the most part are shaded with
beautiful elms and willows. To the right of us is a mountain, to the left
a lake...."[1]

Another was: "Why stay in New York when I had a village green? It isn't everyone who has a village green to write about and I fancy I am about as happy as a peasant of the vale as ever garnished a melodrama, although I have not as yet danced on my village green, as the melodramatic peasant usually does on his."[2]

And, continuing, his offhand praise of the local Waterford citizenry is couched in a certain sly Maine style of seemingly ingenuous anti-snobbery: "We know little of Honore de Balzac, and perhaps care less for Victor Hugo.... Jean Valjean, gloomily picking his way through the sewers of Paris...awakens no interest in our breasts. I say Jean Valjean picked his way gloomily, and I repeat it. No man, under these circumstances, could have skipped gaily...."[3]

Ward specifically connected his genre of writing to a fellow Mainer, born at nearby Buckfield, Seba Smith, known for his satire done in poor grammar and rustic speech mannerisms. Smith, who published his first book, based on the invented character of Major Jack Downing of Downingsville, in 1833, a year before Ward was born, achieved a renown that carried him to an editorial career in Portland and New York City. Like Smith, Artemus Ward used funny spellings and dialect to enhance his humor, which was not overwhelmingly political, although his foolishness really tickled President Abraham Lincoln's funny bone and, in an oblique fashion, played a key role at a crucial moment of the Civil War. This story has been told over and over again and will be presented in more detail later in these pages.

But first, some examples of the kinds of things Artemus Ward wrote and then how he got from sylvan Waterford, Maine, into the national limelight.

In the misspelled mode, he had statements like the following:

"Old man Townsin's Fort was to maik Sassyperiller. 'Goy to the world! another life saived!' (Cotashun from Townsin's advertisement)...."

"Cyrus Field's Fort is to lay a sub-machine tellegraf under the boundin billers of the Oshun, and then hev it Bust...."

"My Fort is the grate moral show bizniss & ritin choice famerly literatoor for the noospapers. That's what's the matter with *me*."

As Seba Smith had pictured his Major Jack Downing in fictional encounters with President Andrew Jackson, so, too, did Ward posture himself on a visit to Abraham Lincoln in Springfield, Illinois, right after the railsplitter's election when he was being besieged by office-seekers:

"'Good God!' cride Old Abe, "they cum upon me from the skize—down the chimneys, and from the bowels of the yearth!' He hadn't more'n got them words out of his delikit mouth before two fat offiss-seekers from Wisconsin, in endeverin to crawl atween his legs for the purpose of appyin for the tollgateship at Milwawky, upsot the President eleck & he would hev gone sprawlin into the fire-place if I hadn't caught him in these arms. But I hadn't more'n stood him up strate before another man cum crashin down the chimney, his head striking me vilently agin the inards and prostratin my voluptoous form onto the floor. 'Mr. Linkin,' shouted the infatooated being, 'my papers is signed by every clergyman in our town, and likewise the skoolmaster!'"[4]

Ward's father died when he was thirteen years old. The boy had already established a reputation in Waterford as a cut-up by locking all the hens in town in the schoolhouse and creating an odorous mess that took two days to clean. Plainly, his mother, alone, could not manage him and he was sent off to northern New Hampshire to learn printing at the *Lancaster Weekly Democrat*. He was soon fired for, as we would say today, "goofing off." Sent back to Maine, to the *Norway Advertiser*, he worked there until the newspaper folded, then had a brief stint at the *Skowhegan Clarion* before moving on to Boston.

In the big city, he produced his first published writing, using the pseudonym "Lieutenant Chubb," and turning out seven stories for a short-lived publication called *The Carpet-Bag*. Next heard from, he was in Tiffin, Ohio, not far from Toledo, employed by the *Seneca Advertiser*, and this job was followed by one at the *Toledo Commercial*. In the fall of 1857, Charles Farrar Browne, not quite yet Artemus Ward, was offered the position of city editor of the *Cleveland Plain Dealer*, one of five dailies in the Ohio city.

On January 30, 1858, his first column containing the name *Artemus Ward* appeared under the title "Letter From A Side-Showman," concerning a "show bisness in Cleeveland; have a show consisting in part of a California Bare, two snakes, tame foxies, etc., also waxworks..." and with statues of "our saveyor General Taylor and Doktor Webster in the ackt of killing Parkman [a sensational murder in Boston]."

The *schtik* (to use a show biz term) about a crazy traveling animal circus was a running gag that caught on and furnished continual silliness for Mr. Artemus Ward, whose name was becoming known, to exploit in column after column. He added a "Cangaroo" to his imaginary menagerie and the marsupial was a perfect foil for all sorts of comments and adventures; for example, having Governor Salmon P. Chase of Ohio, a noted abolitionist, say on seeing it, that "the chained beast reminds me of three milyuns an a Harf of our unfortyunate cullered brethren which are clankin their chanes down in the Slaive Ollergarchy...." For those without a taste for politics, there was excitement and suspense when the kangaroo escaped from his cage. The common council of the town where this happened passed a resolution to help poor Artemus recapture his kangaroo. Seven hundred citizens "jined in the pursoot" and finally they "cawt him," but he continued "very troublesome," yelling and kicking up his legs "from mornin til nite."[5]

At this point, when *Artemus Ward* is beginning to become a name embedded in American consciousness, it might be well to ask where that curious moniker came from. There was in American history a real-life Artem*as* Ward (note the *as*), a Revolutionary War general, no less, from Massachusetts, who fought beside George Washington at the Siege of Boston

Another Artem*us* Ward biographer, Don C. Seitz, trying to answer this question, digs into Maine history, indeed the history of Waterford. A Mainer himself, Seitz reports that the Massachusetts General Court had given veterans' bonuses to men who had joined Sir William Phips's 1690 expedition against Quebec, and that almost a century later, the Boston lawmakers turned Waterford over to three of their descendants, but the record also reads: "and Artem*us* Ward is joined." Grandfather Brown was an agent for that land, so Seitz goes on to write that the budding humorist, "chuckling at his shaky worktable in the *Plain Dealer* office," needing a name for his showman—and his own persona—chose that one out of some long-buried memory.[6]

Note: Charles Farrar Browne's surname was originally *Brown*. He added the *e* once he became famous, an attempt at some spurious or humorous touch of class, or both.

In 1860, the writer of these "Artemus Ward" columns in the *Cleveland Plain Dealer* realized he was not receiving any royalties for his work, which was being syndicated to other newspapers. He was only earning his fourteen-dollar-a-week salary. The notion of going on a lecture tour began to intrigue him. Reportedly, he had his first run at public speaking while attending a ball in Cleveland where he was asked to talk to the attendees and, because of shyness, refused. The next day, however, he stated in his column that he had given "a dignified and striking effort" and reproduced it, "as follows," in three column inches of totally blank space, at the bottom of which he added the notation: "immense and prolonged applause."

It was his dalliance with the idea of lecturing and the appearance of his stories in the New York City-based magazine *Vanity Fair* that got Ward in trouble in Cleveland. The owner of the Ohio newspaper, J. W. Gray, saw an advertisement placed by *Vanity Fair* in his own publication, touting "Artemus Ward, the Great American Showman." Furious, he told his upstart columnist that anything he wrote belonged to the *Plain Dealer*. The young Mainer argued back that the lecture notes were *his* property, but made an offer that for $1,200 a year the *Plain Dealer* could own his whole output exclusively. Publisher Gray said no. Therefore, on November 10, 1860, Artemus Ward resigned his job at the Cleveland daily.

Before long, he was en route to New York City and an exciting new life, hobnobbing with the Bohemian literati of the future Big Apple. As a published author in *Vanity Fair* and *Punch*, he was inducted into a group actually called the Bohemian Club that met at Pfaff's Restaurant on lower Broadway. Among the regulars there were Walt Whitman and Thomas Bailey Aldrich, the Portsmouth, New Hampshire, novelist who wrote the best-selling classic, *The Story of a Bad Boy*. Charles Godfrey Leland was then the editor of *Vanity Fair* and the writer of several books, some favorable ones about witches and another, *Algonquin Legends,* which were transliterated stories from American Indian lore, including those of the Maine Indian tribes. When Leland left his position at *Vanity Fair,* Artemus Ward succeeded him.

His fellow Bohemian Club members also encouraged him to go on the lecture circuit, and his first professional engagement occurred November 26, 1861, in New London, Connecticut. The title he gave his talk was "Babes in the Wood." This had absolutely nothing to do with the things he said on stage. After a tour of New England that took him to Boston, Salem, Massachusetts, and Concord, New Hampshire, he made his debut in New York City on December 23, 1861. A snowstorm limited the attendance but he received a favorable review in the *New York Times.*

"Artemus Ward, Showman, could be imagined as a burly, middle-aged person in seedy apparel. But *Mr. Browne* was a tall, slim, and gentlemanly looking young man, rather careful in dress, with an imperturbable expression of face, which adds very materially to the effect of the droll philosophies that are propounded by him."[7]

His comedy included comment on current political events. An example: attributing the recent flight of the Union Army at Bull Run to a rumor that there were three customhouse job vacancies in nearby Washington. Or, on the suspension of specie (gold coin) payments by Northern banks, he said he "trusted that the banks would not claim originality for the move. He had friends who had suspended specie payments several years ago and others who had stopped paying in paper as well."[8]

In later years, when he had mastered his technique, Ward had a sure-fire opening for his act. He would come out onto the stage and simply stand there, saying nothing. As the minutes went by, the crowd grew restless. People began stamping their feet, shouting out, clapping rhythmically. Finally, he would hold up his hand for silence and announce: "Ladies and gentlemen, when you have *finished* with this unseemly interruption, I shall be glad to continue...."[9]

And most of what came from this early example of a stand-up comic was basically nonsense, a gag, like: "I met a man in Oregon who hadn't any teeth. Not a tooth in his head—[pause]. Yet that man could play on a bass drum better than any man I ever met...." Or a longer, if no less ridiculous, disquisition, such as: "You may lie down on the ground and let a kitten walk over you with perfect safety, but if you put a heavy dray horse in the place of the kitten, you immediately experience a disagreeable pressure," or "we can easily hold in our arms an infant and experience delight; but it would be very difficult for us to perform a similar experiment with a corpulent gentleman who is in a state of unconscious inebriety."[10]

All of this random silliness was, to quote Don Seitz, "delivered with a gravity that was wholly delicious."[11]

While he was enjoying himself with the crowd at Pfaff's Restaurant, Artemus Ward also met an extraordinary female habitué of the place and seemingly lost his heart to her. Adah Isaacs Menken was quite a lady. She had been born Adah Bertha Theodore in New Orleans, to a French

Creole mother and "free Negro father of mixed color." Strikingly beautiful, she was married four times, and in one of these marriages—to musician Alexandre Isaacs Menken—she converted to his religion of Judaism. Thus a Google bio of her is headlined: "First American–Jewish Superstar." Despite divorcing Menken, she remained faithfully Jewish to the end of her days and a rabbi presided at her funeral. An actress of some note, her biggest hit was in a drama called *Mazeppa,* about a famous real-life Ukrainian rebel who was executed by being tied naked to a wild horse which was then set loose. Playing a man, dressed in skin-color tights, Adah was a sensation in the part. She also took male roles in blackface minstrel shows as Mr. Bones, and once impersonated Edwin Booth as Hamlet. It was claimed that among her illustrious friends were Mark Twain, Walt Whitman, Bret Harte, our own Henry Wadsworth Longfellow, Charles Dickens, Algernon Swinburne, and Alexandre Dumas, Sr. She was said to have been linked romantically to the latter two and also to have been wooed by poet Dante Gabriel Rossetti. She drank champagne in public and smoked, cared not what society thought of her, and published two books of her poetry. Dickens is quoted as saying, "She is a sensitive poet who unfortunately cannot write."

It was in the spring of 1862 that Adah achieved stardom in the play *Mazeppa,* or *The Wild Horse of Tartary.* She performed it in Boston at the Old Howard Theater and was later in San Francisco when Ward made his first—and memorable—visit to the West Coast. Meanwhile, she had changed husbands, giving up a boxer named Heman for a comic author, Robert Henry Newell. There was a time in this period when she dallied with Artemus. It is believed he proposed to her and was rejected, but they remained friends, nevertheless.

In that same spring of 1862, on May 17, *Artemus Ward, His Book,* a collection of humorous stories, appeared in print and provided the occasion for the Maine funnyman's "big break"—the incident that catapulted him into history and national renown.

The date was September 22, 1862. The site was the White House. Artemus Ward was not present, except in book form. Secretary of War Edwin Stanton has described what happened. Upon the order of President Lincoln, the War Cabinet had assembled. Stanton wrote: "The President hardly noticed me as I came in. He was reading a book of some kind. It was a little book. He finally turned to us and said:

'Gentlemen, did you ever read anything from Artemus Ward? Let me read you a chapter that is very funny.' Not a member of the Cabinet smiled; as for myself, I was angry and looked to see what the President meant. It seemed to me like buffoonery."12

The *chapter* that Lincoln read aloud to them was entitled: "A High-Handed Outrage at Utica." This tall tale was done in the writer's usual misspelled vernacular and narrated in his capacity of Showman, with his circus animals and waxworks. The plot revolved around a "big burly feller" who broke into the wax depiction of the Last Supper and pulled out the figure of "Judas Iscarrot" by its feet, dragging it off on the ground and beating it as hard as he could.

"'What under the son are you about?' cried I.

"Sez he, 'What did you bring this pussylanernus cuss here for?' and he hit the wax figger another tremenjis blow on the hed.

"Sez I, 'You egrejus ass, that air's a wax figger—a representashun of the false 'postle.'

"Sez he, 'That's all very well for you to say, but I tell you, old man, that Judas Iscarrot can't show hisself in Utiky with impunarty by a darn site!" and with that he smashed in Judas's head. Showman Artemus Ward said he sued the guy and "the Joory brawt in a verdick of Arson in the 3rd degree."

The president laughed heartily when he finished reading and most of the cabinet showed they were amused. Not so Secretary of War Stanton. Responding to his frown, Lincoln put the book down and explained, "Gentlemen...with the fearful strain that is upon me night and day, if I did not laugh I should die, and you need this medicine as much as I do." It was his prelude to the announcement of an earth-shaking decision he had made and was now ready to share with them: the issuing of the Emancipation Proclamation.

Stanton's attitude immediately changed. This dour Ohioan described the aftermath in these words: "I have always tried to be calm, but I think I lost my calmness for a moment, and with great enthusiasm I arose, approached the President, extended my hand and said: 'Mr. President, if reading chapters of Artemus Ward is a prelude to such a deed as this, the book should be filed among the archives of the nation and the author should be canonized....'"

Needless to say, Artemus Ward never did get canonized, but the publicity he received (and helped stir up) from the president's action made him a "hot property" as a lecturer. The story circulated that Thomas Maguire, owner of the San Francisco Opera House, posed a query to him about his availability and that the exchange went like this:

Maguire: "Mr. Ward, what will you take for forty nights in California?"

Ward: "Brandy and water."

The wisecrack version of this negotiation was soon making the rounds on the West Coast and creating what we would today call "a buzz" about this Artemus Ward guy, even well before he arrived at the Golden Gate.

For he soon did go west, and with him went his new agent, E. P. Hingston, an English show manager and Americanophile, who had pronounced himself "a Longfellow enthusiast."

Hingston had gone to work for Ward in 1863, and their trip together, particularly its overland return, which spilled into 1864, has all the raffish elements of a hippie classic like Jack Kerouac's *On The Road,* but in the opposite direction, west to east.

In the summer of 1863, before he left for California, Artemus Ward made two interesting trips, one to the South, or rather, to a Yankee-occupied section around Memphis, where he met and supped with General William Tecumseh Sherman; the other was his usual pilgrimage back to Waterford, where this time he "astonished the natives by strolling about in a gorgeously figured dressing gown, wearing a smoking cap...with a big gilt tassel hanging off of it."13

Folks in Waterford had still not quite gotten accustomed to the eccentricities of the youngster they knew as Charlie Brown. People still talked about how he and a childhood friend, Dan Setchell, met in the Waterford village store and pretended it was by accident and carried on like mad men. Often Ward was seen cavorting through town with children, whooping and doing handsprings. Wrote John J. Pullen, "The impression grew that he was a likeable but shiftless fellow who, for some unaccountable reason, had become famous 'outside.'"14

Then Charles Farrar Browne was off to San Francisco, traveling by sea and crossing the Isthmus of Panama. Hingston was sent ahead as an advance man. The audiences in 'Frisco were enormous, as many as 1,600, each paying a dollar in gold (as opposed to 25 and 50 cents elsewhere). Adah was in the city with new husband Newell, starring in her hit *Mazeppa*. During off hours from his lectures, Ward hung out with her and also some of the local literati, like Bret Harte and Joaquin Miller.

His next stops with Hingston were the mining camps farther east. But there was also the question of how they would return to the opposite coast, and Ward won a toss, opting to go via Utah, since he wanted to meet Brigham Young and the Mormons.

Adah threw a farewell party for them, attended by all of the "literary colony of which [she] was the queen." Bret Harte followed upon Ward's departure with an article that defined the Maine man's humor in a particularly felicitous manner, emphasizing its quintessentially *American* quality, to wit: "humor of audacious exaggeration—of perfect lawlessness, a humor that belongs to the country of boundless prairies, limitless rivers, and stupendous cataracts...that fun which overlies the surface of our national life, which is met in the stage, rail car, canal, and flat boat, which bursts out over campfires and around bar-room stoves...."

This was essentially the life on the road that Ward and Hingston were living, starting by stagecoach to Placerville, California, then to Carson City, Nevada, and into Virginia City, Nevada, which biographer Pullen intimates was one of the high spots of Artemus Ward's short life.

Virginia City! The name conjures whiskey-soaked visions of gold and glitter—wealth hewed out of the bowels of the earth by dirt-caked miners who also crowded into rip-roaring saloons with cowboys, gamblers, dancing girls, et. al.—the Wild West, in short, at its bawdiest. Actually, this boisterous scene was only about four years old when Artemus Ward and E. P. Hingston descended upon it. The Comstock Lode, a massive silver bonanza, had been discovered just prior to the Civil War, and the Union's need for specie led to boom times. So when our entertainer from Maine and his advance man came riding in on the stage from California, the place was really hopping.

Today, Virginia City is a tourist center. To read its publicity, you'd think the only writer or humorist who ever graced its honky-tonk environs was Mark Twain. Certainly, Samuel Clemens was one of its stars. He was a columnist who had started writing for the *Virginia City Enterprise* in the summer of 1862. It was here that he first signed his work *Mark Twain*—and met Artemus Ward, who helped him get his first short story, "The Celebrated Jumping Frog of Calaveras County," published, which gained him his first national attention.

There was never any doubt that Mark Twain and Artemus Ward would be attracted to each other's company. They had a number of things in common besides using catchy noms de plume. They had equally come from good families that had moved to "remote frontier areas." Each had lost his father in 1847. Both had been printers' apprentices. Their older brothers were useless, Twain's (Orion Clemens) an incompetent and Ward's (Cyrus Brown) a drunkard. They were almost the same age. And equally wild and crazy, besides.

The long-lasting image of the two of them together in Virginia City is, after a night of drinking, their cavorting on rooftops, jumping from one to another, blithely endangering their lives in more than just a fall. A Virginia City policeman below took aim at them with his service revolver, judging they were robbers. The editor and owner of the *Enterprise*, Joseph Goodman, stopped the cop by telling him who those daredevils were. Ward had performed in town to great acclaim and Twain, of course, was already a local fixture.

During the week Artemus Ward remained in Virginia City, he and Hingston inspected the mines, frequented all of the bars, and took over the *Enterprise* office, which they made their headquarters. There were evening-long drinking bouts, and following one of these binges, Ward, Twain, and another writer, William Wright—he called himself Dan de Quille—ended up passing out in the same bed. Twain, writing later about such days in Virginia City, could attest: "They were the wine of life; there have been no others like them."

In reminiscing years afterward, Twain remembered Ward in blackface atop a table in the Meloden, a twenty-four-hour Virginia City gin mill, reciting Thomas Bailey Aldrich's "Ballad of Baby Bell." It was 2:30 A.M. As Twain writes it, Ward was "reciting a poem about a certain infant," interrupted every few lines by shouting and pounding on the tables until he finished to "a long, vociferous, poundiferous, and vitreous jingling of applause, and, himself, said slurringly: 'Let every man 'at loves *his* fellow man, stan' up—stan' up and drink health and long life to Thomas Bailey Aldrich—and drink it stan'ing...'" which was amended after his auditors tried struggling to their feet, "Well, consider it stan'ing and drink it just as ye are."

On December 29, 1863, Ward and companion made their escape from the fleshpots of Virginia City and arrived in the primitive mining town of Austin, Nevada. The miners there had never had a show put on for them. Afterwards, our Mainer called himself the "Wild Humorist of the Plains."

While in Austin, Ward, on New Year's Day 1864, wrote a letter to Mark Twain, addressing him as "My Dearest Love," and telling him Austin "is a wild, untenable place, full of lion-hearted boys." He also mentions having blackened his face at the Melodeonard [*sic*] and making a "gibbering, idiotic speech."

"Love to Jo Goodman and Dan," he goes on, then declares that "some of the finest intellects in the world have been flouted by liquor," and warns Twain, "Do not, sir...flatter yourself that you are the only chastely humorous writer onto the Pacific slopes."15

Soon he and Hingston were off again, over the Diamond Mountains. Two days after they had passed by Spring Valley Station, an attack by hostile Indians killed two men and scalped them. On January 10, our travelers were in Salt Lake City, where Ward was laid low and bedridden for three weeks, probably from typhoid fever. Oddly enough, eating canned oysters made him feel better. And he did get to meet Brigham Young. "Artemus Ward Among the Mormons" eventually became one of his most popular acts.

Although the content of this show had no more to do with the title than had been the case with "Babes in the Wood," Mormonism and its then notorious practice of polygamy afforded opportunities for laughs. Ward wisecracked that all "the pretty girls of Utah mostly marry Young," and he had complimentary tickets printed that read: "Admit the Bearer and ONE Wife."

The trip out of Salt Lake City across the Rockies to Denver was grueling, and prompted Ward's sardonic remark that an "overland journey in winter is a better thing to have done than to do." Its survivors were also likely to arouse the same awe as "a Christian coming back alive from a trip to Mecca."

Back in the East, Artemus Ward was as much in demand as before. He settled in New York City and once the Civil War ended, could state complacently that "the Star Spangled Banner is waving round loose again and there don't seem to be anything wrong with the Goddess of Liberty beyond a slight cold." During the summer of 1865, in addition to his usual trip home to Waterford, he performed for the only time in Maine—three shows, one each in Biddeford, Portland, and Lewiston. Six months later, he embarked on a trip to the defeated South, making appearances in Mississippi, Alabama, Georgia, and South Carolina. That the former Rebels greeted him warmly was perhaps due to his having done a benefit performance in the North where half the proceeds had gone to benefit Jefferson Davis's family. To the criticism he received from Northerners about this, he referred in his best deadpan manner to a statement he'd made that he'd "stay away from General Robert E. Lee if Lee stayed away from Maine" and that "Lee must have heard him since Lee never did come to Maine."

It was during this period that Ward also issued one of his most enduring pronouncements, which is still repeated today: "I am not a politician and my other habits are also good" (sometimes attributed to Will Rogers). Lesser known is Ward's companion quip: "I have allers sustained a good moral character. I was never a Railroad director in my life."

In June of 1865, Ward mentioned in a letter to an admirer that he had "a liberal offer to go to England on a lecturing tour." He was then still living in New York City, engaged in writing "a book of travels, giving my experiences among the Mormons." The letter also noted that he spent portions of the summer every year in Waterford.

Maine was rarely ever completely out of his thoughts, sophisticated and world-wise as he had become. Like latter-day Maine humorists, he worked local idiosyncrasies into his material. He would talk about Washington Hale, a real-life Waterford resident who kept a hotel frequented by bad characters, including one who had robbed a savings bank in nearby Norway. Ward called the proprietor "Honest Old Wash." Or there was this tale of the hard-faced Maine farmer, anxious to get back to his duties on the day of his wife's funeral, continually looking at his watch throughout the service, but finally announcing happily, "It was just 2:20 when we got her in."

On the question of his Farrar Brown ancestry, he once replied: "I should think we came from Jerusalem, for my father's name was Levi and we had a Nathan and a Moses in the family. But my poor brother's name was Cyrus, so perhaps that makes us Persians."

He could be self-deprecating, too, telling the story on himself as related to him by Colonel George L. Beal of Norway who had a soldier report indignantly that he'd gone to a show in Baltimore to hear the famous Artemus Ward, "and by Gawd, it was none other than that gol-darned cuss of a Charles Brown we used to know up to Norway."

Waterford-bound one March day, saying goodbye to his friends in Madison Square, "Me thought I would have nice times among the squir-rels and bluebirds and dandelions down in Maine." But alas, it snowed. So, grumpily, he could write, "Standing late at night in the great dismal depot at Portland, it occurred to me that when, many years ago, the Indians sold the land upon which that beautiful and brilliant city now stands, for a jug of indifferent rum, they considerably cheated the Whites...."[16]

Less dyspeptically, he did include a sort of grudging paean to his native state: "Here there is maple syrup, virtue, shrewdness, strong arms and big chests, pickerel, rosy cheeks, and true hearts...and scenery that knocks Switzerland into a disordered chapeau, and air so pure that the New Yorker is sorry he can't bottle some of it and carry it to the metrop-olis for daily use."[17]

But he was soon back to picking on Portland again. When the invi-tation to England arrived and Ward began planning his trip, he wrote a friend in that Maine seaport and said he had thought of leaving from there, except "I am told your steamers depart punctually but seldom reach the other side. I would not die in springtime, unless it was strictly necessary."

So he left from New York on June 2, 1866, aboard a ship called the *City of Boston* and arrived in Great Britain safe and sound. Yet irony continued to hover over his offhand smart-alecky talk about not want-ing to die in the spring. For it was a little more than two weeks shy of official springtime when, the following year, Artemus Ward did die—and on the "other side"—in London.

He was only thirty-three years old.

His trip to England had been a great success, a tour de force, his friend Henry Watterson had declared. Watterson was a Kentuckian Ward had met and befriended in Cincinnati, who happened to be in England and the two saw a lot of each other. The Southerner, later well known as "Marse" Watterson, founder and editor of the *Louisville Courier*, also considered his Maine friend's hectic pace to be a "sort of suicide." Ward suffered from tuberculosis, and by December 1866, when he and Watterson had dinner together, the latter thought the entertainer looked ghastly. On New Year's Day 1867, Ward had to cancel three shows. A trip to the better climate of the south of England did him little good. Nor was he a compliant patient. As the story goes, he was refusing to take his medicine, although a friend was urging him to do so and said he would do anything for the sick man. "Would you really do anything for me?" asked the humorist. "Yes, of course," said his friend. Ward shot back, "All right, you take the medicine."

On March 6, 1867, Charles Farrar Browne—aka Artemus Ward—breathed his last labored breath. The funeral was held at the Savage Club in London, of which he'd become a member, and which resembled the Bohemian Club of his early New York days.

While the British appreciated American writers like Emerson, Hawthorne, Thoreau, and Longfellow, it was said they "idolized" Artemus Ward.

However, our humorist never ended up in Westminister Abbey as our poet Longfellow did. For a memorable epitaph for Artemus Ward, the world had to await the tribute paid him by Mark Twain in 1871, four years after his demise.

It was a performance the late Charles Farrar Browne would have loved (or given himself), in its joshing lack of pomposity, sly digs, and absence of seriousness. Twain started his lecture by saying that, although it was advertised to be about "Several Distinguished People," he would confine himself to Artemus Ward and the subject had been born in Waterford, Maine, in 1834.

"His personal appearance was not like that of most Maine men. He looked like a glove stretcher. His hair, red and brushed well forward at the sides, reminded one of a divided flame. His nose rambled on aggressively before him with all the strength and determination of a cow catcher, while his red moustache—to follow out the simile— seemed not unlike the unfortunate cow. He was of Puritan descent and prided himself not a little on being derived from that stern old stock of people, who had left their country and home for the sake of having freedom on a foreign shore, to enjoy their own religion, and, at the same time, to prevent other folks from enjoying theirs....

"Ward never had any regular schooling: he was too poor to afford it, for one thing, and too lazy to care for it, for another. He had an intense ingrained dislike for work of any kind; he even objected to see other people work....

"He tried every branch of writing, even going so far as to send to the Smithsonian Institute—at least so he, himself, said—an essay entitled 'Is Cats to be Trusted?'... It was in Cleveland that he wrote his first badly spelled article, signing it 'Artemus Ward.'... When he went to England, his reception was of the nature of an ovation."

Twain continued in this teasing vein all the way to his conclusion when, as the *Brooklyn Eagle* put it, "he pathetically alluded to the death of Artemus Ward, expressing himself with exquisite taste." And, oh, yes: he did pronounce Artemus Ward "America's greatest humorist."

1. Nancy Chute Marcotte, *This Is Waterford*. Norway, ME: Waterford Historical Society, 2003, p. 31.
2. Ibid.
3. Ibid.
4. John J. Pullen, *Comic Relief: The Life and Laughter of Artemus Ward, 1834–1867*. Hamden, CT: Archer Books, 1983, pp. 30–31.
5. Don C. Seitz, *Artemus Ward*. New York, Harper and Brothers, 1919, p. 33.
6. Ibid., p. 25.
7. Ibid., p. 105.
8. Ibid.
9. Pullen, p. 45.
10. Seitz, p. 56.
11. Ibid., p. 57.
12. Ibid., p. 113.
13. Ibid., p. 124.
14. Pullen, p. 61.
15. Seitz, p. 144.
16. Ibid., p. 295.
17. Ibid., p. 297.

Asa Meade Simpson
Courtesy Coos Historical & Maritime Museum, CHMM 972-18c

OREGON

One of the jokes told by Artemus Ward, and reproduced in the previous chapter, began: "I met a man in Oregon who hadn't any teeth." If you remember, its illogical punch line made it what we used to call "a shaggy dog story." There wasn't any point, but the effect could be hilariously funny.

Even more illogical, perhaps, was the Maine humorist's choice of Oregon. He might have assigned the toothless man in question to any state of the U.S. We can even rightly ask: had Artemus Ward ever been in Oregon? We know he was in California and Nevada and Utah and Colorado. Or did *Oregon* just have a humorous ring to it somehow?

Connections between Maine and Oregon, on the other hand, do exist. Probably not too many Mainers are aware of our best-known tie— the naming of Oregon's largest city. This is not a fable. All of the pertinent history books tell how Maine-born Francis W. Pettigrove and Bostonian Asa Lovejoy flipped a coin to determine the name for a settlement they planned to erect on property jointly owned by them along the banks of the Willamette River. It was a 640-acre parcel midway between Oregon City and Fort Vancouver, originally referred to as "the Clearing." But obviously, if it were to amount to anything, it would need a more distinctive title, even one derivative of certain celebrated cities in the east. Lovejoy, a lawyer who flouted the honorific of "General Lovejoy," opted for his venerable hometown of *Boston;* Pettigrove said no; although born in Baileyville, Maine, and raised in Calais, he wanted *Portland,* the city where he'd been a merchant and from which he'd left for the West Coast.

It was at a dinner in Oregon City where Lovejoy and his wife, Pettigrove and his wife, and a friend came up with this notion of naming the proposed city on the Clearing. They agreed on flipping a coin to decide. After winning the first toss, Pettigrove gallantly allowed a rule change, making it two out of three to win. And since he did garner two out of three, so Portland the putative site became. Needless to say, all of these doings were utterly theoretical at the time, if not a bit of a spoof.

The coin, by the way, used in those historic tosses had come from Maine. It was a commemorative copper penny celebrating "Old Times Down East." This dinner party entertainment happened in 1845, the same year, it turned out, that the two partners laid out lines for the Portland they hoped to build.

Actually, not until three years later, 1848, was Oregon admitted as a territory of the United States. But since the early 1840s, Americans had been headed that way. In 1843, a "great emigration" took place when 900 settlers entered an area of North America whose ownership was still disputed by Great Britain. Oregon grew into an issue in the presidential election of 1844, as staunch U.S. nationalists chanted "Fifty-four Forty or Fight," the 54°40' being the boundary claimed by our federal government. Yet in 1846, the U.S. accepted a compromise at 49° and before Oregon achieved statehood in 1859, Washington State was carved out of the top part of this immense territory in the Pacific Northwest.

Francis Pettigrove had been among the earlier emigrants to the new land. In 1842, while running a shop in Portland, Maine, he was given an opportunity to bring a stock of goods to Oregon. Along with his wife and their only child, he took ship for the West Coast, but the vessel was blown off course to Hawaii before he was able to reach the Columbia River and Fort Vancouver (today Vancouver, Washington). From there, he hired a Hudson's Bay schooner and sent his goods to Oregon City, where he did quite well in disposing of them.

Interest in Oregon had been sparked by its fur trade after John Jacob Astor established a fur post at the mouth of the Columbia River. Francis Pettyigrove went into the trade, too, once he'd decided to stay in the West and bought a warehouse in Oregon City. His land deal with General Lovejoy occurred because he had purchased half a share from the first owner of the plot, a "Tennessee drifter" named William Overton.

Pettigrove, who had married Sophia Roland in 1842, prior to leaving for the West, did not stay in Oregon all that long. On the Portland property, he built the first house, first warehouse, and first road, but in 1851, suffering from malaria, he moved north with his wife and family into Washington State, where he helped to found the Puget Sound community of Port Townsend. In the same year, his dream municipality of

Portland, rapidly filling up with people, was incorporated as a city.

From then on, Pettigrove vanishes—at least from the history of Oregon.

What other ties, then, do we in Maine have with this distant state, which is like a mirror image of ours, loaded with evergreens and sporting a magnificent coastline, only, as some wag once said, "with the ocean on the wrong side."

A few years ago, while traveling along the Oregon coast with one of my daughters and going south along the ocean, we came upon a series of delightful small state parks. One was named Shore Acres. And here, to my great surprise, I was introduced to the historical personage of Asa Meade Simpson, a native of Brunswick, Maine.

On an informational panel within the confines of the park, a reproduced nineteenth-century photograph depicted stern-faced Asa Simpson with a full white beard. The placard revealed he'd been born in Maine in 1826.

Naturally, I was at once interested, and searched the park's gift shop for material on this hirsute gentleman from down home. Two publications were available, which I bought: *The Simpsons of Shore Acres* by Stephen Dow Beckham[1] and *The Uncommon Life of Louis Jerome Simpson* by Judith and Richard Wagner.[2]

Unlike the first park we stopped at, simply a lovely beach, this property included, besides a rocky shoreline, beautiful world-class gardens, and a set of handsome buildings—in other words, it was a showplace. From the books I purchased, I learned all this was not the work of Asa Meade Simpson, but of his eldest son and heir Louis Jerome Simpson, who had sold the entire complex to the State of Oregon in 1942. But it had been the old Mainer's money—earned in lumbering and shipping—that had made possible the creation of this impressive estate.

My two biographies dealt with both individuals. The father, a Mainer, was naturally of more interest to me initially. The patriarch, I soon learned, was the originator of the Simpson Lumber Company and shipbuilding operations at Coos Bay, the nearby city in the general area. Then I was struck by a descriptive sentence meant to help characterize him: "Thin, resolute, and pugnacious, he [Simpson] was thought by many to be the model for novelist Peter B. Kyne's *Cappy Ricks.*"

I had never heard of Peter B. Kyne, nor of Cappy Ricks, the hero of a series of Kyne's novels. On the Internet, author Kyne was identified as a best-selling writer in the 1920s of latter-day Horatio Alger stories about individuals navigating the perils of the business world through sheer grit and superior wiles. The fictional Cappy Ricks was described as "a crusty yet soft-hearted Scots sea captain, a real go-getter who owns the Dollar Steamship Lines." Thes most popular of Kyne's many novels was titled *The Go-Getter*. Published in 1922 by William Randolph Hearst, it sold more than half a million copies worldwide, telling of a World War I veteran who "becomes a successful businessman with Cappy Ricks and Ricks's Logging and Lumbering Company."

So the life of a son of Maine who did so well on the far-off West Coast that he was incorporated in the popular fiction of his time seemed perfectly apropos for inclusion in a collection of Mainers who went into the world.

Asa M. Simpson's curriculum vitae begins with his father, Thomas Simpson of Brunswick, who married three times. The man's first wife was from the still-prominent Pennell family of Brunswick (a section of the town is called Pennellville), and she left him a son, Thomas Jr. His next wife, Mary Wyer, was Asa's mother. To her were born seven children and all but one lived to maturity. She was a devout Congregationalist and Asa Meade was named for a prominent minister of that same faith. She died three years after Asa's birth. Father Thomas waited exactly a year, then married again and sired five more children.

Thomas Simpson, Sr., was a master shipbuilder and gentleman farmer. Son Asa received a primary and partial secondary education, while working summers on the family farm, and then was apprenticed to a shipbuilder, emerging at age twenty-one certified as a master shipbuilder, able to handle crews in creating new vessels. He also built houses and bridges. For a time in 1848–49, he joined his half-brother, Thomas Jr., and both worked in the shipbuilding center of Bath.

Although gold was discovered in 1848 at California's Sutter's Mill, it took time for the news to have an impact throughout the east. Thus do we hear of forty-niners, not forty-eighters. Asa Simpson and two of his own brothers, Isaiah Hayes Simpson, a year younger, and Lewis Pennell Simpson, four years older, were swept up in the gold rush fever. All of Asa's savings—$2,500—were invested in a 1/32 share in a ship, the *Birmingham*, on which he could carry lumber and general goods around

Cape Horn to California. He and his siblings sailed in November 1849 and reached San Francisco on April 7, 1850.

Some goods sold well, but the lumber didn't, so the brothers decided to try their hand at gold mining. Their only question was how to get to the gold fields. All small boats for the river trip were in use, causing Asa, the master shipbuilder, to construct a skiff they could take to Stockton. The mines they finally reached were on the Tuoloume and Stanislaus Rivers. Asa didn't exactly strike it rich, but amassed a neat nest egg of $1,500 before deciding that prospecting was a dangerous business. For him, it was back to San Francisco, while brother Lewis went off to Sacramento.

In the early decades of the nineteenth century, Maine was the lumber capital of the world. The Simpson boys must have been familiar with all the logging around Brunswick. In San Francisco, Asa still had some of the lumber he'd shipped from Maine on the *Birmingham* and heard there was a market for it in Stockton. There, in the autumn of 1850, he joined forces with an old acquaintance from Maine, S. R. Jackson, and together they sold the boards brought from home. "The retail lumberyard made Asa solvent again," wrote the Wagners in their biography.[3]
In time, this Stockton business was turned over to yet another Simpson, half-brother Andrew, who'd joined the Forty-niners. Moving on to Sacramento, the ever-entrepreneurial Asa opened another successful lumberyard.

While doing this, his keen business sense scented opportunities no one else was seizing. Lumber for use in California was still being shipped from the East Coast, all the way around South America. Although great tracts of merchantable timber were available on the West Coast, there were very few sawmills. Therefore, Asa sought opportunities to cut western logs, and set up sawmills near Truckee, in Crescent City, and at Mendocino, while also investing in shipping to service his retail trade. Headquarters for the A. M. Simpson and Brother Company were established in San Francisco. Asa had partnered there with Robert Wyer Simpson, the oldest sibling of his own mother's brood, twelve years his senior.

Of the six male children Mary Wyer contributed to the extended Simpson family, all at one time or another went west. So, too, did two of the offspring of Thomas Simpson, Sr.'s, third wife. Maine's population had grown fast after the Revolution, but by the 1840s and 1850s the lack of good farmland was the engine of the exodus that began spilling out of the state. Lumbermen themselves, were heading west—mostly to the Middle West—where there were large pockets of Yankees. Asa's wife, Sophia Dwight Smith, was from Racine, Wisconsin, but her folks were New Englanders and the couple met in California.

Restless as Americans tend to be, California could not hold the Simpsons forever.

The Wagners write: "Asa's wide-ranging explorations of Oregon began in 1851. He needed ships to probe the bays and rivers. Questions had to be answered. Were timber tracts useful and available? Did sites afford locations for mills as well as for loading wood products? One early ship Asa had a share in, the *Potomac*, wrecked on the Columbia River bar in 1851. Asa had her towed to Portland for repairs and dispatched his trusted brother Lewis to supervise her loading lumber and pilings in preparation for sailing to San Francisco."[4]

At first, Asa had his eye on Astoria, Oregon, way up north near the Washington border, where John Jacob Astor's fur-trading post had been established. He bought a sawmill but found it had been badly constructed and shut it down. Finally, a much more unsettling happenstance turned him away completely from this region of Oregon. One of his ships, the *Michigone*, loaded with his lumber, went down in a storm off the mouth of the Columbia River. All hands were lost, including the captain, who was his younger brother, Isaiah.

Not until 1855 was Asa's attention drawn to Coos Bay, much farther south on the coast. On the "north bend" of Coos Bay, he discovered large trees growing to the water's edge, lots and lots of them. As the Wagners put it, "The unspoiled timber growth, natural water passages, lack of hostile natives, and new prospects of coal all combined to argue for great potential here. The reason for building a sawmill at Coos Bay was to provide deck loads of lumber for the schooners carrying coal. Schooners were not fitted to carry coal without a deck load, and coal was the reason to come to Coos Bay."[5]

It is an unusual geographical setting where the communities of Coos Bay (a city of 15,000), North Bend, and Charleston are found. A long inlet from the open ocean leaves an extended sandbar—the so-called north bend—with a flow of seawater continuing northward, until it debouches into a spacious lake-like body, on one side of which the municipality of Coos Bay has developed. This sheltered harbor created by nature is a perfect place for good-sized ships.

But entering from the often-wild Pacific can be treacherous. So it was in May 1856. Aboard the ship *Quadratus* on a flood tide as she crossed into the channel opening was Lewis Simpson, bringing a used sawmill his brother Asa planned to install at Coos Bay. The captain missed the channel and *Quadratus* grounded on a sand spit and was subsequently pummeled by "breakers," powerful waves that appeared to be breaking the vessel apart.

A woman passenger, a Mrs. McDonald, who had her young son with her, panicked and went into hysterics. She could see land just a few hundred yards away. She demanded a lifeboat be launched to take her and the child to safety. Lewis Simpson volunteered to go with her and so did one of the mates whose name was Marsden. The small boat was soon swamped, then overturned by the waves and only Marsden escaped alive. The bigger boat ironically was driven ashore near Charleston and no one aboard her was hurt. Some of the cargo was even salvageable.

As soon as Asa heard of the tragedy, he hurried to Coos Bay and spent a month searching for his brother's body. All in vain. He called the event "the most serious knock down" he had ever had. Besides the personal loss, there were business losses, as well. But he saved enough equipment from the wreck of *Quadratus* to start his sawmill at Coos Bay. Eventually, to safeguard ships entering or leaving the bay, he acquired a tugboat.

Next came a Simpson shipyard. Brother Elbridge Gerry Simpson arrived from Maine in North Bend, where the shipyard had been sited, and built *Arago*, the maiden ship in the Simpson fleet. Named for a nearby landmark, Cape Arago, she was followed by the two-masted schooner *Blanco*. This Oregon shipyard, which lasted until 1903, in the end turned out fifty-three sailing vessels. A fifty-fourth emerged from another shipyard acquired by Asa at Marshfield, the city that had its name changed to Coos Bay in the mid-twentieth century.

Asa Simpson's relatives handled these Oregon operations: his cousin William R. Simpson, who was known as "Little Bob," and "Big Bob," that older sibling of his, Captain Robert Wyer Simpson, whose size had gained him his nickname, since he weighed 210 pounds. Captain Bob became known, too, for his political partisanship. When, in 1884, the GOP chose Maine's James G. Blaine as its presidential standard-bearer, Captain Bob sent Blaine-Logan banners to all Simpson properties and ships and ordered them flown day and night "until Blaine is elected." But Blaine lost to Grover Cleveland.

Another Maine Republican import by the Simpsons to the West was prohibition, which had been in place back home since 1856. It was instituted in their Oregon workplaces by the business manager of their sawmill at North Bend, a man named C. M. Merchant. Asa, who is described as straight-laced, opposed to gambling, smoking, and chewing tobacco, and in later life, a strong temperance supporter, saw how the ban saved money and extended it to all his enterprises.

Asa Meade Simpson has been described as "a very distinguished man, always formally attired." He achieved the title of "Captain" Simpson by commanding some of the tugboats he owned, but a few people called him "Stovepipe" Simpson due to the type of high hat he habitually wore. Its height added to his six-foot-one stature. Later, allegedly, he switched to a fashionable derby. Other characteristics were: "Often he was silent.... When he spoke, he was direct, forceful, at times salty.... He could quote Scripture or the poets, and in a more relaxed mood, he was known to spin many a good yarn...."[6]

His Maine-inspired habits extended to frugality. He would always shave himself rather than spend a quarter for a barbershop shave. "The old Captain was hanging on to every penny of his millions," according to Frank Lamb, who wrote a history of Hoquiam, Washington, where the Simpsons also had mills.

They had begun their thrust north across the Columbia River around 1868. Hoquiam, even farther north at the entrance to the Olympic Peninsula, became a Simpson target thirteen years later. The lumber they manufactured was shipped from this port city and eventually went directly to Australia, Mexico, South Africa, the Philippines, Hawaii, Fiji, and Japan. A shipyard, as well, was built in Hoquiam.

It has been said Asa Simpson's "empire ran the length of the Pacific" and "his lumber built homes and buildings on at least four continents."[7] Despite his Yankee frugality, he was neither a miser nor a skinflint zealously guarding every bit of his gold. One story concerning his nonchalance about money was told by his son Louis, who had taken over the company's holdings in Oregon. Finding himself short of cash to meet a payroll, Louis wired his father to bring $15,000 with him to the North Bend headquarters. When Asa arrived, he went first to the shipyard to inspect the newest ship they were constructing. Eighty years old at the time, the old gentleman flew into a fury because his master builder, K. V. Kruse, had deviated from his instructions in the formation of the ship's hull. He yelled to his son, "Louie, get me a broadaxe!" and with it, he chopped the hull's main beam so badly the whole thing had to be rebuilt. His father's rampage was bad enough, but son Louis, horrified in more ways than one, suddenly exclaimed, "Dad, where's the money you brought!?" The reply was an over-the-shoulder casual remark of "Oh, it's in that black bag I tossed on the lumber pile."

Another dispute Captain Simpson had with builder K. V. Kruse approached sheer comedy. It had to do with a difference of opinion on the location of a "head" aboard a Simpson vessel being readied to go to sea. Asa told Kruse to put it under the forecastle deck instead of in the forward deckhouse, where Kruse wanted it. His argument to his boss was that the deck was too low. His boss then proceeded to show him he was wrong by squatting backwards into the place. However, there wasn't enough room for him to lower his trousers. Backing out, he cracked his skull on an overhead beam. But instead of conceding the problem, he commanded Kruse to have a niche cut in the beam to allow for more headroom. Since Captain Simpson was returning to San Francisco the next day, Kruse stalled about cutting the beam, so the octogenarian took an ax and did it himself, notwithstanding which, as soon as he was gone, Kruse located the comfort station where *he* wanted.

Stephen Dow Beckham sums up this doughty Maine tycoon in the following paragraph: "Not only his shipbuilders but also his mill managers and even his sons had to be wary when the director of the Simpson companies came to town. L. J. Simpson's secretary at the turn of the century, Mrs. Frances McLeod, more than once had to flee the office when word came from the lower bay that Captain Simpson had been sighted on an incoming vessel. Louis would say to Mrs. McLeod, "Get out quickly!" And in a frenzy to clear the decks and leave everything in the office quiet and orderly, the secretary dumped her papers, account books, and letters into drawers and scurried away for a holiday until the old captain again left town."[8]

No wonder Peter B. Kyne, who had actually worked as a bookkeeper for the Simpsons, had lots of material to draw on for his novels.

Yet no one was a softer touch than Asa M. Simpson. Panhandlers who approached him on the street were always rewarded with a coin or two. He was charitable to a fault. A fund for wounded Civil War soldiers in New York received $1,000. YMCAs in San Francisco and Oakland were given donations. Another $1,000 went to the Oakland Ladies Relief Society. Money was sent to the Catholic Sisters of Charity Hospital in Portland. When a Protestant hospital protested through a lady named Charlotte and asked for similar treatment, he gave them the same amount, but jokingly made out the check to "Sister Charlotte." With those of his own family members who'd remained in Brunswick, he always supplied money at Christmastime. The funds would go to certain of his kin who would earn "agent's fees" for dispersing it to the rest of the clan.

With his workers, he was always fair and decent, considering the times. He was never anti-union and provided workmen's compensation to injured employees, although the law did not require him to pay them anything. Half pay went to the injured and a full year's pay to the family in case of a fatality.

Furthermore, Asa Meade Simpson was cosmopolitan enough to take his wife on two grand tour trips to Europe, and he frequently went back to Maine. He visited Brunswick fifteen times, and in a local cemetery, established memorials for his two brothers who'd perished in Oregon. A throwback to his upbringing was also evident in the white paint and neatness of his company's installations, something that gave them a Maine look.

Asa himself died in his ninetieth year in Oakland, California, on January 10, 1915. He had been at work in his office until the week before. Command of his empire devolved upon eldest son Louis Jerome Simpson, the creator of Shore Acres, who had associated himself totally with Oregon and even ran, albeit unsuccessfully, for governor of the state.

1. Stephen Dow Beckham, *The Simpsons of Shore Acres*. Coos Bay, OR: Arago Books, 2003.

2. Judith and Richard Wagner, *The Uncommon Life of Louis Jerome Simpson*. North Bend, OR: Bygones, 2003.

3. Ibid., p. 5.

4. Ibid., p. 6.

5. Ibid., p. 9.

6. Ibid., p. 18.

7. Beckham, p. 18.

8. Ibid.

Kosrae, looking much as it did many years ago.
Photograph by the author

10

ISLANDS WAY OUT IN THE PACIFIC

We have seen that Asa Simpson's ships were taking his lumber far out into the Pacific—to Australia, Fiji, the Sandwich Islands (Hawaii). Other Mainers, much more purposefully, were also out on the wide expanses of the world's largest ocean, so far from their home state, and among the islands that dot it.

Whaling was one of the earliest occupations that attracted Americans to these distant waters, while religion wasn't far behind, in the vocation of missionary to the hitherto "heathen" populations of the scattered archipelagoes. Business, too, as with the Simpsons, entered the mix. Even in the very first decade of the nineteenth century, navy man Edward Preble was escorting American merchant ships home from the Dutch East Indies.

But back to religion. For the moment, let us focus our attention on the Bangor Theological Seminary, Maine's supplier of Congregational recruits to this proselytizing effort. One graduate whose name cropped up previously on these pages is Cyrus Hamlin, who went to Turkey and founded Roberts College. Elias Bond, class of 1840, was a noted missionary in Hawaii. Before 1866, the school had its first native Hawaiian student to train. Therefore, we read in a history of the school that "not only were men going out to serve home mission fields, they were scattering far and wide to serve the far-flung missionary stations. There was, for example, Ben Galen Snow who came to the Seminary from across the river in Brewer. He was thirty-two when he was graduated from the school...."[1]

This is the Mainer, of course, who inspired this book in the first place.

The good reverend, born in Orrington and raised in Brewer, and his wife, Lydia Vose Buck Snow, originally from Robbinston, were part of the stream of missionaries being sent to the Pacific under the auspices of the Massachusetts-based American Board of Commissioners for Foreign Missions, an arm of the Congregational Church.

This organization had been dispatching missionaries to Hawaii since 1819. By the 1850s it had expanded its reach. The Snows' initial assignment was to Kusaie (now universally known as Kosrae), a small remote island off by itself in the much larger spread of the Caroline Islands of Micronesia.

The year was 1854. Reverend Snow, a Bowdoin graduate, class of 1846, had finished his studies at Bangor Seminary in 1849, waited until September 1851 to marry (you couldn't be an unmarried missionary), three weeks later was ordained at his home church in Brewer, and in November, shipped out with his bride, first stop Hawaii. On board the *Esther May* with them when they left Boston was Dr. Luther Gulick, a medical missionary, and his wife. In Honolulu a month later, they were joined by yet another pair of Americans assigned to Micronesia, the Sturgeses of Indiana. It should be noted that no Protestant Christian missionaries had ever gone to these remote outposts before.

To help safeguard them, if it were possible, they carried a letter from the king of Hawaii, Kamehameha III, the grandson of the fabled monarch Kamehameha I, who had united the Sandwich Islands into a single domain. Consequently, in his friendly message to "all chiefs of the island in this great ocean to the westward, called Caroline Islands, etc.," the Hawaiian sovereign highly recommended "these teachers of the most High God Jehovah" who were coming their way. "A part of them are white men from the United States of America and part of them belong to my islands," the king wrote, adding that he had seen the value of such teachers, how they, the Hawaiians, had been "given to war" and now were at peace, how his people were enlightened and no longer lived "in ignorance and idolatry." The royal letter ended with an exhortation to the Lord God Jehovah "to make these new teachers a great blessing to you and withhold from you no good thing. [signed] Kamehameha."[2]

On July 15, 1852, the trip from Hawaii began on the schooner *Caroline*. They first landed in Kiribati, among a group of atolls then called the Gilbert and Ellice Islands. They tried to have Kamehameha's letter translated into a native language by an English-speaking trader but he refused, angered by snide remarks they made about polygamy because, only later did they learn, he had four wives. In Kosrae, it turned out, the *Togusra,* or supreme chief, knew English.

This man, Awane Lepalik I, or "good King George," allowed the

Reverend and Mrs. Snow to stay on Kosrae with their helpers, a converted Hawaiian couple, Daniel and Doreka Opunui. The *Caroline* had docked in Lelu Harbor and a house on the adjoining islet of Pisin was given to the Americans for their quarters. The other missionaries aboard the *Caroline* continued on to Pohnpei, a major Micronesian archipelago.

At first, the conditions on Pisin (or Dove Island, as Snow called it) were still quite primitive, even though the Americans had a shelter. Here is how the Mainer described his maiden "island home":

"Such mingling together of hogs, pigs, cats, rats, lizards, old barrels, old boxes, ropes, paddles, bottles, guns, rags, old bits of canvas, mosquitoes, and so on, as there were in the house, we would never become accustomed to. And the felicity of being in a rainy latitude under a leaky roof, so that while eating we would be obliged to get up and move our table to a less drenching spot, and while trying to sleep, we would change our pillows to the other end of the bed that they might be kept a little drier, and let our feet take the shower bath...."[3]

But the natives finally built him a waterproof dwelling and life commenced to look up. Here is the Reverend Snow in a better mood:

"Upon one side of the islet is a beautiful sand beach on a reef which affords an excellent place for bathing at high water, and for a walk at low tide. On another side, within a rod or two of my south door, I can sit on a wall of stone and catch fish with a pole at high tide...."[4]

The point of the mission, needless to add, lay not in seeking creature comforts but in saving souls. Therefore, Reverend Snow must have been gratified, indeed, to be able to write after only several months on Kosrae that the local people had begun filling a "capacious hall for worship." He was learning to speak their "dialect" and living among them "in such rectitude that they understood the gospel from seeing it active in his life."[5]

Today on Kosrae, Sunday service is a must for all visitors to attend, of whatever religious persuasion, to witness a spectacle of the locals wearing their best finery (women must come with hats and long dresses and men with trousers and dress shoes and collared, flowery Hawaiian-style shirts), and the hymn-singing of both choir and congregation is truly sweet-sounding, catchy and touching. Everything—lyrics, sermon, dialogue of any kind—is in the Kosraean language, but it doesn't matter to the onlookers. It is your old-time religion, brought from Maine and adapted to a tropical clime and culture.

Indeed, a visiting church historian from Boston has been reported as flabbergasted, once the Kosraean rites were translated for him, because they were identical to those of nineteenth-century New England. Kosrae has also been dubbed "the Saudi Arabia of Christianity" due to its devout followers, the most observant in the Pacific, they boast.

Pre-Christian Kosraeans, likewise, had a thriving religion. It was based on nature and ancestor worship. Their gods were called Inut and they governed agriculture, climate, all human action, and the souls of the dead. A particulary important deity was the goddess Sinlaku, who ruled the heavens and breadfruit, which was an important food crop.

On Kosrae, and in the Lelu district where the missionaries were housed, there are ruins of an earlier civilization that are considered "one of the true marvels of the Pacific world."[6] Immense walls, 20 feet high, their rocks weighing tons, were apparently constructed between 1100 and 1200 AD. They are currently cloaked in jungle but can be toured with some effort. The relatively unexplored interior of Kosrae is also thought to contain more such ruins; a legendary "King's Mound" was recently discovered, where a monarch who transgressed their religion about the year 1200 had been killed and buried.

During the Reverend Snow's years on the island, priests of the former gods and goddesses, particularly Sinlaku, were still in evidence and blamed the Christian interlopers for angering the heathen powers when sicknesses such as a flu epidemic attacked the population.

These "blueskins," as the hostile Kosraean clerics were called (from the pale bluish color of the conger eels they considered sacred), were not the only hazard Benjamin Snow had to face. In the years 1852–56, the number of whaling ships stopping at Kosrae reached seventy-six. The main problem Snow faced was keeping the women of the island from going out and spending all night among the crews. Such practices—and the venereal disease that resulted—were taking a serious toll on the natives, whose numbers were diminishing. Snow was able to persuade good King George to prohibit this state of affairs, but did not have equal success with the monarch's successors. In the matter of modesty, since most natives of both sexes wore a minimum of clothing or none at all, he had more luck. The men began donning trousers and the women wrapped themselves in Mother Hubbard dresses Mrs. Snow provided.

King George was truly supportive. He ordered all work stopped on Sunday and for people to attend church. He had his younger son, Aliksa, move in with the missionaries. He had written back to Kamehameha that he would be "a father to Mr. and Mrs. Snow" and kept his word. When his people in church had to stand for the benediction, they were reluctant at first because local custom dictated no one could be on the same level as the royalty. But King George gave them permission and, despite their nervousness, they did stand. Smoking and drinking also ended under prodding by the teetotalers from Maine.

Church services were soon removed from Reverend Snow's house to King George's much larger cookhouse in order to accommodate the numbers who wanted to attend, at least seventy-five at this point. Lydia Snow helped clothe the women for worship, making calico gowns.

Another reform was that King George broke completely with the whalers and other white adventurers who frequented Kosrae. Beachcombers were no longer welcome, and deserters from whaling ships were rounded up and returned to their captains, who always had trouble recruiting and retaining enough manpower. Grateful for the king's help, they became amenable to his new missionary-inspired policy of keeping local females off their ships.

By 1866 two stone churches had been built on Kosrae. King George ordered his people to contribute their labor free of charge.

As long as this amenable monarch was alive, the Snows and their Hawaiian helpers found their work eased. His death in September 1854 unfortunately brought trouble. A high chief named Sesa seized power. Reverend Snow warned the Council of Chiefs that if they made Sesa their togusra, or king, the missionaries would leave. So instead, the council elected King George's son, who wasn't as supportive as his father had been, but neither was he hostile.

With a succession of different native leaders on the island came setbacks for the Reverend Snow. Nele Lepalik VI, the king in 1856, had two wives and allowed women to go again to the whale ships. The pagan religion revived in certain areas and the minister from Maine discovered that some of his parishioners were indulging in adulterous affairs. He forced the culprits to make public confessions of their sins before the church congregations.

Three kings passed away on Kosrae during the Reverend Snow's tenure. The idea of classes—royalty and commoners—started to diminish. In a church body set up by Snow, both groupings were included, which would have been unthinkable in the past.

When Opunui, his Hawaiian assistant, suddenly died, the Reverend Snow felt bereft enough to write, "I have lost friends at home, near and dear ones, but now my only brother is taken and I am left alone. There is none to take his place."[7]

Loneliness was an occupational hazard for missionaries, and in later years, when Benjamin began keeping a diary, he often expressed this emotion so many thousands of miles away from his roots in Maine. Yet while working on Kosrae, he occasionally had taken trips to an even smaller and more isolated island in the southern part of the Marshall Islands.

This was an atoll called Ebon. One of its attractions for the reverend was an available printing press, which he could use, among other things, to prepare a bible in Kosraean, a language he had thoroughly learned. The Snows left Kosrae in 1862 for a trip back to Maine and then the reverend, by himself, returned to the Pacific, but this time to Ebon, while Mrs. Snow remained at her family's home in Robbinston with their daughter, Carrie. His diary for 1868, written on Ebon, was later found in a house in Robbinston.

Each diary entry usually began with a comment about the local tradewinds, which were "strong," "squally," or "pleasant."

So January 1, 1868, commences with "Strong trades" and next, excitedly: "Sail ho!"—a ship arriving. It was the *Joseph Cogan*, carrying supplies, and Snow went on board to see if any letters in "the Ponape bag" were for him. None were that New Year's Day, but he did get "a good fill of newspapers from the captain, who is also a Catholic and very kind. Gave me a bag of potatoes."[8]

Another later "Sail ho!" was even more propitious for the missionary in his incredibly isolated outpost. This time, the chief officer of the ship was named Captain Willis and he was from Hilo on the "Big Island" of Hawaii. The Reverend Snow not only received mail from home, but *two* bags of potatoes—"Irish and sweet"—plus a box of oranges.

His own mail went out in return. One letter was to Peking, China, to someone whose Maine-sounding name was Blodgett, while other missives were dispatched to Koloa, Hawaii, on the island of Kauai, to missionaries "Reverend Dole and Smith." The latter was Dr. James W. Smith, a medical doctor who had arrived in 1842, became ordained in 1854, and led Koloa Church until 1869. Dole, it goes without saying, is a name intimately connected to Hawaii and not just because of its association with pineapples. Daniel Dole was a fellow Mainer, originally from Skowhegan, and his wife was a Ballard from Hallowell, of the same family as the since-famous midwife, Martha Ballard. Their son, Sanford Ballard Dole, is probably the best-known American in the nineteenth-century history of Hawaii, serving as president of the short-lived independent republic that overthrew Queen Liliuokalani and governed until the former Sandwich Islands were absorbed into the United States. Old Reverend Dole put most of his effort on Kauai into running an English language school, where he conducted his religious services on Sunday, and later founded the famous Punahou School on Oahu.

Tidbits of Snow's life on Ebon appear as the diary days stretch out. Hardships, to be sure, like: "We had to walk home in water up to our middle" when he and Kapali, a Hawaiian Christian, had gone somewhere by canoe and had their canoe stolen, and on top of the discomfort, the fifty-one-year-old reverend had suffered a leg cramp. But such trials were mitigated by small joys: "It is pleasant to see the girls keep my little blue pitcher filled with lilies."

"Pretty good meeting but the Hawaiians talked too long" was his assessment of the religious activity on Ebon in January 1868. It was evident from Snow's use of the plural that Kapali had several of his fellow Sandwich Islanders visiting. We see this again when Snow later tells of "engaging passage for the Hawaiians to other islands."

The Ebon printing press was in use. One day, Snow "struck" a hundred calendars. He translated Luke into the Ebon dialect for a tract he distributed. All those potatoes he was eating, he reported, were making him fat. He now weighed 184 pounds, consuming spuds three times a day. Work was continuing on the church he was building. He had to go to another village to help a man named Charley Andrews make a will. The poor guy had an abscess on his liver.

There seemed to be plenty of people around with Anglo-Saxon names—whalers and often some none-too-savory characters. Snow writes, "Nugent has been having a regular drunk. Black Dan and Tom keeping him company. Captain Emery instigated or influenced him to buy the liquor. Oh, what a scourge this Captain Emery is...."

One night, the missionary had a poignant vision. Coming home to his quarters, Snow saw lights on in the dwelling and found himself actually thinking he would see Lydia and his children inside.

His entry for January 20, 1868, announced the fact that he had decided to go back to America. Previously, he had written in his diary, "My heart and head trouble me." And after stating in writing that he'd made up his mind to leave the tropics, "those islands yet in darkness," he complained of an old illness reoccurring and causing him to take "a good dose of sulphur and cream of tartar."

Home certainly must have been on his mind when he subsequently dined with a sea captain, unnamed, who was a native of Calais, Maine. Three of this man's brothers, who worked at a shipyard in East Boston, were identified but only by their first names: John, Hugh, and Henry.

The prospect of going home "excited" Reverend Snow, he admitted. In the diary, it becomes almost an obsession, mentioned again and again. He said he was glad his wife Lydia's return had gone unnoticed in the Maine newspapers. Anonymity was what he wanted for himself, too—"Stealing my way home." His *bowels*, he declared, had for some time been "out of order"; he was "not getting good sleep"; felt "bilious."

If all worked out well, he'd be able to attend the "semi-centennial" of the Bangor Theological Seminary in July 1870. After a stop in Hawaii for a meeting, he would board the fastest boat to California and travel nonstop to Maine, straight through to Bangor via Chicago, the Great Lakes, and Portland. Lydia would be asked to meet him in Bangor.

A bad dream disturbed Snow, in which he claimed to see "a dead man rise out of a coffin and kiss me." This spectre looked like a certain "Reverend E. Carpenter," he wrote. But there were happy dreams, as well, such as smiling appearances by Lydia.

"September 6. Saw my dear wife last night in my dreams. Our embrace was so affectionate that when I waked up [*sic*], my lips pained me—it seemed so real. Shall it ever be real?"

This diary ends on the last day of December 1868. He had to dose himself with castor oil. There were still mundane duties to perform. Andrew Fisher wanted Snow to marry him to the daughter of Lemaik.

Snow would, he said, if the girl and her parents were willing. "It may open the way for several others to do the same who are living in wickedness now."

His final note was that the year just ending had been: "a year of suffering...and a year of great loneliness as to the companionship of wife and children," but, he added, "a year of great comfort in work and Jesus."

The Snows had two children, both apparently born during their stay on Kosrae—Caroline, or "Carrie," in 1856 and Frederick Galen in 1858. Obviously, they had gone to Maine with their mother by the time the reverend was keeping his diary on Ebon, quite likely due to the lack of adequate schooling anywhere in mid-nineteenth-century Micronesia. In his diary, Snow told of "writing to my darling Carrie." Fred had several stories told about him. One was his sailing in 1884 on *Morning Star*, one of a long series of missionary ships by that name, after her launching at Bath, Maine. He was listed in the annals of the Lincoln and Sagadahoc Counties Congregational Conference, which recorded the event, as the son of Reverend Benjamin Galen Snow, and his job was ship's engineer. Some reports had him as captain of *Morning Star*. But he was also reputed to have lived on Hawaii, owning a plantation and raising pineapples, sugar, and cattle.

Home ho! The vision of Maine, of family, did turn out to be a reality for the Reverend Snow in these last years of the 1860s. He most likely made it to the celebration at Bangor Theological Seminary in 1870. Afterward, his whereabouts are fuzzy, as are the dates. The only certainty is that in 1877 he suffered a stroke. There are hints he had returned to the Pacific by then with Lydia. Was he at Kosrae? Was he at Ebon? Or still commuting between the two? Other information would have us believe he was with his son Fred at the latter's plantation digs in Hawaii. But in 1877, Frederick Galen Snow would have been only nineteen years old, hardly the age at which one amasses an estate. The other firm date is 1880—the Snows were residing in Brewer when the reverend died.

That his legacy can still be seen in packed church services every Sunday on Kosrae is no doubt the most obvious result of his lifetime work. Even while the Reverend Snow was alive in 1874, and possibly living in the Kosrae area, it has been asserted the infamous local pirate "Bully" Hayes himself went to church there, proclaiming (or pretending) he'd been converted. By the same year, too, Reverend Snow's efforts could also be seen fruitful in that the native population, once feared headed toward extinction, was palpably on the rise.

The mention of Bully Hayes inevitably brings to mind our second Mainer out here—Harry Skilling (alternative spellings: Skillin or Skillings). The main branch of this family in Portland is still extant and so numerous that for some years it printed a "Skillin Family Newsletter." Among its past distinguished members can be found Samuel Skilling, who in the eighteenth century owned land with Thomas Westbrook; Samuel Skilling, Jr., commander of Portland's forces during the French and Indian Wars, and considered "a military genius"; and a Simeon Skillings, Jr., who married a great-granddaughter of General Jedediah Preble and owned land in connection with the heirs of Commodore Edward Preble.

Harry N. Skilling, the black sheep, was probably born in 1845. His older brother, Theophilus, had gone off to California in the gold rush and Harry is thought to have shipped out on a whaler at the age of twenty-five. In the far-out islands, he was known as a "trader." But also, in words the family newsletter actually printed, "the greatest scoundrel unhung."

His own descendants claimed he was a pirate who killed many people. One of these descendants, a distinguished Kosraean judge, Harry *H.* Skilling, wrote about his ancestor's narrow escape from death during the period 1899–1914, when Imperial Germany controlled the Caroline Islands: "The fact was, since he was a pirate and had killed many people, the Germans were after him. He was caught in Pohnpei and brought back to Kosrae to be executed.... He was then brought to see his family before being executed. They did not kill him anyway because he had many children in Kosrae and they decided to leave him there."9

This narrative of Judge Skilling's helps establish the fact of Harry's arrival at Kosrae earlier than the German period. He allegedly came from the island of Nauru, where he had married Jenny, a native woman. Her sisters and father and brother had fled with Harry and his family to Kosrae because of continuing turmoil on Nauru, which is out in the middle of the Pacific and noted for its deposits of phosphates. Harry had been a trader in this fertilizer, but the Naurans, drunk most of the time and supplied with guns by Bully Hayes, had made life too uncomfortable for him.

To be sure, Harry was no angel. Once established in a homestead at Sansrik on Kosrae, courtesy of the reigning king, Harry proceeded to kill his own brother-in-law for stealing his cigars.

He also proved to be a good friend to Bully Hayes, who had an even worse reputation, accused of murder, rape, blackbirding (or kidnapping natives to sell as slaves), thievery, and child sex-abuse. On his ship, the *Lenora*, Hayes arrived at Kosrae in March 1874.

A wild time was in the offing. Also on Kosrae was another group of refugees from Nauru, both white traders and natives. They were making trouble, and the king of Kosrae pleaded with Bully Hayes to take them somewhere else. We have a description at this period from one of the *Lenora's* crew, Louis Becke, an Australian, of Harry Skilling aboard the pirate brig before she sailed. He called Harry an "Adonis," stretched out on a pile of sleeping mats, "with clean-cut features, dark brown curly locks, and drooping moustache." Becke refers to him as "the ideal sea-rover," and how he appeared equally devoted to his four wives, "a man who simply laughed at wounds and death and a dangerous antagonist, as some of his fellow traders had good reason to know."[10]

The situation on Kosrae grew all the more dangerous when Bully Hayes's ship, trying to leave, was sunk off an islet called Utwe Ma. The survivors, back on shore, caused untold problems, especially by abducting young island girls.

Begged by the king to get Bully Hayes to stop this practice, Harry and Louis Becke went and talked with him. But the pirate captain was in a foul mood and they had to retreat before his "black rage."

Yet later on, Harry agreed to look after Hayes's property and good relations were restored. Harry's idyllic life was further pictured by Becke in his writings, such as finding this "sybarite" Mainer "lying in a hammock, smoking his morning pipe, while two of his wives, Rosa and Taloe, combed his long ringlets." Becke wisecracked it was "Harry's cure for a headache."

The whole crisis on the island was finally on its way to ending with the arrival of a British man-of-war and Bully Hayes's arrest. But the wily pirate managed to escape, find Harry, get a rifle and ammunition from him, and disappear, after receiving a promise that his place on Kosrae would be protected. When the Kosrae authorities and the British officers demanded Harry surrender the pirate captain's belongings, the man from Portland not only threatened to shoot the first person who stepped on his land, but also warned them against tampering with an American citizen.

Not long afterward, the British navy ship left and Bully Hayes was soon killed in a fight with his ship's cook.

Numerous descendants of Harry Skilling remain on Kosrae. He had one son, Fred, who became—of all things—a minister and fathered eleven children; he also had three daughters, one of whom married John Sigrah, the last king of Kosrae, who reigned from 1910 to 1947. The royal ruins of Lelu, possibly through this last connection, are owned by the family of a Sidney Skillings.

During my stay on Kosrae, the Sigrahs were still in power. Rensley Sigrah was the governor and Aaron Sigrah his administrative assistant. The latter, a handsome, friendly young man, talked proudly about his Maine heritage. And he jokingly expressed a fear that if he met his Pine Tree State relatives, "They wouldn't exactly think I was from Maine," referring to his Micronesian looks.

Perhaps by now Aaron has been to the Portland area and met his long-lost cousins. Others from Kosrae *have* traveled to family reunions.

So there is a closeness to America in this distant Pacific land, where our dollar is the official currency, and the form of government resembles that of an American state, with an elected governor and legislature and an independent judiciary. Kosrae is one of the four components of the Federated States of Micronesia, which has a special relationship to the United States. Our armed forces protect them and our State Department handles their foreign matters, but otherwise they run their own affairs.

Originally, these islands were controlled, like the Philippines, by Spain, but after the Spanish–American War, the Carolines were sold to Germany. World War I ended that situation, and the Japanese, who had fought on the Allied side, took over. Their grip on Micronesia was not loosened until the end of World War II. Remnants of their military occupation are still visible on Kosrae: sunken ships in the water, rusting tanks, and pillboxes on the beaches. There is also one horrifying memory—the fact that an order came from Tokyo to the local commander to massacre all of the Kosraeans before the island was abandoned to the Americans. The natives were to be lured to a public meeting and machine-gunned. Fortunately, the local commander disobeyed.

The population of Kosrae is now more than 8,000. In the Reverend Benjamin Snow's day, it was closer to 300. He well can be said to have helped them avoid extinction. Churches of his Congregational denomination currently serve about 99 percent of the population. They have been rebuilt since the days when he officiated at Lelu, but they still have the style of nineteenth-century New England churches. The visitor is assured, "Dr. Snow would recognize them immediately."[11]

1. Walter L. Cook, *Bangor Theological Seminary: A Sesquicentennial History.* Orono, ME: University of Maine Press, 1971, pp. 26–27.

2. Segal, *The Sleeping Lady Awakens,* p. 92.

3. Cook, p. 27.

4. Ibid.

5. Ibid.

6. Segal, p. 7.

7. Ibid., pp. 96–97.

8. Benjamin Snow Diary. Orono. ME: Special Collections, Folger Library, University of Maine. March 10, 1868.

9. *Skillin Family Newsletter.* Spring 1986, Fall 1988.

10. Ibid.

11. Segal, p. 285.

Nathan Clifford
Courtesy Maine Historic Preservation Commission

James Shepherd Pike
Courtesy Calais Free Library

NATHAN CLIFFORD, DEMOCRAT
AND
JAMES S. PIKE, REPUBLICAN

Two men from Maine, in juxtaposition, help illustrate through their lives the story of an epoch of American life that saw the United States almost come apart, fight a ferocious internal war, and start to unify again. These two politicians, Nathan Clifford and James Shepherd Pike, came from different parts of Maine, the former from York County, the latter from Washington County, just about as far apart as possible. Outside of Maine, each achieved a certain notoriety: Clifford rose to the top of the legal profession and filled a long-term seat on the U.S. Supreme Court; Pike became a nationally known newspaper columnist and Washington correspondent for the *New York Tribune*, the nation's most popular newspaper in its era. Both were diplomats, Clifford in Mexico during the Mexican War, and Pike in the Netherlands at the time of the Civil War. And their politics, while they were of opposite parties, had a certain convergence, as our country struggled over the issue of slavery and what to do with the freed slave population once the Civil War ended.

Since Nathan Clifford was the older of the two men, by not quite a decade, and began his career in public affairs earlier, we will begin with him.

Newfield, near the New Hampshire border, was the York County town Nathan Clifford would call home after 1827. It was a small but bustling place then, with close to 1,300 inhabitants, and is not much bigger now in the twenty-first century (1,328). It remains true that Clifford was not a native-born Mainer; his roots were in Rumney, New Hampshire, in the southwest White Mountains country. At age nineteen, having finished a course of study in a local law office, he walked the sixty-plus miles to Newfield carrying his worldly possessions wrapped in a kerchief attached to a stick slung across his shoulder—a literary image rather more congenial to a Horatio Alger novel than reality. In any event, Nathan Clifford never looked back.

One reason Newfield struck Clifford as it did was to be found in the house where he boarded. This was the home of Captain James Ayer, a prominent citizen of the town, and inside lived Hannah, his beauteous sixteen-year-old daughter. Within a year, on March 20, 1828, the two were married.

No explanation has ever been given of Nathan Clifford's connection, if any, prenuptially, to the Ayer family. While he lived in the captain's home, he also had his law office in the house of the captain's cousin, Dr. James Ayer. The Ayers, incidentally, were the leading landowners of this area in and around the Little Ossippee River watershed.

That Clifford could so easily and quickly establish himself as a practicing lawyer in Maine was the result of a state law allowing reciprocity of licensure to lawyers trained in other states, including New Hampshire. The social position of his soon-acquired father-in-law no doubt helped guarantee a steady stream of respectable and well-paying clients.

The young man's charm, ability, and dogged hard-work ethic had to be as important as family connections in contributing to his success. But he also exhibited a trait of Yankee independence, if not cussedness, which quietly commanded guarded appreciation. It was in the matter of politics. The initial trouble was that Newfield happened to be a Whig town—and Clifford happened to be a Jacksonian Democrat. Although Captain Ayer controlled the levers of power as Whig Party chief, Nathan Clifford stuck to his populist guns and refused to change his allegiance.

If he were going to have a career in elected politics, he would have to win over his neighbors, only a bare handful of whom were Democrats. But within three years, win them he did. In an election where Andrew Jackson was trounced in Maine by John Quincy Adams, Clifford was elected to the Maine State Legislature by a wide margin.

Despite the Adams win in the Pine Tree State, the lawmakers of both bodies who gathered for the 1831 session (the capital was still at Portland) were, in the majority, Democrats. So, too, was Governor Samuel E. Smith. As a freshman, Nathan Clifford was placed on the rather trivial Committee of Bills on the Third Reading and the far more substantive Education Committee.

One of the earliest of Clifford's speeches showed his propensity not to shy away from being a contrarian. What he was proposing was to *raise* a tax—specifically the bank tax—from half a percent to a full one percent. His opponents immediately countered with a modern-sounding charge: this tax increase would drive capital out of Maine. Clifford retorted that he was convinced such wouldn't happen; otherwise, he wouldn't be supporting the measure. Then they tried a different tack, claiming that one-third of all bank stock in Maine was owned by widows and orphans. "Nonsense," said Clifford, most holders of bank stock were wealthy individuals and he never saw any tears shed by them over the dependents of needy farmers when their capital assets, like a pig or a cow, were seized for debt. Whether this particular bill passed or was defeated has not been revealed by Clifford's principal biographer, his grandson, Phillip G. Clifford.[1] The next act of his statehouse debut, on March 22, 1831, brought forth what was to be his signature contrariness throughout a long life in politics. One might as well call it by its real name: Clifford's defense of slavery!

This was 1831. Abolition was not yet fashionable in the North. Although Maine had come into the Union as a *free state* in 1820, linked with *slave state* Missouri in the famous "Compromise," the backlash Down East against the "peculiar institution" was only starting to stir. Even later, as we shall see with James S. Pike, Republican attitudes were far more focused on stopping the *spread* of the practice than in emancipating the blacks. Nathan Clifford's attitude on March 22, 1831—along with many other Democrats—was that states' rights should prevail. Slavery was a local institution and permitted by the Constitution. The occasion for airing his feelings on the subject was a resolution the legislature had just passed approving the abolition of "negro servitude" in the District of Columbia. The Honorable Gentleman from Newfield arose to have his colleagues reconsider their action. The State of Maine, he insisted, had no business juridically involving itself in this matter.

The first-year member went on to say that interference of this sort by the North in the affairs of the South was the cause of treasonable murmurs about secession coming from the region, and he further added his conviction that, if left alone, slavery would die away on its own volition.

So, very early on, Nathan Clifford made a name for himself as a debater and forthright defender of his opinions. When, in 1832, the new capitol building in Augusta was opened, he received recognition of his up-and-coming status by being placed on an important committee—that of Contested Elections.

It was during the 1832 session, too, that Clifford first tangled with William Pitt Fessenden, whom we met earlier as the grieving fiancé of Henry Longfellow's deceased sister. Now a Maine Whig leader, eventually to become a major Republican figure—U.S. senator and secretary of the Treasury—Fessenden was pushing for support of the National Bank, which Whig leader Henry Clay was trying to have rechartered in Congress. The Jacksonians were opposed even to having a National Bank, never mind continuing it.

Clifford led the opposition's fight in Maine and wrote home to Hannah that W. P. Fessenden was responsible for "scurrilous" articles about him in the *Portand Advertiser*. "I have had the pleasure in thwarting that Gentleman in nearly every project which he has started during the session and hope to have the pleasure of defeating him again."[2]

On another major issue of 1832—that of settling Maine's northeast boundary with Canada—Clifford's skills were recognized when he was put on a special select committee to deal with the matter.

At stake was nothing less than the future shape of Maine. The peace treaty negotiations ending the American Revolution had not delineated the state's northernmost border. Both sides—England and the U.S.— had been quarreling about the final lines ever since. The king of the Netherlands had been brought in as an "unbiased arbitrator." But his proposals, which Clifford's committee considered, were rejected out of hand. Maine would lose too much of the territory it hoped to gain up toward the St. Lawrence River.

Clifford's advancement in the legislature was further highlighted when he was made chair of another special committee handling this conflict and, toward the end of the session, when by an overwhelming vote, he was elected speaker pro tem to fill in during the illness of the regular speaker.

It was all but inevitable that in the next legislature, after his reelection, he would be made speaker, though only twenty-eight years of age. Additionally, he was also moving up in Democratic Party affairs, having been picked as a Maine delegate to the Baltimore Convention—the first-ever such gathering of national Democrats, which unanimously chose Andrew Jackson to be its presidential candidate again.

The country boy had moved out into the big world. Before then, he'd never been farther away than Boston, and suddenly, by stagecoach, he was off to Providence and then on a sixty-six-hour ride to Washington, D.C., prior to ending up in Maryland. "I have seen most of the great men of our country, Jackson, Calhoun, Clay, Webster, etc.," he wrote his wife.

A hint of restlessness becomes evident in his correspondence afterward, and more than a hint of quiet dissatisfaction with his financial affairs. When alerting his wife that he had been chosen chairman of the state Central Committee of Correspondence, he was quick to add it was "an honorable station *without profit*." In the winter of 1834, he was again made speaker of the Maine House of Representatives. Telling his wife he had "engaged board [in Augusta] at the Mansion House kept by Rogers with fine accommodations," he added the caveat: "but I expect I have to pay for them." By February it was rumored that he planned to leave Newfield and the office of speaker—gossip he vigorously denied— but with subtle intimations of something else to come in his life. He had written home in January that he did not "expect to be in the legislature again" (and told his wife to burn the letter), since it was "no place to make money" and the "honor" of it soon wore thin. Before long, the secret was out: discreetly, Clifford had been lobbying for the soon-to-be-vacated job of Maine attorney general. The same day that as speaker he adjourned the legislature in March 1834, he was nominated for the law post by Governor Robert P. Dunlap and immediately confirmed. The pay was $1,000 a year, far more than the legislature paid. Clifford kept the attorney general position until 1838.

Even while he was Maine's top lawyer, he had his eyes on federal office. He offered himself for U.S. senator in 1837, but the legislature chose someone else. The following year, Clifford went for York County's congressional seat and won. In December 1839 he was off to Washington again, and this time from Providence by train, not jouncing for three days in a stagecoach.

Nathan Clifford served two terms in Congress. While seeking his third term, he was defeated in a Democratic primary. John F. Kennedy once said that successful politicians not only have to be capable; they must also be lucky. And luck, in politics, comes in all sorts of shapes. Unbeknownst to Clifford at the time, losing his seat in Congress was the best thing that could have happened to him.

There were other elements of luck, as well. In the 1840 presidential election, to Democrat Clifford's horror, incumbent Martin Van Buren lost to a war hero running for the Whigs—General William Henry Harrison—"Old Tippecanoe." Clifford referred to him as "an imbecilic old man, a mere child." His inaugural was held in March 1841 and by April, Harrison was dead, carried off by an infection after a mere month in office. Another disguised stroke of luck for Clifford. Vice President John Tyler was not really a Whig at all and ended up with no support from either party. James Polk of Tennessee, the Democrat, was elected president just as Clifford was losing his party's nomination back home.

That left the Maine lawyer and faithful Democrat available for a patronage post. It was also good luck for Clifford that he had become bosom friends with fellow Democrat James W. Bradbury, Longfellow's classmate, who had been his roommate in Augusta when both were in the state legislature. Bradbury was now a U.S. senator from Maine. Accordingly, in 1846, when President Polk sought an attorney general for his cabinet, Senator Bradbury offered Clifford's name and rounded up the other senator, John Fairfield, plus numerous powerful Maine Democrats. Also, Polk wanted a New Englander. Completing Clifford's lucky star in this instance was the fact that he represented the Van Buren faction which had opposed Polk for the nomination, and his appointment could help heal the rift in the party. On October 23, 1846, Clifford wrote one of his supporters, former Maine governor Hugh Anderson, "I have accepted the offer of attorney general of the United States and entered upon its duties."[3]

James K. Polk is noted as the president who added more land area to the United States than any other, including Thomas Jefferson. The means by which he did this was the Mexican War. Hostilities between the two neighbors had already erupted before Clifford became Polk's attorney general. On May 11, 1846, the president told Congress, "War exists and exists by the act of Mexico herself." Prior to its end two years later, with the signing of the Treaty of Guadalupe Hidalgo, Attorney General Clifford was involved in it. He had not been on his new job even two weeks when he was asked to facilitate the calling-up of volunteer regiments in Massachusetts and New Hampshire. Soon he was known as the foremost proponent of the war among the cabinet members. For that reason, he was chosen in March of 1848 to go to Mexico on a special mission: bringing the Guadalupe Hidalgo treaty, as subsequently amended by the U.S. Senate, for Mexican acceptance. Polk explained: "It was a case of emergency and no time was to be lost. I thought of Mr. Clifford, the attorney general...as a fit person and one who was already informed of all my views." Secretary of State Buchanan concurred and, just like that, Nathan Clifford moved into yet another phase of his public career—diplomacy.

There was no little adventure in what he was undertaking—entering Mexico as an American envoy in 1848. The country, often lawless at the best of times, was going through a period of great unrest. Bandits were taking advantage of this situation, and on one occasion, Clifford had to wing with a pistol shot the leader of a gang trying to rob his stagecoach. Yet he would write his wife, "I am in no danger. I keep myself well armed. We are just as safe as you are. These rascals are mighty fearful of well-armed men, especially Americans."

It may have been with thoughts like this that, several months later, Clifford considered bringing his wife and some of his children to Mexico. He had been successful in his mission. The Mexicans had accepted the amended treaty, which had given California, New Mexico, Arizona, etc., to the U.S., and, as his reward, Clifford was named "Envoy Extraordinary and Minister Plenipotentiary to the Mexican Republic"—a fancy name for ambassador. In accepting the job, the Maine man stipulated he wanted leave enough to return home in order to take members of his family back with him to Mexico City. By February 1849 he was ensconced with them at the American Legation in the Mexican capital. However, due to D.C. politics, his tenure was not to last long. In the 1848 presidential election, the Whigs, using a war hero again—General Zachary Taylor—were victorious over the Democrats. Clifford knew his days in Mexico would be numbered as soon as his friend James Buchanan was no longer secretary of state. Before the end of 1849, Clifford and his family were back in the USA and he was a private citizen once more.

Although Nathan Clifford had acquired a name and considerable prestige, he still had to make a living. Newfield no longer sufficed as a place to practice law. Portland beckoned; his friend John Appleton, soon to be a congressman, urged him to relocate and so he did. Clifford did not entirely divorce himself from electoral politics in the years that followed—in 1850, he tried for U.S. Senate but lost to Hannibal Hamlin for the Democratic nomination, and in 1853, he unsuccessfully challenged his old nemesis, William Pitt Fessenden, for the same office. Meanwhile, immense political changes were happening in the nation and Maine as the future of slavery turned into an ever more divisive issue. Maine Democrats split over it and so did the national party. Whigs—and antislavery Democrats—morphed into the Republican Party. At home, old-time Democratic stalwarts like Clifford, James Bradbury, Hugh Anderson, and John Appleton remained "soft" on slavery; others, like Hannibal Hamlin and the Morrill brothers, Lot and Anson, went from Democratic leaders to Republican superstars. The legislature in Augusta changed hands to a perpetual GOP majority. A Democratic "last hurrah" before the Lincoln era was seen in the presidential victories of Franklin Pierce (1852) and James Buchanan (1856), and the latter event, the elevation of his old boss at the State Department, played a major part in Nathan Clifford's life. More good luck. On November 25, 1857, he was informed by his friend, Congressman John Appleton: "My Dear Sir, you will be nominated as soon as the Senate is ready to receive nominations. There can be no doubt of this and you may safely proceed quietly to make your arrangements."[4]

Thus did Clifford learn he now would have a *lifetime* job—justice of the Supreme Court of the United States.

A letter of congratulations from a Massachusetts friend mentioned that "Greeley and others of that ilk" were not pleased and had begun carping against him in the *Tribune* and other papers, but not to worry— "a good selection has been made, for there is nothing which these fellows particularly dread than a Judiciary who will fearlessly and impartially expound the meaning of the Constitution."[5] One wonders if James S. Pike, who went on Greeley's payroll in 1850, was included among that "carping ilk"—and, not coincidentally, Clifford was confirmed in the Senate by a mere three votes.

Justice Clifford remained on the Supreme Court until his death in 1881—almost a quarter of a century. He was there throughout the Civil

War, and despite his unswerving loyalty to the Democratic Party and sympathies toward the Southern point of view, remained totally loyal to the Union.

Two examples of judicial actions among his many decisions are of special interest: the Neal Dow case and the Electoral Commission of 1876.

The first involves a Maine figure of considerable notoriety, even international fame. Neal Dow, originally a Portland fireman, could claim the title of the originator of Prohibition, an issue he promoted in the Maine legislature to produce the Western world's earliest ban on alcoholic beverages. Made mayor of Portland on this issue in 1855, he had his initial run-in with Nathan Clifford when arrested, under his own law, for ordering city liquor for "medicinal purposes"; he was prosecuted by lawyer Clifford but ably defended by William Pitt Fessenden.

Twenty-one years later, the Supreme Court case involved Neal Dow in his capacity as a Union general in Louisiana during the Civil War. His troops of the 13th Maine had raided a plantation and taken from it a supply of sugar and various articles of silverware. The owner, however, was not a Confederate rebel but a loyal resident of New York State, and this man, Bradish Johnson, sued General Dow as responsible for his loss and won a judgment in a Louisiana court. The sum was $1,454.81, but Dow refused to pay a penny.

Undeterred, Bradish Johnson pursued his claim after the war. It came before the U.S. Circuit Court in Maine and, in those days, U.S. Supreme Court justices also sat on federal circuit courts. When the Johnson-Dow case came to Portland, the presiding judge was Nathan Clifford.

The key to a decision was whether or not the court in Louisiana, then a state that had seceded, had any validity in a case against a U.S. citizen.

Had the decision been left to Judge Clifford, the answer would have been yes. He followed the Democrats' line of reasoning that the Southern states, in seceding, had never left the Union. Yet Clifford recognized his own bias and felt the case should go to the U.S. Supreme Court, rather than be judged by him alone. In order to effect this, he needed another judge besides himself to render an opposing view, which would remand the case to the higher court. Finding a federal judge in

New Hampshire to sit with him, he so proceeded.

National politics then entered this case. The 1876 presidential election was in full swing. That year's Republican nomination had gone surprisingly to Governor Rutherford B. Hayes of Ohio, rather than to James G. Blaine of Maine, but Blaine, a devout GOP man, was out in Ohio campaigning for Hayes when the circuit court in Portland gave its split decision. Blaine used the occasion to attack Judge Clifford and through him, the Democrat running for president, Governor Samuel Tilden of New York. With typical Blaine hyperbole, he asked his audience whether Clifford's decision "would not enable the man who owned the field at Appomattox to collect ground rent from Grant for the...destruction of its fences and crops," and added, seldom has "so menacing a cloud" hung over a "free people." Blaine's distortions of the case were immediately challenged and even the local Republican U.S. attorney rebuked him.

With Justice Clifford dissenting, the U.S. Supreme Court went on to decide that Louisiana, at the time, was "a captured province in the possession of an invading army" and that no court within it thus had any jurisdiction—i.e., finding for Neal Dow.

Blaine's outburst had come toward the end of what, until the election of 2000, was the most highly contested presidential race in American history. The electoral vote was questioned and, as in the year 2000, Florida's count was at issue; but in 1876, also were those in South Carolina and Louisiana, plus a single disputed elector in Oregon.

At first, it seemed as if Democrat Tilden had won. But once the Republicans challenged the votes in those three Southern states, which they controlled, a battle for the presidency ensued so intense that some feared it might lead to another Civil War. The 2000 controversy was ended by a vote of the U.S. Supreme Court. The 1876 battle was settled by votes of an Electoral Commission, set up by a divided Congress (Republican Senate, Democratic House). On this fifteen-man body, whose word would be final, were to sit five senators, five representatives, and five Supreme Court justices. Ostensibly, the majority would be controlled by the latter quintet, whose political views were balanced: two Democrats, two Republicans, and one Independent (whom the Democrats thought was in their camp but who soon withdrew in favor of a Republican leaner).

As the senior member of the court, Clifford was made the chairman of the Electoral Commission. Despite his partisan bias, he ran the meetings with scrupulous impartiality, winning praise from all involved. When it came to voting, he was always on the losing end of the 8–7 decisions by which every disputed elector was given to the Republicans and Rutherford B. Hayes elected president.

Far from the public view, though, a deal had quietly been arranged—often called a "Devil's Bargain"—between top Republican and Democratic leaders. In exchange for ending their electoral fight, the Democrats in the South were promised the withdrawal of all remaining federal troops from former Confederate territory—a promise that was kept. The era of Jim Crow was about to begin.

In 2004, not long before his death, William Rehnquist, then chief justice, published a book entitled *Centennial Crisis: The Disputed Election of 1876*. Several critics saw it as his answer—or apologia—for the court's role in the 2000 election. It's a fairly straightforward account of the events of 1876. He only briefly touches on the Devil's Bargain, but he does have a bit to say about Nathan Clifford, including these remarks: "He was a loyal Democrat, steeped in the tradition of Jacksonian democracy. He held high public office in the days of Democratic ascendancy before the Civil War and was something of an anachronism afterward,"[6] and also was "a large man, in robust health, and willing to work hard,"[7] plus that he had written "none of the [Supreme Court's] important constitutional opinions."[8]

Furthermore, Rehnquist noted that Clifford had stayed on the court long afterward, hoping for the election of a Democratic president who could replace him with one of their party members. His death in 1881 missed by three years the opportunity that arose once Grover Cleveland won the White House in 1884 against none other than James G. Blaine.

The other half of our duo of Maine politicians, James Shepherd Pike, died one year after Clifford, in 1882.

He was also eight years younger, having been born in 1811, and on Maine soil, although Calais, more so than any of our cities, has intimate ties with Maritime Canada. The first thirty-four years of Pike's life (apparently, he was often called "Shepherd" or even just "Shep") were spent mainly in his hometown, engaged in various businesses, first clerking in local stores and then expanding into banking, shipping, and speculating in Maine and New Brunswick forestlands. His schooling was skimpy, as he'd been expelled by the parson who served as his schoolmaster, but he was an avid reader to the end of his days. By the time he was thirty-five and possessing a tidy nest egg, Pike "lay down hard work," as he put it.

Politics had already enticed him. In 1834 the Calais *Boundary Gazette*, of which Pike was part owner and full-time contributor, saw light as a new Whig newspaper in the state. Maine and particularly the Washington County area was still staunchly Democrat, and this journalistic venture did not survive more than three years. But James S. Pike had been amply bitten by the writing bug.

One of Pike's notable forays out of Maine was to Pomfret, Connecticut, for the purpose of marrying Charlotte Grosvenor, and then back to Calais went the young couple. They had one child, a daughter, who was six years old when her mother died unexpectedly, and she had to be raised by her widower father.

By then, Pike had already started his practice of spending winters in Washington and writing columns on D.C. politics for various Whig newspapers, among them the Portland *Advertiser,* the Boston *Atlas,* and the Boston *Courier*. In so doing, he perforce became known to Horace Greeley, the famous editor and publisher, whose *New York Tribune* was the most important of Whig organs in an epoch when all newspapers were unabashed partisan mouthpieces.

As one might expect, on the issues of the day James Shepherd Pike was diametrically opposed to Nathan Clifford—slavery, without question, leading the list of divergencies between them. Yet other different slants on problems separated the two with only slightly less fervor. On a worldview scale, it might be said the Whigs, lineal descendants of the Federalists, were the moneyed, snobby bunch, big business and the like. The Democrats, close to the earth, were the agriculturists and yeoman craftsmen, fiscally tightfisted and States' Righters, rather than for strong central government. When James Pike entered the political scene in Maine, the Democrats were still enjoying an advantage because they had been the victorious proponents of Maine's effort to break from Massachusetts.

In the long run, the dynamics of the slavery battle, coupled with another moral crusade—Neal Dow's Prohibition initiative—were to undermine the Democrats in Maine. A third element in the political mix in the 1840s was *Nativism,* but *anti-Catholicism* would be a more apt description, since the "foreigners" bashed were mostly refugees from Ireland's potato famine. Protestant Maine had received a goodly number of them.

Pike, it was said, wanted no part of the Know-Nothings, who in Maine torched Catholic churches and especially shamed themselves by tarring and feathering a priest who, during a visit to Ellsworth, tried to say mass for a group of parishioners. To the man from Calais, these Protestant bullies were merely trying to deflect the Whigs' attention from their antislavery stance. Pike had no love for papist Irish and French Canadians, but it was only because they flocked to the Democrats. And neither were his violent feelings against the Southern "Slave Power" tinged with concern for the poor Negroes—just the opposite: he thought blacks ignorant and uncivilized. Slavery, to Pike, was simply a means by which the Southern states were trying to take over the country. Its spread had to be stopped and its practice contained in what he called "a Negro pen" along the Gulf Coast in Dixie. As for the constitutional argument employed by Democrats such as Nathan Clifford, Pike shot back that he believed the pro-slavers were destroying the "very foundation of the Constitution."

His stinging words to them were: "You and your doughface allies in the North are perverting it [the Union] to the pestilent uses of human servitude...an Ethiopia in the South is inevitable." ("Doughface," it should be noted, was a slang term often hurled at Nathan Clifford.)

Such heated rhetoric even led Pike to push for disunion in his editorials. Allow the North to secede from the Union, rather than bow down to the ascendant Slave Power.

It was the Kansas–Nebraska Act of 1856 that really stirred the pot. In Maine, it especially resounded because one of its provisos was repeal of the Missouri Compromise of 1820, by which Maine had become a state. The new law now allowed slavery wherever states would permit it, and furthermore, tightened up the Fugitive Slave Act by making all Northerners liable to imprisonment for not helping recapture escaped slaves. A year later, the Dred Scott case was decided by a pro-Southern Supreme Court and insured that slaves would always be slaves, even in free states.

Politically, these events caused the birth of the Republican Party. Most Northern Whigs joined it, as did many antislavery Democrats, and James S. Pike and his kid brother, Frederick A. Pike, who was elected to Congress in 1860, made the transition to the GOP easily. The older Pike sibling had twice tried for Congress and once for state senate—all unsuccessfully—running as an underdog Whig. His last campaign in 1850 had coincided with his move to write for Horace Greeley, and ever afterward, he confined himself solely to doing what he could for candidates as a member of the Maine Republican State Committee.

A series of communications to Pike in the late 1850s characterizes his work as one of the party's activists.

Hannibal Hamlin wrote from Hampden on September 12, 1858 (Maine voted in federal elections in September): "I forwarded $150 to the State Committee," that his total contribution was $500–600, and also, "I have worked hard in your district. I feel confident all will go right."

A letter from party chair John L. Stevens to Pike a month earlier was likewise about money. Ruefully, he begins, "Had Coburn been nominated [lumber baron Abner Coburn, the richest man in Maine], I could have called on him for $1,000...." Worse, the actual nominee, one of the Morses from Bath, was not being at all financially forthcoming. "He still declines to pay the $200" (which Maine Republican candidates were assessed for the privilege of running).

Four days later, Stevens, who was an ordained minister and a one-time co-owner of the *Kennebec Journal* with James G. Blaine, informed Pike he was sending him "another hundred and you may rely on $300–400 more." Two more checks were sent on the last day of August, one of $200 and one of $50—"to help the 6th District in its need."

In early September, as the election neared, Stevens discussed the Democratic candidate, Bion Bradbury. Another $80 was added to the G.O.P. war chest. "Bion will be beaten. Our only trouble spot is the 3rd [District]." Finally, on September 17, Stevens wrote: "Well, the fight is over and we have licked them. Washington and Hancock [Counties] have done nobly.... Bion might give you large credit for his defeat."

In a postscript ten days later, Stevens added: "There can be no doubt that the Republicans of Washington County were shrewd in selecting you as their state committeeman."

With such a sterling record of service to the Republican Party—which Pike continued during the 1860 campaign—it was natural he would seek a patronage position once the Lincoln administration took office. He had always looked forward to foreign travel; so, too, apparently, had his second wife, whom he married in 1855. She was the former Elizabeth (Lizzie) Ellicott of Avondale, Pennsylvania, a Quaker who had once promised to marry Salmon P. Chase, Lincoln's famed secretary of the Treasury. Despite this rivalry for the same fair hand, Pike and Chase did turn out to be close friends. A letter that Chase wrote to Miss Ellicott after her engagement to Pike teasingly reminded her how they had both expressed a longing to visit Europe, but she should not worry. "When I am elected president, Mr. Pike shall have a diplomatic appointment and you shall enjoy old world sights for me."

Well, the Pikes did go to Europe, but it was courtesy of President Abraham Lincoln. And there has been speculation that a number of Lincoln's overseas diplomatic appointments went to *Radical*—i.e., anti-slavery—Republicans such as James Shepherd Pike. Fierce abolitionist rhetoric did better in the Old World, it was felt, than at home, where Lincoln and Secretary of State William Seward were doing all they could to keep the border slave-owning states from leaving the Union.

Pike signed his columns *JSP,* and those initials were becoming ever better known for heated writing in the months of 1860 and 1861 leading up to South Carolina's secession. The lame duck Democratic administration of James Buchanan came in for special Pikean vitriol: "Such another pack of Miss Nancies to oppose treason and bullying, the world never saw," he labeled them. No longer pushing disunion, Pike was now calling for *emancipation.* But he would only be fulminating on this side of the Atlantic until April 1861. His appointment as minister to the Netherlands had arrived from the White House. On April 27, Pike and Lizzie set sail for Europe. Fifteen days previously, the Confederates in Charleston Harbor had attacked Fort Sumter.

Pike's notebook impressions from the Continent were eclectic, to say the least. There might be descriptions of scenes that struck him in Holland—example: "They sell cabbages from the boats—boats with loads of 3,000 cabbages take the places of wagons in other countries...they use rushes for lathings because of the scarcity of wood...wooden shoes everywhere prevail with the poorer clad.... The buildings all rest on piles...." Or a set of figures: "The salaries of the Ministers at the Hague: Russian $16,000; English $18,000; French $13,000; Hanover $3,750; Denmark $3,000"—no mention of his own pay ($7,500), but a posting of wages in the American Army: "Major General $5,724; Colonel $2,844; Captain $1,662...." He might jot down a simple opinion: "The House of Orange...a good family," or a more decided prejudice: "I am disgusted with the Americans I meet who come abroad.... Just looking to 'live comfortably.'... I have no words to express my contempt of the whole crowd." Odd facts crop up on Pike's pages: "The loans of France in 1854 were $400 million." Then a slam at his own profession: "The world is entirely too full of books. The most of them, like the everywhere present newspaper of modern times, serve only to dissipate the mind and weaken the understanding...." Dutch expenditures for 1860; the population of France from 1802; word pictures of the cattle markets at Rotterdam and Delft; and, once the newness of his position had worn off, this admission of a disappointing discovery: "The diplomacy of the Hague is thus no longer significant. And as the diplomatists have little to do, they become correspondingly fastidious and lay great stress on ceremony and etiquette."

It was not as if Minister Pike had nothing to do. American diplomacy during the Civil War had one all-important task—keep the European countries from recognizing the Confederacy. Some, like England, seemed on the verge of doing so and had already announced a neutral position in the fighting, *ipso facto* treating the Rebels as co-belligerents with the Union.

One of the more serious effects of this situation soon had Pike embroiled in a potentially real Dutch-American clash. A Confederate raider, the ship *Sumter,* captained by the notorious privateer Ralph Semmes, approached the small port of St. Anne on the Dutch West Indian island of Curacao. In Union eyes, the Confederate mariner was nothing more than a pirate and should have been denied access by the Dutch. This was done at first but an angry Semmes then ordered "gunnery practice," with his cannon aimed at the harbor. Shells began exploding not far beyond the council chamber where the Dutch authorities were conferring. A hurried vote allowed this aggressive visitor to sail in and anchor. Consequently, albeit by intimidation, Captain Semmes had established the Dutch government's accounting him a co-belligerent, accorded equal rights with the U.S. Navy.

Word of this incident reached Pike in the Hague. He swiftly complained to the Dutch foreign minister, Baron Van Zuylen. And while an argument raged for several months, it grew all the more vociferous once it was learned the *Sumter* was subsequently admitted to still another Dutch Caribbean port in their South American colony of Surinam.

It thus seemed as if Pike had suffered a major diplomatic defeat. Both Pike and his boss, Secretary of State Seward, did not mince words in making their strong displeasure apparent to Van Zuylen. The Americans' obvious fury finally pushed the Hague government to a seeming compromise that actually favored the North: the Dutch closed all their ports to *both* Rebel and Yankee shipping, and since the Confederates had much more need of open ports, Pike and the State Department were satisfied.

Pike soon realized, after this incident, that the U.S. needed to win the support of European governments and people through strong actions, not simply strong words. Nothing would be more effective, he felt, than a declaration that all slaves in America were to be freed. Holland, particularly, would feel the effect, since emancipation sentiment there was running high—so high, in fact, that in June 1862 the Dutch ended slavery in every one of their colonies. In his discussions with any and all Europeans, Pike emphasized that the Lincoln government was a force for ending slavery. Letters home to his friend U.S. Senator William Pitt Fessenden, urged pressure on the president to make a dramatic emancipation gesture. The first open indication that Lincoln would do so came at the cabinet meeting on September 22, 1862, where he warmed up his audience with Artemus Ward's humor.

The action did not work the instant magic Pike thought it would. But as Pike's biographer, Robert Franklin Durden, writes, "Lincoln's emancipation policy slowly made itself felt in Europe."[9] English working people started flocking to pro-Northern demonstrations, and it was reported that pro-Confederate Britons had clammed up; France, too, showed similar signs of sympathy for Lincoln's gesture.

The question of the freed slaves' future was essentially held in abeyance until the close of the war. Pike had rather startling ideas of his own—the "Negro pen," for example. Originally he had seen freedmen occupying areas of the Deep South, possibly Gulf Coast states, with white enslavers removed. "The whole of the West India Islands" was another possible destination. But, he finally concluded with a sigh, it might have to be both.

Some of Pike's notions were briefly picked up in Congress. Senator James Lane of Kansas, a veteran of pre-Civil War guerrilla fighting there, was professing a similar solution. "I hope the time should come when the footprints of the white man should not be found on the soil of South Carolina." But his bill to set apart a large area in western Texas for blacks never made it out of committee.

The war inevitably drew toward a close. Entries in Pike's notebook for February–May 1865 record the progress the Union had achieved. "We are all rejoicing over the fall of Richmond, and the more that its capture is the reward of the patience, the pertinacity and the ability of General Grant."

Some pages later, there is a stark, funereal sketch entitled "Drapery for a Union." With it, Pike wrote these words: "Now five days that we have been shocked and stunned by the news from America of the most diabolical crime ever committed on the continent—the murder of Abraham Lincoln and the attempted assassination of Mr. Seward.... All Europe has been astonished at the intelligence."

By the end of Pike's tenure in Holland, he could write with more familiarity about "all Europe" because, in the meantime, he and Lizzie had done a good deal of traveling. After settling the problem of Captain Semmes's incursions, not a lot of pressing matters required Pike's attendance in the Hague. The Confederates did not even bother to post an agent in the Netherlands.

England and France were the major points of visitation, although Minister and Mrs. Pike did manage trips to Germany, especially the Rhineland and the city of Frankfort. Lizzie Pike's increasingly poor health also necessitated stays at health spas on the Riviera and in Scotland.

Pike's language skills were poor. He knew nothing of Dutch nor did he try to learn it, and he repeated the quip of an Italian friend that it sounded like a man talking German with a hair in his throat. The Mainer stuck to trying French, the language of diplomacy, which he spoke poorly.

So it was easiest for him to travel in England. He enjoyed attending Parliament and, as a former political reporter, felt at home watching and even meeting such luminaries as Gladstone, D'Israeli, John Stuart Mill, and John Bright. One literary light he was able to make friends with, as Longfellow had, was Thomas Carlyle, the great historian. Pike first encountered him at a reading by Dickens of his *Pickwick Papers,* where both he and Carlyle laughed like crazy, along with the audience. Pike wrote that he himself roared until his "jaws ached." Carlyle mirrored some of Pike's jaundiced views toward the Negro question, stating: "The South says to the Naygur, God bless you and be a slave! The North says, God damn you, and be free!"

In France, Pike developed a strong aversion to the Emperor Napoleon III. The *casus belli,* in this case, was the French dictator's invasion of Mexico, undertaken while the U.S. was distracted by the Civil War. He wrote to Senator Fessenden that the Europeans saw American tolerance of this violation of the Monroe Doctrine as a sign of weakness, and he urged strong action—something Secretary Seward delayed until after Appomattox.

Finally, with Lincoln's death in April 1865, it seemed clear that changes would be forthcoming in the restored Union's overseas representation. One by one, Pike's colleagues were being replaced. Pike jumped the gun by submitting his resignation in the spring of 1866. Bidding goodbye to Holland's Queen Sophie, he found her quite upset by the rumor that his replacement might be General Daniel Sickles, a highly controversial ex-congressman who had once openly shot and killed a man for dallying with his wife. (Sickles got sent to Spain.) On June 21, 1866, Pike and Lizzie arrived at Boston, then went to New York. Pike's prejudiced comment at the time foreshadowed the shift later to emerge in his writings. He was quoted as condemning the population of New York because "those who are not German are Irish, those who are not Irish are Chinese, and those who are not Chinese are [African Americans]."[10]

The most famous—or infamous—writing to come from the pen of James Shepherd Pike was a book entitled *The Prostrate State,* published in 1873. Prior to that year, an article of his in the *Tribune* had provided a foretaste of his venom. Headlined "A State in Ruins," the state being South Carolina, it appeared before Pike had ever been to the Palmetto State. Pike's complaint could be summed up in his statement that "300,000 white people, composing the intelligence and property holders of the state, [were] put under the heel of 400,000 pauper blacks, fresh from a state of slavery and ignorance the most dense." This column also contained an apology for "the wild crimes of Ku Klux youth."

Two major sources Pike used here were the biased comments of a Republican U.S. senator, William Sprague of Rhode Island; a property owner in South Carolina known for his wealth, alcoholism, and stormy marriage to Kate Chase, the daughter of Salmon P. Chase; and of Wade Hampton, a former Confederate general and leading Democrat.

Politically, within the Republican Party, Pike had been on a sort of rollercoaster ride. Originally a Radical, he had switched gears and followed Horace Greeley into a splinter group, the *Liberal* Republicans, running their own candidate (Greeley) for president. That the Democrats nominated Greeley, too, was meekly accepted. But the combined ticket found itself swamped by Grant's reelection bid. One of the Liberal Republicans' major planks was removal of federal troops from the South.

Pike's book on South Carolina, in which he drew a devastating, but distorted, picture of the "carpetbagger" government in the state, enjoyed widespread credibility since its author was touted as a "prominent Republican Abolitionist from Maine." It may have played a role in softening Northern indignation over the abandonment of the blacks in the Devil's Bargain of 1876.

But because of his perceived flip-flop, Pike found himself in a political limbo back in Maine. His brother's congressional seat had already been lost in an intraparty squabble to Eugene Hale, a crony of James G. Blaine, who was running the Maine Republican Party. Pike himself had been heavily criticized in the Calais press as a traitor for having supported Greeley in 1872.

His racism, nevertheless, remained on display. In the *The Prostrate State,* according to biographer Durden: "He frankly admitted that his pride of race was 'incontinently shocked' when a 'thick-lipped, wooly-headed' Negro on the floor of the House [in South Carolina] dared criticize a white man."[11] Pike is also quoted as saying that to allow the situation in South Carolina to continue was a "testimony against claims of Anglo-Saxon blood."[12]

Upon returning from Europe, Pike bought an impressive home twelve miles south of Calais, along the St. Croix River, which he called

"The Mansion House." One of his chief pastimes was to go on drives and so, with his own money, he posted a dozen granite milestones to mark the road to and from Calais.

In 1876 he quietly cheered the decision to pull the last federal troops from the South, and not so quietly, wrote editorials in the *New York Sun* skewering the GOP for stealing by fraud those elections in South Carolina, Louisiana, and Florida.

When James Shepherd Pike died in 1882, he did not forget his native city. Calais was left a substantial bequest in his will. This was enhanced by donations from his younger brother and another local citizen. Although the small handsome building on the waterfront is called the Calais Free Library, it also serves as a memorial to James S. Pike.

1. Phillip G. Clifford, *Nathan Clifford, Democrat, 1803–1881.* New York: G. P. Putnam's Sons, 1922.

2. Ibid., p. 37.

3. Ibid., p. 145.

4. Ibid., p. 268.

5. Ibid., p. 269.

6. William H. Rehnquist, *Centennial Crisis: The Disputed Election of 1876.* New York: Alfred A. Knopf, 2004, p. 143.

7. Ibid.

8. Ibid., p. 146.

9. Robert Franklin Durden, *James Shepherd Pike: Republicanism and the American Negro, 1850–1882.* Durham, NC: Duke University Press, 1957, p. 83.

10. Ibid., p. 159.

11. Ibid., p. 209.

12. Ibid., p. 215.

Lillian Bayard Norton, "Madame Nordica"
Courtesy Maine Historic Preservation Commission

MADAME NORDICA

It was an odd future to predict for a little country girl who lived in western Maine during the nineteenth century. Lillian Bayard Norton had written a childhood poem and it was shown to "Aunt Eunice," a Farmington neighbor who had the reputation of being a witch. The resulting oracular pronouncement was: "You will sail the seven seas and crowned heads of Europe will bow before you."

Who would believe that sort of thing in the shiretown of Franklin County, still one of Maine's least populated areas. Farmington *is* the home of a branch of the University of Maine, specializing in teacher education, but *international* is not a word one would attach to this section of the Pine Tree State.

Yet in the Norton family, back in the 1860s, there *was* a foreign touch. Of the five Norton daughters, one of them married a Cuban, Emilio Castillo, whose father had to flee his island home and who somehow ended up at the Abbott Family School in Farmington, run by Reverend Samuel Abbott, brother of Jacob Abbott, a writer of the popular *Rollo* boys' books. Then, too, some of the Norton girls had exotic first names: Imogene (the one who married Emilio), Ione, and Wilhemina Kossuth (her middle name in honor of a Hungarian hero), although more prosaically there was Annie and baby Lillian, who had replaced another Lillian, deceased at the age of two.

Many years later, in the 1930s, a new post office was built in Farmington as part of the New Deal's effort to provide more work. The interior included a WPA mural and on it was depicted the town's most famous citizen, the opera diva who'd won international fame as Madame Nordica. But in a nice touch, she was seen as six-year-old little Lillian Norton, wandering in the local woods, listening to the songs of birds.

The Nortons had an extensive history in Farmington. Great-grandfather Ephraim Norton, of a family prominent on Martha's Vineyard, had moved north in what was then still Massachusetts, cleared a patch of Maine forest, and settled. The area became known as Norton Woods, and several generations preceded the second Lillian's birth in 1856. Her father was Edwin Norton, "a dignified, cautious gentleman of the old school," and her mother, Amanda Allen Norton, "beautiful in person and gracious in manner."

Mother Amanda was the daughter of a well-known local character nicknamed "Camp Meeting Allen," who was considered the "most famous revivalist in Maine." A spirited woman, as well as beautiful and gracious, Amanda added a touch of the out-of-the-ordinary to the family's everyday milieu. For example, when her Cuban son-in-law's exiled father could not go back to his homeland to attend to the estate he'd left behind, she taught herself Spanish and went in his stead.

Both of young Lillian's parents were musical. Her mother played the piano and her father the fiddle—allegedly in secret. But the two of them did sing openly in the local Methodist church.

Edwin had quit farming and opened an inn, the Blue Mountain House, by the time Lillian was born. The resort did not prosper, and in 1864 he sold it and moved the family to Boston. Lillian was only seven years old. Yet her mindset forever fastened on Farmington as her home, and she has been described by one biographer as a woman who never wanted to be "alienated from the hard and vigorous soil from which she sprang."[1]

Quite definitely in the Norton family, little Lillian was not seen as a future opera star. All of the girls sang, but it was said her sisters *paid* Lillian not to sing. The future songstress of the brood was actually Wilhemina Kossuth, or "Willie," who matriculated at the newly opened (1867) New England Conservatory of Music. In 1868 sixteen-year-old "Miss Willie Norton of Boston" had a debut of sorts singing with the Franklin County Musical Institute at Farmington's First Parish Congregational Church.

One year later, the Nortons were back in Farmington and Willie sang again. But a terrible thing happened next. That October, the budding teenage soprano took ill; the diagnosis was typhoid fever and in November, Willie died.

Several years went by after this stunning tragedy. The Norton sisters must have stopped paying Lillian, for Mother Amanda heard her youngest warbling and thought she displayed as much talent as Willie. So Lillian, then fourteen, was taken to Willie's old teacher, Professor

John O'Neill, and auditioned for him. The upshot was her admission to the New England Conservatory.

After four years, Lillian Norton made *her* debut singing at Bumstead Hall in Boston on June 11, 1874. Four months later she made her first professional appearance—that is, she was paid to sing—in this case, a dollar and a chicken drumstick. She was also, she said, once paid with a jug of maple syrup.

Looking back on her career, she could reflect honestly, as she did to a group of girls seeking stage careers, "I have not leaped into success. It has been a long, painful, and often demeaning struggle." Furthermore, staying on top was a constant effort. "Others have passed me and won triumphs to which I thought myself entitled...." And she warned them: "No woman should enter upon an operatic career unless she feels she has within her the power to conquer fate."[2]

One spur for young Lillian was seeking success as a singer in order to assuage her mother's grief for the loss of Willie. After Boston, she went to New York City at the invitation of Madame Max Maretzek, who had sung at La Scala, and completed lessons with her while tentatively entering the opera scene in Manhattan. Her first favorable review came in the *New York Herald* following a concert at Steinway Hall.

But her first protracted commercial engagement had her conservatory professor, John O'Neill, absolutely aghast. She went traveling on the road with a brass band, that of impresario Patrick Sarsfield Gilmore, who paid her a hundred dollars a week plus expenses for her and Amanda.

The initial tour of the Gilmore Band was in the Midwest. Lilly, as she was called, was a smash hit in Cleveland. Planning a trip to Europe, Gilmore included her in his plans.

Before Lilly left, she and Amanda made a visit to Farmington, where she sang in the local Methodist church. The *Farmington Chronicle* described a reception of "encore after encore" and commented, "Farmington is justly proud of this talented young lady...this being the place of her nativity...and feels a deep interest in her welfare."[3]

The Gilmore group sailed for Liverpool on the ship *City of Berlin*, but had to leave behind three band members who were deserters from the British army. In England, they had great success, particularly their attractive young singer, Lillian Norton. In Dublin, though, they were hissed when they played "God Save the Queen." Gilmore, Irish himself, hurriedly changed the atmosphere by at once leading his musicians into the popular song, "St. Patrick's Day."

The tour covered fourteen cities in the British Isles; Amsterdam, Rotterdam, and the Hague in Holland; Brussels and Antwerp in Belgium; and Paris, where Lilly told her mother when they walked past the opera house, "One day, I'll sing there." While in the French capital, an agent stole money from the band and Gilmore had to borrow cash from the Nortons, which he eventually paid back double. Appearing at the Trocadero in Paris, Lilly sang "The Marseillaise" and "was encored and applauded," reported the *New York Times* correspondent. It was also in Paris that Lilly's connection with the brass band ended. She and her mother decided she should concentrate on a straight operatic career, and the best teachers were in Europe. It helped, too, that the husband of her sister "Onie" (Ione) sent funds enough for her to continue her lessons.

For operatic aspirants, Italy was the promised land. Lilly and Amanda were soon off to Milan. She was accepted as a pupil by a master teacher, Antonio Sangiovanni, who had her commit ten operas perfectly to memory. He also had her change her name. She became *Giglia* (Italian for *lily*) and *Nordica* (of the *north*, as derived from Norton). *Giglia* didn't last long outside of Italy, but *Nordica* stuck for the rest of Lillian Norton's life.

It was quite a while before the American girl in Europe had *Madame* attached to *Nordica*. Yet her operatic career soon began by playing in the smaller cities of Italy. She first sang in *La Traviata* in Brescia (present population around 150,000) and achieved an absolute triumph in the role of Violetta. The audiences went wild. There were continued cries of *"Nordica! Bellissima Violetta! L'Americana Nordica! La gentilissima Violetta!"*

She wrote her father, "I have had a grand success and no mistake. Such yelling and shouting you never heard. The theater is packed.... It makes me laugh to see men and women cry and wipe their noses in the last act...."[4]

But she was still at heart an American girl from New England, for she told her dad to send her newspapers, adding, "Sometimes it does seem as if I should die off with nothing to read in English."

News reached Milan of her success in Brescia. Opera buffs from

Milan started flocking to the Lombardian provincial capital. A benefit Lillian performed there created a howling furor.

Mother Amanda, accompanying her daughter, acknowledged in a letter home that she was "horrid homesick," as they went from one Italian venue to another. In a fancy restaurant, the two Mainers ordered lobster, not realizing what they were served would be clawless crustaceans from the Adriatic, "hard-fleshed and tasteless." Lillian sang *Rigoletto* in Aquila, another provincial capital near Rome, and in Venice she inadvertently almost caused a riot. Traveling in a gondola with her mother, she heard people singing on the Grand Canal, so she joined in with them. Immediately, everyone else stopped singing to listen to her magnificent voice. Afterward, every other gondolier pursued her to ride in their picturesque craft, creating an incredible Italianate scene.

Word came that she had been invited to sing in Czarist Russia. En route to St. Petersburg, mother and daughter stopped in Vienna and Miss Nordica sang with a number of celebrated European opera stars in works like *Mignon, Huguenots,* and *The Masked Ball.*

The Nortons' experiences, once they got to Russia, were a mixed bag of triumph and travail. Amanda's homesickness was a real problem, made all the worse when word reached them on Christmas Eve that her husband, Edwin, had died in Boston. They had been married forty years and she wrote pathetically of her longing to go back to Farmington and see "the dear old home" where "were passed so many happy days and years with him when I was young and cared for nothing more than his approbation and always agreeable society."[5]

In Russia, Lillian was performing as a member of the St. Petersburg Opera and giving concerts, often at the command of the czar. On March 5, 1881, Lillian sang for him for the last time. Eight days later, Czar Alexander II, a noted liberal, was assassinated by a radical bomb-thrower, and Russian politics changed completely. All of Alexander's reforms were overturned by the reactionary czar who followed him, with fateful consequences for Russia and the entire world. Amanda's acid comments on the situation showed an amazing foresight: "You might as well give the government into the hands of Orang-outangs [*sic*].... Who can tell what will be the end? I pity the nation!"

Meanwhile, Lillian's career moved ahead swimmingly. True to her prediction, she received a contract from the Paris Opera. Singing

Marguerite in *Faust*, the twenty-four-year-old Lillian was a smash hit among the Parisians.

However, there was one sour note. It came from a fellow American, a music reviewer named Henry Haynes, who panned her in the overseas American press. Here was a lesson in opera politics. One was supposed to pay off these people for favorable comments, and Haynes was venting his anger at not having been bribed. But Amanda, gritty Mainer that she was, struck back sharply, and biographer Ira Glackens writes, "Before her fiery and sardonic maternal counter-attack, the detractors and commentators, the mockers, advisors and critics, retired in confusion and none was ever heard of again."[6] Here's a sample of Amanda's justifiable venom: "Haynes is a blackmailer whose opinion could be bought for a few hundred francs to the detriment of anyone...."[7]

Among indications of support for Lillian was an envelope containing a check for $10,000—most unexpected—and it came from a second cousin on her mother's side, Frederick Allen Gower, who was fairly close to her in age.

Much about Lillian Norton's life, right to the very end of it, has the feeling of high drama, outsized intensified emotions, love and death romanticized, etc. Thus, in the real-life story of cousins Frederick Gower and Lillian Norton lies the stuff of a libretto.

Lillian fell in love with her kinsman, who had amassed a fortune out of his association with Alexander Graham Bell, organizing telephone companies in Europe. Lillian wasn't doing badly herself, enjoying a salary of $12,000 a year from the Paris Opera, but Gower was reputed to be worth $1.5 million. He had bought a house for his mother in swanky Brookline, Massachusetts, for $25,000, and the engagement ring he'd put on Miss Lillian Norton's finger had cost $1,000—both breathtaking sums in those days.

Soon Lillian and Frederick were slated to be married. It took a critical eye like that of Mother Amanda to see that this opera story might not end happily. She grumped of her prospective son-in-law, "He is scientific and rich, but he knows nothing about art." Nor did he seem to care for it, either—and Amanda fretfully surmised he thought of Lillian's singing as merely a job and would not want his wife to continue a stage career.

Frederick and Lillian were married in Paris on June 22, 1883, by the mayor of the city's 8th *Arrondisement.*

A trip home to the U.S. followed during September, and a big family reunion was held in Farmington. Lillian's sisters, Annie and Onie, came from Boston, and their grandfather, "Camp Meeting" Allen, hale and hearty at eighty-three, was also present. On September 28, 1883, "The Lillian Norton Gower Concert" was held in Farmington's Music Hall, with the celebrated Danish pianist Otto Bendix as accompanist, plus a selected chorus joining the hometown diva. The program, after scripture reading by Reverend Allen, included songs from two operas, *The Barber of Seville* and *Mignon,* as well as additional music by Mozart and Rossini, while the chorus chimed in on "Auld Lang Syne." Admission was 25, 35, and 50 cents, and half the crowd was made up of Norton and Allen relatives. The proceeds were donated by the families to buy streetlights for Farmington.

Shortly thereafter, in Boston, the New England Conservatory hosted a "Welcome Return" concert for its successful alumna.

Unfortunately, her marriage was not the same success. As Amanda had feared, Frederick Gower did not appreciate Lillian's career. When he took her back to England, Amanda followed and a climactic scene occurred. The businessman husband burnt the wife's theatrical costumes and music scores, and the mother protested so vigorously she was ordered out of the house. Her no doubt tearful daughter fled with her— another bit of opera in real life.

Subsequently, there was even greater drama. Frederick Gower disappeared in the most extraordinary manner: he literally vanished into thin air on a solo balloon flight across the English Channel. Neither Lillian nor anyone else ever saw him again. In due time, with Frederick declared dead, his estate was probated and found to have disappeared, also. Lillian had to go back to work.

Settling in England, she picked up where she had left off, enthusiastically received and sought after. One performance she gave was at Buckingham Palace, where the Duke of Edinburgh and the Prince of Wales "warmly admired her." She also sang at Albert Hall and then took a trip to Germany, to the famous Wagner Festival at Bayreuth, where she would often sing in the future.

Accustomed to lots of traveling, it was not surprising that, when she heard of the fatal illness of her dear uncle, Woodward Norton, she quickly crossed the Atlantic and arrived in Farmington while he was still alive. At the farm on Titcomb Hill, the Nortons' ancestral home, she crooned the old farmer's favorite tunes and he heard her and knew his famous niece had come "from the great world" to see him.

Before long, Lillian was back in London with Amanda. There, on November 28, 1891, her seventy-year-old mother unexpectedly died. At age thirty-five, Lillian was now suddenly and entirely on her own.

Much of her operatic work in the ensuing years alternated between the Met in New York City and the Wagner operation in Bavaria. One of her Manhattan co-singers was a beautiful young American girl, Emma Eames, raised in Portland and Bath, Maine. A co-singer at the Bayreuth *Festspiel* was a handsome Hungarian baritone named Zoltan Dome, and Lillian was attracted to him. Ira Glackens is playfully cynical in this instance, for he archly writes, "If love is blind, it is also deaf, for she thought he sang divinely."[8]

Lillian's connection with the Wagners and Bayreuth developed slowly. In 1892 she traveled to Bavaria and auditioned for the real power behind the festival, Frau Wagner, the composer's second wife, born Cosima Liszt, the daughter of Franz Liszt. Not only was she hired to sing in Richard Wagner's *Parsifal* but, as she said, "I lived right with her (Cosima Wagner) for three months and it was a great privilege... She taught me the German and helped me in every way...." When she went on to the role of Elsa in *Lohengrin,* the first performance of the opera at Bayreuth, some Germans were indignant that such a Teutonic heroine was played by an American. Nor was Lillian shy about her own national pride, once stating that when she went to sing, she felt "the eye of the musical world was upon me and that the stars and stripes were in my keeping and must be brought forth in victory."[9]

Nevertheless, she was still very much taken by her Hungarian leading man, Zoltan Dome, who played opposite her in *Parsifal.*

An interesting fellow American female on the international circuit in those days was Lillie de Hegemann-Lindencrone (née Lillie Greenough in Cambridge, Massachusetts), married to a Danish ambassador, who had something piquant if not catty to say about this operatic relationship in a sprightly memoir she published entitled *The Sunny Side of Diplomatic Life.*

"Madame Nordica has been singing throughout the season," Lillie reported. "She has a promising *affaire de coeur* with a tenor called Dome, Hungarian by birth and, I should say, anything by nature. He is handsome, bold, and conceited and thinks he can sing *Parsifal.* Madame Nordica, I believe, has sung for nothing, on the condition that her fiancé should make his debut here, previous to taking the world by storm." Lillie de Hegemann-Lindencrone would have us believe, when the cast appeared for their encores, Parsifal (Dome) "came out with the others and looked more like an Arab beggar than anything resembling a Parsifal." Lillie continued, "Nordica took her fiancé off the next day," and concluded that she didn't think the American opera star's life would run smoothly with Dome.[10]

She was right. Although the couple wasn't married right after *Parsifal,* they did eventually tie the knot and proceeded to have the troubles predicted for them, with the Hungarian running through Lillian Nordica's money and committing a series of infidelities.

Meanwhile, Nordica had been commuting transatlantically to Manhattan, where in 1893 she became employed at the Met as a member of the company. On one occasion, appearing with her in Mozart's *The Marriage of Figaro* was fellow Mainer Emma Eames. After three years, though, the New York public was jolted in November 1896 by the headline "OPERA WITHOUT NORDICA." She was leaving and her replacement was Nellie Melba, a younger Australian soprano. The competition between these two women had spilled over from the stage. When a fancy restaurant concocted a soon-to-be famous dessert called "Peach Melba." Lillian's partisans rushed in with a not-so-long-lasting "Chicken Nordica." The messy public divorce of the American diva and her Hungarian consort was even incorrectly blamed on Nellie Melba.

So Lillian Norton was alone again, having to fend for herself as an independent soloist, rather than regularly part of an ensemble. She sang here, she sang there—the *New York Evening Sun* called her "an American Brunhilde as world renowned as the Goddess of Liberty down the bay." She made plans to create an American Bayreuth, an opera house on the Hudson River, with an open amphitheater, an institute of music, and an annual festival. One unique feature was to have a board of directors consisting entirely of women.

Madame Nordica had become a suffragette. In later years, she was to devote more and more time to the campaign to allow females to vote in the United States. In any event, the grandiose plan for a Wagnerian-style music complex in the New World came to naught, but Lillian continued to sing on, whether it was to a huge Methodist convention in New Jersey or to thousands in Valley City, North Dakota, or singing "Dixie" to a frenzied audience in Richmond, Virginia.

Romance entered her life once more in the person of George Washington Young, a multimillionaire who gave her a "fabulous necklace of emeralds" while still in the process of divorcing his wife.

After their marriage in London, the couple eventually returned to America, and in August 1911 Lillian showed off her latest beau to her hometown and relatives during a memorable week spent in Farmington.

A photograph of these two (by now middle-aged and plumpish) newlyweds shows them surrounded by an entourage of Mainers in front of the Norton homestead. The pictured event was from a reception at the farmhouse following the "Great Farmington Concert" where her cousin Hiram led Lillian up onto the stage to perform before an adoring crowd. She was introduced by Farmington's leading citizen, David Knowlton, and she sang "Home Sweet Home" while looking in the direction of her own childhood manse.

Among the crowd of her kinsmen was Franklin Norton, a young cousin she had discovered during a trip to Martha's Vineyard and whose education she assisted. The visit also included trips to the nearby Rangeley Lakes where Lillian fished and caught a specimen of the famous local trout. They also stopped at the old Allen Camp Ground in the town of Strong, and she entertained the worshippers by singing the favorite hymn, "Nearer My God to Thee."

On a much larger stage, she was next in San Francisco for the groundbreaking of the Pacific Exposition slated for Golden Gate Park. President William Howard Taft also participated in these opening ceremonies, and Lillian, wearing an enormous hat, rode with him in the presidential car to receive the cheers of 200,000 people. Once Taft lifted the first golden shovelful of dirt, Lillian sang "The Star-Spangled Banner." While still in San Francisco, she also attended a suffrage rally and spoke in favor of an initiative to allow California women the vote. Men in the audience called to her and promised to approve it if she sang for them. She did sing and, as it turned out, the ballot initiative passed.

But problems, too, were looming for Madame Nordica. It seemed her third husband wasn't quite the moneyman he'd made himself out to be. He had encountered financial losses. To bolster his funds, he formed a Maine holding company and talked his wife into investing in it. Yet further losses resulted.

Another difficulty became the diminishing quality of Lillian's aging voice. She was a realist and once stated with good old Maine frankness: "A prima donna dies three deaths: when her beauty fades, when her voice fails, and when the breath leaves her body."[11]

She gave two last American concerts—one in Boston that was disastrous (she had a cold) and another in New York that was a triumph. In Manhattan, too, there was a "monster suffrage pageant" at the Metropolitan Opera House. Teddy Roosevelt appeared and gave his first major speech in favor of women's suffrage. Madame Nordica came dressed as Columbia, wearing a star-studded crown, and sang the national anthem.

Then she was off to Australia. Why "Down Under?" A theory was advanced that she wanted to invade the homeland of her purported rival, Nellie Melba, and show the Aussies what a magnificent singer she was. More likely she needed the money. Concerts had been arranged in Sydney and Melbourne for a company Madame had assembled. They also traveled to New Zealand and performed, stopping to play in Hobart, Tasmania, too, before returning to Melbourne.

Incidentally, on her way to Australia from the States, Lillian first landed with her crew in Honolulu, and she managed to arrange an hour-long visit with the former Hawaiian monarch, Queen Liluokalani. The queen, who had been deposed in an 1893 coup by American colonists, was notably musical, the composer of more than 200 pieces of music. The most famous is still heard today, the hauntingly beautiful "Aloha Oe," a song of farewell. Madame Nordica sang it for the queen, before reboarding her Australia-bound ship.

Once back in Melbourne, Lillian had a sensationally successful concert, but soon fell ill due to neuritis, and remained sick for the next three weeks. Her schedule was tough—she was to leave for Batavia in the Dutch East Indies, perform a concert there, then fill other singing dates in Manila, Singapore, Hong Kong, and Shanghai. The last leg would be to take the Trans-Siberian Railroad and travel across Russia to Paris and London.

Her ship, *Tasman*, left from Sydney. She went aboard with those members of the company who had stayed with her (a few split off), and on Christmas Eve 1913 *Tasman* anchored in the harbor of Port Moresby, New Guinea. The next leg took them into the Coral Sea, but ten miles off course during a dark night, they hit a reef. Eventually maneuvered free by the captain, *Tasman* was in no shape to continue on her route. By then it was New Year's Eve, and the stricken ship, in the midst of a bad tropical storm, set out for nearby Thursday Island, part of the Prince of Wales group controlled by Australia.

For the next three months, Lillian Norton remained a patient in the tiny tin-roofed Torres Strait hospital on Thursday Island, overcome by exposure, nervous exhaustion, and bronchial pneumonia.

It was a period of severe suffering. The heat was terrible, the mosquitoes just as awful, and probably worst of all was the incessant, sleep-depriving noise made by myriad frogs all night long. Refreshing swims in the sea were impossible because of sharks and saltwater crocodiles.

A welcome distraction came in the form of a fellow patient—an American boy taken off a round-the-world trip with a San Francisco boys' club due to illness, and left stranded on Thursday Island. The famous Madame Nordica sang to him, among other acts of kindness, but the young fellow, George McDonald, died on February 13, 1914. Lillian paid for a grave and gravestone that bore the inscription: "Far Away—From Home—from his countrywoman, Lillian Nordica."

She was not far from death herself. After young McDonald's passing, she was finally able to leave Thursday Island and sail to Batavia. There, at the Hotel des Indes after two weeks of convalescence, she succumbed to sudden heart failure on May 10, 1914.

Allegedly, her last words were "I'm coming, Mother." By her side was a fellow Mainer—Franklin Holding of Lewiston—a violinist and "assisting artist" in her company. Although two of his stringed instruments had damaged wood because of the heat, he was still able to play for her as she lay on her deathbed. When the music began, she asked what it was. "Your violinist," she was told. "Isn't it beautiful?" she replied. "I love to hear him play."

Holding, who was to die soon himself at the age of twenty-seven, performed her favorite songs until the very end. A Maine Writers Research Club publication on Lillian Nordica's life comments, "It is pleasant to know her last days were cheered by the presence and the beautiful music of the boy from her home state."[12]

Her memory has not been forgotten. Her funeral was held in London at the King's Weigh House Church, where she had been married five years earlier to George Washington Young, who, by the way, promptly tried to break the new will she had dictated on Thursday Island. Her faithful, longtime accompanist, E. Romayne Simmons, whom she called "Simmie," had arranged in Batavia for her body to be shipped to England.

At home in Farmington, a group was formed in 1927 to perpetuate her memory. They bought the old Norton homestead and turned it into a museum. Her costumes and props are displayed—exotic things in a down-home Yankee setting. During World War II, a Liberty ship built in South Portland was named for Madame Nordica. It was also nicknamed the "Lucky Lillian," having survived a bombing attack in Belgium and torpedoes fired at her in the Atlantic.

What did Lillian Norton think about the role of luck in her own life?

Always down-to-earth despite the colorful, exciting world in which she worked and traveled throughout her career, Lillian once stated in an interview, employing typical Maine frankness, that her success had come from "much misery," a "great deal of hard work," and "a little luck—yes, a very little of that—it's not good to have too much luck."

1. Ira Glackens, *Yankee Diva: Lillian Nordica and the Golden Days of Opera.* New York: Coleridge Press, 1963, p. 14.
2. Lizzie Norton French, "Madame Nordica," extract from *Just Maine Folks.*
3. Glackens, p. 36.
4. Ibid., p. 56.
5. Ibid., p. 80.
6. Ibid., p. 96.
7. Ibid., p. 100.
8. Ibid., p. 150.
9. Ibid., p. 170.
10. Lillie L. de Hegemann-Lindencrone, *The Sunny Side of Diplomatic Life.* New York: Harper and Brothers, Publishers, 1914.
11. Glackens, p. 255.
12. Maine Writers Research Club publication.

Cyrus H. K. Curtis, 1921
National Photo Company Collection, Library of Congress

13

THE SATURDAY EVENING POST

How many Maine people know that the most successful American magazine of all time had its origins, so to speak, in Maine? At least the creator of the latter-day *Saturday Evening Post* was a man from Maine—Cyrus H. K. Curtis of Portland. But in discussing his career, it also seemed appropriate to include a Maine author who gained his start at this same publication and for many years, before he took to novel-writing, was a regular contributor—Kenneth Roberts.

These were two Mainers who went elsewhere, at different times, but were connected by their unique talents and devotion to the media phenomenon that left such a mark on American life.

If he'd just been plain old Maine Yankee Cyrus Curtis, would the native Portlander in our story have reached the heights he did in the world of American publishing? One wonders. He wasn't simply at par with his schoolmates, growing up in the pre-Civil War era when practically no one in Maine bore a surname that wasn't unmistakably Anglo-Saxon. Poor little Cy had to carry those extra initials, making him Cyrus H. K. Curtis, and the *H. K.* was inescapably foreign: it stood for *Hermann Kotzschmar*—which would have been quite a mouthful for the kids on the Portland streets.

Still, there is a redeeming feature to this tale. Young Curtis neither resented nor felt ashamed of the German gentleman for whom he'd been partially named. Hermann Kotzschmar was a well-respected figure in Portland, having arrived in the United States as a result of the European revolutions of 1848, when many a German liberal had to flee monarchist repression. It was said that Cyrus's father, a Portland businessman and amateur musician, had met Herr Kotzschmar in Boston and induced him to remove to Portland.

The elder Curtis was also named Cyrus (his Maine-sounding middle name was Libby) and he was, indeed, a music lover. He played trombone in the Portland Band and acted as the group's conductor at rehearsals. Both he and his wife sang in their church choir, where, in fact, they first met. Thus it was not so strange he would give his son middle names derived from his musical friend.

Strongly rooted in Portland as the organist for the First Parish Congregationalist-Unitarian Church, Hermann Kotzschmar soon became a major force for promoting classical music in Maine's largest city. His Kotzschmar Piano School instructed hundreds of students throughout the half-century he taught. His most noted student is judged to be John Knowles Paine, called the "Patriarch of American Music," an organist, composer, Harvard professor, and founder of Harvard's Department of Music—located in Paine Hall, of course. Included in the young Mainers Kotzschmar influenced, too, was his namesake, little Cyrus, who first heard the maestro perform on Sundays in church.

Cyrus H. K.'s biographer, his son-in-law Edward Bok, relates how as a boy the future publishing king "as often as he could...would watch Kotzschmar play the organ,"[1] and also how, at age thirteen, after he bought a small hand melodeon from a friend, he would go listen to Kotzschmar, then rush home, take up his own instrument, and try to imitate the master from memory. Since he couldn't read music, and neither he nor his family could afford lessons for him, he simply "picked out the notes on the melodeon."[2]

Every Sunday he would look forward to hearing Kotzschmar in church, try to reproduce what he'd heard from memory on his melodeon, and, eventually, improvise melodies of his own.

Bok describes Cyrus H. K. Curtis's steadfast devotion to organ music in the following paragraph in his book, A Man from Maine: "All through Mr. Curtis's life has this love of music, particularly sacred music, developed within him and proved his chief outlet. He has become articulate through his fingers; seated at the organ he expresses his nature as he rarely does in words. What other men say by word of mouth, he says with his organ. It is his confidant; his solace in perplexity; his means of expression."[3]

During his later business life, once he could afford it, Cyrus Curtis bought a parlor organ. He originally paid for the instrument through the ingenious device of placing an ad in one of his publications, running it for an entire year, and charging himself. Every evening at home, he was sure to spend time on this organ. Curtis also played the piano—

again by ear—but much preferred organ music.

One of his several houses was in Wyncote, Pennsylvania, a small rural community northwest of Philadelphia. There, in the music room of the mansion he installed a magnificent, full-sized organ with 158 stops. Bok made sure to say in his book, "The playing of this beautiful instrument is his daily delight."4

Not only did Cyrus H. K. Curtis indulge his personal predilection, but as a memorial to Hermann Kotzschmar, he also donated another even more splendid organ to his native city.

The Kotzschmar Organ, located in Portland City Hall, has been called the oldest municipal organ in the United States. Curtis had it constructed in 1912 by the Austin Organ Company of Hartford, Connecticut. Ranked as "truly one of the nation's musical treasures," this ensemble of six actual organs includes five manuals for the hands, a thirty-two- note pedal board and 6,857 pipes.

This enormous organ complex, considered one of the largest of its type in the world, was dedicated and initially played on August 22, 1912. Cyrus Curtis was present in person to turn over his gift. The attendees in the auditorium quite naturally gave the hometown-boy-made-good a prolonged, rousing, standing ovation. A few, perhaps, remembered him when he'd been a newsboy selling papers on the Portland streets.

The Kotzschmar Organ is still in constant use. Since 1981, when the Portland City Council decided it could no longer afford the upkeep, a private group of citizens, Friends of the Kotzschmar Organ, has raised the needed funds. On April 15, 2008, a special concert marking the 100th anniversary of Hermann Kotzschmar's death was held in Portland's Merrill Auditorium and the music included a composition by John Knowles Paine, as well as pieces by Haydn, Bach, Mendelssohn, and even two pieces written by Kotzschmar himself: "Rejoice in the Lord," a sacred work, and, on the popular side, the "Commercial Street Polka."

Cyrus Curtis was known for his modesty and dry Maine wit. He evidenced no special pride about any musical prowess he might exhibit. In that regard, Edward Bok tells several stories.

As a boy, young Cyrus was a vocalist at a Sunday school convention in Boston's Tremont Temple, joining a quartet that included a girl originally from Maine named Lillian Norton. In later years, when asked if he could sing well, Curtis would reply, "Yes, of course. Why, I once sang with Madame Nordica."

On another occasion, his daughter and only child, Marie Louise, had her fancy music teacher listen to her father play the organ. A "lesson" was then arranged so Jean-Paul Kirsteiner could teach Cyrus Curtis about "simple harmony"—the use of triads, etc. To please his daughter, the multimillionaire publisher did allow himself to perform before the expert, although protesting he knew nothing about music and merely improvised without knowing what he was doing. The brief recital was made even briefer when the instructor abruptly interrupted, telling Marie Louise, "Positively, I have nothing to tell him. I have never heard anything like this in my life.... The man does nothing wrong."

Curtis responded, "Bah.... Just fingering a lot of chords. Half the time I don't know how I am going to get out."

The publisher's love of music, inherited from his own parents, descended to the third generation in Marie Louise's devotion to the art. In 1924, she founded a new music school in Philadelphia and named it for her father. Thus did the Curtis Institute of Music appear on the American scene, soon to become one of the world's premier training grounds for performers and composers (deemed the *absolute best*, I was told by my closest boyhood friend, who heard it from his older brother, Leonard Bernstein, one of Curtis's most illustrious graduates). Following the death of her husband Edward in 1930, Marie Louise Bok spent much of her life helping to develop the school, and in 1943 married its director, Efrem Zimbalist, the noted violinist and father (with his first wife, an opera star) of actor Efrem Zimbalist, Jr.

As already hinted, Cyrus Curtis commenced his business career as a newsboy in Portland quite by accident, it seems. As the story goes, one Fourth of July he asked his mother for money—some change—so he could buy a few explosive missiles to add to the noise of the local celebration. Her answer was that if he wanted more spending money than the change she had already given him, he would need to earn it himself. Consequently, the boy went back out on the street with only the three cents he had left.

A pal of his approached, carrying three copies of a local newspaper called the *Courier* and looking fairly glum.

"What's the matter?" young Curtis asked.

"Can't sell 'em," answered the other lad. "I'm stuck with 'em."

"I'll sell 'em," said Curtis. "I'll give you three cents for 'em."

Done deal. Cyrus H. K. Curtis entered the newspaper business. The fact that it took him four hours to get rid of his stock, making him too late to go and buy firecrackers, was of little import. He went home with *nine cents*, a three-fold profit, jingling in his pocket.

The next day, he bought nine cents' worth of *Courier*s, sold them, and his hoard of change grew to eighteen cents.

But very quickly, Cyrus was introduced to the realities of the market. Other newsboys—bigger newsboys—had their territories. The new kid on the block promptly got squeezed out, usually physically.

What Cyrus did next we would today call "thinking outside the box."

The Civil War was in full swing. Garrisons of soldiers were quartered in the Casco Bay forts that ringed Portland Harbor. Fort Preble was one Cyrus could see from the waterfront, and it occurred to him that here was a potential source of newspaper buyers. Right away, he sought out the *Courier's* circulation manager and proposed he be given a day's worth of newspapers and see whether he could sell them at the fort. No one else had this territory.

The manager agreed. They worked a way for Cyrus to get his load of papers and rush to the sailboat ferry to Fort Preble. Every last copy was bought and, moreover, the soldiers paid him five cents for each one, not three cents, covering the cost of his transportation. The twelve-year-old went home feeling the rush of excitement from his first big business venture.

On top of that, word went around Portland about his exploit. The business manager of the *Portland Press* took notice. He offered Cyrus a steady job, a weekly salary (two dollars), and an exclusive paper route. The security involved led the lad to accept, even though it meant getting up at the crack of dawn, since the *Press* was a morning paper.

Half-seriously, he would later say, "That is why I never grew. I never had enough sleep and I was always on my feet."

Despite the fact the young Cyrus Curtis had shown himself to be a budding Republican, he switched jobs once more and went to work for the *Portland Argus*, the most Democratic newspaper in Maine. One day in April 1865 he came into the office and a fellow newsboy greeted him with: "*Your* president has been shot!"

Shortly before this, Cyrus already had taken his first stab at publishing. Along with a friend, Walter Goold, he started a weekly newspaper for boys called *Young America*, selling for two cents a copy. The initial issue appeared on April 5, 1865. They had found a printer who, for five dollars, put out four hundred copies. Had they all sold, the boys would have made a three-dollar profit. But none sold. Walter bailed out of the project. Cyrus, as Edward Bok wrote, "found himself 'left cold,' as sole proprietor of a paper, with five dollars of debt on his shoulders."[5]

Some other teenager would have given up on the spot, paid off the printer, and gone on to a different pursuit. Not Cyrus. Seeing that if he continued his publication, he would owe five dollars more every week, he decided to buy his own press. Money he'd earned already had given him a small nest egg; he used five dollars of it to pay off his creditor, then traveled to Boston to buy himself a printing press. He found a used hand press for two and a half dollars, invested fifteen dollars in a font of type, and went into business by himself. A week after the first printing of the *Young America*, he had a new issue out, bearing his name alone on the masthead. Content included juvenile jokes like: "Why is a man with a cork leg never to be forgotten by his friends? Because he has been remembered," plus a serialized short story and "Enigmas" for his readers to solve. In this brief publishing venture, he even received a column of advertising and also a lesson in bill collecting, stubbornly pursuing the purchaser of a printing job he'd done and finally getting his money, but only after he'd been kicked down a flight of stairs several times. Eventually he was clearing eight dollars a week and had two hundred dollars invested in his printing plant.

That is, until the Fourth of July, 1866.

Any student of Portland history knows how, during the local Independence Day festivities, an errant firecracker caused the start of a conflagration that swiftly destroyed most of the city.

The flames not only leveled Cyrus's uninsured printing plant on Middle Street, but also wiped out his family's home on Wilmot Street. He was sixteen years old and had started high school. In the aftermath of the Great Portland Fire, he knew he could no longer enjoy the luxury of an education. He had to go to work.

It was the dry goods business in Portland that beckoned to begin with, at a store called Leach, Bartlett, and Parker, where he commenced by lugging around huge bundles of cotton goods. For a time he dreamed of having his own such store where the Preble House once stood on Congress Street. After three years, however, an offer of work came to him that led to the exodus from his native hearth. At age nineteen, he accepted a position in the Boston dry goods emporium of George R. Davis Company, which paid him two dollars more a week than he was earning in Portland.

We are now in Horatio Alger country. The career of Cyrus H. K. Curtis shows that, no matter what, he was always looking ahead; thus, while clerking in Boston, he took to selling advertising inches on commission for a publication known as the *Traveler's Guide*. His immersion into the lifeblood of all newspaper and magazine publishing had begun, and his knowledge of ad selling expanded into dailies, too, when he took a job at the Boston *Times*. The editorial side of the "fourth estate" was covered, as well, because he started putting out a weekly journal, the *People's Ledger*.

In the beginning he had a partner, but he was soon the sole proprietor and staff. The vicissitudes of his one-man operation can be imagined. The help of a Scottish-born printer named W. C. Allen proved essential to the survival of the business, which reached a 30,000 circulation. So was Cyrus's iron will to pick up the pieces after a second city fire—that of Boston in 1872—devastated him once again. In 1876, at the time of the U.S. centennial observation in Philadelphia, he went to the City of Brotherly Love to attend the celebration but also to investigate a cheaper printer for the *People's Ledger*. The potential savings turned out to be so great that he decided to move his paper and himself to Pennsylvania.

This time, though, he was not going to relocate alone. The year before, he had married a Boston girl, Louisa Knapp, a private secretary for—of all people—Dr. Samuel Gridley Howe and his wife Julia Ward Howe. The Curtises had their first and only child, Marie Louise, on August 6, 1876, and three months later, Mrs. Curtis gave her assent for their displacement to Philadelphia.

In later years, after Cyrus Curtis achieved his immense success, it was remarked that he had emulated Benjamin Franklin by transferring his abode from Boston to Philadelphia. Also, the flagship of Curtis's publishing empire was the *Saturday Evening Post,* and this fantastically popular periodical came in a direct line from Franklin's *Pennsylvania Gazette,* which he'd started in 1728. The name had been changed to the *Saturday Evening Post* in 1821 to avoid confusion with other *gazettes* published at the same time.

But in Curtis Publishing Company history, before the *Saturday Evening Post* rose like a rocket into the magazine firmament, there was the preceding success of the *Ladies' Home Journal.*

The genesis of Cyrus H. K. Curtis's first big magazine hit was a column he himself was writing for a four-page weekly he had started in Philadelphia, the *Tribune and Farmer.* Aimed at rural housewives, this continuing op-ed piece was called "Women and Home."

Mrs. Louisa Knapp Curtis, never one to beat around the bush, told her husband these articles of his were awful and ridiculous and he should stop them.

"All right," he snapped back. "You write it,"

She did—and that small seed grew into the publication that became the *Ladies' Home Journal.* Under Louisa Curtis's editorship, coupled with an unprecedented advertising campaign, the magazine blossomed. Well-known women authors like Louisa May Alcott began appearing on its pages. By October 1889, when Mrs. Curtis felt she should turn over her duties and stick to mothering their daughter, the *Journal's* circulation was heading toward a million. For its new editor, Cyrus chose Edward W. Bok, a naturalized Dutchman and writer, who one day would marry the little girl Louisa Curtis had left publishing to raise. Bok stayed with the *Ladies' Home Journal* for the next thirty years.

The *Saturday Evening Post* naturally built upon the success of this earlier mass publication. Edward Bok has written, "During all his busy days establishing the *Ladies' Home Journal,* Mr. Curtis never lost sight of his pet idea to create a paper for men."[6] Apparently, such an *idée fixe* had come from his youthful reading of the business stories of a long-forgotten writer named Richard B. Kimball. Curtis believed that knowledgeable business stories, put into the hands of businessmen, could be a journalistic gold mine, although pundits in the magazine world disagreed with him.

Eventually, the Curtis Publishing Company, through Cyrus's efforts, took over the remains of the operation that had once been Benjamin Franklin's. It was still a weekly and was down to a subscription list of 2,000. Curtis bought the whole kit and caboodle for $1,000.

Next, he set out to find an editor. He had his eye on the former editor of *Cosmopolitan,* a man named Arthur Sherburne Hardy, who had since joined the State Department and was U.S. minister to Persia. Curtis contacted him and they arranged a date to meet in Paris, France.

But meanwhile, another possibility arose. The name of George Horace Lorimer was proposed to Curtis, not necessarily as top editor, but in his capacity as a promising young journalist, now working for the *Boston Post.* It seemed Lorimer had business experience, having worked for Armour and Company in Chicago, but had left to go to Colby College in Maine and study journalism. Curtis met Lorimer in Boston, offered him a job, which he accepted, and prepared to go meet Minister Hardy in France, a meeting that never actually took place. Nor was it necessary. The few weeks Lorimer was at work in Philadelphia convinced Cyrus he was the man for the *Saturday Evening Post* job.

Maine's Kenneth Roberts embellishes this story in his autobiographical book, *I Wanted to Write.* He, too, worked at the *Boston Post,* but after Lorimer had left. The first time the Kennebunker asked for a raise (only two dollars a week), it was, much to his surprise, granted by the paper's owner, Edwin A. Grozier. The reason, Grozier candidly confessed, was that his refusal to give George Lorimer a two-dollar raise had led the talented journalist to go off to Philadelphia. Said Grozier, "I've always been sorry we let Lorimer go the way we did. If you ever meet him, I'd be glad to have you tell him so."[7]

Roberts thought to himself at the time: It seems obvious to me that I'll never meet Mr. Lorimer.

But through reputation alone, the budding newspaperman from Maine had great respect for Lorimer, commenting on how he had taken over Curtis's "newly acquired, sick-looking *Saturday Evening Post*...a moribund affair," and one decade later, "Lorimer's editorial genius made it the greatest magazine in America. Cyrus Curtis wouldn't have traded him for the Philadelphia Mint."

Of course, by the time these memoirs were penned in the late 1940s, Kenneth Roberts had not only met George Lorimer, he had written innumerable *Saturday Evening Post* pieces for him. In fact, the first two freelance pieces Roberts ever sold were bought by the *Saturday Evening Post.*

Lorimer had been hired in 1899. He was tough. When his boss, Mr. Curtis, relayed the news to him that Mrs. Curtis didn't like a certain article, he snapped, "I'm not editing the *Post* for your wife." Curtis never said another word on the subject and not long afterward increased Lorimer's salary.

Roberts referred to the man as "that granite-faced but tender-hearted editorial genius." Their relationship probably really got underway in 1919, when Roberts, an officer in U.S. Army Intelligence, went to Siberia as part of an expedition sent by President Woodrow Wilson to intervene in the Russian civil war that followed the Bolshevik revolution. Before embarking, Roberts wired a telegram to Lorimer offering to write stories from this complicated battlefield in the Far East. Lorimer wired back that he was interested in articles on the social, political, and economic situation.

While on active duty Roberts had trouble trying to find time and permission to write. He complained frequently about "the utter stupidity of that Siberian expedition," which ended with the pull-out of American troops. But if nothing else, he did manage to see a good deal of the world.

Aside from Siberia, a generally dreary place, Roberts spent a good deal of time in Japan, visiting Nagasaki, Kyoto, and Kobe before proceeding to Manila, which he described as "a magnificent city of stately buildings, of far distances, made beautiful by American taxpayers and doomed from the first to inevitable destruction by Filipino incompetence or Japanese aggression...."8

While in the Philippines, he managed to interview Emilio Aguinaldo, the former rebel leader, whom he characterized as "the little wrinkled brown man who had defied the American army."

This was one piece he sold to Lorimer. Another was a story from the Siberian fighting about something called the "Svetlanskaya Front."

When Roberts was finally able to be in Philadelphia, he and Lorimer lunched in the private executive dining room on the top floor of the elaborate Curtis Building the *Saturday Evening Post* owner had had constructed at Independence Square in 1909. The two men talked about the *Boston Post,* Edwin A. Grozier, and the two-dollar raise.

Kenneth Roberts
Courtesy Maine Historic Preservation Commission

Lorimer remarked that if he'd gotten the measly increase, he'd most likely still be in Boston.

It wasn't long before both were engaged on a more elaborate and sustained writing project, one that sent Roberts abroad once more. The subject was immigration into the U.S., when in that era the country was open to almost anyone who wanted to come. Lorimer was a strong conservative who wanted restrictions, particularly on Eastern and Southern Europeans. Roberts shared his exclusionist views. "Screamed at each other like Italian ditch diggers" was an expression he used quite naturally in his autobiography.

Agitation over immigration was as heated a subject after World War I as it is in the U.S. in the twenty-first century. Lorimer expressed his intentions for the *Saturday Evening Post* series. Roberts was to write on it in the following terms: "We've got to hammer at immigration until Washington and the country at large wake up to what's happening...."[9]

Kenneth Roberts was only too happy to oblige. His trip was to take him to England, Ireland, Scotland, France, Germany, Czechoslovakia, Poland, Austria, maybe Greece and Constantinople, the Balkans, and Russia. The message he sent back was that America should shut its doors. He wrote later: "I'd seen consular officers shed tears of fury at the unending streams of slum-stunted throngs pouring through their consulates to become added burdens to America,"[10] and he spoke of the "hordes of emigrants" wanting to enter the U.S. who "could be as undesirable as every American consular officer in Europe knew them to be...and as I emphatically found them in France, Belgium, Holland, Poland, Italy, and wherever my wanderings took me that winter."[11]

Upon his return from Europe, Lorimer made Roberts the *Post's* Washington correspondent, a position he would hold for many years. Roberts also worked unofficially as an advisor to the House Immigration Committee, headed by Republican congressman Albert Johnson. A former newspaper editor from the State of Washington, Johnson is considered the godfather of our first quota system, which was heavily weighted toward letting in mostly Anglo-Saxon and Teutonic Europeans. Two books by Roberts, containing his articles on the subject, were published at the time: *Europe's Morning After* and *Why Europe Leaves Home*. To his chagrin, they did not sell very well.

Obviously, the *Saturday Evening Post* dealt with many other concerns besides immigration. It attracted writers of distinguished reputation, such as Frank Norris, Willa Cather, Jack London, Rudyard Kipling, Theodore Dreiser, Sinclair Lewis, H. G. Wells, and Stephen Crane. Peter B. Kyne, the novelist who had worked for the Simpsons in Oregon, also appeared there in print. Some critics attacked the magazine's generally pro-business slant, but Lorimer also published muckraking radical David Graham Phillips, author of *The Treason of the Senate,* who blasted the rich and their political allies.

In 1916, after the *Post's* circulation had gone above two million, Lorimer brought on board a twenty-two-year-old artist destined to become a veritable icon for the magazine and one of America's most popular painters of all time. Norman Rockwell did *Post* covers throughout the next forty-five years. So identified with Rockwell is the *Saturday Evening Post* that a Google article on the publication had to be sub-titled "More to its pages than just Norman Rockwell."

While this success was happening and the flagship of the Curtis Publishing Company was reaching toward the three million circulation mark, what of Cyrus Curtis? As one reads Edward Bok's biography of him, the picture that emerges is of a doughty, canny, self-contained Mainer, his fingers always on the pulse of his enterprise, but never an interferer. He hired good men to run his magazines and let them do it their way, but he watched closely. There was also a Down East terseness to his decision-making, when it became necessary. Bok relates the story of a labor-management dispute that couldn't be settled. Mr. Curtis was called in as a third-party arbiter and he listened to both sides, then asked, "What do you want me to do?" Decide who is right, he was told, the company or the workers. "That's easy enough. The men are right," he replied. After a pause and a peek at his watch, he inquired, "Is that all?" and, hearing no answer, left to do other things.

Such a crisp style—he was described as a "little general with snapping black eyes"[12]—combined with a prodigious reputation for fairness, gave him total respect. He was also scrupulous in fulfilling his obligations, once taking years to track down a creditor to whom he owed four cents.

"Everyone around him may lose their heads. Mr. Curtis never does," Bok wrote. "He sits silent and quiet, the picture of placidity. He lets everyone else do the talking." When Curtis does finally enter the conversation, Bok says he does it with only the fewest words. "He has been known to attend three successive board meetings of a bank of which he is a director without uttering a word. 'Nothing to talk about,' he explained. 'Why use up time?'"[13]

Cyrus H. K. Curtis, the newsboy from Portland, had slowly turned into a poster boy of American big business, up there (or almost) with the

Fords and Rockefellers and Carnegies and J. P. Morgans—and although he did not try wholly to emulate them in the splendor of his trappings of success, he did not live badly, either. He had his mansion at Wyncote, Pennsylvania, a lovely spread back in Maine at Camden, and, to indulge his love of the sea, perhaps the biggest yacht in America, on which, in his later years, he spent considerable time.

Important businessman that he was, Curtis not surprisingly earned a tribute after his death from the Newcomen Society, which supports capitalist ideology through speeches about its foremost practitioners, which are then printed and widely distributed. In an address published as *The Life and Times of Cyrus H. K. Curtis (1850–1933)*, the *Saturday Evening Post*'s resuscitator is especially lauded for his role in developing advertising as a vital ingredient for any successful modern economy. The Newcomen speaker was Walter D. Fuller, then president of the Curtis Publishing Company and past president of the National Association of Manufacturers. He declared unequivocally that Cyrus Curtis "was to advertising what Ford was to autos and Carnegie to steel."

Whatever is thought about advertising now—hucksterism, lies, snake oil—was just as bad if not worse in Curtis's day. Patent medicine was one of the biggest culprits and he refused to run its ads, on one occasion sending back a certified check for $18,000 to buy six pages in the *Ladies' Home Journal*. This same sense of rectitude was likewise backed by a Curtis policy of paying for any reader's loss through an advertisement in their magazines or newspapers.

Curtis's belief in advertising extended not only to those he ran but also to those that promoted his own products. He established regional advertising offices of the Curtis Publishing Company, and so invested in the concept of advertising was he that he unconsciously furnished an amusing anecdote, told both by Walter Fuller and Edward Bok.

It concerned a problem the building superintendent at the company's Philadelphia headquarters was having with soap in the restrooms. People were taking the bars. As a countermeasure, he had them etched with the message: "Stolen from the Curtis Publishing Company." That cut down on the thievery, but there was one inexplicable result. He would put a bar in Mr. Curtis's private washroom, but the soap would be gone the next day; replaced, it would also again vanish. The mystery was solved when Mr. Curtis himself admitted he was throwing the soap out the window. "You didn't advertise what you were doing," he scolded his employee.

Another incident Walter Fuller included in his Newcomen lecture told of a French sociologist, Andre Siegfried, who made the charge that American publishers lived at the sufferance of advertisers.

Cyrus Curtis's rejoinder sounds like that of a Mainer. "Mr. Siegfried is said to be a professor of sociology in Paris.... But his statement that publications in the U.S. are run by moneyed interests who bribe their publishers with advertising is so absurd and ridiculous that it shows he doesn't know what he's talking about. Consequently, he is just as likely to be ignorant of sociology and his title of professor to be a misnomer...why bother with him?"[15]

By 1932 the *Saturday Evening Post* had $22,557,621 in ad revenue, three times that of any other magazine except Curtis's own *Ladies' Home Journal.*

A year later, Cyrus Curtis died. By then he had amassed other journalistic properties: the *Country Gentleman,* aimed at a rural audience, which reached a two million circulation mark, and the *Philadelphia Public Ledger,* the *Philadelphia Evening Express,* and the *Philadelphia Press,* all daily newspapers. His wife Louisa had died in 1910; he remarried shortly afterward, gaining stepchildren and grandchildren from his new wife, and pursued his charitable activities, like the Kotzschmar Organ. Two other notable Curtis legacies are the Curtis Hall Arboretum, a section of his estate in Wyncote, Pennsylvania, of forty-five acres with more than fifty types of trees, and Curtis Island in Penobscot Bay, Maine, containing a Coast Guard lighthouse and maintained by the town of Camden.

Kenneth Roberts, as we know, went on to become a world-class novelist. He did not stay long with the *Saturday Evening Post* once George Lorimer retired in 1936. But Lorimer had also helped get the Kennebunker established in the field of historical fiction by serializing *The Lively Lady,* an early Roberts work, in the *Post.* When Lorimer's son brought the news to Kennebunkport that his father had said Roberts's work was better than Robert Louis Stevenson's, Roberts responded, "Hey, hey! Who would work for any other editor if he could work for Lorimer?"[16] Also: "I cannot say too often that unless I'd been able to have the support of the *Saturday Evening Post* between and during novels, I couldn't possibly have written fiction of the sort I had set my heart on doing."[17]

Those novels by Roberts are mostly about Maine. We know, too, that he contemplated writing one about the true adventures of Edward Preble and Henry Wadsworth in North Africa, but had to settle for including an episode about the Derna expedition in his last major work, *Lydia Bailey.*

Whether Kenneth Roberts ever met Cyrus Curtis is unknown. He never mentions him in his autobiography. All his contacts at Curtis Publishing seem to have been with George Lorimer.

The final word on the Portland newsboy-made-good will have to come from son-in-law Edward Bok, writing a decade before the old gent's death.

"There I leave him with every faculty alert, with his face set toward his native East, eager for further accomplishment in the great game of business and in his later joy of service for others; a man full of that sterling quality that is inherent in the rock-ribbed character of a man from Maine."[18]

1. Edward W. Bok: *A Man from Maine*. New York: Charles Scribner's Sons, 1923, p. 29.
2. Ibid.
3. Ibid., p. 31.
4. Ibid., p. 32.
5. Ibid., p. 14.
6. Ibid., p. 149.
7. Kenneth Roberts, *I Wanted to Write*, p. 67.
8. Ibid., p. 121.
9. Ibid., p. 145.
10. Ibid., p. 144.
11. Ibid., p. 146.
12. From an anonymous publication called *Concerning Cyrus Curtis, Publisher, Written by the Editor.*
13. Bok, pp. 129–30.
14. Walter D. Fuller, *The Life and Times of Cyrus H. K. Curtis, 1850–1933.* Newcomen Society, London: 1948.
15. Ibid., p. 23.
16. Roberts, p. 204.
17. Ibid., p. 205.
18. Bok, p. 275.

Edna St. Vincent Millay, January 1933
Carl van Vechten photograph, Library of Congress

EDNA ST. VINCENT MILLAY

In her family, they called this sprightly red-haired lass "Vincent." The odd middle name, the story goes, honors St. Vincent's Hospital in New York City, where an uncle's life had been miraculously saved shortly before Edna's birth. Quite likely, she didn't mind responding to a boy's name; certainly, she always enjoyed being different. No doubt, in any case, she still would have been the poet—and controversial lady she became—under whatever name she went by.

This future Pulitzer Prize winner was born in Rockland, Maine, on February 22, 1892. Two sisters followed: Norma in December 1893 and Kathleen in May 1896. The trio of attractive females had a noteworthy distinguishing feature: one was brunette (Kathleen); another blonde (Norma); and the eldest (Edna) a flaming redhead. Their parents divorced in 1899 and the little misses were brought up by their mother. Edna's closeness to her siblings can be discerned in a teenage letter she wrote them while staying with an aunt in Massachusetts. "Who are the most provoking little brats in the world?" she asked rhetorically. "Answer: Hans and Fritz Katzenjammer—alias Norma and Kathleen Millay."[1]

The setting for their mostly fatherless childhood, in which they were likely as mischievous as the comic-strip German-American characters, was Rockland's neighboring town of Camden. Specifically, it was a section of one of Maine's most beautiful coastal towns nicknamed Millville. This was a tough, working-class area, and the three girls were often left by themselves while their mother, a visiting nurse, was out on her rounds. To Edna, it was "the bad section of town where the itinerant mill workers lived...restless streams of mill workers" of whom the Millay children were afraid. On one occasion, the three girls had to fling themselves against their front door and bolt it when, apparently, some of these scary strangers tried to break in and hung around outside for what seemed like hours. Environmentally, too, Millville was none too healthy. The river behind the Millay house was perennially stained from discharges of the dyes these woolen mills were discarding.

On their father's side, the Millays were French Protestant Huguenot descendants—the original surname possibly having been *Millais* or *Millet*. The mother's ancestors were solid Anglo-Saxon Yankees—with names like *Buzzell* and *Emery*, about as quintessential "old Maine" as you can get. Cora Buzzelle (she added an *e* for some reason) and Henry Tolman Millay, following their marriage, moved to Union, Maine, where Henry was a high school teacher and superintendent of schools. Their first apartment was actually in nearby Rockland. But once the marriage broke up, Cora and her girls lived a peripatetic life—moving to Rockport, Maine, then to Newburyport, Massachusetts (where Cora had grown up), then back to Knox County, Maine, and Camden, where they settled.

Edna matriculated at Camden High School. She played basketball on the girls' team, was a member of the Latin Club, and participated in the Genethod (a Welsh word meaning "daughter"), a Bible study group at the Congregational church. Edna also became fairly proficient at playing the piano. Seemingly, her life had all the hallmarks of an average small-town feminine existence of that era. If there were any hints of straying beyond the norm, they were to be found in her literary interests—not just that she joined groups of young ladies who *read* to each other—like the Genethod, the S.A.T. Club, and the Huckleberry Finners—but that she *wrote,* including songs and poems.

Edmund Wilson, the famed literary critic who later in vain wooed Edna to be his wife, once described her mother, and the same uncanny sense he had about Cora may well have applied to Edna. "But it was the mother who was the most extraordinary," wrote Wilson. "She looked not unlike a New England school teacher, yet there was something almost raffish about her. She had anticipated the Bohemianism of her daughters."[2]

The exotic red hair of the Camden high schooler may have advertised that flair. At age fourteen, she already had had a poem printed in *St. Nicholas Magazine*, a national journal for young people. Entitled "Forest Trees," it wasn't exactly Bohemian stuff, with lines like "Monarchs of long forgotten realms, ye stand; Majestic, grand...." But soon afterward, she was on the editorial board of the *Megunticook*, Camden High School's student-run magazine.

Mount Megunticook, which, along with Mount Battie and Bald Mountain, overhangs Camden to the west, seems to have exerted a special fascination upon Edna—particularly during foliage season. Of the leaves at the height of fall color, she wrote, "They are so beautiful they almost kill me...." And then, with a glance in the mirror, "...my beautiful hair—all autumn-colored like Megunticook."[3]

Such images were to provide subliminal inspiration when Edna began, at still an early age, to try to write real poetry. Her extraordinary poem "Renascence" may have been started in 1912. Early that year, news came that Henry Millay was seriously ill, maybe dying. He had removed to the remote Penobscot County town of Kingman, Maine, where he was superintendent of schools and chair of the Board of Selectmen. Edna was dispatched on an arduous voyage to comfort him in his last hours. She journeyed by boat from Camden to Bucksport, then by train to Bangor, and finally by sleigh to her father's bedside. On March 4, 1912, she could write home: "Papa is better and they think he will get well." Also penned were snippets about her adventures in this heavily forested wildland area. A Dr. Somerville took her driving every day and one time, as she wrote, "I pointed to a snowy mountain and asked what it was. Doctor told me it was Mount Katahdin. Yes, I've seen it! Beautiful!" They went "sleighing right straight up the Mattawamkeag River to Spragues Mills" and she saw a deer hanging on a tree, allegedly killed earlier by a bobcat.[4]

Returning home, the twenty-year-old Edna finished "Renascence," submitted it for inclusion in *The Lyric Year*, an anthology of a hundred competitively chosen outstanding new American poems, and her work was accepted for publication.

That summer of 1912 was important to Edna's future in another way, too. Her sister Norma had been waitressing at one of the Camden establishments catering to people "from away"—the Whitehall Inn on High Street. The season's end was always celebrated by the staff with a masquerade party. Edna attended, danced a waltz with Norma, won best costume, then sat down at the piano and played her own composition, "The Circus Rag." In the flush of applause, it was suggested she recite her prize poem, which she did to a rapt audience.

Among those who heard the attractive redhead was a vacationing woman named Caroline Dow, a Vassar graduate, on summer break from her job as head of the YWCA Training School on East 52nd Street in New York. Edna didn't know it that evening of the party, but her life was about to change dramatically.

Going to college had never seemed an option for the Millay kids. Vassar! Undoubtedly, Edna had heard of the famous women's school in Poughkeepsie, New York. And here was this nice Miss Dow—later to be called "Aunt Calline"—wanting to raise a scholarship for the promising young poetry writer who had so impressed her. Plus, another vacationing woman also had listened to Edna recite "Renascence" that night. Charlotte Bannon had gone to Smith. And she set about trying to gain admittance for Edna to *her* alma mater.

In broad, symbolic terms, the striking theme of "Renascence" was suddenly borne out in Edna's own reality. The very first stanza opens upon a provincial narrator's view of life—unmistakably experienced from Camden, a town sandwiched between mountains and the sea.

All I could see from where I stood
Was three long mountains and a wood;
I turned and looked another way
And saw three islands in a bay....

The verse is spoken by a person who has died and is comfortable six feet under until a stormy rain erupts and he/she is revived, reborn—a *renascence*, in other words, and the language is strong, simple, and strikingly poetic.

Edna finally had to make a wholly amazing decision: Vassar or Smith? She chose Vassar, in a sense acknowledging her wanderlust and desire to escape her roots. As she told Cora, she picked Vassar because she'd get to know girls from Persia, Syria, Japan, India, and one from Berlin. There wasn't a single "furriner" at Smith. Plus, "Lots of Maine girls go to Smith. Very few to Vassar. I'd rather go to Vassar."

The printing of "Renascence" had attracted the notice of two literary-minded Harvard graduates from Davenport, Iowa, who wrote to "Vincent Millay," thinking she was a male. Arthur Davison Ficke and Witter "Hal" Brynner both had poems in the *Lyric Year* collection, but both thought Millay's was the best. They regretted it wasn't given the top prize, or any special prize.

Alerted by Vincent that she was a female, they refused to believe it. "No sweet young thing of twenty ever ended a poem where this one ends," they wrote to her in Maine. "It takes a brawny male of forty-five to do that."

Her riposte was: "When a woman insists she is twenty, you must not call her forty-five." For absolute proof, she added: "The brawny male sends his picture."

These two guys became great friends of hers, especially Arthur Ficke.

Vassar, it turned out, could not begin for Edna until she had taken a semester of prepatory work at Barnard. "Her life in Camden was over" is the comment at this point of Nancy Milford, author of *Savage Beauty: The Life of Edna St. Vincent Millay*. The budding poet herself had mixed feelings, as this passage from her diary attests: "Some people think I'm going to be a great poet and I'm going to be sent to college so that I may have a chance to be great...but I don't know—I'm afraid...."[5]

Edna entered Vassar as a freshman in 1913. A twenty-one-year-old freshman was a rarity on any campus, but it was said she only looked about twelve. Yet her classmates accepted her and she was popular. Right off the bat, her poem "Interim" won the Miscellany Prize for the best undergraduate piece of poetry. In her second year, she had the lead in the Sophomore Party Play. She wrote the baccalaureate hymn for the Class of 1917, and another of her plays, *The Princess Marries the Page*, was performed and she played the princess. The foreign girls she had hoped to meet did not appear in droves, but she drew close to Elaine Ralli, whose family was Greek—and rich. Some of her favorite moments with her friends occurred when she would convulse them with stories about Maine, using a comic but authentic Down East accent.

If anything, her age was merely a handicap in that she had a tendency to revolt against what she obviously considered childish parietal rules of restraint. Senior year saw the worst cases of her free-spirited disobedience. She went into New York City to the opera and stayed overnight without permission. For that she was grounded—in Vassarspeak, she was "campused," not allowed to leave the Poughkeepsie premises, except she did, stayed away overnight again, gave the mistaken impression she was with a man, and was caught.

The faculty voted to suspend her indefinitely. Graduation was impending and Edna St. Vincent Millay would not be allowed to receive her degree.

Suddenly, her case was a cause célèbre. They would be playing her music at the ceremony, singing her lyrics, Cora pointed out to the president of the college, but she couldn't be there. Half of her class, more than a hundred girls, petitioned to let her join them—and in the end, the authorities relented.

Whereupon Norma sent a letter addressed to "Highly Esteemed Edna St. Vincent Millay, A.B.... Oh—my baby, cute thing—How things are changing. I realize now you don't really belong here anymore. You belong in New York."

Where else would she go to live after college except Manhattan? Bohemianism, as it was still called then, had migrated from its concentration around Pfaff's Restaurant on lower Broadway during Artemus Ward's day into the area known as Greenwich Village. The Washington Square Players and other little theater groups sprang up. In the summer of 1915, George Cram Cook, one of a surprisingly numerous contingent from Davenport, Iowa, started an off-off-off Broadway extension in Provincetown, Massachusetts. Eugene O'Neill became involved with the Provincetown Players, as did Floyd Dell, another Davenporter, poet, and playwright, who also edited the *Masses*, a leftist antiwar journal.

In such an atmosphere, "Vincent" fit right in. She began her New York career looking for work as an actress. The Provincetown Players, their summer run finished, played in the Village in the winter. Floyd Dell's play, *The Angel Intrudes,* was being cast and Edna landed a part in it. The show opened right after Christmas, 1917, to be followed by another Dell work, *Sweet and Twenty,* in which she was also featured. For Edna, too, there was an on-again, off-again, love affair with Floyd Dell.

The *Masses* was not a popular publication with the authorities once the U.S. went into World War I. In April 1918 Dell and his associate, Max Eastman, were put on trial under the Sedition Act—a trial that was prolonged and eventually included the pro-Bolshevik journalist John Reed as a defendant. All of these men were part of the "gang" Edna hung around with. Another member was Max Eastman's roommate, Eugen Boissevain.

This fellow differed significantly from the others of the crowd—not an American, but Dutch despite his French name (the descendant of

Appearing in a play by Alfred Kreymbort in 1917 are (left to right) Luie(?) Earl, Marjorie Lacey-Baker, Norma Millay, William Zorach, Edna St. Vincent Millay, and Kitty Cornell. Peter A. Juley & Son photograph, Library of Congress

Huguenot exiles in Holland), a businessman, and a widower. His late wife, the beauteous Inez Milholland, was a Vassar graduate and the two of them had visited the Poughkeepsie campus while Edna was enrolled. Inez Milholland, a practicing lawyer, was nationally known for her untiring and outspoken campaigning for women's suffrage. It was at a Los Angeles rally in November 1916 that she collapsed, and her death followed ten weeks later. Her bereaved husband Eugen (*Ugin*, to Edna and the "gang" in New York) went to room with his buddy Max Eastman, who had also been linked romantically to Inez before her marriage.

Meanwhile, Edna lived her wild life in the Village—perhaps tempered by the fact that she had brought some of Maine with her: sister Norma, and even mother Cora. First, she and Norma lived at 139 Waverly Place; when Cora came, they moved to West 19th Street and

Mother Millay was put to work sewing costumes for the Provincetown Players.

With the war over, some of the pressure (although not all) against peace activists eased and Edna came out with an antiwar play she had been writing. *Aria da Capo* is considered her most famous work for the stage. It was produced in December 1918, highly acclaimed by critic Alexander Woolcott, and reprinted the following year in *Reedy's Mirror*, the St. Louis weekly magazine edited by William Marion Reedy, an influential literary entrepreneur said to have also helped writers such as Emily Dickinson, Ezra Pound, Edward Arlington Robinson, Amy Lowell, Carl Sandburg, and Vachel Lindsay. In addition to *Aria da Capo*, Reedy also printed some of Edna's sonnets.

Miriam Gurko, the author of *Restless Spirit: The Life of Edna St. Vincent Millay*, capsulizes *Aria da Capo* in the following terms: "The senseless tragedy of war is poised against the empty, incongruous fripperies of an indifferent harmony which hastens to brush the horrors of war out of sight."[6]

Edna's own "fripperies" of lifestyle, as America edged into "normalcy" and Greenwich Village into the Roaring Twenties, were those of a rising young writer. She even did satiric stories for *Ainslee's Magazine* under the pseudonym Nancy Boyd. Her Vassar play, *The Princess Marries the Page*, opened the New York season for the Provincetown Players. She directed the performance and played the leading role. *Vanity Fair* published some of her poems and Nancy Boyd stories. Edmund Wilson, on the staff there, fell in love with her poetry and, after he met her, with the poet herself.

In Nancy Milford's biography, there is a play-by-play description, often explicitly sexual, of Edna's many loves during this period, both men and women. Marriage was proposed to her, by "Bunny" Wilson, for one, and rejected, while she herself made advances to several males; in the case of Hal Brynner, who turned her down, he was bisexual, but leaned toward the gay side.

After a summer in 1920 at Truro on Cape Cod, the Millays came back to New York City and once more changed addresses—to 77 West 12th Street. "She found New York a wonderfully open world after the limitations of Camden and the schoolgirl confinements of Vassar," writes Miriam Gurko.[7] The year 1920 saw a book of her poetry, *A Few*

Figs from Thistles, emerge, and it contained arguably her most famous lines, as she put her poetic finger on the zeitgeist of the era her own "fast" lifestyle was helping to create:

My candle burns at both ends;
It will not last the night;
But ah, my foes, and oh, my friends—
It gives a lovely light.

Nancy Milford opined that this single quatrain helped "make her the most widely read poet of her generation," since that stanza "became the anthem of her generation" and the "Jazz Babies took it as their rallying cry."[8]

It has been reported that Edna wrote this "First Candle" poem, as she called it—otherwise "First Fig" in her manuscript—while frequenting a favorite Greenwich Village hangout—Romany Marie's Café. The locally famous lady in question, a Romanian Jewish immigrant, has borne the title the "Queen of Greenwich Village," and in Robert Schulman's book about her, there is a section on "Edna, the little lady poet."[9]

Marie describes Edna: "She'd sit in a corner and either think or read something [that is, when she was alone, without her friends like Arthur Ficke or Hal Brynner]. Many times," Marie goes on, "I'd say: 'You want something?'

"'Oh, Marie, Marie,' Edna would answer. 'Yes, a lot of Turkish coffee.'

"And then," said Marie, "she'd turn over the drained cup and say: 'Read it to me [the coffee grounds].'"

In doing this form of fortune telling with Edna, Romany Marie was always careful to be cheerful. "Edna needed cheer," she said. The motherly café owner knew Edna wasn't making a living from her poems and plays and wasn't happy doing the Nancy Boyd stuff, so, also knowing that *Vanity Fair* was considering Edna's work, she looked in the bottom of the coffee cup one night and said, "I see coming up a new proof that you *are* loved for your poems as much as for yourself." Two days later, her poems were accepted by the magazine and Edna came in to embrace Romany Marie and tell her, "Marie, you were a bridge for me over two empty days."[10]

Included in this biography is also a cameo portrait of Edna with her on-again, off-again lover, Floyd Dell, taken from the *Quill,* a Village magazine: "Floyd Dell, with white face and longish hair, hanging on the words of Edna, the great poetess herself chatting titterishly, very much as any flapper—and the complacent Villagers unconscious of these divine presences."[11]

Restless all the same, Edna left for Europe in 1921, with Paris her initial destination, like so many young American wanna-be's. She met Scott Fitzgerald and other émigrés, and while in the City of Lights, finished a book of her poems she called *The Harp-Weaver and Other Poems.* Yet to her the most thrilling place she visited was Albania. Cora came over and they were in England together, allegedly tracing the Buzzell ancestry. But there was another agenda. Edna had had an affair in Paris with a Frenchman named Daubigny and she was pregnant. Cora had met the man and detested him. Using her nurse's training, Cora went roaming the English countryside, searching for a certain herb called alkamet, which had abortive powers—and found it—and employed it to induce a miscarriage in her daughter.

When the Millays were ready to go back to the States, it was 1923— and that was to be a stupendous year for Edna.

In April, she received a Pulitzer Prize for *The Harp-Weaver and Other Poems, A Few Figs from Thistles,* and eight sonnets published the year before in *American Poetry*—the first woman ever to win a Pulitzer for poetry. And on July 18, 1923, she married Eugen Boissevain.

As usual, Edna St. Vincent Millay was doing the *un*usual. Eugen (Gene to many people by then) was certainly an offbeat casting choice for her—no intellectual, no Bohemian wit, no literateur, but a seemingly phlegmatic Dutchman (he was also half-Irish) who imported coffee from the Dutch East Indies. Charlie Ellis, married to Norma, pin-pointed the attraction of this affable, big bear of a man for his sister-in-law, saying: "He was the mother type...just in the complete attention at all times to her needs." At the moment, Edna needed all the help, support, and security she could get, for she wasn't well physically. A New York press headline told the story:

POETESS BRIDE TO GO UNDER KNIFE
HONEYMOONING ALONE IN HOSPITAL

The marriage ceremony was performed in a garden of Eugen's country estate at Croton-on-Hudson, New York. Present were Edna's sisters and two of her ex-lovers, Arthur Ficke and Floyd Dell. The bride, whose veil had been improvised from a roll of mosquito netting, looked wan and pale. The next day, she was to be driven into Manhattan for an operation to remove her inflamed appendix. "If I die now, I will achieve immortality," she declared.

However, the operation was a complete success and the real honeymoon took place a little less than a year later when she and her husband went on a wedding trip halfway around the world, sailing to the Far East and continuing on to Europe, where, among other things, they dropped in on Eugen's family.

The itinerary included Java in the Dutch East Indies and its capital Batavia (did Edna know of Madame Nordica and her sad end in that city?). The newlyweds had no health problems there. They also stayed in the Java interior with a friend of Eugen's and climbed an 11,000-foot mountain. But they did experience a few bouts of illness on their adventurous trip—the flu in China and dysentery and tropical fever in India. Nor was the visit to Eugen's family in the Netherlands an unqualified success. Edna was not warmly received and the couple never went back.

Home by Christmas of 1924, they proceeded to purchase a country home of their own. It was at Austerlitz, New York, a still-rural spot today not far from the western border of Massachusetts, on the New York side of the Berkshires. They called this sylvan pad Steepletop, reputedly from the nickname for a local plant found in abundance on their property. The couple also kept a home in Greenwich Village at 75 Bedford Street.

Now, if not *immortal,* "Vincent" was at least well-known enough to be included in prestigious company. Earlier, in 1923, she was invited to contribute a poem at the unveiling in Washington, D.C., of a statue of three leaders of the women's suffrage movement. Edna's piece, appropriately enough, was called "To Inez Milholland," in which she sought to immortalize her husband's late wife. Another memorial celebration found her at Bowdoin College in 1925 for the hundredth anniversary of the famous Class of 1825 that had given America Longfellow and Hawthorne. The invitees were Robert Frost, Carl Sandburg, Professor Irving Babbitt of Harvard, and Edna. She was the star, the students not only wildly applauding at the end of her reading, but madly stomping their feet. This was the only time she and Robert Frost ever appeared on the same stage, and she may have come away with a jaundiced view of the old farmer. President Kenneth Sills of Bowdoin had wanted to set up a dinner for the speakers with the governor of Maine, but Frost grumpily vetoed the idea.

Some years later, perhaps as sour grapes, Edna was to mutter in a letter to her friend Arthur Ficke, "I wondered why I, having once been awarded this prize [the Pulitzer] in 1923, never received it afterward, although Robert Frost and E. A. Robinson seemed to be taking turns receiving it year after year." The Pulitzer Prize judges, she thought, had an easy time with those two because, as she put it, "if their private lives, both sexual and political, were not thoroughly blameless, I have never heard about this."[12]

Her own life, she didn't have to tell Ficke, both politically and sexually, was hardly blameless. She had actually been arrested and jailed in Massachusetts in 1927 while picketing the Sacco-Vanzetti trial. Tongue-in-cheek, she argued, this single act had prejudiced the "aged professors of Harvard [on the Pulitzer board] against her subsequent work," and she concluded: "The judges must have felt entirely happy and at ease in their minds the moment either Robinson or Frost published a new collection of poems."[13]

Gardiner's Edwin Arlington Robinson won the Pulitzer three times, in 1922, 1925, and 1928. Edna's hyperbolic rejection of her fellow Mainer may have contained a touch of sexist envy. Livermore Falls's Louise Bogan, whose career led her to become the poetry reviewer for the New Yorker magazine, received a much different reception. Thanking Edmund Wilson for sending her samples of Bogan's work, Edna gushed: "Who is this person? I never even heard of her. I was quite thrilled by some of the poems. Isn't it wonderful how the lady poets are coming along? 'Votes for women' is what I sez!" In the ensuing years, these two Maine females were to become mutual admirers and close friends.

One person who later commented on this fact was Deems Taylor, the music critic and composer. He and Edna had collaborated on an opera—an American opera, in English—commissioned by the Metropolitan Opera. The story, however, was set in ancient England and based on a tenth-century Anglo-Saxon chronicle. The King's Henchman opened on February 17, 1927, won a huge ovation, became a big success, and sold in book form, too.

The 1930s brought the death of Edna's mother in 1931. Cora had been living back in Maine, and Edna had her body brought to Steepletop and buried on the estate. She and Eugen were spending a good deal of time at this New York retreat of theirs. Yet according to Toby Shafter in her book *Edna St. Vincent Millay: America's Best Loved Poet*, it seemed confining. "Vincent especially sometimes felt closed in at Steepletop and longed for the endless horizon of the ocean of her native Maine."[14] After all, one of her lines of poetry had proclaimed, "More sea than land am I...."

The opportunity for Eugen and Edna to add a nautical mix to their lives occurred in 1933. The two of them had stopped at the Bailey Island, Maine, summer home of two friends, Esther Root and humorist-writer Franklin P. Adams. From that tongue of land jutting into Casco Bay, they could spy an island in the distance with a single house on it. Thus did Ragged Island come into their lives. It had formerly been owned by a literary Maine man, Elijah Kellogg, Jr., a minister who wrote poetry and popular prose books for young people, one whole series of them set on "Elm Island," his name for Ragged Island. Eugen and Edna bought the entire property of fifty wild acres and Kellogg's house (he had died in 1901), which they renovated. Eugen set out lobster traps and Edna swam in those frigid waters and wrote lines like: "There you row with tranquil oars and the ocean shows no scar from the cutting of your placid keel."[15]

There was more travel in the 1930s—to the French Riviera, to the Virgin Islands, Puerto Rico, Haiti, Cuba, Charleston, South Carolina, and Florida—a fire at a Sanibel Island hotel destroyed one of her manuscripts. A collection subsequently published, *The Buck in the Snow*, had a distinctly Maine image in its title. But a new vogue in poetry had arisen, inspired by T. S. Eliot, and described as "intellectualism" and "obscurantism." Then the Second World War broke out and its effects were hard on Eugen: Holland was invaded and occupied by the Germans, the Japanese overran the Dutch East Indies, and his source of revenue was cut off. Edna wrote propaganda poems. She excoriated the Germans in "The Murder of Lidice," honoring the Czech village wiped out in revenge for the resistance's killing of SS leader Reinhard Heydrich; for D-Day, she wrote "Poem and Prayer for an Invading Army." Snobby critics took her to task for such unliterary conduct, prompting a counter-snicker that poor patriotic Edna had been more attacked because of her gung-ho verses than traitor Ezra Pound had been for his lavish praise of Fascism.

With the war over and gasoline rationing ended, Eugen and Edna returned to their country retreats. In the summer of 1946, spending her time in Maine, Edna wrote her poem, "Ragged Island."

So to speak, you could take the girl out of Maine, but you couldn't take Maine out of the girl. Miriam Gurko had this to say: "There often seemed in Edna Millay an echo of the New England conscience, the heritage of the Puritan colonists, which amounted to an almost rigid inflexibility of principle, and which Edna might have absorbed from her early life in Maine."[16]

Life got tougher for Edna as the decade of the 1940s drew to a close. On August 30, 1949, Eugen died suddenly following an operation at Deaconess Hospital in Boston. They had had what was known as "an open marriage," tolerating affairs with others, even saying they were like two bachelors living together, yet needing each other and never even dreaming of separating. Edna became ill and stayed ill for a long time after Eugen's death.

In her correspondence with her Bailey Island friend, Esther (Tess) Root Adams, we get a glimpse of her mood and situation.

"Dear Tess, Ragged Island is not for sale.... As soon as I can bear it, I shall go back there. Possibly next summer. I don't know.... Tell John [her caretaker] to board up things as best he can and carry on.... When I go to Maine again, I shall go straight to Ragged [and thus can't visit her at Bailey Island].... P.S., ask the tax collector, Gladys Thurston, to send me the tax bill *under my own name* [since Eugen was dead]."[17]

This letter went out from Steepletop on August 4, 1950. On October 9, 1950, there was another letter to Tess and this one, too, had to be from Steepletop. It concerned a visit Tess was planning to make to Edna. She was to come after lunch and leave before dinner and, "No, my dear. Don't bring me any lobsters. And don't bring me any seaweed."[18]

Ten days later, on October 19, 1950, Edna stayed up all night reading proofs of a new translation of *The Aeneid*. She was later found lifeless at the bottom of her staircase. There are at least two suppositions concerning the cause of her death: one that she suffered a fatal heart attack while climbing the stairs; the other that she fell—maybe drunk or doped up (she was addicted to morphine)—and broke her neck.

Today Steepletop, which was Edna's major home after World War II, is now a National Historic Landmark. Her sister Norma inherited the property, which includes 700 acres plus house and gardens. It is currently owned by the Edna St. Vincent Millay Society, a nonprofit group which, starting in 2005, organized a "Steepletop Festival" featuring readings about her and of her own work, even including Nancy Boyd pieces, plus a discussion and concert performance of *The King's Henchman* opera.

Camden girl Edna St. Vincent Millay still has a lot of fans out in the wide world.

1. Allan Ross, ed., *Letters of Edna St. Vincent Millay*. New York: Harper and Brothers, 1952, p. 8.

2. Ibid., p. 191.

3. Nancy Milford, *Savage Beauty: The Life of Edna St. Vincent Millay*. New York: Random House, 2001, p. 56.

4. Ross, p. 13.

5. Milford, p. 77. According to Milford (p. 37), Edna called her diar "Ole Mammy Hush-Chile."

6. Miriam Gurko, *Restless Spirit: The Life of Edna St. Vincent Millay*. New York: Thomas Y. Crowell Company, 1962, p. 115.

7. Ibid., p. 131.

8. Milford, p. 160.

9. Robert Schulman, *Romany Marie: The Queen of Greenwich Village*. Louisville, KY: Butler Books, 2006, p. 74.

10. Ibid.

11. Ibid., p. 96.

12. Ross, p. 295.

13. Ibid.

14. Toby Shafter, *Edna St. Vincent Millay: America's Best Loved Poet*. New York: Julian Messner, Inc., 1957, p. 174.

15. Gurko, p. 171.

16. Ibid., p. 246.

17. Ross, p. 373.

18. Ibid.

John Frank Stevens
Moffett Studio portrait, Library of Congress

15

JOHN FRANK STEVENS

Unless you look for it, you'll undoubtedly walk right by without notic-
ing the small statuette on a table just inside the entrance to the Maine
State Library in Augusta, Maine. You've already had to go down a set of
stairs and through a low-wattage electronic-style security gate meant to
detect any books taken out surreptitiously. Even if you do catch sight of
the curious, un-library-like object, you may not be interested enough to
examine it.

The figurine, the color of bronze, seems to be about two feet high.
It depicts, in miniature, a hardy, muscular man with a nineteenth-century moustache, wearing heavy, bundled-up winter clothing, and staring
straight ahead in a determined, no-nonsense fashion.

If you are intrigued enough to stop and peer, this is what an accompanying plaque says: "The statuette of John Frank Stevens, near the general reference desk, is a reproduction of the great bronze statue of
Stevens by Gaetano Cecere, which stands at Marias Pass in Summit,
Montana. The statue represents Stevens at the age of thirty-six, when he
discovered Marias Pass through the Great Divide of the Rocky
Mountains."

Left unsaid is that John Frank Stevens was born and raised in nearby
West Gardiner, Maine.

Why this man from Maine has been memorialized in such a remote
wilderness area of the West dates back to the year 1889. At the time,
John Frank Stevens was an assistant principal engineer working for the
Great Northern Railway, which under its legendary chief, James J. Hill,
was trying to build a railroad along the uppermost rim of the country
from Minneapolis to Puget Sound. By 1887, the hard-driving Hill had
pushed his line into Montana, to the town of Havre, just about halfway
across the state. Yet the hardest part would soon have to be faced—
breaching the barrier of the Rockies. How could a pass be found
through the Great Divide where a railroad was able to run?

When Stevens first went to work for James J. Hill, he had been working low-level railroad engineering jobs for more than twenty years. Actually, he had studied teaching at the Farmington Normal School, preparing for a career in education. But after one year in the classroom, he found it much too sedentary an occupation and soon began learning the engineer's trade by doing it himself—starting in Lewiston, surveying lots and staking them.

In 1873 he left Maine for the Middle West, where an uncle of his was an engineer in Minneapolis. More apprenticeships ensued in Colorado, New Mexico, and Canada, where he initially crossed paths with James J. Hill in gaining an assistant location engineer's job with the Canadian Pacific.

The word "location" in his job description meant exactly that—a roving scout going out into wild, untouched country, trying to locate optimum routes for future trains to travel. These years of adventure roaming the great outdoors for the Canadian Pacific and Great Northern, Stevens declared "the happiest of my professional life." They were not without a modicum of danger. On one occasion, marooned with another man by seven feet of snow blocking a mountain pass, he was anxiously listening to talk of cannibalism from his companion before a rescue party reached them. More seriously, on another occasion, hiking with three other men to Spokane, Washington, they discovered they were being stalked by a gang of thugs who planned to rob them, thinking they were smuggling opium. A member of this gang was later hanged for a brutal murder. Stevens's other close calls included being treed by five wolves and attacked with knives by Italian workmen, furious because he had buried a dead mule they had planned to eat.

His assignment in 1889 was to find Marias Pass, a possibly legendary opening in the mountains between Montana's western border and the plains of eastern Washington State. An Indian legend spoke of a gap at one of the headwaters of the Marias River, and in the 1850s, a surveyor named Isaac I. Stevens (not a relation) claimed he'd heard of the site—stating that "a little dog" had told him about it. No whites believed him and most of the local Indians were of the Blackfoot tribe, who maintained the area was full of evil spirits and off-limits to them. Meriwether Lewis had tried to find the pass, without success, but named the river after a cousin of his, Maria Wood.

Accordingly, the linchpin of James J. Hill's effort to take his northern railroad to the Pacific was to find Marias Pass, if such existed. John Frank Stevens started out late in the year 1889, in November. Unable to secure a Blackfoot guide, he found a Kalispel Indian named Coonah to take with him. Coonah had been living among the Blackfoot, supposedly having fled his own tribe because he had killed a member of his clan. As a guide, he was useless, totally ignorant of the country, and physically, too, he lacked enough stamina to keep up with Stevens and had to be left at their campfire. Wearing snowshoes, the Mainer struggled ahead and on December 11, 1889, discovered that Marias Pass was indeed real. He tromped through it until satisfied he was on the Pacific slope. Too far from their camp to return, he walked around and around all night to keep from freezing and in the morning returned to find Coonah's fire had gone out and the Indian was almost frozen. Finally, the two got back safely to the Blackfoot Agency. All along, the temperature had been more than 36 degrees below zero.

Stevens sent word to James J. Hill, describing his vision of how the projected railroad could navigate this stretch of the Rockies. His reward was not only the sculpture eventually erected but also a job as chief of surveys for the Great Northern's remaining traversal of the distance to the Pacific. Some pretty rough terrain still had to be crossed, especially the Cascade Mountains, and once more, Stevens discovered a way. So the company gave him another honor. They called this breakthrough via the Skykamish River, Stevens Pass.

Naturally, James J. Hill had good reason to be pleased with John Frank Stevens. The Marias find was characterized as "the lowest and best pass across the Rockies in the United States," and it shortened Hill's route by a hundred miles, saving him untold thousands of dollars. Whoever had the idea for the statue isn't clear, but it was placed at the exact spot where Stevens had paced all that frigid night.

The Maine man's value to his boss seemed to increase almost every year. In 1893 Stevens was appointed Great Northern's chief assistant engineer, and in 1895 became chief engineer. In 1897 he helped supervise work on a tunnel through the Cascades. A year later, though, James J. Hill misjudged his man. Stevens wanted time off for a vacation. Hill said No. Stevens said goodbye and quit. Hill predicted he would be back in a year.

For the next five years, these two strong-willed men were like a comedy routine. The engineer went to work in British Columbia, but his ex-boss kept calling him for advice. An increased salary and bonuses for his old job were dangled as bait by James J. Hill, but to no avail. This was followed by an offer to make Stevens the chief manager of a new railroad Hill had acquired, the Chicago, Burlington, and Quincy—also turned down. Hill was furious and Stevens was sure their days of working together had ended. Instead, Hill came right back with an offer of general manager of the whole Great Northern operation while being chief engineer simultaneously. It was an offer Stevens couldn't refuse.

The railroad Stevens now managed, as second only in authority to owner Hill, had doubled in size since he'd joined the staff seventeen years earlier. It now ran six thousand miles of track.

But the West Gardiner man grew restless in his top jobs. He even worried that Hill would promote him further, into a very top desk job that would "require the practice of diplomacy which I was temperamentally unfit to exercise."[1]

Freed of his Great Northern responsibilities in 1903, John Frank Stevens was consequently available when one of the greatest engineering challenges in world history was ready to acquire his services.

The building of the Panama Canal had begun in 1904—and stalled.

Initially, the federal government had asked Stevens to head up a commission in the Philippines to build railroads throughout those islands. Before he could leave for the Far East, however, he was contacted by a prominent New York lawyer, William Cromwell, on behalf of President Theodore Roosevelt. The isthmian project's chief engineer, John F. Wallace, had just resigned and "Jim" Hill had recommended Stevens to be his replacement. Cromwell, co-founder of the famed law firm Sullivan and Cromwell and the president's chief negotiator concerning the canal, asked the Maine native point blank if he'd accept.

Not until he had talked to his wife, Stevens said. He and the former Harriet T. O'Brien of Dallas had been married almost thirty years by then. She urged him to take on this great task. A move to Panama wouldn't faze her. She had been adapting to out-of-the-way places and raising children in them ever since their wedding day in 1877.

Besides, in Stevens's opinion, conditions in Panama could be no worse than what might have confronted him in the Philippines. He'd been in tropical climates before, and encountered malaria. Still, before acquiescing, he went to Oyster Bay, Long Island, and had a long talk with Teddy Roosevelt. The president agreed to the main condition Stevens insisted upon: the engineer would not promise to stay until the canal was finished, but only until the success—or failure—of the project had been assured.

Neither the tropical climate nor ever-present yellow fever had caused Stevens's predecessor to resign abruptly. John F. Wallace had clashed with the Isthmian Canal Commission, which had oversight of the dig, and had exchanged particularly harsh words with the group's ultimate boss, Secretary of War William Howard Taft.

Once Stevens came on board, he traveled to Panama, accompanied by Theodore P. Shonts, the head of the Isthmian Commission. They found an absolutely chaotic situation.

The work to traverse Panama had actually been started almost twenty-five years earlier, in January 1880, by a French company, whose leader, Ferdinand de Lesseps, had built the Suez Canal (1859–69). This attempt to duplicate his feat in Central America having failed, de Lesseps sold his rights to the U.S. government in 1893. When Stevens arrived in 1905, he was appalled to find the work the Americans had started in 1904 had been done as inefficiently as the rudimentary efforts of the French. Even more appalling was the extent and nature of his task, which seemed to have little to do with engineering.

Yellow fever had absolutely decimated the French workers. Up to that time, medical science had not discovered how mosquitoes were linked to fatal diseases like malaria and yellow fever. From 1881–89, de Lesseps's company had watched 22,000 of its employees die.

Stevens's Panama career commenced stormily enough. His successful opposition to a union shop came only after a major battle with the American Federation of Labor. Yet one of his top priorities was to build adequate housing for all of the workers and to provide them with sanitary conditions. This pioneering public health campaign had him working closely with Dr. William Gorgas, who was often derided by his profession for his insistence that mosquitoes were carriers of disease. In defending Gorgas and keeping him in Panama, the tough engineer had to show some of the diplomatic and political savvy he claimed not to have.

It seemed that not only his fellow doctors were upset by Gorgas's single-mindedness about mosquitoes. Secretary of War Taft and Theodore Shonts of the Isthmian Commission also wanted the forward-looking doctor canned. Stevens intervened with Teddy Roosevelt, telling him, "You must choose between Shonts and Gorgas." The president consulted several of his medical friends. They told him: "Keep Gorgas."

A huge effort was soon underway in Panama to get rid of mosquitoes and their breeding places. The deadly fever ravages diminished accordingly. Dr. Gorgas proclaimed Stevens a hero for having supported him.

On another absolutely key canal question, Stevens had to be as much or even more of a politician. In choosing Panama as the Central American route for ship traffic between the Atlantic and the Pacific, a fundamental decision had to be made before all else. Was it to be a sea-level canal, essentially built straight from one side to the other at the same depth? Or was it to have locks, with the water inside them moving up and down, allowing the ships, in effect, to navigate different heights of land?

This was, or should have been, an engineer's choice. The French had started their canal out as a sea-level type. But Stevens viewed the scene and particularly feared a problem caused by the periodic flooding of the Chagres River. He felt the answer was an 85-foot-high lock and so informed his superiors at the Isthmian Commission. But its members were all for a sea-level canal. So, too, was President Theodore Roosevelt.

Stung by the news of the president's choice, Stevens hurried to see him, argued, appealed, and finally convinced the former Rough Rider that the lock solution was the only one. Then Stevens had to make the same case to Congress. The measure barely passed in the Senate but Congress finally did adopt a lock canal and high-level lake approach. Furthermore, Teddy Roosevelt appointed Stevens to the Isthmian Commission.

Having won his bureaucratic battles with Roosevelt's help, Stevens used the tool he knew best—railroad work—to push along the overall construction. One of the first phases, already started by the French, was the Culebra Cut, and an immense problem was what to do with the dirt and debris they excavated. Stevens devised a small railroad to take away these spoils and thus they handily removed 100 million yards. He also revived an abandoned Panamanian railroad that had once run from

Panama City on the Pacific to Culebra on the Atlantic.

America's master historian, David McCullough, writing about this period in his book on the building of the Panama Canal,[2] includes an interesting sidelight on the relationship between the president and John Frank Stevens.

"Theodore Roosevelt had taken a great liking to John Stevens. Stevens, in addition to his other attributes, was a reader of books" and, like Roosevelt, Stevens would read a book he enjoyed over and over again. "Stevens's favorite of all was *Huckleberry Finn*, which he read continually, and this to Roosevelt was the mark of the finest literary discernment."[3] The president also characterized Stevens as a "backwoods boy," "a rough and tumble westerner," and "a big fellow, a man of daring and good sense."[4]

Nevertheless, it was a bit dicey for this inveterate politician to have to handle a man accustomed to the freedom of action of a corporate executive in the heyday of free enterprise.

By contrast, the canal was a government enterprise, publicly financed, and having to play by D.C. rules. The free-booting policies of a James J. Hill, under which Stevens had gained his business experience, did not apply. For example, first of all was the question of letting out the construction contract.

Stevens essentially wanted a monopolistic situation—one where a syndicate of contractors would be organized and made answerable to him. He would pick the best companies for each individual task and there would be no bidding. Although Stevens had prevailed in earlier controversies, he did not get his way again. Roosevelt opted for putting out the contract with open bidding.

Another political disturbance was created by Stevens's handling of a labor dispute. As we have seen, he wanted no truck with unions. One day, he was besieged in his office by steam-shovel operators and engineers. They demanded a pay raise and threatened a strike. Stevens was a big man, powerfully voiced, and after he heard them out, he simply thundered, "You all know that strikes don't get you anywhere. Now, get the hell out of the office and back to work!" The incident was reported to the men's union in the U.S. and complaints were made to Roosevelt, who was more pro-labor than most Republicans. Counterpressure was brought by Stevens, and no doubt other pro-business persons, and the president responded by issuing an executive order rearranging the Isthmian Commission to make it more efficient.

The principal change was to strengthen the power of the chairman and make the heads of the different departments all members. Since the chief engineer was the most important of these, it gave Stevens much of the centralized clout he desired. The chain of command effectively became Roosevelt–Taft–Shonts–Stevens. The order to effect this transformation was delayed, however. It would get better press, the White House thought, if it were signed during Teddy Roosevelt's unprecedented trip to Panama in November 1906.

With TR's accustomed fanfare, he and his wife set forth on the new battleship *Louisiana* for a two-week voyage. Deliberately, the president had chosen the rainy season as the time to make his "inspection," wanting to see the work in the very worst of conditions. He wasn't disappointed; it poured throughout his visit. Yet there were plenty of photo ops and one became quite famous. It showed Teddy at the controls of a giant steam shovel. Presidents of the United States had been pictured in many odd poses, but never anything like this.

These shovels were working on both sides of the Culebra Cut. Roosevelt was traveling on a train—most likely one employed in removing dirt—when he spied some of the huge machines and ordered a halt. It was raining hard, but TR jumped out and proceeded to climb up onto the nearest steam shovel. Its operator, A. H. Grey, moved aside for the nation's chief executive. During the next twenty minutes, Teddy Roosevelt remained at the controls, asking nonstop questions while he tried to manipulate the mechanical digger. All of this was caught in a camera shot flashed around the world.

Engineer Grey, incidentally, did manage to get a word in edgewise. Probably still smarting from the confrontation with Stevens, he bent the president's ear about the fact that, unlike locomotive engineers, steam shovel operators received no extra pay for overtime.

It is unlikely this tidbit of bellyaching was the seed of an eventual breakdown of the relationship between Theodore Roosevelt and John Stevens. David McCullough is frank about intimating the impetus came from Stevens himself. "What went sour for Stevens," he wrote, "is a mystery that Stevens chose never to explain."[5]

Only three months elapsed between Roosevelt's gallivanting stay at the construction site and the rupture between the two men. The president had declared upon his return to Washington how pleased he was with the progress made in Panama. But it was not long before trouble, seemingly unaccountably, arose. On January 22, 1907, Theodore Shonts resigned to take a nongovernmental position. The president appointed Stevens to replace him. At last, one might think, Stevens had the full power and responsibility he had wanted. But one item had eluded him—the choice of contractor. The open bidding process he had opposed had awarded the prize to a New York City company called Oliver and Bangs. Stevens didn't like them—especially after they announced they planned to bring Southern Negro convicts to do the work.

A little more than a week after Shonts's resignation, Stevens fired off a six-page letter to Roosevelt. It was a strange document, full of what might be deemed whining. The chief engineer complained about the disruption to his home life the job was causing and the fact that he could be earning much more money doing something else. Enough hints were in his language so it could be considered that he was offering his resignation—but no *unless* was included. The final lines were absolutely infuriating to a man with as short a fuse as Teddy Roosevelt.

Stevens had written: "There has never been a day since my connection with the enterprise that I could not have gone back to the U.S. and occupied positions that to me were far more satisfactory. Some of them, I would prefer to hold, if you will pardon my candor, than the presidency of the U.S."[6]

The president called in Secretary of War Taft. They briefly conferred, then cabled Stevens that his resignation was accepted. However, the stubborn Mainer did win one battle. Instead of going ahead with Oliver and Bangs, it was decided the U.S. Army should run the show and, at Taft's suggestion, Lieutenant Colonel George Washington Goethals was put in charge.

Stevens's last day as chief engineer was March 31, 1907. Before he left for home, he was given a hero's farewell at a huge reception on April 6. A petition bearing 10,000 names was presented, pleading with him to stay. Instead, Stevens asked the crowd to extend the same loyalty to Goethals they had given to him, and he also made sure to praise Dr. Gorgas for his invaluable contribution.

In turn, Stevens was lauded, particularly by his successor. Goethals called Stevens the "Genius of the Panama Canal" and added he was "one of the greatest engineers who ever lived, and the Panama Canal is his monument."

On the other hand, Teddy Roosevelt never got over what he felt was a slight on his office—and his pride. He never spoke to Stevens again and never mentioned him, even in the section of his autobiography dealing with the canal.

It was unlikely that Stevens brooded over the snub. He hadn't been kidding—nor bluffing—when he maintained he could have a much better paying job in the United States. He was quickly offered the presidency of the Boston and Maine Railroad, and soon after, James J. Hill hired him away to run the Spokane, Portland, and Seattle Railway, and to beat rival railroader Edward H. Harriman in a race to go through central Oregon. But in 1912, Stevens left the West and settled in New York City, where he worked as a railroad consultant and he and his wife lived comfortably on Park Avenue.

James J. Hill died on May 29, 1916. He and Stevens were great friends, despite their occasional ups and downs, and the latter always had a photo of Hill on his apartment's living room mantel. Alongside it—surprisingly—was a picture of Theodore Roosevelt.

On January 18, 1917, Harriet O'Brien Stevens passed away. Their children were grown and one might have expected that at age sixty-four, all alone, John Frank Stevens would pass into a quiet and comfortable retirement.

But the next thing anyone knew, Stevens was in war-torn Russia, tasked with the responsibility of getting this giant country's railroads untangled from the mess they were in.

The imperial government of Russia, then engaged on the Allied side in World War I, came to a crashing end on March 18, 1917, when Czar Nicholas abdicated. A new provisional government was put in place and America's secretary of state, Robert Lansing, learning the railroad problem was hurting Russia's war effort, wanted an American commission to solve the crisis. Eventually, two commissions went, one to deal with political matters, headed by former secretary of state Elihu Root, and the other to concentrate solely on getting the railroads in shape. This commission was led by Stevens.

Like Kenneth Roberts and the American military expedition dispatched by President Woodrow Wilson, Stevens and his commission entered Russia via Vladivostok. The Trans-Siberian Railroad was the main lifeline to the heart of Russia in the west and it had to cope with a shortage of locomotives and cars and a pile-up of supplies in the Pacific ports. Even to begin his work, Stevens needed to cross all of Russia to the capital at St. Petersburg, (then called Petrograd, and later Leningrad), an arduous trek he finally made.

The politics on the American side were almost as complicated as on the Russian. Stevens quarreled with Elihu Root and with David Francis, the American ambassador, a former Democratic governor of Missouri and friend of Woodrow Wilson's, who was said to be jealous of Stevens.

The latter proposed an ambitious plan—too ambitious—for the Americans to supply Russia with 2,000 locomotives and 40,000 railroad cars. Nothing came of it, and after this whole Russian whirlwind was over, Stevens would write sarcastically, "Both the Wilson and Harding Administrations supported me wholly—That is, they left me completely alone—on my own."[7]

Without the resources he requested, Stevens did the best he could. He failed to unsnarl a tie-up of 8,000 to 12,000 freight cars in Moscow but he later did get six million bushels of wheat delivered to the hungry Muscovites.

The outbreak of the Bolshevik revolution caught Stevens in Moscow. He fled east and ended in Manchuria, in the city of Harbin. Earlier, he had set in motion the organization of a Russian Railway Service Corps of American engineers to assist the Russians, and he was in Harbin when the group left San Francisco. He met their ship in Vladivostok, briefed them, then they all took the same ship when she left, intending to go back to the States. Stevens felt his mission was over since the Communists controlled so much of the country.

Still, they disembarked in Japan first and stayed until the Bolsheviks were driven out of Vladivostok. Then Stevens and the corps went back into Russia.

Besides the American troops who arrived in Siberia at this period, there were also Japanese soldiers (Kenneth Roberts disliked them intensely) and, most significantly, a military body known as the Czech Legion. These were Czechs and possibly Slovaks, captured by the

Russians while fighting in the Austro-Hungarian army and held in Siberia. Enough had been freed to form a fighting force, and its primary goal was to regain their homeland. They had fought the Bolsheviks and driven the Reds out of Vladivostok. Moving west by train, they managed to pass through the Japanese and white army (Czarist) lines without firing a shot. Stevens stayed on during all this confused civil war activity until 1922. He had gone back to Harbin in Manchuria, where he disbanded the Russian Railway Corps in March and finally left in the late fall as soon as the Japanese had evacuated their last troops.

On the way home, he was wined and dined by Chang Tso-lin, the Manchurian warlord, and feted in Japan, as well.

By December 1922, John Frank Stevens's last great adventure had ended. But not the honors that were to come to him. The statue in Montana was erected in 1925 and a big ribbon-cutting ceremony held in July of that year. Three months later, West Gardiner had a gala homecoming for its illustrious native son. Maine Supreme Court justice Albert Spear, a boyhood classmate of Stevens's, was the organizer, the local Grange hall the venue, and the crowd estimated at two hundred. Governor Ralph Owen Brewster spoke, and Justice Spear presented the honoree with a "Resolution of Respect."

His heartfelt thanks included these words: "Never in the past had I visualized in my mind such a welcome back to the dear old town and its warm-hearted people. To feel that one is not forgotten by his old acquaintances, no matter what time or distance intervenes. It's a great source of happiness."[8]

Away from Maine, still in 1925, was Stevens's winning of the John Fritz Gold Medal, the highest mark of achievement for any engineer in America. Previous recipients had been notables such as Lord Kelvin, George Westinghouse, Alexander Graham Bell, Thomas Alva Edison, Orville Wright, Guglielmo Marconi, and George W. Goethals.

In his acceptance remarks, Stevens cited these forerunners of towering stature. In speaking of a recipient's duty to respond, he first joked that "about all that is required of him is that he should look pretty," and then he pointed to the medals he was wearing and added, with a kind of droll Maine humor, "I am somewhat in the condition of the gentleman who came into conflict with the law who upon being asked whether he was guilty or not guilty, replied that he could not tell until he had heard

MAINE IN THE WORLD

what the lawyers had to say...."[9]

Reminiscing, he spoke of the more than half a century (fifty-four years) "since I, a raw lad, without money, influential friends, or technical training...cast my hat into the ring and decided upon an engineering career."[10] And he felt lucky that his work took him "from the petty trumpery of civilization into the wide open spaces and among the mountains." His ending was to state "that while material wealth has passed me by...I have not lived wholly in vain and...can claim membership with those great minds who have previously been so signally honored at this place."[11]

John Frank Stevens lived another eighteen years, not dying until 1943 at the age of ninety. He won more honors, gathered honorary degrees, and received more medals, including the French Legion of Honor, the Japanese Order of the Rising Sun, the Czech War Cross, and the Chinese Order of the Striped Tiger.

His most cherished honor was to have been elected president of the American Society of Civil Engineers. He admitted it was one attainment he had always wanted but never thought possible because he lacked an engineering education. A Normal School teaching certificate was his highest earned degree.

If you go into the Maine State Library in Augusta, be sure to take a look at this extraordinary son of Maine in statuette form.

1. Odin Baugh, *John Frank Stevens: American Trailblazer*. Spokane, WA: The Arthur H. Clark Company, 2005, p. 72.
2. David McCullough, *The Path Between the Seas*. New York. Simon and Schuster, 1977, p. 490.
3. Ibid.
4. Ibid.
5. Ibid., p. 503.
6. Ibid., p. 504.
7. Baugh, p. 214.
8. Ibid., p. 218.
9. Presentation of the John Fritz Gold Medal to John Frank Stevens, March 23, 1925, Engineering Societies Building, 29 West 39th Street, New York.
10. Ibid.
11. Ibid.

The Maxim family gathers around the machine gun.
Hiram Stevens Maxim is second from the left.
Courtesy Maine Historic Preservation Commission

16

SANGERVILLE

Sangerville, Maine, is one of those small towns in America that you drive toward and wonder whether you've passed through it. In this case, having taken a side road, Route 23, for a shortcut if you're heading to Moosehead Lake, it's hard to discover when you've outdistanced the collection of houses that is Sangerville and entered the more industrial-looking community of Guilford.

Yet Sangerville is not just your ordinary run-of-the-mill Podunk, although it is certainly still today a very rural place in the heart of Pisataquis County, another of Maine's least inhabited areas. In the year 2000, Sangerville's census reported a population of 1,270 persons. Six years later, it had actually dropped to 1,256. However, one of its satellites, South Sangerville, was cited that same year of 2006 because it won a tie for fifth place in the increase of Grange membership throughout the state—six new members.

Another example of Sangerville's bucolic status comes from an article in the *Boothbay Register* on February 7, 2007. Pat Waldman, who writes a column in that Lincoln County newspaper, starts out: "We took our annual journey up to Sangerville" and adds that a snow-and-sleet storm was encountered. The sight of an iceboat on Adams Pond brought back "fond memories of many iceboat sightings in the past."

Another sighting, or the report of one, wasn't as pleasant—"a large coyote pack" in the nearby woods, and all pets had to be kept indoors.

Pat Waldman also went to Sangerville to take in the "Homemade Jam Session" in the East Sangerville Grange Hall. "The show includes warm-hearted humor and tall tales, foot-tapping rhythmic music, friendly neighbors, fresh-baked desserts and hot coffee and tea" and constituted a delightful throwback to times "when entertainment was of a simpler nature and more fun."

I myself can never think of Sangerville without remembering my dear friend, the late Honorable Donald Hall, when we were in the Maine legislature together. "Hallsy," as his wife Dot called him, was a

Sangerville-born-and-bred Christmas tree farmer who represented the town and its surrounding communities for many years. Don Hall was one of the kindest, nicest, and wittiest men I have ever met. His store of Maine expressions made him famous among our more urbanized and suburbanized members. Two lines among those I can remember and print were said of someone (member, lobbyist, etc.) who was none-too-bright, "He's number than a pounded thumb"; and of an incompetent,: "useless as teats on a bull." He was a gutsy legislator, too. Although a farmer himself, he sponsored a bill to restrain pesticide usage. During a hearing before an angry crowd of farmers (I was there, too, as a co-sponsor), Don got so riled up at their "foolishness" that he suffered one of the all-too-frequent heart attacks that helped end his career.

So much for Sangerville and its incontrovertible boondocks setting. But what sets it apart from any other out-of-the-way small town?

Let's begin with the nickname its own Sangerville Women's Club helped formulate and advertise on public plaques. The ladies made Sangerville into the "Town of Two Knights."

It seems totally inconceivable, but this little town of Sangerville sired two men who not only went on to world fame, but also, as British citizens, won honors that entitled them to be called "Sir."

These two men are Sir Hiram Maxim and Sir Harry Oakes.

Not to be nit-picky, but the "Town of Two Knights" is not quite technically accurate. Sir Hiram Maxim is the knight, a title in the British pecking order just shy of nobility. On the other hand, Sir Harry Oakes was made a baronet, the lowest rung on the nobility ladder yet higher than a mere knight. Coincidentally, pre-Revolution Maine produced another similar pairing: Sir William Phips, a knight, and Sir William Pepperrell, a baronet. But, of course, we were then a part of England.

That the twentieth century should witness two Americans so honored—from a tiny Maine town, no less—seems more like fiction than anything else. Possibly, in both cases, their gritty Maine upbringing underlay the stubborn doggedness that kept them chasing such success until they achieved it.

The Maxims were another Huguenot family, chased from France, that found itself eventually in Maine. Following a brief stay in England, the early Maxims headed to Massachusetts but ultimately went north to Maine. Sir Hiram's father, Isaac Weston Maxim, settled in Sangerville, married Harriet Boston Stevens, daughter of Deacon Stevens of nearby Abbott Upper Village (his nickname was "Old Brimstone"), and began to raise a family. Hiram was born on February 25, 1840.

When the family left Sangerville, he was still young, but the memory of those days remained clear in his mind. In a later letter to his son Hiram Percy, he wrote about "the kind of life" he lived in Sangerville— "a poor little bare-headed, bare-footed boy with a pair of blue drill trousers, frayed out at the bottom, open at the knees, with a patch on the bottom, running wild but very expert at catching fish. I think I was nine years old when I left Sangerville."[1]

The family and Hiram's travels generally occurred in and around the same region of upper Maine: to French Mill, Milo, Orneville (no longer on the map), and East Corinth. Ultimately, the fourteen-year-old Hiram worked as an apprentice to a carriage-maker. Then the Maxim family returned to Sangerville and for the next four years, young Hiram worked at carriage-making and repairs in Abbott Lower Village. During this period, his first inventions saw the light of day—an automatic mouse-trap to rid the local gristmill of pesky rodents, an improved tricycle, and a silicate blackboard. At age twenty he was off to the "big metropolis," Dexter, Maine, where he was a decorative painter and wood-turner. Longer travels took him to Canada and various northern states before he finally settled down to a steadier job with his uncle Levi Stevens in Fitchburg, Massachusetts.

This last employment signaled his permanent departure from Maine, although the home state was never out of his mind. For example, in 1890, wanting to test the invention that made him famous—the machine gun—he chose Lake Wasookeag in Dexter for the tryout. Local folks watched from a safe distance while the Maxim gun sprayed 666 bullets per minute into the deserted waters. Hiram Maxim was just ten miles from his Sangerville home when that historic experiment took place.

While in Fitchburg, one of the gadgets he worked on was a "Drake's automatic gas machine." It wasn't surprising that this inventive chap would be hired by Oliver Drake in Boston. In this capacity, Hiram "designed several density regulators, as well as an automatic sprinkler for extinguishing fires."[2]

Soon, though, he was off to New York and a position with the Novelty Iron Works and Shipbuilding Company. But he had also gotten more worldly wise. His earlier inventions had not been patented. Now, when he made improvements like automatic gas machines and locomotive headlights, he protected and assigned them to the Maxim Gas Machine Company. Later, he opened a branch in England, too.

Traveling about New York State, he met Spencer D. Schuyler, president of the U.S. Electric Lighting Company, who made him chief engineer of a pioneering commercial effort to cash in on Thomas Alva Edison's invention. Their offices were in the old Equitable Building at 120 Broadway, and eventually the company was bought by Westinghouse. Schuyler had told Maxim that if he could "light a house in New York" with the *lamps* (lightbulbs) he was working on, he could sell their stock for 200 cents on the dollar.

This set off a competion between Maxim and Edison in developing the "incandescent carbon lamp." If a book by Sir Hiram's son, Hiram Percy, can be believed, his father lost the race to patent this revolutionary form of lighting by a single day.

The filial biography is entitled *A Genius in the Family: Sir Hiram Stevens Maxim Through a Small Son's Eyes*[3] and it should be noted the author never saw his father again after he reached the age of fifteen. A publisher's statement includes this quote: "Born in Maine in 1840, Maxim was a paragon of Yankee resourcefulness and of Yankee eccentricity."

The latter quality is well depicted by a scene out of Hiram Percy's memory. They were living in a wealthy section of Brooklyn at the time. His father was president of Maxim and Welch, builders of steam engines and gas generating machines. Down the sidewalk, home from work one evening, strode the pater familias, elegant in a long Prince Albert coat, a high silk hat on his head. But when he reached their picket fence, instead of opening the gate, he simply vaulted over, coattails flying and holding onto his topper.

"With my father, one never knew what was going to happen from one moment to the next," Hiram Percy wrote admiringly.[4]

One elaborate memoir concerned a challenge made to the young son by a Brooklyn drugstore proprietor. The boy wanted a dog he saw in the store. Its owner jokingly said he could have it upon receipt of a *two-headed* coin. Hearing of this, the future Sir Hiram went to work and created a penny with a Lincoln head on either side. That the druggist reneged on his promise didn't seem a problem for Hiram Percy, who was content to focus on his father's cleverness.

Other anecdotes told about the machine-gun inventor included an attempted holdup when Sir Hiram simply seized the gunman and threw him over a fence, and how, in New Jersey, seeking a man who had swindled their Irish serving girl, Sir Hiram opened up the man's water valve and gave drink to a bunch of cows he was trying to keep thirsty. Another image is that of this top-hatted businessman blowing beans at a policeman who was romancing a housemaid. Hiram Percy also described his father in church (the family often went to hear Henry Ward Beecher, brother of Harriet Beecher Stowe), and how the elder Hiram Maxim yawned a lot and fidgeted. One of his favorite sayings was "Remember the Sabbath and go fishing," rather than the familiar injunction to keep the Sabbath holy.

For a while, the family lived in Fanwood, New Jersey, before moving back to Brooklyn. Uncle Frank, his father's youngest brother, came from Maine to help paint the house. Hiram Percy remembers that "like all the rest of the breed, he [Frank] was remarkably profane. However, his profanity, like my father's, was never vulgar.... It was poetic; it had rhythm."[5]

Hiram Percy's memories also included a trip with his father to the 1876 Centennial Exhibition in Philadelphia. He was particularly impressed by the huge Corliss Steam Engine on display and by a 1,440-pound meteorite. Somewhere in his memory, too, was an image of Sir Hiram hypnotizing a chicken. There was a lasting mental picture of himself as a small boy (the Maxims were back in Brooklyn by this time) running behind his dad, who had his silk hat jammed down on his head, jogging toward Brooklyn Hall, and limping home; in Hiram Percy's words, "He certainly resembled a big and very mournful Newfoundland dog." Once back at their house on Union Street, his father yelled out to his mother, the former Jane Budden, "Jane, you almost killed me. It was you who made me go out and exercise!"[6]

His father, too, would bring home mercury to show his children, and the first time pretended it was hot to the touch. He would take them crabbing near Coney Island to catch blue crabs and at home give them arithmetic lessons, saying, "Let me show you how we used to do it when I was a boy down in Maine. Percy, go down to the kitchen and fetch me a handful of beans."

Maine was still very much in the Maxim family's purview. Sir Hiram's parents and a number of siblings had moved from Sangerville to the town of Wayne, just outside Augusta. Hiram Percy visited them in the summers, sometimes with his parents, sometimes alone. He recalled seeing a cage full of bears in the Lewiston train station when traveling with his folks. And Sangerville made an indelible impression of the sense of wild nature the Pine Tree State still exudes. "No spot on the face of the earth appeals to me quite so strongly as these Maine woods," he wrote. "Whether it is something inherited from my early ancestors who did their part in beating back this wilderness, I do not presume to say, but when vacation time comes, I think first of the Maine woods. They represent the last of the extensive wild areas in New England."[7]

Meanwhile his father, the offspring of that sylvan environment, was in America's largest city, working on such esoteric, boundary-breaking projects as standardizing carbon filaments, manufacturing dynamos and arc lamps, and perfecting a process for producing pure phosphoric hydrate.

One would not have predicted that Sir Hiram would ever become an expatriate. His first trip to Europe was in 1881, ostensibly to attend the Electric Exhibition in Paris. A letter home, dated September 7, 1881, was full of red, white, and blue, star-spangled patriotism. "I am an American and see things like an American. So I say Paris is all hollow show, a complete sell. New York is the finest city in the whole world and our own United States is the best country and don't you forget it."[8]

Yet two years later, when he began working on his automatic weapon invention, the die was being cast for his eventual estrangement from hearth and home. His patriotism had led him to offer his machine gun first to the U.S. War Department. The gunnery "experts" there deemed it not worthy of American military standards.

MAINE IN THE WORLD

While in Paris, where Sir Hiram made his earliest preliminary sketch of a machine gun, he had also made some English contacts, including Lord Moulton, who would later be director of Munitions Supply for the British in World War I. Another important person he met once he went to London was Albert Vickers, who headed the giant Vickers armaments manufacturing company. In time, Sir Hiram merged his Maxim Gun Company with Vicker,s and the resulting firm's name was Vickers, Son and Maxim Ltd. Well before World War I began, the Maxim and Vickers operation was producing machine guns in Kent, England. They were used to great effect in the Sudan at the battle of Omdurman, and remained the standard British army machine gun throughout World War I.

More than a decade before that conflict, in 1900, Maxim changed his citizenship, and the following year, Queen Victoria knighted him in recognition of his services. Although his family had stayed in the United States, the inventor did not often return there. One time was in 1914, when he actually traveled to Sangerville for the town's centennial celebration and visited his birthplace in the Brockway Mills section. Those festivities also included a moving picture showing Sir Hiram and King George V inspecting the famous Maxim gun.

Two years later, Sir Hiram died at his home in Streatham, England.

It has been stated that in his lifetime, he took out 271 patents. Besides the machine gun, these included such useful devices as a prototype curling iron, an apparatus for demagnetizing watches, an aerial torpedo gun, coffee substitutes, and various oil, steam, and gas engines. Before the Wright brothers' success, he had produced a flying machine, but his airplane, powered by steam, was too bulky to be practical. In the end, even here he had a magic touch. His "Captive Flying Machine" turned into a big hit at British amusement parks.

Sir Harry Oakes

There is nothing in the story of Harry Oakes to indicate he knew of or admired Sir Hiram Maxim. Nor does anything suggest the contrary— being aware of his Sangerville townsman's extraordinary success and the reward Maxim received at the Court of St. James. It seems hard not to imagine a spark of subliminal knowledge in the mind of the younger son of William Pitt Oakes, even after the family moved "down the road apiece" and settled in nearby Foxcroft.

Sangerville had come into existence in 1801, named for Colonel Colin Sanger, who owned the land it occupied, and by 1808, four of the thirteen settler families were named Oakes. Some, at least, could be found among the gentry of this hardscrabble region. Harry's grandfather, Colonel William Oakes, was immortalized in a bit of local poetry that went:

> Colonel Oakes with beaver hat
> Gold-headed cane and silk cravat
> Was quite sublime, inspiring, grand
> Lord of mansion, stock and land

Harry's father, William Pitt Oakes, was a college graduate, something quite rare in those parts. He'd gone to the originally Baptist institution in Waterville—Colby College. A better education for his boys, Louis and Harry, was a prime motivation for the family's move to the Piscataquis County shiretown seven miles away. In what is now Dover-Foxcroft, the local high school was as highly regarded then as it is today. Harry was not only able to go on to college, like his father, but to a crackerjack school, Bowdoin College, which in many people's eyes, was the Harvard of Maine.

A degree from Bowdoin was almost *de rigueur* for admittance into the Maine "establishment," the small group that dominated the public life of the state during the end of the nineteenth century when Harry Oakes was a student. But this quiet, intensely private young fellow had no intention of carving a successful career for himself in his native state. He wasn't shy about having ambition, and on a bigger scale than was usual Down East. Asked what he planned to do after graduation, he invariably replied, "I am going to make a million dollars." Just as invariably, when asked how he'd do it, he'd say he didn't know.

One inkling was when he talked about gold prospecting. Lots of Mainers had been among the forty-niners who had headed west after the famous California strike. Fifty years later, this sort of adventure, forgetting the number of failures on the West Coast, still had appeal for a dreamy young man from Maine. At Bowdoin, Harry spoke of a recent find of gold "in a place called the Klondike." But once he'd finished his studies in Brunswick, he initially took a more practical path—to become a doctor, enrolling at Syracuse University's medical school and working his way through with a part-time job at the Carter Ink Company.

He did this for two years, hating every minute, and souring on the idea of practicing as a physician, which anyhow didn't pay very well in those days.

It so happened the Klondike gold rush he'd mentioned to his college classmates, begun in 1896, was going into its third year of success. At Bonanza Creek in the Yukon, the population had swelled to 30,000 souls, crammed into Dawson City, a once tiny village. Stories about this excitement were appearing in the eastern U.S. newspapers, along with advertisements to join the crowd. Harry Oakes, back in Foxcroft, Maine, decided he fit the bill for the rugged individualist who could win fame and wealth up there in northwest Canada.

Actually, Harry wasn't too physically rugged. He was short and slight, but wiry and stubbornly determined. In addition, he had family backing. His mother dipped into her savings to pay for his travel and equipment. Brother Louis, in the lumbering business in Greenville, promised to send Harry $75 a month, asking only that he be given shares in whatever Harry found. Sister Gertrude, who was going to work as a stenographer in Washington, D.C., agreed to part with any money she might have to spare.

Thus, off Harry went, and for fourteen years, he was not seen in Foxcroft again.

His route took him to New York City and by train across the U.S. to Seattle. The next leg brought him to Skagway, in Alaska, where he had to spend the winter before heading to Dawson, some 400 miles to the north. Harry's medical training came in handy. He found work at Skagway's hospitals, while during his spare time he read everything he could on geology and mining.

Spring arrived. In fits and starts, Harry made his way toward Dawson City (today, population 881, but back then, bigger than Vancouver). The new train from Skagway only ran as far as its tracks were laid. The neophyte prospector had to cover the rest of the journey on foot, lugging all his equipment.

In Dawson City at last, Harry learned he was a *cheechako*, or tenderfoot, with a lot to learn. One thing he discovered fast was that he didn't want to stay in Dawson. All of the fruitful gold-bearing areas had long since been staked out. Alaska was just across the border, so he went there. Geoffrey Bocca, in his biography *The Life and Death of Sir Harry Oakes,* writes, "Within a few months of his arrival, he was as hard bitten as any veteran. He learned the mystery of toughness."[9] And that mystery was not "the ability to punch and kick and knife"—and in any case, he was too undersized to indulge in much violence. No, toughness in the prospecting field was stick-to-itiveness, the knack of never weakening, and to live a Spartan existence day after day and year after year until he struck it rich.

If he ever struck it rich. Toughness, of course, included never entertaining such a doubt. A quick strike by Harry and a partner in Alaska netted them about $6,000 in gold dust, but most of this was paid to workers they hired in exploiting a vein that turned out to be merely a small pocket of the precious metal, not a bonanza. In the fall of 1899, gold was discovered in Nome, and like thousands of prospectors and miners, Harry set out for the Alaskan location on the Bering Strait. He and another partner used a boat—and landed by mistake on the opposite shore of the Bering Sea in Siberia, where some Russian Cossacks briefly held them under arrest. Once back in Alaska, Harry endured more years of exhausting work with little or nothing to show for it.

Author Bocca writes, "In time, Harry Oakes became something of a legend in the Northwest for his single-minded fanatical determination.... Harry's capacity for hard work was regarded with something like awe."[10] Louis Oakes still helped his brother with regular donations and Gertrude Oakes sent as much as she could eke out of her meager salary.

Since Alaska wasn't producing a living for Harry, he finally was drawn to Australia. There were minor gold boomtowns at Coolgardie and Kalgoorlie, and Harry, now described as "an iron-hard little fellow with almost no physical weaknesses," found himself laboring in a climate as hot as Alaska and the Yukon were cold. His "hardness" extended to his personality: gruff, rude, quick-tempered, and ostensibly mean-spirited. Leaving Australia, Harry spent time in New Zealand and, temporarily, he abandoned gold-seeking and farmed, growing flax. Here, in a sense, he did strike it rich—banking $30,000. But it was just to be a nest egg for financing future prospecting.

One of his new efforts brought him into California's Death Valley. He wasn't much of a success in the desert, either. After yet another failed attempt in the Belgian Congo, he heard about recent gold strikes in Ontario. Despite his initial skepticism—"Ontario has a rotten reputation [for producing gold]," he insisted, yet decided at last to go see for himself. From Toronto, he rode a train to a small Ontario mining town that had the now rather unforgettable name of Swastika.

As Google puts it in a piece on Harry Oakes, it was in Swastika that he met Roza Brown. "Ms. Brown has been described as unusually ugly, malodorous, and was accompanied by snarling dogs." She was alleged not to like prospectors, but boarded them for a fee. She also claimed to have been born of royal Hapsburg descent and spoke with a Hungarian accent. Something attracted her to Harry Oakes, to the point of being friendly toward him, and this hard-bitten Yankee soon learned Roza knew more about gold mining in Canada than anyone else he had ever met.

In the course of one of their conversations, she suggested Harry should go east of Swastika to a place called Kirkland Lake and start looking for gold there.

Harry was skeptical. No gold had ever been found at Kirkland Lake, he argued. She countered that no one had ever prospected the site properly.

The story of Kirkland Lake and its fabulous finds is a complicated one. It involves an English veteran of the Boer War who emigrated to Canada in 1907 and four years later stumbled upon a rich vein of gold in the Kirkland Lake area. It involves Harry and a whole different kind of prospecting—this time, at Roza's suggestion, digging through the card files of the claims office to see if any claims had or were about to expire. Here he struck pay dirt—claims on the verge of ending, made in the name of the Burrows brothers.

But Harry totally lacked the money to do anything about this. Desperate, he approached another group of brothers, four miners, whose last name, of all things, was Tough, made them partners with him in exchange for the needed cash to stake claims, and set off with two of these Tough brothers in 52-below-zero weather to literally drive spikes into rocks in and around Kirkland Lake. They had laid out fifteen claims and were recovering from their exertions when William Wright appeared. He had learned of the claims lapse and was disappointed that Harry and the Toughs had beaten him, yet settled for nailing down some adjoining claims. Before long, Wright and Harry Oakes became partners, and all around Kirkland Lake, the two of them picked up new sites.

The rest of the story concerns Harry's "prospecting" for money—capital with which to exploit the gold contents of his properties. He even went back to Maine and tried to get a boyhood chum, Eugene Whittredge, now a prosperous dentist in Foxcroft, to invest—with no luck. In the role of a prospector seeking to develop his own finds, Harry was bucking history, at least in regard to Canadian gold-mining; no one had ever done so before. In 1914 Harry incorporated Lake Shore Mines Ltd., with an authorized value of $2 million in $1 shares. But only his family kept helping him buy needed equipment. He dropped the price of his shares to forty cents, and still found no takers. Most other men would have given up and sold out cheap.

When World War I commenced, Bill Wright, Harry's partner, joined up as a private to fight in the British army. Meanwhile in Canada, Harry soldiered on and then, drilling under Kirkland Lake, found a major vein on his property, 40 feet in width, producing ore that sold from $60 a ton to $20 a ton. Investors were suddenly interested, especially two financiers from Buffalo who brought a whole trainload of buyers to see the Kirkland Lake mine. Harry sold half a million shares on the spot.

Sheer grit had carried Harry Oakes forward to the point where, in 1921, he could relax. His millions had been made. His Lake Shore Mine was deemed the second richest in the Western Hemisphere. Those who had stuck with him had also become wealthy. Bill Wright returned safely from the war, was vice president of their company, and owned 250,000 shares. Brother Louis Oakes, sister Gertrude Oakes, Harry's mother—all profited immensely. Even Charlie Chow, a Chinaman who had accepted Harry's shares instead of cash at his bar and boardinghouse, benefited greatly.

Had Horatio Alger been writing Harry's story, it would have ended then.

His transition from a gold-mining roughneck in the wilderness to a gentleman tycoon was certainly the stuff of fiction. Those hard years had forged his character, according to Geoffrey Bocca. "What thin veneer of culture Bowdoin had given him many years before had long since worn away. The new luminary in the Canadian financial heavens knew nothing of polite conversation or how to dress. He had forgotten how to use a knife and fork. At elegant parties, to which he was invited, he would spit the pips of grapes across the table. Like many hardened prospectors, he looked years older than his age. His face was lined like an old man's and he would chew and mutter to himself...."[11] This was the Harry Oakes who set forth and built an elegant chateau at Kirkland Lake, but found it lonely and decided to take the first vacation of his life on a cruise around the world, perhaps with an unacknowledged secondary motive of finding himself a wife.

He did so on his second world cruise, which followed the death of his mother in 1923. Aboard ship, he met Eunice MacIntyre, an Australian from Sydney, who was three inches taller than Harry, a "great beauty," always pleasant and charming. She had been visiting her sister, who lived in Mozambique, and was on her way to England, but learned in Capetown that her father had died at home. She hurried off to Sydney, Harry went with her, and the two were married in Australia that June of 1923.

Initially, they returned to Kirkland Lake to live. The road to a real tycoon's life started with the birth of their daughter in 1924. Harry bought a palatial home in Niagara Falls, Ontario, where King Edward VII had once stayed with the previous owner. The Oakeses turned it into a Tudor castle and it included paneling from Cardinal Wolsey's room at Hampton Court in England. Also in that year, Harry decided that, for political and financial reasons, he would become a Canadian citizen.

From the richest Canadian to an English nobleman was a natural progression. En route, he had also assembled a number of stunning dwellings—the two mansions in Canada at Kirkland Lake and Niagara, three in the U.S.—The Willows at Bar Harbor (a favorite of his wife's), and two swanky addresses at Palm Beach; in England he had a posh pad in London's Kensington Gardens and a country home in Sussex. The peripatetic Harry Oakes had a hard time staying anywhere for an extended time.

His eventual farewell to Canada occurred over a money matter. Like

Portrait of Sir Harry Oakes
Courtesy Niagara Falls (Ontario)
Public Library

many a self-made multimillionaire, he hated taxes, and it griped him to discover he was the single largest taxpayer in the Dominion. Insult was added to injury when the party he favored—the Liberals—were turned out of office by the Conservatives. The Liberals had promised him a lifetime appointment as a senator. The Conservatives, however, under Prime Minister Richard Bennett, presented him instead with a quarter-million-dollar tax bill for lands and parks he had donated to the nation—and no doubt had taken a tax loss for doing so.

In his furious reaction, Harry first just moved out of Canada. He had met an Englishman in Palm Beach named Harold Christie who was an important figure in the Bahamas, and Christie persuaded the mining magnate to come live in Nassau. There Harry added to his collection of manors by buying Westbourne, a magnificent estate near the Nassau Country Club.

As a resident of the Bahamas, a Crown colony, Harry Oakes was now eligible to receive British honors and he angled for them, traveling back and forth to London and spreading his money around to important English charities. He also got himself elected to the Bahamian legislature.

This was in 1938. A year later, he achieved his goal. On June 8, 1939, Harry Oakes of Sangerville, Maine, was included on King George VI's Honors List. A baronetcy was given him: he was now Sir Harry Oakes, and Eunice MacIntyre of Australia became Lady Oakes.

Less than three months later, World War II broke out in Europe. The Bahamas made a nice haven, particularly once France fell and the Battle of Britain commenced. Those idyllic islands in the Caribbean also provided a convenient spot where the Churchill government could park England's former King, Edward VIII, who had abdicated in 1936 to marry the American divorcée, Wallis Simpson. Now known as the Duke and Duchess of Windsor, the couple had barely escaped from the south of France, and British intelligence was fearful the Germans might kidnap them if they stayed in Europe.

So Churchill's solution was to pack them off to the Bahamas by making the duke the governor of this Crown colony. One aspect of how this happenstance affected Harry Oakes was that he and Eunice temporarily gave up their Nassau home so their Royal Highnesses could have a place to stay while Government House was renovated to their liking. Another result was that, as Geoffrey Bocca writes, "an odd and yet understandable friendship sprang up between the former king of England and the rough old gold prospector."[12] It was not exactly that they became bosom buddies. You could only be friends with Sir Harry, Bocca says, if you "did not approach him too closely."

There now entered the lives of Sir Harry and Lady Eunice a personage with a name that sounded far more aristocratic than theirs: Count Marie Alfred Fouquereaux de Marigny.

Yet he was not French, but a British subject, a native of the Indian Ocean island of Mauritius, which had been English since the Napoleonic wars and contained a colony of French royalist émigrés and their descendants. In May 1942 de Marigny joined the Oakes family by marrying their oldest child, daughter Nancy. He was thirty-two and the bride eighteen, and she was his third wife. Lady Oakes was horrified, but Harry was much more accepting, reportedly telling de Marigny after they first talked, "Frenchie, you are an SOB for marrying my daughter, but I like you."[13] Such inconsistencies grew ever more consistent with

Harry in the following year—that is, the multimillionaire's strange behavior increased. Money worries were actually depressing him as the output of his mines diminished and—most bizarrely—he had personally taken to bulldozing all the trees on his Nassau property, whereas before he had declared—in reference to his Maine boyhood—that he loved trees. Sir Harry slept with a loaded automatic pistol on the bed table beside him. He drank heavily and was not a happy drunk. Only in Maine, it seemed, did he soften. His brother Louis still lived in Greenville (Gertrude had died in a ship accident), and he also enjoyed visiting Bowdoin, which gave him an honorary degree and put him on its board.

During the night of July 7, 1943, the handgun by Harry's bed was of no help to him. In the darkness, someone entered Harry's bedroom. Despite a raging rainstorm outside, the baronet was sound asleep when he was murdered.

Confusion remains as to exactly how Harry was killed. Four holes were found in his skull; some accounts say these were bullet holes; but a more plausible supposition is that they were made by a sharp pointed instrument rammed into the sleeping man's head again and again.

Whoever did it then tried to set Harry's body and whole house afire.

Harry's son-in-law, Count de Marigny, was accused of the crime and arrested. It is not really necessary to go into the convoluted details of his trial and acquittal on the basis of flimsy circumstantial evidence. It is merely important to point out that the police investigation was woefully blundered, due in large part to the Duke of Windsor's insistence, in his capacity as governor, on bringing in a pair of careless, unskilled police detectives from Miami. Their actions, especially in the poor job they did with fingerprints, has left the sensational killing of Sir Harry in a muddle of conjecture ever since de Marigny's trial ended with a verdict of not guilty.

Harry's charred body was interred in Maine, in a cemetery of the town now known as Dover-Foxcroft. Probably this homecoming would have pleased him. He has also left a few other memorials elsewhere: The Willows in Bar Harbor is now the Atlantic Oakes Inn; his former house in Kirkland, Ontario, is currently a museum dedicated to his life; and Niagara Falls, Ontario, has an Oakes Park on land he donated, an Oakes Garden Theater, and Oak Hall, his thirty-seven-room Tudor mansion, is the headquarters of the Niagara Parks Commission.

It has been more than sixty-five years since Sir Harry Oakes was brought to that Dover-Foxcroft mausoleum where he still lies. And it is over ninety-two years since Sir Hiram Maxim passed away. There are no signs yet that a *third* knight might emerge from Sangerville, Maine. But who would ever have thought, looking at this remote community in remote Piscataquis County, that even *one* of its native sons, never mind two, would reach the heights they did?

1. P. Fleury Mottelay, *The Life and Work of Sir Hiram Maxim, Knight, Chevalier de la Legion d'Honneur.* London: John Lane, The Bodley Head; and New York: John Lane Company, 1920, p. vi.

2. Ibid., p. viii.

3. Hiram Percy Maxim, *A Genius in the Family: Sir Hiram Stevens Maxim through a Small Son's Eyes.* New York: Harper and Brothers Publishers, 1936.

4. Ibid., p. 14

5. Ibid., p. 34.

6. Ibid., p. 80.

7. Ibid., p. 151.

8. Alice Clink Schumacher, *Hiram Percy Maxim.* Cortez, CO: Electric Radio Press, Inc., p. 11.

9. Geoffrey Bocca, *The Life and Death of Sir Harry Oakes.* Garden City, NY: Doubleday, 1959, p. 39.

10. Ibid., pp. 42–43

11. Ibid., p. 72.

12. Ibid., pp. 113–14.

13. Ibid., p. 122.

Movie director John Ford
Courtesy Maine Historic Preservation Commission

17

JOHN FORD

Had John Ford, the extraordinary Hollywood film director, ever made a crime or film noir picture, the murder of his fellow Mainer, Sir Harry Oakes, might have offered an apt subject for a gripping script. He could also have worked in his western milieu by showing the Sangerville native digging for gold in Death Valley. A cantankerous individualist like Harry and the theme of corrupting wealth once gained would have been grist for John Ford's mill.

But at the time of the mystery killing in Nassau, Ford was an officer in the U.S. Navy, making war documentaries, and that summer of 1943 he was traveling all over the U.S., to South America and even India, having just finished his epic *The Battle of Midway.* Neither is there anything to indicate he ever took notice of or actually knew about Sir Harry Oakes.

John Ford was a Portland boy and a different breed from the Maine people we have encountered so far, who, except for Native Americans and those of Huguenot background, were all descended from the first wave of Anglo-Saxon immigrants who settled Maine. The movie director's folks were in the next major wave to come—Irish Catholics driven by famine—and none too welcomed by the original Protestant population.

Ford's family lived on Munjoy Hill in Portland. Their name was Feeney. Years afterward, once he'd achieved fame, John Ford claimed he'd been born in Cape Elizabeth, Maine, as Sean Aloysius O'Fearna. Further research into Maine's birth records reveals this claim of a more Gaelic-sounding moniker to be a bit of Fordian blarney. The Cape Elizabeth registry has him plainly listed on February 1, 1894, under the name of John Martin Feeney, Jr. So does his enrollment at Portland High School and his death certificate.

His father had emigrated from Galway, leaving a small, impoverished farming community called Spiddal. Once in America, he went from Boston to Portland, met and married Barbara (Abby) Curran, who'd been born on the even more impoverished Aran Islands, and together they raised a family of six children (with five others dying in infancy). John Sr. would work at whatever he could, lobster fishing, farming (when living at Cape Elizabeth), and saloon-keeping in the Gorham's Corner section of Portland, another Irish enclave. (Since Maine was a dry state, his "saloon" must have been an early "speakeasy.") It was said that in his own Munjoy Hill neighborhood, John Feeney, Sr., also served as an "unofficial alderman."

Jack Feeney, as they called his namesake, was the youngest of the six children who had survived. At Portland High School, he earned another nickname—"Bull" Feeney—because of his fierce play as a fullback on the football team, which in his 1913 senior year won the state championship.

This bruising, surly looking Irish kid wasn't solely a jock. He had literary tastes and anything about show business attracted him; he soon found an usher's job at the Jefferson Theater. Stars of the stage, playing the New England circuit, often performed in Portland. One was De Wolfe Hopper, a leading man, and Jack was assigned the task of providing him with bottles of ale (illegal in Maine) and when he succeeded, he was rewarded with a dollar tip.

He had his first introduction to acting as a walk-on in a play starring Sidney Toler, later famed on the screen in the part of Charlie Chan. Ford told of a veiled woman in a beautiful fur coat coming to the 6:00 A.M. mass where he was serving, who turned out to be a tearful Ethel Barrymore. Yet even more than the stage, the movies fascinated him. Whenever he got a nickel, he would rush to the nickelodeon. His favorite silent films, no surprise, were westerns.

Scott Eyman, in his seminal biography of John Ford, writes of this period, "For a boy in provincial Maine, the movies, and California, the place where some of the movies were being made, seemed impossibly glamorous, a place of golden sunshine and boundless opportunity."[1]

While Jack was still in high school, an older brother of his, Francis ("Frank") Feeney, was actually establishing himself in the fledgling motion picture industry in California after stints in it in New Jersey and Texas. In the hills above Santa Monica, a studio had leased some 18,000 acres in which to shoot westerns. Thomas Ince was the impresario behind this venture, and the area, complete with the set of a western town, was called Inceville. Frank Feeney had changed his surname to Ford (after the automobile, he claimed), and he both directed and acted in these epics of the American frontier Ince kept producing.

For some years, the Feeney family had heard nothing from Frank, who had been a black sheep needing to leave Portland after he made a local girl pregnant, married her, and the marriage broke up. But by 1913 the news reached Munjoy Hill that Frank was doing well in Hollywood, directing and producing at Universal Studios. In June 1914 Jack Feeney was graduated from Portland High. Had he planned to go on to college? There is a mystery about whether or not he registered for the University of Maine. But for summer break, he decided to join his older brother on the West Coast and, he said, "bum a couple of weeks of free board" from "Francis Ford."

Once Jack decided to stay in the Los Angeles area, he, in turn, became "John Ford."

The November 1914 issue of the *Raquet*, Portland High's alumni magazine, carried the following notice of Jack, but hadn't yet caught up with his name change. It was reported that "John Feeney is closely associated with the Universal Film Company at Hollywood, California."[2]

This expatriate from the Pine Tree State carried an amalgam of two traditions across country. As Scott Eyman wrote, "Jack would always emphasize his Irishness.... But he was always that staunchest of New Englanders, a Maine man, with an abiding memory of a New England town, that is to say an ideal community of enduring values...," and also "his Maine upbringing had given him a valuable lesson in modesty, for you do not put on airs if you live in Maine; the worst thing a Yankee can be is a snob. He had, in short, learned the emotional dynamic that would inform practically every film he would ever make."[3]

The young whippersnapper from Portland, Maine, started by learning the business from the ground up; any odd job would do: handling props, doing stunts, acting in bit parts, go-fer, assistant directing. Scott Eyman writes that "the Californians took one look at the skinny redhead and came to a cruel but more or less accurate estimation: hayseed."[4]

His brother Frank was the director for many of the pictures made at Universal in those days. There is some indication brother Jack also had parts in some of D. W. Griffith's productions. In the most classic of these, *The Birth of a Nation*, young Ford was apparently a hooded Ku

Klux Klansman night-riding in the South. Later, he would claim the hood blinded him and he fell off his horse, came to, and found Griffith hovering and calling for whiskey, but the whiskey was for Griffith himself. This story, as so many of John Ford's were, had to be taken with a grain of salt. Indisputable, though, was the fact that the Munjoy Hill cowboy was a terrible rider—looked like "a sack of walnuts" on a saddle.

Still, he did often talk about the fun of those early years in the picture business—even enjoying the horse-riding stuff, when he and other extras would be Union cavalrymen galloping in one scene, then change their uniforms from Yankee blue to Confederate grey and charge back. Jack would often be a double for Frank, who acted as well as directed. One time, standing in for his brother in a Civil War movie, he was blown up when too much gunpowder was used, and ended in a hospital for six weeks with a broken arm.

Several stories are told about John Ford's debut as a film director. One of them includes horses again. Carl Laemmle, the German-born Universal top executive, was visiting a western set on which Jack Ford was working as a prop boy, but this brash Irish kid pretended he was a director and ordered the cowboys in the scene to congregate at the end of the main street and come racing toward the camera, plus some were to fall off their horses on cue. This was Ford's own story, and he embellished it by adding that an impressed Laemmle, when the company needed a director for a two-reeler, said, "Try Ford. He yells loud."[5] The other version is that Frank got him his first directing opportunity.

Several western two-reelers later, the first *feature* film Jack directed, starring Harry Carey, was made in 1917. It was called *The Soul Herder*. Ford and Carey would make four films together during the next four years.

Several of these collaborations began earning Jack Ford the reputation of a talented director from whom good westerns could be expected. *Straight Shooting* was done in 1917 and *Hell Bent* in 1918, and were pictures of note. Workaholic Ford soon cranked up his production skills, turning out sixteen features in the next two years, plus a number of two-reelers. Reviews in trade papers were consistently flattering to him.

The Iron Horse, a full-length feature film appearing in 1924, has been called John Ford's earliest masterpiece. It is another western, to be sure, but with a whole different theme—the coming of the transcontinental railroads that in historical reality put an end to the Old West. There was an epic story here, based on the real-life drama of two railroads, the Central Pacific and the Union Pacific, meeting at Promontory Point, Utah, on May 10, 1869, where a golden spike was driven to unite their opposite tracks. The symbolism was raw and plain—that of a nation unifying at last after a horrendous civil war.

Ford, who used locations in Mexico, New Mexico, northern California, and Nevada, caught that same epic spirit in his style of camerawork; much of the film was shot in snow, giving it an added quality of gritty realism. He hired genuine Indians to play themselves, although he also slipped them in to supplement the skimpy number of Chinese extras he had to play coolie railroad workers. Over a mile of actual railroad track was laid and the two locomotives available were photographed from various angles to look like more than just the pair. The star was a new actor, George O'Brien, a first-generation Irish-American like Ford, whose father was the police chief of San Francisco. He and Jack Ford were to become best buddies.

The Iron Horse opened in New York City and received glowing compliments in the press. Its premier in Los Angeles was at Grauman's Chinese Theater and, amid a swirl of hyped publicity, a genuine locomotive, the *Collis P. Huntington,* named for one of the Central Pacific's tycoons, was towed down Hollywood Boulevard. Again, we hear from Scott Eyman: "With *The Iron Horse,* Ford found his theme: a people triumphing over sectionalism and parochialism to stand together, not just on May 10, 1869, but for all time."[6]

The kid from Maine was signed to a new contract, starting at $1,500 a week, big money in the 1920s.

The new decade brought some other changes into Jack Ford's life. For one thing, he left Universal and went to work for William Fox, whose studio eventually morphed into Twentieth Century Fox. But the most momentous event in the long term, as it turned out, was his marriage. The bride, who had been married previously, bore the unprepossessing maiden name of Mary Smith. But she was the daughter of a Wall Street financier and from a distinguished Anglo-Saxon line of North Carolinians. She was a Protestant, too, as well as a divorcée, so they weren't married in a Catholic church, but at a ceremony where Irving Thalberg, the future illustrious studio head, was a participant.

At the Ford house on Odin Street in Hollywood, there was always a steady stream of visitors. Possibly the most interesting was an old fellow, a retired cop, or, more exactly, a former frontier marshall, and his name was Wyatt Earp. Years later Ford would make one of his most enduring westerns about this hero from the gun-slinging Wild West days. In *My Darling Clementine,* Earp would be played by Henry Fonda; the setting was Tombstone, Arizona, and the picture's extraordinary climax, the epic gunfight at the OK Corral. It was western myth-making at its finest, based on historical events and once-living personalities.

Ford's road to the role of chief poetic interpreter of the American West advanced another big step in 1927, albeit disguised at the time. Ford was directing a war movie called *Four Sons,* which had been posited as an *art film,* and was never much of a success in the end. On the set, a husky young college kid was earning summer money as a prop boy and handyman, His name was Marion Morrison, and he played football for the University of Southern California. Millions of moviegoers since 1929, when he got his first acting gig, know him as John Wayne.

John Wayne and John Ford, in due time, would be thought of as almost synonymous. However, Ford's first film to win him an Oscar for best director was *not* a western.

The Informer takes place in Ireland, although shot on a sound stage at RKO Studios. Adapted from a short fiction piece by Liam O'Flaherty, *The Informer* was also marked by the unforgettable performance of Victor McLaglen in the lead role, which earned *him* an Oscar for best actor. *The Informer,* according to Scott Eyman, gave Ford "a critical reputation he would never lose and bestowed on him a leadership role within the industry."[7]

All of this happened in 1934. It was not until 1939 that the first of Ford's truly bombshell westerns made their debut.

Among the movie projects proposed at this time was one that involved Maine. In 1921 Ford tried to promote interest in a film based on Henry Wadsworth Longfellow's beloved poem, "The Village Blacksmith," claiming "every man, woman, and child who can speak English throughout the world has read 'The Village Blacksmith' and one out of every three people know the entire poem by heart." As a Portlander like the poet, Ford deemed himself perfect for directing the picture, and besides, the work was in the public domain, free for the taking— but no one bought his sales pitch.

The Iron Horse had been good, but it was a silent flick. With dialogue, so much more could be done. Ford had seen the possibilities in another short story, this one called "Stage to Lordsberg," which he'd read in *Collier's* magazine. It had been written by Ernest Haycox, and Ford bought the movie rights to it out of his own money ($7,500), had one of his favorite screenwriters, Dudley Nichols, whip up a script, and picked John Wayne, then at Republic Pictures, stuck doing B westerns, to have the key role of the Ringo Kid.

Meanwhile, in the jumbled business world of Hollywood, there were complications. Ford had connected himself to an independent producer, Merian C. Cooper, maker of the original *King Kong* movie. Cooper, in turn, in 1936, had merged his Pioneer Pictures with David O. Selznick. The "Stage to Lordsberg" project met fierce opposition from Selznick, who saw it as "just another western" and maintained it needed name stars like Gary Cooper and Marlene Dietrich, not relative unknowns such as John Wayne and Claire Trevor.

The film *was* made, no thanks to Selznick, produced by Walter Wanger at United Artists, and its title changed to plain *Stagecoach*. Shot on location in Monument Valley, Navajo country, it was an immediate critical success and even made money. It also made John Wayne, and today is considered a groundbreaking classic. Orson Welles said he saw it thirty times in order to study Ford's directorial and cinematic techniques before venturing into his *Citizen Kane* masterpiece.

The next Ford blockbuster was *The Grapes of Wrath*. Seemingly, John Steinbeck's novel offered material different from anything Ford had done before. Yet the "Okies" who fled the plains during the Great Depression for the promised land of California were, in fact, merely impoverished descendants of the settlers of the early West. Although John Ford was to give different versions of his political beliefs and have close ties to outspoken conservatives like John Wayne and Ward Bond, he initially always described himself as a Franklin Roosevelt Democrat. When *The Grapes of Wrath* opened in January 1940, Ford had another critical success. The *New Yorker* extolled it as "a great film of the dust plains, the highways, the camps, of the sky above, and of a nameless, evicted people," and other critics called it "one of the cinema's masterworks" and "a genuinely great motion picture." During the 1940

Academy Awards, Ford won his second Oscar for best director.

Before the year 1941 ended, with America suddenly and tragically entering World War II, Ford was able to make yet another hit movie, which increased his growing reputation. This was *How Green Was My Valley,* set not in Ireland but in another Celtic land—Wales. Once more, he was transposing a popular novel to the screen. It was also his first film with Maureen O'Hara. It was the only one of Ford's films to win an Academy Award for best picture. At the same time, he picked up another Best Director Oscar, on his way to a later record-setting fourth win in that category.

Pearl Harbor Day, December 7, 1941, found John Ford having dinner at the home of an admiral in Alexandria, Virginia. In some respects, he had already prepared himself for the conflict. Since 1939 he had been organizing a unit known as the Eleventh Naval District Motion Picture and Still Photographic Group. Even two months before the U.S. was at war, in September 1941, Ford had been inducted into the navy as a lieutenant commander and some of his field photo operatives had been out filming. The home this unconventional naval officer eventually found for his unconventional bunch of cameramen was in the OSS, as a photographic component of the cloak-and-dagger boys' outfit. Ford's boss there was as innovative and creative as Ford, himself—"Wild Bill" Donovan—a former Wall Street lawyer who rarely, if ever, played by the book.

Two of the documentaries Ford made during the war, *December 7th* and *The Battle of Midway,* won special recognition, and the latter picture has been called "one of Ford's greatest achievements."[8] It was filmed under battle conditions and Ford was right in the thick of the fray on that northern Pacific island at the end of the Hawaiian chain when the Japanese bombarded it from the air. Inside one of the main targets, the powerhouse, he was photographing the strafing enemy planes when a piece of flying concrete hit him on the head and knocked him cold. Coming to, he grabbed his camera back and began shooting again, only to be struck by shrapnel that left a three-inch hole in one of his upper arms. Taken to the infirmary, he was patched up, dosed with tetanus vaccine, and returned to keep on filming.

From the island of Midway itself, there was no way Ford could initially know the extent of the crucial American victory. It was the turning point of the war in the Pacific. Out of the raw footage he had shot, Ford spliced together the seventeen-minute film that gained him lasting acclaim and an eventual rank of rear admiral in the naval reserve.

Within six months, the director found himself back in the middle of war action, but on the other side of the world—North Africa—where in Tunisia he once more faced enemy fire. To hear him tell it, his penchant for overdramatizing, if not outright fibbing, had him under fire twenty-four hours a day for six weeks, on short rations and losing thirty-two pounds. He also displayed mock displeasure upon finding his producer, Colonel Darryl F. Zanuck, waiting for him in Algiers. Grumped Ford (allegedly), "If I ever go to Heaven, you'll be waiting at the door for me under a sign reading 'Produced by Darryl F. Zanuck.'"

Ford was at the height of his powers just before, during, and right after World War II. Some of his idiosyncrasies had reached the level of legends. Scott Eyman's title, *Print the Legend,* is a takeoff on a movie drector's approval of the *take* of a scene being filmed. "Print it!" will come as the command, and then on to the next piece of the script.

Some elements of Ford's style were, indeed, legendary: His consistently chewing on a handkerchief while directing. His pipe and the black eye patch (after losing the sight in one eye). The quixotic alcoholism that could involve him in benders lasting a week or more, but never when he was working. His unpredictability and cruelty, both psychologically and even physically, like the time he knocked down an old actor who had solicited him for money for an ailing wife, and then sent the man a large check. His occasional roving eye for females other than his wife, who tolerated these lapses, the most significant of which was a protracted relationship with Katherine Hepburn. There was also Ford's "gang" (his *stock company*), a precursor of Frank Sinatra's "Rat Pack," revolving around John Wayne, Ward Bond, and Henry Fonda, writer Dudley Nichols, and other pals, who often joined the director aboard his yacht *Araner* for binges of "serious drinking and serious fishing."9 The nickname of "Pappy," which was all John Wayne ended up ever calling him.

He made movie after movie, most of them above average, if not always rising to the quality of his Academy Award-winning productions—films in the "classic" category of *Young Mr. Lincoln, Stagecoach, Drums Along the Mohawk, My Darling Clementine, She Wore a Yellow*

Ribbon, They Were Expendable, Mr. Roberts, Fort Apache, The Searchers, The Man Who Shot Liberty Valance, and numerous others, all first-run features.

His last Academy Award—for best director—came in 1952. This was for *The Quiet Man.* Starring John Wayne and Maureen O'Hara, it is generally acknowledged to be his most popular picture. A *Saturday Evening Post* story formed the basis for it, in the February 11, 1933, issue, written by a Maurice Walsh and telling of a former boxer who returns to his home village in County Kerry and falls in love with and marries a local girl. It was an Irish tale Jack Ford had wanted for years to make into a film. In 1946 it looked as if impresario Alexander Korda might hire Ford and Merian Cooper's independent Argosy Pictures to produce the movie version for him in Ireland, with Spiddal, Ford's ancestral home, as the location. Nothing came of the idea. In the end, Argosy arranged with Republic Pictures to shoot *The Quiet Man,* again on location in Ireland and in Technicolor. Only now the setting was no longer in Galway at Spiddal but in County Mayo in a little town called Cong, home to what is now a major tourist hotel, Ashford Castle. Many of Ford's crew were billeted in this elegant hostelry, which had actually been reconstructed some years before, by a member of the Guinness family, upon the ruins of a thirteenth-century Norman castle.

Cong itself was transformed. The villagers had never had electricity and Ford supplied the wiring for them, to their expressed delight. But when told they had to pay for it henceforth, they indignantly protested they didn't need it.

Scott Eyman makes the comment about this movie that "casting was a nightmare of nepotism." Director Ford had two of his brothers—Frank and Eddie—playing parts. Maureen O'Hara had two brothers in the film, Barry Fitzgerald had one brother, and John Wayne had four of his children appear briefly. Victor McLaglen's son Andrew was second assistant director, and *The Informer* star himself was also on the set.

After the pcture was completed, Ford's own complicated relationship to his heritage is well represented in a letter he wrote to the wife of an Irish friend after the picture was made—how, once her husband had escorted him to his plane at Shannon Airport to go back to the States, he had burst into tears. "It seemed like the finish of an epoch in my somewhat troubled life. Maybe it was a beginning. Can I still come back? Don't be surprised if I show up in the very near future. Galway is in my blood and the only place I have found peace...." Then he added, "*The Quiet Man* looks pretty good. I even like it, myself."

As for his other *actual* homeland, Portland, Maine, Ford made yearly visits to "the beautiful town that is seated by the sea," as Longfellow dubbed it. He stayed at the Eastland Hotel and made pilgrimages up Munjoy Hill to the family manse on Sheridan Street. There was also another Feeney home on Peaks Island out in Casco Bay, where the family spent summers and raised a garden they fertilized with seaweed. On Peaks, too, was the Harold T. Andrews Post of the American Legion, where John Ford was a lifetime member.

The last years of John Ford's life were dogged by illness—an abdominal cancer had diminished him to a "shrunken figure" in a wheelchair when, on March 21, 1973, he was brought to the Beverly Hilton Hotel to receive the Medal of Freedom award from President Richard Nixon. Originally, Ford had not been a fan of Nixon's—he was an unabashed Jack Kennedy supporter, but now he felt grateful for Nixon's ending the Vietnam War (his grandson was involved), and upon receiving the medal, exclaimed, "God bless Richard Nixon!" The president, who said he had seen "virtually all" of Ford's 140-plus movies, must have appreciated the salute—he was in the middle of Watergate—but he had also by executive order elevated Ford from rear admiral to full admiral for the evening.

That same evening, as well, John Ford received the first ever Life Achievement Award from the American Film Institute.

Approximately five months later, on the last day of August 1973, John Ford died. Pappy was gone.

But the John Martin Feeney story, at least for Maine, doesn't end there.

In July 1998, a quarter century after his death, a John Ford Festival took place in Portland. The night of July 11, 1998, an audience of 800 packed the newly refurbished Merrill Auditorium in Portland City Hall for a special gala where a twenty-one-piece navy band and the choir of the First Congregational Church of Gorham, Maine, presented music from Ford's films.

The *Maine Sunday Telegram* had headlined the festival:
PORTLAND HONORS A MOVIE LEGEND
NATIVE JOHN FORD

Actors, film historians and
hundreds of others recall
the director of famous westerns

Speakers during the week-long celebration included actor Harry Carey, Jr., actor Claude Jarman, Jr., and Patrick Wayne, son of John Wayne and a godson of Ford's, who had likewise worked on his films. Also participating were two Navajos, paying their respects to Natani Nez, "Tall Soldier," their name for Ford. These were Billy Yellow, ninety-six years old, who spoke no English but chanted a prayer in the Navajo language, and Chief Jefferson Begay, who told how Ford had honored his people "by depicting them so accurately and beautifully."

The final ceremony was the unveiling on July 12 of Ford's statue in a monument plaza at Gorham's Corner. A 10-foot-high work, the sculpture shows Ford in his director's chair, while spaced around him are half a dozen granite blocks engraved with the names of the films for which he won Academy Awards, including the two wartime documentaries. A crowd of 300 at that Sunday dedication included the philanthropist who had put up the money for this permanent display.

Her name was Linda Noe Laine and she was from Louisiana. Her father, James Albert Noe, had been governor of Louisiana in 1936. She herself became friendly with John and Mary Ford when one of his pictures, *Horse Soldiers,* was being filmed in her state. On a trip to Portland in 1996, it upset her to discover his hometown had no memorial whatsoever to him, so she commissioned the statue and made arrangements for its placement at the confluence of the several streets forming Gorham's Corner, where Ford's father once dispensed illegal booze.

A small plaque on the site indicates, in a sense, the historical background of the Feeney family: "Here settled the first Irish immigrants of the 1840s. They lived here for a hundred years until they prospered and moved on."

This theme was picked up, too, by Mrs. Laine in her remarks, saying that John Ford's own life followed the script of many of his films, demonstrating how America allows any individual to rise to society's heights.

"To think that this son of Irish immigrants could rise to be one of the most celebrated American directors in one generation...Mary and

Jack would be very proud and pleased to be represented here in Gorham's Corner."

Maine now remembers this native son, but so, too, does the world. In an academic look at John Ford's place in universal culture can be found this encomium from Professor Ronald L. Davis in his *John Ford: Hollywood's Old Master*:

"He has been compared to Walt Whitman, Mark Twain, William Faulkner, and Charles Ives for, like them, he stands as an American original. Yet famed director Frank Capra went further: 'A megaphone has been to John Ford what the chisel was to Michelangelo: his life, his passion, his cross.'"[10]

1. Scott Eyman, *Print the Legend: The Life and Times of John Ford*. New York: Simon and Schuster, 1999, p. 38.

2. Ibid., p. 45.

3. Ibid.

4. Ibid., p. 51.

5. Ibid., p. 55.

6. Ibid., p. 89.

7. Ibid., p. 160.

8. Ibid., p. 268.

9. Ibid., p. 167.

10. Ronald C. Davis, *John Ford, Hollywood's Old Master*. Norman, OK: University of Oklahoma Press, 1995, p. 3.

Mark Walker
Photo from Maine Roots: Growing Up Poor
in the Kennebec Valley. Camden, *ME: Picton Press, 1994.*

18

THE RADICALS

In the 1936 presidential election, only two states did not vote for Franklin D. Roosevelt: Maine and Vermont. Some wise-aleck pundit, remembering Maine had spawned the political cliché of "As Maine goes, so goes the nation," simply due to the fact it voted for federal offices in September rather than November, changed this platitude to the more sardonic: "As Maine goes, so goes Vermont."

These two northern New England states, so Republican they could resist the attraction of the New Deal as a way out of the Great Depresson, were as poor, if not poorer, than the rest of country. Their people—theoretically, at least—suffered in stoic Yankee silence. Always inured to poverty, these rural folks may not have felt much of a difference. But such harsh conditions did nurture individuals who revolted against the status quo.

One was Mark Walker, who grew up in the 1930s in North New Portland, a tiny community in Franklin County, western Maine, an area that remains sparse, undeveloped, and, some would say, redneck conservative to this day. After leaving Maine, Mark Walker wrote two books about his life experiences. One was appropriately titled *Maine Roots, Growing Up Poor in the Kennebec Valley,* and the other, *Working for Utopia, 1937–1953,* told of his participation in left-wing activities, especially the Trotskyist movement of the Marxist International.

Mark Walker, one can argue, came right out of the bedrock of Maine's population, Anglo-Saxon Protestant back to his earliest ancestor, Captain Richard Walker, who arrived in the Massachusetts Bay Colony in 1629, and to Solomon Walker, one of the refugees from Portland after Mowat's bombardment who were given land in the Carrabassett Valley in 1783. A Walker daughter was the first white child born in this New Portland.

Our previous chapter about John Ford introduced the first major wave of immigration into Maine that was neither Anglo-Saxon nor Protestant: the Irish Catholics. A second Roman Catholic group was of

French Canadians, coming south from Québec after the Civil War to work in the textile and shoe factories, then cropping up in certain Maine urban settings. Another twentieth-century radical we will examine, Raymond Luc Levasseur of Sanford, is a descendant of this migration, a whole generation removed from Mark Walker, but from a subculture equally as conservative, churchly, and God-fearing as the folks in northern Franklin County.

Besides, Maine has also produced, or helped to produce, some rebels on the other side of the aisle—radical right-wingers like Mildred Gillars, the "Axis Sally" of World War II, and George Lincoln Rockwell, founder of the postwar American Nazi Party—who will be touched upon in this chapter.

Mark Walker

The town of New Portland exhibited an economic pattern all too familiar in Maine. Some parts of the state experienced it earlier than in this western enclave—when agriculture stopped prospering. The 1849 gold rush attracted energetic fortune-seekers like Asa Meade Simpson, but similar exoduses were still occurring almost a hundred years later, as Mark Walker reports. He remembers a sort of "golden era" in New Portland lasting until the 1920s, when prices suddenly plummeted and the competition of train-transported produce from the West devastated the farmers of Maine. The New Portland of his early youth—he was born as Malcolm Marcellus Walker in 1919—had two general stores, an Odd Fellows Hall, a turning mill, a gristmill, a harness shop, and two churches.

Yet soon physical evidence of a local decline was there for the boy to see in abandoned farms, fields growing up to "brush and conifers," orchards untended, and farm buildings falling to ruin. Relatives had left—brothers of his grandfather—one to California, one to Kansas, one to Washington, D.C. Mark's comment was, "The transformation of New Portland from a thriving commercial center to a stagnant backwater was symptomatic of the sickness of the whole region and the dissolution of a way of life."[1]

His father, Cephas Walker, like many men in the area, was a jack-of-all-trades—skillful logger, teamster, river driver, farmer, and later mail carrier. His mother, Josephine Williamson, was from a similar long-time local farming family. They had seven children, six boys and a girl, and Mark was the second oldest.

Schooling was in the proverbial one-room schoolhouse, containing forty pupils, to which the children were taken in a horse-drawn school bus. Mark might have ended like his parents with no higher than an eighth-grade education had it not been for an untoward and never-expected set of circumstances.

The Walkers, in addition to all the things they did to earn a dollar, rented living quarters on their farm to hired hands. A handsome young man named Earl Moulton was among them, and pretty soon, Mark's mother, not happy with her husband, was attracted to him. The final crisis in her marriage occurred when Cephas Walker sold some heifers she'd been raising without even consulting her, never mind obtaining her acquiescence.

Josephine ran off with Earl Moulton, literally abandoning her children. Yet this shocking event, condemned even by her own father, had a silver lining where Mark was concerned. The kids had to be farmed out, since Cephas could not care for them alone. Mark and two of his brothers were placed at the Good Will-Hinckley School near Skowhegan, which had been in operation since 1889 to help educate children whose families experienced difficulties.

This fine institution still exists and is going strong. When Mark entered in 1931, it had fifteen resident cottages (ten for boys, five for girls) on 2,000 acres.

The pedagogic philosophy of George Walter Hinckley, the philanthropist who endowed the institution, could not have been more nineteenth-century individualistic. Even Mark Walker, Marxist though he became, was touched by it, and, writing about his school years, could state with a straight face, "G. W. Hinckley also never asked for and would not have accepted any public funding.... He had his own ideas about how the school he had founded should be run and he didn't want any guidance or dictation from politicians, however well-intentioned. Thus he raised the money to build the school and keep it running from private contributors. I have always admired him for that. And back then, if you didn't bother the state, the state left you alone."[2]

On the other hand, the youthful exile from Franklin County was being exposed to ideas other than a Hooverian mind set. He came upon little blue books of leftist writings, and he would quote in class statements from Eugene Debs, Clarence Darrow, and even Karl Marx.

"I knew there was a Depression in the land," Mark writes, "and had heard of bank closings and Bonus Marchers in Washington. I knew of Hitler in Germany. I had heard of labor organizing strikes led by the Congress for Industrial Organization, but all these things had little meaning for me."[3]

From the adults on campus, all he heard was that Franklin D. Roosevelt was a dangerous socialist and the country's salvation lay in returning the Republicans to national power.

To this end, the head of the school, N. H. Hinckley, approached Mark before the 1932 presidential election about starting a "Herbert Hoover Clean Politics Club" among the students. The boy's political leanings, however, were on a much different track. Mark had come to admire Huey Long, a populist and potential Fascist, whose book, *Every Man a King*, had impressed him. Furthermore, he had written to Senator Long asking for a dozen copies of the tract, and a package of them had arrived.

In turning down N. H. Hinckley's proposal, Mark answered that he would prefer Huey Long to Herbert Hoover if he'd ever start a club, which drew the wrathful response from Hinckley that there would be no Huey Long club or any Huey Long literature in the school. What copies Mark had were confiscated.

Despite such shenanigans, Mark left Good Will-Hinckley with a warm feeling, insisting, "I have never forgotten what Good Will did for me and my family when we needed help. Since I have been able, I have in my turn helped Good Will assist other needy children."[4]

Upon graduation, Mark would have liked to attend Bowdoin. He was actually accepted, but only four scholarships were available and he failed to receive one. So his only other alternative was to go to work."

He made a stab at trying to sell magazine subscriptions in southern Maine, in New Hampshire, in Massachusetts, and even in Washington, D.C. Unsuccessful everywhere, he had to be sent home from the nation's capital by Traveler's Aid, and in Lawrence, Massachusetts, he found himself so broke he skipped out on his hotel bill.

Back in New Portland, he stayed with his father, who had married again and started another family. On the farm, he cut wood for his dad and peeled the logs they sold to the paper companies for pulp. But all the while, Mark chafed at remaining in Maine. Quietly, he was saving to buy a 1936 Model T Ford. The year was 1937, he was eighteen, and he contacted a buddy from Hinckley, Preston McCann, who was willing to share his adventure of driving off to Boston.

Their first address was Charlestown, in Sullivan Square, boarding at a rooming house, and Mark's first job was distributing shopping newspapers for the Rogers Distribution Service, followed by a dishwasher's job in the Century Restaurant, where the pay was just as low but he got to eat better. Anyhow, Mark declared himself "glad to be away from Maine" and "pleased to be here in this center of culture and history." Soon, the New Portlander found himself living right in the heart of Boston, off Scollay Square on Howard Street, half a block from the venerable and notorious Old Howard Burlesque Theater. He resolutely declared, "For me there was no longer any question of another humiliating retreat to Maine."[5]

So far, the teenager from Maine was simply one among thousands of fortune-seekers in the cities of the U.S. at a time when conditions were hardly propitious. If anything made him a tad different, it was the fact of his being blind in one eye, the result of a childhood accident, but this affliction was neither discernible nor crippling. It was undoubtedly his economic condition rather than any physical handicap that directed him to enter the political arena by responding to a leaflet he picked up advertising a rally of the Young Communist League.

The year 1937 was politically turbulent throughout the world; even in normally placid Maine, there was labor strife—the most violent strike in the state's history—when the Lewiston-Auburn shoe workers tried to organize.

Attending his first political rally, Mark Walker was among 300 Communists and their sympathizers and received an introduction to the vagaries of a "party line" that had to be followed no matter how it zigzagged.

Only a few months before, President Roosevelt had been hammered by these people as a Fascist. Now, the mantra had changed to promoting a "Popular Front"—the Communists teaming up with other leftists and even middle-of-the-road liberals against the "real" Fascist menace—

Hitler, Mussolini, the Japanese military in Manchuria, and Franco in Spain. Mark joined up in the West End branch of the party on the back side of Beacon Hill, which consisted of about fifteen members, ages sixteen to twenty.

At one of these meetings, an ugly incident took place. Mark had befriended a young man his age from suburban Dedham named John Hamilton. and without warning, the party leadership turned on Hamilton and accused him of being a traitor. Why? Because Hamilton had been seen talking to a group of Trotskyists. True enough, Hamilton admitted; he had been trying to convert them. His defense wasn't accepted and a motion was made to expel him. Mark sought to back up his friend. For his trouble, he too was kicked out.

Like a true Mainer, he indignantly proclaimed, "No one can tell me with whom I might legitimately hold a conversation."[6] But he didn't abandon his Marxist outlook, saying he continued to believe in socialism, if starting to have a dim view of its Stalinist version.

Going to live in Dedham at Hamilton's home, Mark also accompanied his friend to meetings of the Young Peoples Socialist League (YPSL), a branch of the Trotskyist Socialist Workers Party.

In addition to its other happenings, the year 1937 was the time when Leon Trotsky was granted asylum in Mexico. It had been an entire decade since Stalin had forced him out of the USSR. In 1940 Stalin would have his rival murdered in Mexico City, but the split inside the formerly united Communist Party of the Soviet Union still continued.

Mark Walker's Trotskyist connections soon led him in another employment direction. There was a Trotskyist Sailors Union of the Pacific (SUP) with an East Coast affiliate, the Seafarers International Union (SIU). Through his contacts among Trotskyist seamen, Mark was able to get the papers he needed to ship out on a merchant vessel. Before heading to New York City to fnd such work, he hitchhiked home, saw his sister in Auburn and his father (now a mail carrier) in New Portland, and, using his thumb again, bummed rides to Manhattan. At the union hall, he signed up for picketing duty, since he was told it would better help him land a job. The SIU was protesting outside the offices of the Maritime Commission on lower Broadway, condemning management's use of something called "the Fink Book"—a printed list that would show if a sailor was a union man. According to Mark, the Fink Book was supported by the Stalinists in two other major maritime unions on the grounds the federal government wanted it, and they were backing President Franklin Roosevelt because they thought he would work with Stalin.

For his work on the picket line, Mark was rewarded with a job on a 6,000-ton freighter, *Harpoon*, destined for San Francisco via the Panama Canal.

The farm boy from a maritime state was going to sea. Most of the voyage was out of sight of land but exceptions sharply remained long afterward in Mark Walker's memory: the landscape of Panama, which was the first lush tropical vegetation he had ever seen; an encounter with blacks speaking a language he couldn't understand; and during an unexpected stopover, once through the canal on the Pacific coast of Mexico, his maiden experience drinking tequila, and getting sick from it.

Arriving in California, the fledgling sailor was paid off at San Pedro, the port for Los Angeles. No immediate work was available. So Mark set out for the East Coast by car. But along the way, an accident landed him in a hospital in the Ozarks town of Rolla, Missouri, with internal injuries that weren't properly diagnosed. Trying to continue his trip by Greyhound bus, he was stricken by excrutating pain and rushed to another hospital, this time in Harrisburg, Pennsylvania. An operation was required, but since he was only nineteen, his mother had to come from New Jersey and give the necessary permission. Two-thirds of the boy's injured liver was removed (it would regenerate), and recovery took three months because crushed vertebrae were also discovered. In the process, at least, Mark was able to procure for himself a glass eye to replace the one rendered useless in his childhood.

The nurses, Mark reported in *Working for Utopia*, were entertained by his Maine accent, but his pronounciation did once cause embarrassment. One day he was brought a meal and noticed a key piece of silverware missing. "I want a fok," he told the nurse, dropping an *r*, as Yankee speakers do. The amazed, if not horrified, look on the woman's face instantly telegraphed to him what he'd sounded like. "A fok to eat with," he quickly added.

The resumption of Mark's nautical career did not resume immediately after he left the Harrisburg hospital in February 1939. Two other highlights of this period were that he became a dues-paying member of the Socialist Workers Party, and he got married to a female comrade named Nina Tucker. Finally, by hanging around the SIU hiring hall, Mark landed a job on a supply ship operating out of Galveston, Texas. On one of her runs, the vessel stopped in South Portland and he had a chance to see his sister again and an aunt and uncle. Also during this time, Trotskyists learned of the murder in Mexico on August 21, 1940, of Leon Trotsky, killed by a Stalinist agent who had infiltrated his bodyguard. Mark attended a memorial gathering for the slain leader at his union's headquarters, where 200 people showed up to hear James P. Cannon, the president of the Socialist Workers Party.

Unfortunately, Mark's frequent absences from his wife were to lead to a mutually agreed-upon divorce in 1941.

By now, the U.S. was edging toward the war raging in Europe and on the high seas since September 1939. A bachelor again, Mark took a job on the SS *Millinocket*, a 3,000-ton freighter owned by the Bull Line, running between Puerto Rico and East Coast U.S. ports. Mark called Puerto Rico "very exciting for a young man only recently from the backwoods of Maine." One of the things he liked about the run was that he could fish off the vessel out in open water.

With the U.S. entry into World War II imminent, Mark found he had to pass a physical to be able to remain in the merchant marine. All of a sudden, his glass eye became a problem, for he would have to have an eye test. Happily, the doctor he saw in Mobile, Alabama, turned out to be particularly friendly because he had visited Maine and liked it very much. Having memorized the eye chart, Mark passed the reading part of the exam easily and his artificial eyeball proved so realistic-looking the garrulous physician never bothered to check it.

His next berth was on a confiscated former Yugoslav ship made into a U.S. Army transport, sailing on November 24, 1941, two weeks prior to Pearl Harbor. Although the U.S. was not yet quite at war, security measures were already tough. Leaders of the Socialist Workers Party had been indicted under a law known as the Smith Act, allegedly for advocating the violent overthrow of the U.S. government. Mark vigorously protested that Socialists only advocated change through constitutional means. Reluctantly, he signed a loyalty oath in order to be able to work.

Their ship was at sea on December 7, 1941, and immediately they had to worry about German subs. Luck was with him. He was aboard the SS *Greylock* when she was attacked outside Halifax Harbor. A torpedo fired at them missed because of skillful evasive action by the skipper. On another occasion, Mark was hospitalized with tropical fever and missed sailing aboard *Greylock* on a voyage to Murmansk. During her return from Russia, she was sunk in the frigid Barents Sea. Seven other ships Mark had sailed on, including the *Millinocket*, were lost during the war. The merchant marine's high casualty rate was second only to the U.S. Marines, but as Mark Walker, good Labor man, points out, not until 1988 were any of them given veterans' status.

Toward the close of the war, Mark found himself in Ohio, working on the Great Lakes. Shortly before FDR's death in April 1945, he married again, despite the efforts of his antagonistic Republican father-in-law-to-be to sic the FBI on him. Mark even attempted politics, was nominated by the Socialists to run for Congress only to be ruled off the ballot by a technicality, but then competed as a write-in for governor of Ohio.

All this while he kept his faith in the Marxist philosophy of an ultimate victory for the proletariat, waiting for, as he put it, "the sweep of radicalization that would accompany the economic crisis we regarded as inevitable...."[7] Ruefully, he had to concede it never came. The Socialist Workers Party suffered a dramatic decline and was down to a mere 500 members nationwide by 1954.

After the birth of their first child, Mark and his wife moved to California.

Never what one would call a *violent* radical, Mark Walker mellowed in his thought process as he grew older. Unlike Irving Kristol, a fellow Trotskyist whom he'd met in New York City in the 1930s, he did not turn sharply to the right, but kept his idealism intact, if more generalized, while leading himself away from the political wars of the past.

Here are some of Mark Walker's concluding thoughts:

"What we once considered a logical and historically ordained progression of human society through ever higher stages of development—from primitive communities to slavery to feudalism to Capitalism, to Socialism, giving way to Communism, the Classless Society, in which the State would 'wither away' has taken detours not foreseen by Marx, Engels or Trotsky"[8] but "ultimately human beings will always seek freedom from tyranny,"[9] and hopefully mankind's affairs can be managed "without poverty and exploitation and without racial, religious, or gender discrimination."[10]

Raymond Luc Levasseur

Since 9/11 and the Iraq War, the word "terrorist" has acquired a distinct meaning in American journalese and political parlance. It is now aimed at Muslim fundamentalists. But we have had prior targets for it, too, in this country. The single most deadly attack in the U.S. prior to September 11, 2001, occurred in Oklahoma City, where two right-wing anti-U.S. government fanatics blew up a federal building and killed 168 of their fellow Americans, including nineteen children at a day-care center on the premises. Some echoes of what was then a rising "militia" movement remain in so-called vigilante groups who have taken it upon themselves to patrol our border with Mexico. Timothy McVeigh, the prime instigator of the Oklahoma outrage, when arrested, was wearing a T-shirt with the motto *Sic Semper Tyrannus*, the words uttered by John Wilkes Booth as he shot Abraham Lincoln to death. A direct line from the Confederacy through the Ku Klux Klan to right-wing agendas of anti-government hotheads like McVeigh is not an unreasonable historic comparison.

On the other side of the coin are those on the left who take the law into their own hands. The 1960s and the 1970s in the U.S., particularly because of the reaction against the Vietnam War, saw spurts of anti-establishment, anti-corporation violence within our country. The Weathermen were one group that achieved notoriety; another was the so-called Ohio Seven, accused of committing nineteen bombings and ten bank robberies over a nine-year period. One of its members, Raymond Luc Levasseur, was from Maine.

He was a native of Sanford, in York County, where his Franco-American grandparents, part of the nineteenth-century exodus from Québec, had settled, findng work in the textile mills and "shoe shops."

In a "Trial Statement" made by Ray Luc Levasseur in 1986, he spoke of this background, saying his grandparents had started such work when they were thirteen and fourteen years old. His own parents began at the age of sixteen. And he himself entered the same workforce when he was seventeen.

"I worked in a mill...where we made heels for shoes. I worked with primarily French Canadian people, people who didn't have much education. I didn't have much good education myself at the time. It was nonunionized labor. All the unions had been broken earlier by runaway shops. It was low pay. It was the kind of money that was difficult to raise a family on. We were subject to speed-ups on those machines."[11]

Levasseur then went on to describe how a schoolmate of his, Albert Glaude, working in another mill, caught his arm in a machine, was pulled into it and mangled to death. "They can kill you very quickly or take a long time to do it," Levasseur stated, and to illustrate the latter thought, cited his grandfather's breakdown in health and his own conviction that "I always thought that those mills had a big part in killing him."[12]

Rather than continue in this same way of life, Ray Luc Levasseur left Maine at seventeen and went to Boston, found work loading docks, and then enlisted in the army in 1967.

The Franco-Americans in Maine, despite experiences of being treated like second-class citizens since their arrival from Canada, have always been strongly patriotic. Levasseur's grandfather, father, and uncles all served in the military. But Ray's twelve-month tour of duty in Vietnam served to change his views about the war. His Trial Statement puts it this way: "I was trained to kill. And I was fully armed and sent to Vietnam. You know there's a lot of vets who came back with post-Vietnam stress disorder. I've worked with those veterans. I didn't suffer any mental illness or syndrome when I came back enraged by what I saw."[13]

After receiving an honorable discharge from the army, the young, politically charged-up Franco-American did not go back to Maine. The civil rights movement in the South became a magnet for him and he was soon in Tennessee, working with the Southern Student Organizing Committee. They were trying to organize workers in meat-packing plants. In 1969 he was in Atlanta at the Ebenezer Baptist Church on the first anniversary of the death of Martin Luther King, Jr., and marched "while white racists stood on the sidelines and spat at us."

Sometime afterwards, back in Tennessee, he was convicted for selling seven dollars worth of marijuana in what he insists was a "setup by a police undercover agent." He was given a five-year sentence, despite the fact that he had never been in prison before and had no previous felony convictions. His conclusion was: "That's the price I had to pay for being a Vietnam veteran opposed to the war and to racism."

For protesting conditions in the county jail, he was classed an "agitator" and sent to the Tennessee State Penitentiary. He now considered himself a political prisoner. Further "agitation" landed him in solitary confinement, where he had nothing much else to do but read. The books he had available—Marx, Lenin, Mao, Malcolm X, Che Guevara, Franz Fanon, Rosa Luxembourg, Emma Goldman, the writings of the Black Panthers—all focused on class struggle and class conflict, and, as he said, "this is how I became a revolutionary."[14]

Tennessee finally released him on the condition that he leave the state. Ray consequently returned to Maine, went to work, saving money to go to school, and, on the side, acting as a state organizer for Vietnam Veterans Against the War. He also did work for an organization called SCAR, which gave assistance to prisoners in Maine jails and ex-convicts after they were freed.

When I was in the legislature in the 1970s, I do remember meeting with representatives of SCAR, which was working with local low-income and social-work groups. I may have met Ray Luc Levasseur. He himself writes about spending time at the Bayside Projects and Kennedy Park in Portland, two of the poorest sections of the city.

The evolution from SCAR, which also organized a Portland Community Bail Fund, to Ray Levasseur's later troubles with the federal government began in 1974 when, in his words, "I went underground because of my commitment to building a revolutionary movement that could grow, sustain, and defend itself at each stage of its development."[15]

His Trial Statement speaks of fear of assassination by the Portland police and harassment by them at his Red Star North Bookstore on Congress Street. He says he began to carry a pistol to protect himself, knowing the risk he ran as a parolee—ten years in jail—if he were caught with a weapon.

His bigger risks started a decade later.

On January 12, 1989, the Associated Press reported that "nine months after lawyers began jury selection, opening arguments have begun in the trial of avowed revolutionaries that has already cost the government millions of dollars."

There were three defendants "among seven people captured in 1984 and 1985, after a long manhunt," and the charge against them was sedition, or conspiring to topple the government by force, the same ancient statute used in Mark Walker's time against the Socialist Workers Party. Those three defendants were Raymond Luc Levasseur, forty-two; his wife Patricia Gros Levasseur, thirty-four; and Richard Williams, forty-one. Each faced a sentence of sixty years in prison and $60,000 in fines; they were likewise prosecuted under the RICO statute, usually used against organized crime gangs. The trial was held in Springfield, Massachusetts, in order to be close to Hartford, which alone has a prison able to house both men and women.

Ray Levasseur served as his own lawyer. He and the other defense attorneys argued the trial was a waste of money since the defendants had already been convicted on bombing charges. They also claimed that the sedition statute, first promulgated during the Civil War and revamped in 1918, was so broad it could be used to stifle any type of protest. Of the eight members of the group, called variously the United Freedom Front, the Sam Melville-Jonathan Jackson Unit, and the Ohio Seven, those not on trial had either pleaded guilty or been dropped from the case. Only Mrs. Levasseur had never been jailed.

Levasseur, who with his wife was arrested in Deerfield, Ohio, had been previously found guilty of bombing, to quote him, "U.S. military facilities, military contractors, and corporations doing business in South Africa," and had received a forty-five-year sentence.

The trial in Springfield, deemed by Ray "the largest sedition trial in the history of the U.S.," ended with his acquittal on the charge of seditious conspiracy. But his prison term for the bombing charges continued.

In August of 2004, another Ray Luc Levasseur bombshell occurred when the federal government released him on parole after twenty years of incarceration.

Portland Press Herald writer Giselle Goodman started her story with the following lead: "The man Portland Police Chief Michael Chitwood described as 'truly a revolutionary' arrived Friday afternoon at the Portland International Jetport, ready to settle back into the city as a changed man." Levasseur was now fifty-seven years old. But Chief Chitwood insisted he still posed a threat, although Levasseur's new wife,

Jamila Levy Levasseur just as stubbornly maintained he was no longer a dangerous person. "We've all changed in thirty years," she told the press. "He intends to lead a law-abiding life," she added, emphasizing "the U.S. Probations and Parole Office would not have approved his coming to this halfway house [Pharos House in Portland], if they didn't believe he was safe."

At the Jetport, Levasseur himself said he couldn't talk about the past because of parole restrictions, but he was happy to be in his home state. "I'm from Maine. This is where I grew up, this is where my family is. It's where my heart is," he informed reporters at an impromptu press conference, and added that he was looking forward to seeing his mother, who would be celebrating her eighty-third birthday in a couple of weeks.

The *Press Herald*'s story ended in an interview with a man named Doug Sneed, who was unbothered that the ex-con would be living near him. "Levasseur has paid for his crimes," Sneed said. "The guy's over fifty years old. He's a grandfather. He's not a threat to society.... What's he going to do, go out and rob banks? What revolution? There is no more revolution. Those times are gone."

Pretty much so. Except Ray Luc Levasseur, while staying within the law, still had a knack for raising hackles. On September 15, 2006, an exhibit of art was displayed at the Woodbury Campus Center of the University of Southern Maine, organized by the USM Art Gallery director and the Portland Victory Garden Project, but its title, "Can't Jail the Spirit," gave hint enough it might prove controversial. Plus Ray Luc Levasseur was to be the opening speaker. Plus, too—and for this reason he told the USM officials the show was "hot"—a centerpiece among the canvases was one by Thomas Manning, a Portlander and sidekick of Levasseur's, currently serving an eighty-year prison sentence for shooting and killing a New Jersey state trooper, an act claimed to have been done in self-defense.

The reaction, once the artwork went up, wasn't just "hot"; it created a firestorm. Maine's two largest police unions and the Maine Association of Police Chiefs immediately protested, objecting to the characterization of Manning as a political prisoner. Former South Portland police chief Robert Schwartz, now head of the chiefs' association, called it "an issue of a convicted cop-killer and convicted bombers that they were making heroes of...." Schwartz also labeled Manning "a homegrown terrorist."

But his remarks were mild compared to the spate of angry comments that poured in over the Internet.

USM President Richard Pattenaude backed down and ordered the exhibition closed.

In true academic fashion, the USM president's action was followed by two symposia—one to rehash what happened, under the title "Changes in Activism, Political Repression, and Subversive Art"; the other, "Controversies on Campus. Who Decides?"

Two years later, Ray Luc Levasseur was back at the Woodbury Campus Center. This was on April 2, 2008, during USM's Human Rights Week, for the showing of a documentary movie about the 1974 prison riot at Attica in upstate New York, during which thirty-one prisoners and nine guards were killed.

The keynote speaker was Ray Luc Levasseur, now living in Brunswick. He was as outspoken as always, stating that in response to Attica, a widespread use of solitary confinement had permeated the country's correctional systems, aimed at isolating what he termed "prison activists" and "jailhouse lawyers." Ray also declared everything happening at Guantánamo had been exported from American prisons and that the conditions leading to the Attica outburst weren't "ancient history at all." They are still the norm, he warned.

Mildred Gillars and George Lincoln Rockwell

Lest it be thought that Maine's radical bent occurred only on the left side of the political spectrum, there are two figures on the far, far right who have Maine ties.

The Pine Tree State, in its past, has from time to time belied its image of peaceful folkways played out in a sublime setting of natural beauty. In Colonial days, there were vicious Indian fighters like James Cargill of Newcastle, who scalped innocent Indian women and children in order to collect bounties; "White Indians," disguised squatters who terrorized landowners; and the "Know Nothings" who burned Catholic churches (Ray Luc Levasseur's parents would have remembered the surge of Ku Klux Klan activity in Maine in the 1920s, particularly aimed at intimidating Catholics).

Mildred Gillars, Portland-born, who lived on Park Street until she was ten years old, is the only Maine person ever convicted of treason against the United States. She is most certainly better known as "Axis Sally," the nickname given her by G.I.s overseas when she was broadcasting for the Nazis from Berlin during World War II. It was one of these broadcasts, just before D-Day, on May 11, 1944, that led to her treason trial, because it had been witnessed by two American POW's doing janitor service in the studio. There had to be actual witnesses to her act, and these two men could say how they'd seen her at work trying to undermine the morale of our servicemen, taunting them about their wives and sweethearts philandering at home, and railing against Jews and President Franklin D. Roosevelt. One of her defenses was that she had gone to Germany, after studying drama at Ohio Wesleyan, and fallen under the spell of a Nazi professor, Max Otto Koischwitz, a former teacher at Hunter College in New York City. Found guilty and sentenced to ten to thirty years in federal prison, she was freed on parole after ten years and lived out a quiet life in Ohio, teaching English and German at a Catholic prep school.

George Lincoln Rockwell, infamous as the postwar founder of the American Nazi Party, was not born in Maine but spent part of his childhood with his father's family at Boothbay Harbor, where he developed a passion for sailing and fishing. Both his parents were vaudeville comedians and actors. "Doc" Rockwell, his father, was a Maine humorist, and some of the elder Rockwell's friends were entertainers such as Fred Allen, Jack Benny, Groucho Marx, and Benny Goodman (the last three being Jewish). While a teenager, young Rockwell was sent by his father to Maine's prestigious prep school, Hebron Academy, where his readings in philosophy and literature led him to drop his interest in religion and consider himself an agnostic. He went on to Brown University for more intellectual stimulation, but left in 1940 and joined the U.S. Navy Air Force. During the hostilities, he fought in the Pacific and was later called back into service as a flight instructor during the Korean War.

Perhaps a tip-off to his future leanings was when he and his second wife, an Icelandic woman, had their honeymoon at Berchtesgaden near Hitler's mountain retreat.

After working for arch-conservative William Buckley and the *National Review*, Rockwell decided American conservatives were not anti-Semitic enough. He launched his American Nazi Party in March

1959, and Doc Rockwell soon disowned him. In August 1967 George Lincoln Rockwell was fatally shot in his car while at a shopping center in Arlington, Virginia, where he had established his party headquarters. His father, on learning of his death, merely commented, "I am not surprised at all. I've expected it." While his parents would have had him buried privately in Maine, they decided not to contest the Nazis for his body. There followed a long dispute over where he could be buried, since he was a veteran who had been honorably discharged. The Defense Department refused to allow a Nazi burial in any public cemetery. In the end, he was cremated, but his ashes were still not allowed into a military cemetery. Incdentally, it was one of his own Nazis, disgruntled after the two had feuded, who shot and killed him. Maine, at least, was spared having George Lincoln Rockwell on its soil.

1. Mark Walker, *Maine Roots: Growing Up Poor in the Kennebec Valley.* Camden, ME: Picton Press, 1994, p. 16.
2. Ibid., p. 122.
3. Ibid., p. 131.
4. Ibid., p. 134.
5. Mark Walker, *Working for Utopia, 1937–1953.* Concordia, CA: Quixotic Press, 2000. p. 52.
6. Ibid., p. 64.
7. Ibid., p. 311.
8. Ibid.
9. Ibid., p. 316.
10. Ibid., p. 317.
11. "The Trial Statement of Ray Luc Levasseur: From the Shadows of the Mills." Google: http://earthlink.net/neoind.statement.html. Page 1.
12. Ibid.
13. Ibid., p. 2.
14. Ibid., p. 5.
15. Ibid., p. 8.

Samantha Smith
Courtesy of the Samantha Smith Foundation

19

SAMANTHA SMITH

A *non-radical* approach to the ideological tensions of the twentieth century certainly characterizes the actions of Samantha Smith, actions which brought her worldwide fame during a particularly ticklish era of the cold war—the early 1980s. This ten-year-old schoolgirl in the small Maine town of Manchester, slightly west of Augusta, was innocently responding to a growing international public concern about the nuclear arms race between the United States and the Soviet Union.

Two years before Samantha got involved, in April 1980, another New England female, Randall Forsberg, who held a Ph.D. from MIT in arms control studies, proposed a solution that had gained enormous attention: simply stop building new missiles capable of delivering nuclear warheads. The "nuclear freeze," as it was called, was an idea that resonated throughout the U.S., as well as in Europe and other parts of the world. By 1982, resolutions in support of a nuclear freeze had been "passed by dozens of town, city, county, and state legislatures throughout the country...."[1] I myself was involved in writing the resolution presented to the Maine State Legislature and negotiating the bipartisan support with which it was passed. Concern had been heightened by Ronald Reagan's capture of the presidency in 1980 and the fear that his anti-Soviet intransigency might be leading to a nuclear war. On June 12, 1982, a gigantic crowd of 700,000 demonstrated for the freeze in New York City's Central Park.

One reason—aside from her sparkling personality—that Samantha Smith's act of writing about peace to the leader of the Soviet Union, Yuri Andropov, in November 1982, struck the public nerve as it did was its reflection of the general worry about world catastrophe seen through the clear, wide eyes of a youngster.

Samantha, born in Houlton, Maine, was the only child of a college professor and his social worker wife who had moved to Maine from "Away." Samantha's father, Arthur, initially taught at Ricker College and then took a job at the University of Maine in Augusta, while her mother,

Jane, went to work for the state's Department of Human Services, dealing with child protection matters. The family established their new home in Manchester, a close commute for both parents.

At age five, Samantha had precociously shown an interest in the outer world by writing to Queen Elizabeth of England. It was really a fan letter, merely expressing her admiration for the British monarch, and in return, she received a gracious note from a lady-in-waiting, thanking her on behalf of Her Majesty.

The notion of writing to a celebrity, therefore, was not entirely unfamiliar in the Smith household when, in 1982, Samantha watched a TV program in which scientists demonstrated how a nuclear war would destroy the earth and its atmosphere, thus ending all life on the planet.

The ten-year-old girl, very alarmed, suggested that her mother write the leader of the Soviet Union and tell him not to go to war.

Jane Smith responded, "Why don't you write him?"

So Samantha did. As she later explained, although she had a typewriter, she thought it would be more personal if she wrote by hand, and she was very careful to make the words legible in her best handwriting. Mother Jane looked up the address for her: Mr. Yuri Andropov, the Kremlin, Moscow, USSR.

Samantha's letter read in full:

Dear Mr. Andropov:
My name is Samantha Smith. I am ten years old. Congratulations on your new job. I have been worrying about Russia and the United States getting into a nuclear war. Are you going to vote to have a war or not? If you aren't please tell me how you are going to help to not have a war. This question you do not have to answer, but I would like to know why you want to conquer the world or at least our country. God made the world for us to live together in peace and not to fight.
Sincerely,
Samantha Smith.

Such incoming letters are commonplace for people who hold high public office. How Samantha's letter found its way to the top office in the Kremlin will forever remain a mystery. Timing had a lot to do with the fact that her missive attracted the attention it did. Instead of a polite reply drafted by a lowly assistant for the boss's signature, Samantha Smith's letter was seized upon for an instrument of policy—what anti-Communist critics were to call propaganda.

How much Samantha knew about the man to whom she was writing is hard to know. It is obvious she had been told by her parents that he was new in his position as head of the Communist Party and consequently of the Soviet Union. But did she know what a hard-liner he was, a Soviet counterpart to the avowedly anti-Communist President Reagan? Andropov had played a major role in suppressing dissent within the Soviet empire by leading efforts to put down the Hungarian and Czech revolts against Russian occupation. In fact, he had been placed in charge of the secret police, the KGB, and was the first Soviet political leader to have come directly to power from that dreaded organization. It was in November 1982 that his predecessor, Leonid Brezhnev, died, and so the new party secretary had barely taken office when Samantha's letter arrived.

Someone close to the top of the Soviet bureaucracy saw an advantage in responding to Samantha, as a way to reinforce the USSR's position that it was a force working for peace. Hard-liners in the U.S. did not shrink from accusing Samantha and her family of being dupes playing into Soviet hands.

It was some five months after she wrote that Samantha first learned something was afoot. A United Press reporter phoned and said a copy of her letter to Andropov had been printed in *Pravda*, the official government newspaper in the USSR.

Samantha immediately wrote another letter—to the Soviet ambassador in Washington, D.C., asking if this were true. The reply was that a letter from Secretary Andropov, translated into English, had been sent to Manchester.

Word soon came from the Manchester Post Office that the letter had arrived.

First stating that he received many letters like hers from "your country and other countries around the world," Andropov in his second paragraph dropped a hint as to why he might have chosen Samantha's for his public response:

"It seems to me—I can tell by your letter—that you are a courageous and honest girl, resembling Becky [Thatcher], the friend of Tom Sawyer in the famous book of your compatriot Mark Twain. This book is well known and loved in our country by all boys and girls."

Anropov's comment about Mark Twain's popularity in the USSR was no bit of political hyperbole. Five years earlier, in 1977, I was in Leningrad with my wife and youngest daughter and saw the longest line of consumers among the many such we had seen in a month of traveling. Ths queue stretched for block after block after block. "What are they waiting to buy?" we asked our Intourist guide. The answer: the newest Russan translation of *Tom Sawyer* and *Huckleberry Finn* had just gone on sale.

In his letter to Samantha, too, Andropov spoke of the U.S.–USSR alliance during World War II, and he restated for her the Soviet announcement that they would never be the first to use nuclear weapons in any conflict. Then he added, "It seems to me that this is a sufficient answer to your second question: 'Why do you want to wage war against the whole world or at least the United States?' We want nothing of the kind. No one in our country—neither workers, peasants, writers, nor doctors, neither grown-ups nor children—wants either a big or 'little' war...."

When Samantha returned from the post office, a crowd of reporters was waiting at her home. In this first encounter with the media, the overwhelming impression Samantha left was of her poise. Her father admitted he was surprised at how well she handled herself. The initial story went out on the AP and UPI wires all over the country, was picked up by the CBS *Morning News,* and appeared on many front pages. The only people not impressed by her notoriety were her schoolmates in Manchester—that is, until the Portland TV station, WGAN, arrived to film her in class.

Ten days after this preliminary burst of attention, the *Kennebec Journal,* the major daily in the Augusta area, was reporting that Samantha was "the hottest ten-year-old girl in the news business." She had been cited in *Time, Newsweek,* and *People* magazines, had been interviewed by the Soviets' Washington bureau chief for a segment on USSR TV, had gone to New York for interviews with Ted Koppel and Jane Pauly, to California for the *Tonight Show,* and finally back to the fifth grade in Manchester.

As to charges that Andropov was simply using this incident to push Soviet "peace propaganda," the *Kennebec Journal* (a staunchly Republican paper) editorialized on April 26, 1983, under the heading SAMANTHA SUCCEEDS WHERE OTHERS FAILED, stating: "Yes, Andropov is a politician. Though not in the American sense of the word. And, yes, there obviously is a measure of propaganda in his response to Samantha's letter. But there's a glimmer of hope, too, uncovered by a ten-year-old girl."

The human interest news peg keeping this story alive centered on the fact that Andropov had invited Samantha to come to the Soviet Union and meet with Russian kids her age. The trip was to be for two weeks, all expenses paid by the Soviet government. The Smiths (her parents were also invited) would fly to Moscow, go to the Crimea to the Artek Youth Camp, and see Leningrad, too.

Samantha's preparations were big news locally. On June 16, 1983, three weeks before their starting date of July 7, the *Kennebec Journal* was writing, "Kids from Kiev will be wearing Colby College T-shirts this summer. That's right, comrades, Colby College, Waterville, Maine." The Smiths had gone to the Colby College bookstore. Although well supplied with material from the Maine Publicity Bureau to give out in the USSR, they also wanted to include mementoes from Colby, Bates, and Bowdoin. Arthur Smith said, "We thought since the Russians are going to be promoting Russia, we should be promoting Maine."

At the bookstore in Waterville, Samantha was given a Colby sweatshirt to wear over her Izod shirts and her Calvin Klein jeans. When she finally boarded her plane, she had a whole box of Maine doodads with her besides the college T-shirts—things like moose and lobster patches, pins with the Maine state seal on them, and calendars depicting Maine's gorgeous scenery.

Described as the "first ordinary citizen to visit the USSR as a guest of the Soviet government," Samantha was also characterized in the press as "an intelligent and cute girl who is still just a girl."

Being herself, showing her great poise at all times, Samantha Smith took the Soviet Union by storm.

The highlight of her visit was indisputably the time she spent with her contemporaries at the Artek Camp on the Black Sea.

There were 5,000 young people accommodated by the popular

summer operation (presumably open mainly to offspring of the more privileged levels of Soviet society). Samantha was greeted by a girl her own age, Natasha Krishina from Leningrad, with the traditional symbols of a Russian welcome, salt and a round loaf of bread. These two girls became "best friends" for the duration of Samantha's stay.

Some Maine tourism boosters may have been dismayed by Samantha's response to the question, " What was your strongest impression of the camp?" since she answered, quite artlessly and sincerely: "The sea, because in America, the lakes I swim in have lots of gunk on them."

During a cruise out into the Black Sea with her camp friends, Samantha, like them, threw a bottle into the water containing a peace message. Hers was: "Hopefully, we will have peace for the rest of our lives."

As soon as she arrived at the camp, Samantha was given a Young Pioneer's uniform of a white short-sleeved shirt, a turquoise skirt, and a turquoise scout's hat. Unlike the others, she did not wear a red neckerchief; that was a symbol of devotion to the Communist Party; her neckerchief was blue and white, the type reserved for visitors. Asked later what she most liked about her stay, Samantha again mentioned the sea but also spoke of the "nice parties" they had.

Did that mean she was up very late? she was asked.

Her answer, no doubt with a twinkle and a smile, was: "*Da.*"

Her goodbye speech to her friends, at a ceremony where she was showered with gifts, concluded: "My stay at sea camp in Artek has been wonderful, very wonderful, and I shall miss my new international friends.... But we will remain friends across the sea. Let our countries be friends, too. Some day I hope to return. I love you, Artek."

Whereupon a tremendous roar of applause erupted.

The remainder of the trip occurred in an atmosphere of continual celebrity. The *Kennebec Journal* reported that "Samantha has been ushered around with the pomp usually accorded high-ranking foreign dignitaries."[2] Occasionally, she ran into fellow Americans. At Yalta, it was Mrs. Charles Schulz, wife of the famed cartoonist and creator of the *Peanuts* comic strip, who gave her a "Snoopy" badge; and in Moscow, at the circus, she was recognized by a man in the audience who jumped up and yelled, "I'm from California!" In Leningrad, she attended the world-famed Kirov Ballet; went aboard *Aurora*, a museum ship in the Neva

River that fired the first shot of the Bolshevik revolution; and in the Smolny Institute, a museum of Russian Communism, she saw Lenin's office, which had been kept intact. She is described as riding through Moscow in a black Chaika limousine with a police escort, generally a perk assigned only to top party leaders. The equally famed Bolshoi Ballet in Moscow was closed for summer repairs, but she had a private tour of its magnificent building and the management gave her a special medal heretofore reserved exclusively for top performers. In return, Samantha gave them a small Maine pin. Other destinations were the ornate Novodevichey Monastery and the circus, of course (there was one in every Soviet city), and an animal show where 150 Young Pioneers were also present.

At last it was time for the Smiths to come home. An Associated Press story reported that a lawyer had been retained by the family to help deal with "an onslaught of media offers." Already, Samantha had been invited to appear on the *Today* and *Tonight* shows, *Good Morning America* and the *Phil Donahue Show.*

This Rockville, Maryland, attorney they'd hired, George Haldeman, had known the Smiths beforehand and had been contacted by Arthur prior to the Smith family's flight to the USSR. Haldeman argued that while some people dismissed Samantha's travels as propaganda, she had enhanced the image of the U.S. to a huge degree. "Ninety-nine percent of the public is in favor," he said. "The one percent are hard-line rightists."

Back in Manchester, Maine, the Associated Press was interviewing locals at Daggett's Country Market, which serves as an informal community hangout. To the question of whether the home folks thought the trip would have changed Samantha, the general feeling expressed by one Manchester old-timer was: "Speaking for the majority, we feel she's a pretty composed girl who handles herself with dignity." The minority opinion, offered by a few, was: "She should be home playing with dolls instead of with politics."

On Monday, July 25, 1983, Samantha and her parents returned to Manchester and a tumultuous welcome. As part of the Old Manchester Day Parade, the three Smiths were riding in a baby blue '65 Mustang, and right behind them in a blue pickup truck were Samantha's playmates on her softball team. When the procession finished up at the

Manchester Elementary School, the kids jumped over the sides of the pickup and Samantha "met them joyously, jumping up and down like the eleven-year-old girl she is." A speech by Governor Joseph Brennan, a key to the town of Manchester, and a bouquet of red roses were other components of the homecoming event. Then, it might well have been thought, Samantha would fade back into a normal Maine childhood once the euphoria had worn off.

The sole big disappointment of the trip had been their inability to have a meeting with Andropov. Too busy with affairs of state was the message a top aide of his had brought to the Smiths. Accompanying the apology were a number of gifts from the big man himself, like a samovar and tray, a pair of 100-page photo albums picturing Samantha's visit, and a magnificent hand-laquered box. On her part, Samantha sent Yuri Andropov a book of Mark Twain's speeches.

Three days later, the local press reported Samantha upstairs in her room, giggling with her best friend, Lynn D'Avanzo, but also getting ready to fly to California for her second appearance with Johnny Carson on the *Tonight Show.*

Samantha's take on all of this excitement was the aplomb you might expect from an unspoiled preteen girl. "Johnny Carson," she said, "was very, very nice even if he did kiss me." But then, quickly, she had to explain: "In California, everybody shakes your hand and then kisses you."

One of the Hollywood personalities who caught Samantha's *Tonight Show* appearances was Robert Wagner, the film and TV actor. That he kept her in mind for a part in a future production he was contemplating had, ironically, an overriding influence on the course of her life.

Meanwhile, the pros and cons of her activity were tossed back and forth. Russian exiles in Richmond, Maine, were unhappy and wanted President Reagan to invite a Soviet schoolgirl to the U.S. to counter "the Communist propaganda value of Samantha's trip." An ex-U.S. ambassador to the USSR, Malcolm Toon, verbally attacked the Maine schoolgirl. Defending her was Dean Rusk, former secretary of state. "Well done," Rusk told her, adding how he was "enchanted by the way you handled yourself for that extraordinary visit. You gave many Russians a chance to see an attractive, natural, and unpretentious young American."

Samantha Smith did not fade from sight. She did television spots for the Maine Department of Inland Fisheries and Wildlife, telling kids what to do if they were lost in the woods. Then, with her mother, she flew to Japan to address a session of the Children's International Symposium for the 21st Century, as one of five Americans who took part. In 1984 Samantha was hired by the Disney Channel to do coverage for children of the presidential campaign, interviewing candidates. The Maine State Legislature had her address them. In Washington, D.C., she met with the children of Soviet diplomats.

Soon word was out that Samantha had a book contract with Little, Brown and Company, the venerable Boston publisher—a photo essay, for the most part, to be called *Journey to the Soviet Union*. Appearing in 1985, it contained a foreword by Dr. Lee Salk (younger brother of Dr. Jonas Salk), a noted child psychologist who owned a Maine summer home on an island in Moosehead Lake. His summing-up of Samantha's experience led him to write: "Perhaps we should cease asking children: 'Why don't you act like a grownup?' and begin asking adults: 'Why don't you think like a child?'"

Other books about Samantha have also been written: *Samantha Smith: A Journey for Real* by Anne Galicich; *Samantha Smith, Young Ambassador* by Patricia Stone Martin—aimed at the children's market— and plays about Samantha have been performed in Maine schools.

Had Samantha's life not been cut so tragically short, it's possible to imagine the brilliant future she might have had. At thirteen, she was already starting on an acting career. Robert Wagner began producing a TV series called *Lime Street,* in which he would also star, and he needed to cast the role of one of his fictional daughters just entering her teens, like Samantha. She took a screen test, thought she'd done a terrible job, and was amazed as well as delighted when told she had the part.

The premise of the show was built around the adventures of an insurance fraud investigator who had homes on both sides of the Atlantic and a family containing two young daughters. Robert Wagner, acting as a director, too, taught Samantha how to dance in preparation for the TV program showing her on her first date. The shooting went well and it was not long before the first episode was to air at the end of September.`

Commuting to Hollywood and other locations for the shooting of the episodes put a decided crimp in her social life in Manchester. She once complained, "I kept missing out on stuff like the Christmas dance, which everybody said was really great. And I missed my best friend's birthday party."

World traveler that she was, Samantha would hardly have been blown away by the prospect of a trip to London. The cast and crew went to the English capital to film the fourth show in the *Lime Street* series.

On August 25, 1985, Samantha and her father, who had gone with her to England, were returning home. It is possible Samantha slept on the tedious flight across the ocean; she'd always slept well on planes. It is easy to imagine Samantha impatiently awaiting her arrival in Manchester, seeing her dog Kim, her twenty mice, her friends such as Jessica Jones, to whom she'd written from London, saying she was bored in her hotel room, but had gone shopping and bought a lot of stuff, "but I'm not telling you what until I get home." Most assuredly, home was all-important to her. As she had said to the press when she'd come back from Russia, "I think Maine is a good place to come home to...."

In Boston, the Smiths transferred to the puddle-jumper Beechcraft 99 Bar Harbor Airlines commuter plane that would take them to Augusta. There was a scheduled stop first at the Lewiston-Auburn airport. It was rainy and misty out, not great weather. And that's where this Cinderella-like story came to a sudden horrific end.

The pilot was off course when he tried to land and flew straight into a grove of trees short of the runway. All eight persons aboard—pilot, copilot, and six passengers—were instantly killed when the aircraft exploded.

Yet Samantha's story was not over.

A thousand people attended the funeral for Samantha and her father in Augusta's St. Mary's church. Vladimir Kulagin, first secretary for cultural affairs at the Soviet embassy in Washington was given special permission to travel to Maine, hitherto off-limits to diplomats from the USSR. He read a message from Mikhail Gorbachev, now the new top man in the Kremlin. Robert Wagner was present, absolutely devastated by what had happened and mournfully stating that now Samantha would never have the first date he had been preparing her for. Governor Joseph Brennan spoke; his office had helped facilitate getting the Soviet representation at these rites.

They were also helpful in the next major effort to memorialize Samantha. The idea of having a statue of her in a public setting was proposed, and a friend of the family, sculptor Glenn Hines of Aroostook County, was enlisted to start the project rolling by making a 37-inch model. The Portland Museum of Art undertook the search for a sculptor to cast it life-sized in bronze. Governor Brennan's staff said they would find an appropriate site on state property.

Today, many Maine people and visitors to Augusta have seen the results of those efforts, which were fulfilled in December 1986 when the finished five-foot-tall work was unveiled. The location chosen was to one side of the front of the Cultural Building housing the Maine State Library, Maine State Museum, and Maine State Archives. Samantha is facing the state capitol building where the legislature and the governor have their offices. In her outstretched hands, she holds a dove of peace she's about to release. By her right leg is a bear cub, coincidentally a symbol for both Russia and Maine (the University of Maine's football team is known as the Black Bears). The plaque reads simply: "Samantha Reed Smith, June 29, 1972–August 25, 1985—Maine's Young Ambassador of Good Will."

The Cultural Building attracts large numbers of Maine schoolchildren, primarily to go through the museum; afterwards, in many cases, they have a tour of the state capitol. It is not unusual to see young people crowded around Samantha's statue.

Following her death, too, there were a good many more tributes to the effort she had initiated of bringing young people of opposing nations together. A group of Soviet kids came to Maine and sampled the various summer camps here, including a Samantha Smith camp. A delegation of American youngsters—Samantha's schoolmates from Manchester and surrounding towns—went to the Soviet Union. The Soviets honored her memory with a postage stamp bearing her picture and even named a mountain for Samantha. Yet as political conditions changed—the Soviet Union itself was to dissolve within four years and the danger of mutual atomic destruction seemed to fade—the urgency of Samantha's initiative seemed harder to sustain. Other conflicts took center stage. Still, it is interesting that Maine should currently contain another conflict resolution camp—the Seeds of Peace Camp in Otisfield—where Arab and Israeli kids and others from warring areas come directly into contact with each other and wind up as friends. This seems an echo of Samantha's example.

I met Samantha Smith once—very briefly. There was a reception for a Soviet delegation visiting the U.S. held at the home of an Augusta lawyer, Severin Beliveau. As a state representative and friend of Severin's, I was invited to attend. I knew Jane Smith slightly. Before her daughter's fame, she had come before the committee I co-chaired in the legislature when we looked at the state's child protection services. Much later, she and I and others worked together, without success, to keep the *Maine Times*, a progressive weekly, from eventually folding. In any event, at this crowded gathering in the Beliveau house, there was the young girl we had all seen on television and read about in the newspapers. She was a bit older, growing taller, not quite yet a young lady but getting there fast. I shook hands with the Russian dignitaries and listened to Samantha speak, impressed, as everyone was, by her poise and charisma. I would not have been much of a politician if I did not think to myself: Boy, when she gets old enough, we Democrats should get her to run for office.

All of that potential went up in the flames of the tragic crash in August 1985. But almost a quarter of a century later, Maine continues to remember her and still marvels at what could be done in such a short, positive life.

1. Wikipedia—Article on Nuclear Freeze.
2. *Kennebec Journal.* Augusta, ME: July 11, 1983.

Sister Priscille Roy, at Natal, Rio Grand do Norte, Brazil, in 1980.
Courtesy of Sister Roy

20

SISTER PRISCILLE ROY
AND MAINE'S FOREIGN TIES

In Brazil's northeasternmost state of Rio Grande do Norte, the capital city, Natal, is now a metropolis of more than a million people. In 1942, when the U.S. established an airfield and naval base at this strategic point where the South American country juts toward Africa, about 34,000 inhabitants lived at the site.

Rapid growth has characterized Rio Grande do Norte's small and formerly neglected corner of Brazil, where poverty—extreme poverty—has always been a constant reality.

In 1967 Maine and Rio Grande do Norte were linked in a federally sponsored (but not fully funded) partnership under a Washington, D.C., umbrella organization called Partners of the Americas.

The group was originally titled Partners of the Alliance and was the brainchild of President John F. Kennedy. Remember his Alliance for Progress? That was a government-to-government initiative designed to better U.S. relations with Latin America and the Caribbean, but Kennedy found it too exclusively governmental. He wanted to add a people-to-people exchange, enlisted a friend to get it started, and today its sixty-plus partnerships constitute the only remnant of the Alliance for Progress still functioning.

In 1973 a Biddeford, Maine-born-and-raised nun, Sister Priscille Roy, of the Order of the Immaculate Heart of Mary—also known as the Sisters of the Good Shepherd—went to Brazil, in part under the auspices of the Maine–Rio Grande do Norte partnership.

Initially, she was located in the back country of our sister state. The natives call this area the *Sertao*, and it is totally unlike the concept most Americans have of Brazil. It is not Amazonian jungle full of lush, green tropical vegetation; on the contrary, it is close to desert country, like southern Arizona, with many species of cacti and other thorny plants, and a dry and barren landscape that can go five years without a drop of rain.

Sister Priscille, a graduate of Biddeford Catholic schools and Saint Joseph's College in Windham, Maine, until assigned to Brazil had been teaching and supervising child-care workers in Massachusetts. Her family, like that of Ray Luc Levasseur, had emigrated from Québec to work in the York County mills.

Interviewing her at the Good Shepherd retirement home in Saco where she now resides, I asked her, "Why Brazil? Was that your choice?"

Knowing religious missionaries usually are just sent where needed, I was surprised to learn she had wanted to do missionary work in Brazil since childhood, after reading a book on religion in the Portuguese-speaking country. As early as 1968, she had been slated to go to Lesotho in Africa, but due to her father's sudden serious illness, could not take the post. The Good Shepherds' mission—the order's first in Brazil—had support not only from Partners of the Americas, but also from the Diocese of Maine and its Rio Grande do Norte counterpart.

The town to which she went was Caico, in the remote southern region, and the name of the particular mission site was expressive of things that frighten many people about Brazil—*Jardim de Piranhas*—Garden of the Piranhas—those ferocious fish with needle-sharp teeth that can reduce a whole animal to a skeleton in a matter of minutes.

When Sister Priscille, after six years of toiling in the back country, was transferred to Natal, she entered an environment no less challenging. This was city poverty, and the dangers from violence and crime were as bad as anything the nature of the *Sertao* had to offer. The home she set up for "women victims of prostitution along with their children in risky situations, as well as ex-convicts and/or household employees in search of health services, etc.," was in the middle of what Brazilians call a *favela*—we would say "shack city"—and it was Natal's worst, nicknamed with typical sardonic *Brazilheiro* humor *Cidade da Esperanca*, or "City of Hope."

I have some memories of the *Centro Bom Pastor* (Good Shepherd Center) that I visited—the rambling house and its grounds amid a background of squalor—but the most unforgettable mental picture is of a small boy they had sheltered. In my image, he is scampering up a coconut palm with the agility of a monkey, laughing happily as he shows off. But only months before, I was told, he had been unable to walk. The soles of his feet had been riddled by chiggers that had bored deeply into his flesh; and, moreover he'd been abused and was unwilling even to speak. Now, from the top of the coconut tree, he kept jabbering at us.

This was only one case of rescue. Another was of two handsome children, brother and sister, who were introduced to me. They were going to school now, thanks to a fund started by Sister Priscille, to which I had contributed, and they had come to thank me. Their mother was a former prostitute whom Sister Priscille had lured away from that dangerous profession and trained to be a seamstress, now earning an honest living.

Nearby in the same grim neighborhood was the school for local children built under Sister Priscille's guiding hand, with funds from the Biddeford-Saco Rotary Club and Rotary International. When a group of us *norteamericanos* were taken to see it, a throng of grinning, shouting kids in blue uniforms mobbed us, much to our delight. (It should be noted that, at least during this era, free elementary education was not provided in Brazil.)

Another *Bom Pastor* effort attempted to fill yet one more social service gap in this world of poverty. Generally, no help whatever was available for the disabled poor. In *Cidade da Esperanca*, a young Brazilian woman named Shirley Carvalho, from a wealthy family, who had early lost one of her legs to elephantiasis, was trying to offer rehabilitation services. Sister Priscille worked hand in glove wth her and we in the Partners helped where we could. And Shirley managed to build a facility that even had a pool for therapy swimming.

The tireless work of the dedicated nun from Maine was likened by some to that of Mother Teresa in India. It was certainly of the same ilk, since she dealt with the inner-city problems of the *favelas* and even created missions at impoverished fishing villages on the Rio Grande do Norte coast. But in 1997 her religious duties intervened. The order elected Sister Priscille to its general council, requiring her to move to their international headquarters in Quebec City where the order had been founded in 1850. She was needed to do administrative work as the second assistant to the general superior. Local newspapers in Brazil were full of praise for "*Irmã Priscille.*" One headline declared, "The Sister Says Goodbye to the People of Rio Grande do Norte But Leaves Behind a Great Work of Love and Charity."[1] She, in turn, was quoted as saying, "I am leaving the warmth and sun of Natal for the cold and snow of

Quebec City in Canada. I am going to feel [and here she used an untranslatable Portuguese word, *saudade*, roughly meaning *intense nostalgia*] for the people and music of Brazil. You are a happy people who like to dance and sing. I am so fond of your culture here." No wonder an article referred to her as "North American born, but Brazilian in her heart."[2] Her two years in Québec were spent in raising money for foreign missions and finding donors to pick up educational costs.

In addition to working with Rotary clubs in her hometown and in Natal—where she received the Jean Harris Award, the highest a Rotary district can give[3]—Sister Priscille also had close ties to the University of New England, another Biddeford institution. In 1990 UNE conferred an Honorary Doctorate of Laws upon this local-girl-made-good, as well as the St. Francis Medal, a tradition carried over from the school's past as St. Francis College.

But back in Maine, retired or not, she hasn't stopped working. She still promotes her Brazil Education Program, seeking stipends for students in primary and secondary grades, or for a seminarian or a sister in religious formation. While the prices of these scholarships are a little higher than I remember them, they still seem an extraordinary bargain: $75 for a primary student; $150 for a secondary student; and $250 for the postsecondary level. In Saco, Maine, just as ardently as she did in Natal, Sister Priscille was pursuing her humanitarian task.

Naturally, my emphasis on Sister Priscille is not in any way meant to denigrate or belittle the efforts of the other members of the Maine–Rio Grande do Norte partnership. It was her many years spent outside of Maine that furnished the raison d'être for her inclusion in this book as an exemple of all Maine is doing in relation to our ever more globalized planet.

No huge compilation, as far as I know, has ever been made of the innumerable examples of cooperation that partnerships such as ours supply—two-way, in most instances—as different peoples get to know each other and interact. From my own participation in the Maine–Rio Grande do Norte exchange, I have lots of memories, both serious and sometimes humorous, of the times we Down Easters have had with the *potiguaries* (literally, "shrimp-eaters") of our sister state. One shining emblem of our effect on each other is that in the heart of Natal there exists the Hotel Maine, and the restaurant on its top floor, with its panoramic view of the expanding city, is called The Augusta. A touch of Brazil we once had in our own capital city was the brightly colored parrot that Governor Ken Curtis, who helped initiate the program, brought back to the Blaine House for his children. Today, four decades later, exchanges continue between the two entities, bringing expertise and friendship north to south and south to north in areas as varied as environmental protection, preventing domestic volence, agriculture, and the arts.

Maine also contributed significantly to the national Partners program when Alan Rubin, a Gardiner businessman, who had led the Maine–Rio Grande do Norte partnership from its beginnings, went to D.C. and ran the entire operation for seventeen years.

But the Partners of the Americas program, while perhaps the first, is far from being the only international program in which Mainers are involved. Portland, for example, has four sister cities around the globe— in Japan, Russia, Haiti, and Greece.

The oldest of these couplings is with Shinagawa-ku (Shinagawa City), one of the twenty-three special wards of Tokyo, located in the southeastern part of the Japanese capital. It contains about 300,000 people, somewhat more than live in Greater Portland, and also has formed ties with three much larger cities worldwide: Geneva, Switzerland, Auckland, New Zealand, and Harbin, China. The invitation for the pairing came from Shinagawa, primarily because of their memories of a Maine-born and raised scientist named Edward Sylvester Morse.

Morse is a fascinating person, an icon to this day in Japan and yet another Mainer who flourished out in the world. A Shinagawa–Portland connection was eminently appropriate since Portland was Morse's birthplace and early home, and Shinagawa was the site of shell mounds he discovered in the 1870s while looking for new species of mollusks. Edward Sylvester Morse, the son of a devout Calvinist minister, had grown up a problem child, expelled from every school he attended, which included the Portland Village School, Bridgton Academy, and Bethel (now Gould) Academy. Yet at the last named, he was encouraged to follow his interests in biology and mineralogy, and before he was twenty, he had discovered a new species of land snail, which was named for him: *Tympanus morsei*. Further study with the famed Louis Agassiz at Harvard led to a career in marine biology, with conchology his specialty. His years in Japan were detailed in two volumes he wrote, *Japan*

Day by Day, 1877, 1878–79, 1882–83, and also led to his world-class collection of Japanese pottery, sold to the Boston Museum of Fne Arts in 1890. His work at Shinagawa has been called "the starting point of modern archaeology in Japan."[4] Among other accomplishments in the island nation, he founded the Department of Zoology at the Imperial University and a marine laboratory, the first in the Pacific, at Enoshima. The emperor decorated him—the first American to be so honored—with the Order of the Rising Sun, and later he received the equally prestigious Order of the Sacred Treasury. His last years were spent as director of the Peabody Essex Museum in Salem, Massachusetts.

With Morse as a lead-in, it was natural the universities in the two cities—Rissho and the University of Southern Maine—would develop special ties. Some 2,000 exchanges of all sorts have occurred between these sister cities. and in 2010 Portland–Shinagawa celebrates its twenty-fifth anniversary.

Portland's Russian connection is with Arkhangelsk (City of Archangel), and was founded three years after the Japan link. The partly ice-free port on the Russian north coast, population 350,000, was then in the Soviet Union and well known to Americans from World War II. Named for a twelfth-century monastery, it was the only place under the Communists allowed to keep a religious name.

As in all of these community-to-community programs, the lifeblood here is that of exchanges. This one even has a Department of Transportation engineering project, as well as a Russian–American Rule of Law Program, contrasting the legal system of Maine with that of Archangel *Oblast,* the Russian' equivalent of a state. Visits, of course, help launch and sustain these activities. Recently, Portland's then-mayor Ed Suslovic led an eight-person delegaton to attend the "Third Annual America Week" in Archangel. Included in the group were two Portland policemen and the mayor's thirteen-year-old daughter Kate, and they allegedly stole the show[5] as a constant focus of attention. It was April, but in Russia even colder than Maine—the North Dvina River was just icing out as it ran through the city and snow showers were a frequent event. Intense seminars were held with the Arkhangelsk Commercial Court on land law and individual bankruptcy. This rule-of-law activity was followed up by a delegation from Maine, including longtime Cumberland County District Attorney Stephanie Anderson, coming to discuss juvenile justice. On the other side of the partnership, Archangel Oblast's governor, Ilya Mikhalchuk, and two of his highway engineers were scheduled to meet in Augusta with Maine Department of Transportaton experts, and several five-person Russian delegations were expected before the end of 2008.[6]

From the frozen near-Arctic to the ever-warm Caribbean is the next transition among Portland's overseas relationships. Their third sister city is Cap Haitien, the largest community in northern Haiti. The most active participant in Portland is a group called *Konbit Sante,* a Haitian Creole term literally translated as "barn-raising for health." Its direct tie is to the municipal department of public health in Cap Haitien, and especially with the 250-bed Justinian Hospital (*Hopital Universitaire Justinien*), although work is also done with the smaller Fort St. Michel clinic on the city's outskirts.

Founded in 2000, Konbit Sante helped arrange the sister city connection between Portland and Cap Haitien. More than 300 exchange trips have been made. Medical personnel continually travel from Haiti to Maine for training, while supplies and medical teams from Maine go to Haiti. Grants have been received to build a pediatric emergency room at the Justinian Hospital, and other donations are earmarked for hookworm eradication and infection control. At Fort St. Michel's clinic, tuberculosis is a special concern. One of the biggest needs Konbit Sante tries to address is finding resources enough to bring clean water to these two medical facilities. Improving the Justinian Hospital's electrical infrastructure is another high-priority goal.[7]

The fourth of Portland's international ties is with the city of Mytilene on the Greek island of Lesbos in the Aegean Sea. A University of Southern Maine/Aegean Culural Exchange has been in existence for more than a decade, its first contact having been made in 1992 when a USM faculty member gave three piano concerts on Lesbos. Most recently, the Maine Street Jazz Quartet played to a packed audience in Mytilene, and in the interim, a number of artists and craftsmen from Greece have traveled to Maine. When Nick Mavodones, a Portlander of Greek heritage, was mayor, an official sister city relationship was set up between Portland and Mytilene.

Nor is Portland the only municipality in Maine to have sister cities. Bangor has two—with Carasque, El Salvador, and St. John, New

Brunswick, a much closer neighbor. One view of the Central American tie can be seen in the December 2006 newsletter of PICA (Peace through Interamerican Community Action), a Bangor-based, labor-oriented organization, best known in Maine for its "Clean Clothes" campaign to keep sweatshop-produced textiles out of our state. PICA apparently also has strong ties to Bangor's Salvadoran counterpart, for it has a "Sister City Committee," a "Sister City Marketing Committee," and a "Youth Adelantando (Advancement) Committee." The newsletter started its lead story with: "Earlier this month a truckload of soldiers arrived without notice in...Carasque in El Salvador's Chalatenango Department and before consulting with local authorities climbed Cerro Coyote, the hill behind the village...." The motive the military gave was that they were inspecting the countryside for environmental damage, but since they had "foreigners" with them, the villagers believed they were linked to North American gold-mining firms.[8]

This same newsletter issue also carried the report of an eleven-member PICA delegation that spent four nights in Carasque. "The gorgeous mountainside town...had the most caring people we had ever met, who never hesitated to try to communicate with us despite the inability of some of us to speak Spanish." Six of the contingent were Youth Adelantando members.

Bath is another Maine city with two sister cities: Bath, England, as one might expect, and Shariki, Japan, which is a story in itself. It seems that on October 30, 1889, an American sailing ship was caught in a typhoon off the coast of Japan. She was the *Chesebrough*, built in Bath, Maine, and she ran aground in the storm and broke up. All of the crew would have perished except for the local Japanese who rode their fishing boats out to the stricken vessel and managed to save four of the Americans while risking their own lives. Two local youths ran forty miles to the prefectural capital in order to summon help. A memorial in Shariki village commemorates this heroic happening.

Friendship between Shariki and Bath was cemented in 1994 and drew a favorable comment from President Bill Clinton, who said in a letter to the citizens of Shariki, "By hosting the Bath, Maine, junior high exchange students, you are contributing to our two nations' efforts to sustain and deepen the good will that exists between us. The exchange program between students of Shariki and students of Bath is a shining example of the value of promoting mutual understanding and appreciation of different cultures...."9 In memory of the 1889 event, there is an annual "Chesebrough Cup Swim Ekiden" in Shariki, a combined swim race and long-distance run.

The list of sister cities continues with Eastport and Husavik, Iceland; Greater Waterville and Kotlas, Russia (a city of 70,000 in the Arkhangelsk Oblast); Brunswick and Trinidad, Cuba; Scarborough and both Scarborough, England, and Scarborough, Ontario; Old Orchard Beach and Miamian, France.

A search of the Internet showed that a woman in South Portland was trying to promote a sister city relationship for Prishtina, which is the capital of Kosovo, originally under Serbia but now, with its overwhelmingly Albanian population, on the verge of becoming independent.

A direct connection exists between the University of Maine and Bulgaria, where the Orono campus has opened a branch in the city of Plovdiv. And some Maine high schools have overseas programs. In Farmington, the Friends of Pueblo Nuevo help a high school in Nicaragua, while Greely Middle School in Cumberland has a sister school in Namioka, Japan.

The latter community is in Aomori Prefecture, as is Shariki, the town linked with Bath. Like Rio Grande do Norte, the entire Prefecture of Aomori is partnered with the entire State of Maine. Its location is in the extreme north of Honshu, Japan's most populous and important island, and the capital city is also called Aomori. The Aomori–Maine connection is one of the most active, with delegations going back and forth on a continual basis. One in 2005 was led by Maine's first lady, Karen Baldacci. There is a permanent Maine–Aomori Sister State Advisory Council, and state government and quasi-governmental agencies such as the Maine Humanities Council, the Maine International Trade Center, the Maine Arts Commission, and others, take part. For the tenth anniversary in 2004, a large contingent from Maine visited Aomori and a "grand reception" was provided by the prefecture's governor. This Maine delegation included groups from Greely Middle School and Bath Middle School. The Mainers arrived at the time of the famed Nebuta Festival in Aomori, a weeklong affair that draws 3.7 million visitors. As part of the festivities, a "Maine Fair" was coordinated with the festival, and Maine lobsters were sold. Simultaneously, in Maine, an

"Apple and Pine Tassel" photo exhibit (apples are a specialty of Aomori) was making the rounds. I remember a stunning showing of kimonos in Maine, done through the work of a good friend of mine, Maggie Kelly of Winthrop, who has been very active with this exchange and accompanied Mrs. Baldacci on her trip.

There is also a Maine–Jilin Province, China, relationship. Fred Richardson, a former Maine state representative who once headed up the Portland–Archangel project, has been instrumental in forming this exchange.

Many nongovernmental international programs also occur in Maine. Lists of them are mind-boggling. I will cite only three, two of which I am familiar with myself, and the third because it has been in the news recently.

This latter is known as Safe Passage, and its moment in the head-lines was, unfortunately, due to a tragedy. Haley Denning of Yarmouth, Maine, the young woman who had started Safe Passage, an organization dedicated to helping the poorest children of Guatemala City, Guatemala, was killed in an auto accident in that Central American country. Her vision had formed in 1994 after a visit to Guatemala City's dump, where she saw "shoeless, dirty children living and working in the dump, trying to help feed their families by picking through the trash for recyclables, a pursuit that nets the equivalent of $4 to $6 a day."[10]

Haley Denning's solution for putting an end to this degrading occupation, which goes "hand-in-hand with glue-sniffing and alcoholism," was education, but in a country, like many in Latin America, where elementary schooling isn't free or requires money to buy uniforms and school supplies, this wasn't easy. So Denning proceeded to raise enough money, selling her car and computer, to equip ninety dump children to go to school. She next went on to build educational centers, and Safe Passage, headquartered by her in Yarmouth, grew into a large organization with an annual budget of $1.7 million.

For three years prior to her death, Henning had been looking forward to launching a hotel training program in a Guatemalan hostelry Safe Passage had leased and rebaptized as the *Posada Lazos Fuertes* (Hotel Strong Ropes). It is located in the popular tourist site of Antigua, a highly picturesque historic city about an hour's ride from Guatemala City. At Denning's death, her organization had 100 employees and was assisting 400 children. To replace Denning, whom the Guatemalans had nicknamed *Angel de Basuero* (Angel of the Garbage Dump), Safe Passage named its accountant, Ed Mahoney.

In Portland, a benefit concert and film showing filled Merrill Auditorium with a capacity crowd of 1,900. Haley Denning, whose thirty-seventh birthday it would have been, was shown with the dump kids in a documentary nominated for an Oscar, entitled *Recycled Lives,* and all proceeds from the evening were added to Safe Passage's budget. A Portland reporter sent to Guatemala City recorded how the work continues, describing a teenage Guatemalan girl, Florinda Xiloj, wearing "a frayed pink jacket held together with safety pins," gazing about at the "exposed wooden beams, flowers bursting from hanging pots and open air balconies" of the plush hotel where she would start her hospitality worker's training, along with twenty other "children of the dump." Haley Denning's death had delayed the program's opening by a week, but it was going ahead.

Sustainable Harvest is another Central American activity headquartered in Maine. The idea is based on the "Extension" programs of American agriculture instituted in the 1930s that helped U.S. farmers become the most modern in the world. Sustainable Harvest, operating out of its primary office in Surry, Maine, works in four Central American countries: Belize, Honduras, Nicaragua, and Panama. It brings in experts to train local farmers to become Extension agents, introducing new techniques and crops to their neighbors. The results, soon evident to the farmers, is an increase in income by using practices more environmentally friendly and better paying than what they've done traditionally.

I have actually observed the program at work in Belize. Along with my wife and one of my daughters, we traveled to Punta Gorda, a town near the Guatemalan border in Mayan Indian country, and out to Boom Creek. There Nana, the Ghana-born director of Sustainable Harvest in Belize, was not only conducting his planting experiments. but had also provided a special kind of wood stove to heat the thatched-roofed huts in which the locals lived and help them cook their food. These stoves need only a fraction of the wood the natives generally burn, thus reducing the cutting down of the rainforest. Sustainable Harvest not only works on food crops but has been reforesting thousands of acres.

Simple techniques are employed: building small silos for grain storage so farmers can hold onto their crops and not unload them all at the same time, thus depressing prices; using rice paddies year after year to avoid the age-old "slash and burn" methods that destroy so much wild land; making worm composting beds; recycling wastes; and setting up vegetable gardens at schools to provide for healthy school lunches. One project we didn't see was underway in Honduras, where several thousand breadfruit seedlings from the National Tropical Botanical Garden in Hawaii were planted in an effort to create a new, large-scale food crop for Central America.

Finally, there is the Seeds of Peace Camp at Otisfield, Maine. In a sense, this is a case of the world coming to Maine for a neutral ground where warring ethnic groups, or rather their offspring, can mingle and, like youngsters everywhere, become friends. It started with Arab and Israeli kids, and its successful means of getting enemies to bond were extended to other hostile entities: Greeks and Turks from Cyprus, Indians and Pakistanis, and Serbs and Croats from Eastern Europe.

Where does Maine fit in, aside from providing a bucolic, peaceful setting? There is what was first called "the Portland Project," in which a group of Portland students of various ethnic backgrounds, children born overseas and brought to America as refugees, and American-born adolescents could participate during the summer in the Seeds of Peace procedures of learning how to live and interact with each other and then spend the school year in bringing those lessons back to—initially Portland, and now Lewiston, too—but really to all of Maine, since delegations travel from school to school, speaking to kids around the state. It is said that more than forty languages are spoken in the Portland school system. Lewiston has a noticeable Somali and Somali Bantu population, and other areas of Maine are no longer as insular as they were.

An example of how these "Maine Seeds" are working can be seen in "the first-ever Portland Color Games" they organized after a season at the camp in Otisfield. The games brought together ninety youths from six Portland area high schools, formed them into random teams, gave each team color-coded T-shirts, and put the teams in competition, the same way it worked at the Seeds of Peace Camp—"seeing people from different schools, people with different beliefs and pasts, working together as a team during the Games."[11]

Maine *is* in the world in a way it never was in the past.

1. *O Jornal de Hoje* (Today's Journal), Natal, Rio Grande do Norte newspaper, November 22, 1997.

2. Ibid.

3. Rotary International Monthly Letter, District 4500, Natal, Rio Grande do Norte: February 9, 1999.

4. Wikipedia article on Edward Sylvester Morse.

5. Handout by the Archangel Committee, the Russian Sister City Committee of Greater Portland, Spring 2008.

6. Ibid.

7. Konbit Sante, Cap Haitien Health Partnership website.

8. *Picante,* newsletter of PICA, Volume 21, Issue 1, December 2006.

9. Letter from President Bill Clinton to the citizens of Shariki, Japan— Wikipedia.

10. *Portland Press Herald.* Portland, ME: January 29, 2007.

11. *The Olive Branch,* Youth Magazine of the Seeds of Peace Program, Winter 2006, Spring 2007.

AFTERWORD

Right up front, I'll admit my choice of candidates to illustrate the theme of *Maine in the World* is more than a trifle arbitrary. The other day I caught hell for not devoting an entire chapter to Edward Sylvester Morse, the nineteenth-century Portlander whom the Japanese adore. Frankly, I'd never heard of him before I'd already chosen my subjects for each chapter. But this is indicative of how *many* Mainers, past and present, are potentally of interest. When I talked about the idea of this book in 2007 at the 14th Annual Washburn Humanities Seminar, Billie Gammon, the doyen of Norlands in Livermore, Maine, where the conference was held, jumped on the notion as an overall theme for the future 15th seminar. And so "Mainers and Their Neighbors Who Went into the World" became the title of the 2008 event.

What a harvest of names and histories came forth! Most of them, as well, are folks I also never heard of, whose stories sound absolutely tantalizing, such as "From Pine to Palm: The Voyage of Captain John Drew," "John Warren: From Hallowell, Maine, to the Society of California Pioneers," "Last of the Saddle Tramps, a Docudrama about Messanie Wilkins from Minot, Maine," "George Dana Boardman, Missionary to Burma," and "Elizabeth Upham Yates on the American Woman Suffrage Campaign Trail, 1894–95."

Teased into the limelight under this rubric are bits and pieces of Maine history forming what one might call a huge cauldron of material. We have only to look at Doug Stover's book, *Eminent Mainers,* published in 2006, wherein he documents "Thousands of Amazing Mainers, Mostly Dead, and a Few People from Away."

Reading a classic Maine book, *The Peninsula,* by Louise Dickinson Rich, about a still very isolated Down East section, the Gouldsboro/ Winter Harbor/Prospect Harbor/Corea region, it was startling to encounter the following quote about local names:

"Quite a few men answer to Ivory and Harvard, and quite a few women to Persia, India, or Ceylon. These last were inherited from their great-grandmothers, who were born in the days when the sails and the lovely sheers of the American clipper ships were familiar on every horizon and in every port in the world.... These names have been handed down in seafaring families as proudly as have been the camphorwood chests, Paisley shawls, and dinner dishes of Canton china brought home from the ends of the earth."[1]

A final postscript to this bit of rummaging through our attic of Maine history in search of the international dimensions of our state and its people comes from the immediate present. Sister Priscille Roy, as I have already noted, maintains her Brazil education work in her retirement. Before me, I have documents she recently sent, following up on donations I made. They contain head-and-shoulder photographs of a young boy and a young girl my money helps support and Sister Priscille's comments about both children.

Of the boy, Joao Fabio de Olveira, she writes, "Joao lives wth his mother and younger brother in a very modest home. The mother does not have a steady job...works cleaning and washing clothes in homes to support her two boys. Joao is intellgent and he does very well in school...."

Of the girl, Luana Celia Rochelly de Lima: "Luana lives with an 'adopted family' under very primitive conditions. She has a sad life story. Yet she does very well in her studies." Included is a translated note from Luana, stating her name, that she is twelve years old and in her first year of high school, and continues, "I was adopted when I was a day old by a very special woman who was very poor [still is, and dying of AIDS]. I love my mother. She's all I have."

Sister Priscille finishes the story, how the adoption came about instead of an abortion, the fragility of the situation, and that "Our Ed Program is providing a food package monthly and seeing to Luana's education since 1995!!! This past March, I bought a 'hammock' and clothing.... She had so little to wear."

Thus does Maine make its contributions in the outer world, as it has done since our inception.

1. Louise Dickinson Rich, *The Peninsula*. Philadelphia: J. B. Lippincott Company, 1958, pp. 188–89.

ANNOTATED BIBLIOGRAPHY

American Friends Service Committee. *The Wabanakis of Maine and the Maritimes.* Bath, ME, 1989.

American Journal of Numismatics. *Correspondence Relating to the Preble Medal,* 1872.

Anastas, Peter. *Glooskap's Children: Encounters with the Penobscot Indians of Maine.* Boston: Beacon Press, 1973.

Baker, Emerson W., and John G. Reid. *The New England Knight, Sir William Phips, 1651–1695.* Toronto: University of Toronto Press, 1998. A very complete biography, almost too complete, of the back-country Maine boy who made good in the complex world of English colonialism in the seventeenth century. Extraordinarily well researched.

Banks, Charles Edward. *History of York,* Volume 1. Baltimore, MD: Regional Publishing Company, 1967; first published 1931–35.

Baugh, Odin. *John Frank Stevens: American Trailblazer.* Spokane, WA: Arthur H. Clark Company, 2005.

Baxter, James Phinney. *Documentary History of the State of Maine,* Volume 5. Portland, ME: 1897.

Beckham, Stephen Dow. *The Simpsons of Shore Acres.* Coos Bay, OR: Arago Books, 2003.

Bocca, Geoffrey. *The Life and Death of Sir Harry Oakes.* Garden City, NY: Doubleday, 1959. A compelling portrait of a Maine-born man consumed by finding gold, whose fame and fortune, once he did, ended in tragedy.

Bok, Edward W. *A Man from Maine.* New York: Charles Scribner's Sons, 1923. Cyrus H. K. Curtis's son-in-law draws a sympathetic picture of his wife's father's climb to the heights of publishing. An able editor himself Bok writes well, if a bit on the hagiography side, in presenting the Portlander who made the *Saturday Evening Post* and the *Ladies' Home Journal* famous and successful.

Boyle, Gerry. *The Legend and Lore of Tate House.*

Burrage, Henry S. *Early English and French Voyages, Chiefly from Hakluyt, 1534-1608.* New York: Charles Scribner's Sons, 1906.

Butler, Joyce. "The Wadsworths: A Portland Family." *Maine Historical Society Quarterly,* Volume 27, Numbers 2-19, Spring 1988.

Calhoun, Charles. *Longfellow: A Rediscovered Life.* Boston: Beacon Press, 2004. My friend Charles has written a fine up-to-date biography of Longfellow.

Chapman, Leonard B. "Colonel Thomas Westbrook," *Portland Transcript,* 1883.

Clifford, Phillip G. *Nathan Clifford, Democrat, 1803-1881.* New York: G. P. Putnam's Sons, 1922. A descendant of the U.S. Supreme Court justice from Maine, Phillip Clifford presents a workable study of his kinsman's busy life. The only extant biography of Nathan Clifford.

Cook, Walter L. *Bangor Theological Seminary: A Sesquicentennial History.* Orono, ME: University of Maine Press, 1971

Davis, Ronald C. *John Ford: Hollywood's Old Master.* Norman, OK: University of Oklahoma Press, 1995.

De Hegemann-Lindencrone, Lillie L. *The Sunny Side of Diplomatic Life.* New York: Harper and Brothers, Publishers, 1914. A favorite of mine, a little jewel of writing from the nineteenth century, done by a Massachusetts girl who married a Danish diplomat.

Dixfield Bicentenary Committee. *The Early History of Dixfield.* Dixfield, ME: 1976.

Durden, Robert Franklin. *James Shepherd Pike: Republicanism and the American Negro, 1850–1882.* Durham, NC: Duke University Press, 1957. Nicely done biography of an obscure but not uninteresting journalist-diplomat from Calais, Maine, who epitomizes some of the nineteenth-century quandary about slavery and blacks in the U.S.

Eyman, Scott. *Print the Legend: The Life and Times of John Ford.* New York: Simon and Schuster, 1999. The best book I found on the career of John Ford, well-written and exhaustive in its research.

Flandreau, Grace. *The Story of Marias Pass.* Great Northern Railway Publication.

Fuller, Walter D. *The Life and Times of Cyrus H. K. Curtis, 1850–1933.* London: Newcomen Society, 1948.

Galicich, Anne. *Samantha Smith: A Journey for Real.* Minneapolis, MN: Dillon Press, Inc., 1987.

Getchell, Jessie. *Long, Long Ago in Calais.*

Glackens, Ira. *Yankee Diva: Lillian Nordica and the Golden Days of Opera.* New York: Coleridge Press, 1963. *Yankee Diva* really brings Lillian Nordica to life, from her childhood in Farmington, Maine, to her death in the Dutch East Indies.

Gollaher, David. *Voice for the Mad: The Life of Dorothea Dix.* New York: The Free Press, 1995.

Goold, Hon. William. *Sir William Phips.* Portland, ME: Maine Historical Society, 1887.

Gorges, Sir Ferdinando. *Briefe Narration of the Originall Undertakings of the Advancement of Plantations in the Parts of America.*

Griffith, George Bancroft. *The Poets of Maine.* Portland, ME: Elwell, Pickard and Company, 1888.

Griffiths, Thomas Morgan. *Maine Sources in the House of the Seven Gables.* Waterville, ME: n.p., 1945.

Gurko, Miriam. *Restless Spirit: The Life of Edna St. Vincent Millay.* New York: Thomas Y. Crowell Company, 1962.

Hall, Joseph D., Jr. *The Genealogy and Biography of the Waldos of America, 1650–1883.* Danielsonville, CT: Scofield and Hamilton Press, 1883.

Howells, Anne Molloy. *Five Kidnapped Indians.* New York: Hastings House Publishers, 1968.

Joe, Rita and Lesley Choyce, editors. *The Mikmaq Anthology.* Lawrencetown Beach, N.S.: Potterfield Press, 1997.

Johnson, Steven F. *Ninnuock (The People): The Algonkian People of New England.* Marlborough, MA. Bliss Publishing Co., 1995.

Journals of the House of Representatives of Massachusetts. Boston: Massachusetts Historical Society, 1942. Volumes: 1739–40; 1740–41; 1744–45; 1746–47; 1759–60. These records published by the Massachusetts Historical Society are invaluable for anyone doing research on eighteenth-century Maine.

Kennebec Journal. Augusta, ME: Scrapbook of stories about Samantha Smith.

Lathem, Edward Connery. *England's Homage to Longfellow.* Portland, ME: Maine Historical Society, 2008. A Dartmouth professor's impeccable research on how Longfellow's bust—the only one of an American—came to be included in England's Westminster Abbey. Recently printed by the Maine Historical Society.

Leland, Charles G. *The Algonquin Legends of New England: Myths and Folklore of the Micmac, Passamaquoddy, and Penobscot Tribes*. Boston: Houghton Mifflin and Company, 1884.

Lenz, Peter A. Editor. *Voyages to Norumbega. Documentary Account of Native American and Euro-American Culture and Contact*. Augusta, ME: Maine Arts and Humanities, Inc.

Lincoln, Waldo. *Waldo: Genealogy of the Waldo Family, 1647–1900*. Worcester, MA: Press of Charles Hamilton, 1902.

Locke, John L. *General Waldo's Circular*, translated from the German. Portland, ME: Maine Historical Society Collections. Volume II, 1859.

Longfellow, Samuel. *Life of Henry Wadsworth Longfellow*, Volume 1. Boston: Ticknor and Company, 1886.

Lounsbury, Alice. *Sir William Phips: Treasure Fisherman and Governor of the Massachusetts Bay Colony*. New York: Charles Scribner's Sons, 1941.

Marcotte, Nancy Chute. *This Is Waterford*. Norway, ME: Waterford Historical Society, 2003.

Martin, Patricia Stone. *Samantha Smith, Young Ambassador*. Vero Beach, FL: Rourke Enterprises.

Mather, Cotton. *The Life of Sir William Phips*. New York: Covici Friede, Inc., Publishers, 1929, reprint. An old chestnut first published in 1697. Reprinted edied with a preface by Mark Van Doren. Most valuable for its view of the great Boston divine's temperament and prejudices as he defends his protégé Sir William Phips against his political enemies.

Maxim, Hiram Percy. *A Genius in the Family: Sir Hiram Stevens Maxim Through a Small Son's Eyes*. New York: Harper and Brothers Publishers, 1936. Hiram Percy Maxim never again saw his father, the inventor of the machine gun, after he reached the age of fifteen. But these memoirs bring the famous British knight, born in Sangerville, Maine, to life.

McCullough, David. *The Path Between the Seas*. New York: Simon and Schuster, 1977.

McKee, Christopher. *Edward Preble: A Naval Biography.* Annapolis, MD: Naval Institute Press, 1972.

Milford, Nancy. *Savage Beauty: The Life of Edna St. Vincent Millay.* New York: Random House, 2001. To me, the best book on Edna St. Vincent Millay. Author Milford leaves out nothing, including the Camden poet's sexual pecadillos.

Morey, David C. *The Voyage of Archangell.* Gardiner, ME: Tilbury House, Publishers, 2005. Presents Rosier's original text with annotations.

Mottelay, P. Fleury. *The Life and Work of Sir Hiram Maxim, Knight, Chevalier de la Legion d'Honneur.* London: John Lane, 1920.

Naval Documents Related to the United States Wars with the Barbary Powers, Volume II. Washington, D.C.: U.S. Printing Office, 1940. An exhaustive compilation of records from the Barbary Wars, containing many valuable documents and writings.

Naval Operations from December 1800–1801, Quasi-War with France, Volume 7. Washington, D.C.: U.S. Government Printing Office, 1938.

Nicolar, Joseph. *The Life and Traditions of the Red Man.* Bangor, ME: C. H. Glass and Company, Printers, 1893. Reprinted by Duke University Press, 2007.

Norman, Howard. *How Glooskap Outwits the Ice Giants and other Tales of the Maritimes.* Boston: Little Brown, 1989.

Paulin, Charles Oscar. *Commodore John Rogers: Captain, Commodore, and Senior Officer of the American Navy*, 1773–1838. Cleveland, OH: Arthur H. Clark Co., 1910.

Pullen, John J. *Comic Relief: The Life and Laughter of Artemus Ward, 1834–1867.* Hamden, CT: Archer Books, 1983. Always a joy to read, Pullen does his usual biographic justice to Maine's quirky but hilarious humorist.

Rehnquist, William H. *Centennial Crisis: The Disputed Election of 1876.* New York: Alfred A. Knopf, 2004. The author is seemingly more important than what he writes about this famed disputed election of 1876. Is it the chief justice's apologia for the 2000 election?

Rich, Louise Dickinson. *The Peninsula.* Philadelphia: J. B. Lippincott Company, 1958.

Roberts, Kenneth. *I Wanted to Write.* Garden City, NY: Doubleday and

Company, Inc., 1949. A fun read. Kenneth Roberts was, if nothing else, always opinionated, but also always a talented writer, whether doing nonfiction or fiction.

Rodd, Francis Rennell. *General William Eaton: The Failure of an Idea.* New York: Minton, Balch and Company, 1932.

Rolde, Neil. *Sir William Pepperrell of Colonial New England.* Brunswick, ME: Harpswell Press, 1982.

_____. *The Interrupted Forest.* Gardiner, ME: Tilbury House Publishers, 2001.

Rosier, James. *A True Relation of the most prosperoous voyage made this present year 1605, by Captaine [sic] George Waymouth, in the Discovery of the land of Virginia.* Through this on-the-spot diary, the story of Waymouth's 1605 voyage to Maine and his kidnapping of five local Indians has been admirably presented for posterity. His account is also published, with annotations, in David Morey's *The Voyage of Archangell,* listed above.

Ross, Allan, ed. *Letters of Edna St. Vincent Millay.* New York: Harper and Brothers, 1952.

Rusk, Ralph L. *The Life of Ralph Waldo Emerson.* New York: Columbia University Press, 1949; reprint.

Schulman, Robert. *Romany Marie: The Queen of Greenwich Village.* Louisville, KY: Butler Books, 2006.

Schumacher, Alice Clink. *Hiram Percy Maxim.* Cortez, CO: Electric Radio Press, Inc.

Segal, Harvey Gordon. *The Sleeping Lady Awakens.* Kosrae State, Eastern Carolines, Federated States of Micronesia: Kosrae Print Shop, 1989. A work of love about one of the most obscure islands in the world. Invaluable as a guide to Kosrae in Micronesia and its history and geography.

Seitz, Don C. *Artemus Ward.* New York: Harper and Brothers Publishers, 1919. Seitz is a sprightly writer, originally from Maine, and his book nicely complements the work of John J. Pullen.

Shafter, Tony. *Edna St. Vincent Millay: America's Best Loved Poet.* New York: Julian Messner, Inc., 1957.

Simmons, Matthew. "When the Creation of America Began." Ch. 4 of *One Land—Two Worlds—Maine-Mawooshen, 1605–2005, The 400th Anniversary of George Waymouth's Voyage to New England.*

Rockland, ME: Island Institute, 2005.

Skillin Family Newsletter. Spring, 1986, Fall, 1988.

Smith, Samantha. *Journey to the Soviet Union.* Boston: Little, Brown and Company, 1985.

Snow, Benjamin Galen. Diary. Folger Library, University of Maine at Orono. The diary is not always easy to read nor to understand where the writer is located, which happens to be in the Marshall Islands. But it is extremely authentic in its depiction of a missionary's lonely life.

Stahl, Jasper Jacob. *History of Old Broad Bay and Waldoboro,* two volumes. Portland, ME: Bond Wheelwright, 1956. Another old chestnut. The all-time definitive work on this section of midcoast Maine.

Thayer, Reverend Henry O. *Sir William Phips, Adventurer and Statesman: A Study in Colonial Biography.* Portland, ME: Maine Historical Society, 1927.

Tiffany, Joseph. *Life of Dorothea Lynde Dix.* Boston: Houghton Mifflin, 1918.

Van Deusen, Glyndon G. *Horace Greeley, 19th Century Crusader.* Philadelphia: University of Pennsylvania Press, 1953.

Wagner, Judith and Richard. *The Uncommon Life of Louis Jerome Simpson.* North Bend, OR: Bygones, 2003.

Walker, Mark. *Maine Roots: Growing Up Poor in the Kennebec Valley.* Camden, ME: Picton Press, 1994.

_____. *Working For Utopia, 1937–1953.* Concordia, CA: Quixotic Press, 2000.

Two unsung volumes I discovered on the shelves of the Portland Public Library. Mark Walker is a good writer, self-taught, and covers well what it was like to be poor in the 1920s, 1930s, and 1940s in Maine and elsewhere.

Woodward, C. Vann. *Reunion and Reaction.* Boston: Little, Brown and Company, 1951.

Wright, Louis B., and Julia H. MacLeod. *The First Americans in North Africa: William Eaton's Struggle for a Vigorous Policy Against the Barbary Pirates, 1799–1805.* Princeton, NJ: Princeton University Press, 1945.

Yankee Magazine. "The Last and Tragic Concert Tour of Lillian Nordica," January 1979.

INDEX

A. M. Simpson and Brother Company, 137
abolition. *See* slavery.
Adams, Esther (Tess) Root, 226
Adams, John Quincy, 160
Admiral Duff, 65
Africa, 60
Agassiz, Louis, 311–12: *Japan Day by Day,* 311–23
Alexander II, Czar, 185
Algonquin Legends of New England (Leland), 3
Allen and Ticknor, 91
Allen Island, Maine, 14, 16
Allen, "Camp Meeting," 182, 187
American Board of Commissioners for Foreign Missionaries, 145
American Nazi Party, 276, 290–91
Amoret, 20, 22, 25
Amori–Maine Sister State Council, 315
Anderson, Hugh, 164, 166
Anderson, Stephanie, 312–13
Andropov, Yuri, 293, 294, 295–97, 300
Andros, Edmund, 37
Angel Intrudes, The (Dell), 218
Appleton, Fanny. *See* Longfellow, Fanny Appleton.
Appleton, John, 166
Appleton, William, 92–93
Archangel, Russia, 312–13
Archangell, 13, 14, 16, 18, 20
Aria de Capo (Millay), 220
Arkhangelsk. *See* Archangel.
Artek Camp, 297–98

Artemus Ward, His Book (Ward), 121, 122
Arundell, Thomas, 14, 15, 22
Atlantic Oakes Inn. *See* Willows, The.
Augusta Mental Health Institute (AMHI), 102
"Axis Sally." *See* Gillars, Mildred.
Ayer, James, 160

Bahamas, 256, 257
Baker, Emerson "Tad," 33–34
Baldacci, Karen, 315–16
Bamford, Thomas, 60
Bangor Mental Health Institute (BAMHI), 102. *See also* Dorothea Dix Psychiatric Center.
Bangor Theological Seminary, ix, 145, 146, 153
Bangor–Carasque, 313, 314
Bangor–St. John, 313, 314
Bateman, Edward, 31
Bath, Maine, 314–15
"Battle of Lovewell's Pond" (Longfellow), 82
Battle of Midway, The (movie), 261, 268–69
Baxter, James Phinney, 21
Becke, Louis, 155
Beckham, Stephen Dow: *The Simpsons of Shore Acres,* 135, 141
Belcher, Jonathan, 49–50, 52–54, 55
Beliveau, Severin, 304
Bernstein, Leonard, 198
Birmingham, 136–37
Birth of a Nation (movie), 263–64
Bladen, Martin, 50, 51

Blaine, James G., 140, 168, 169, 172, 178

Blanco, 139

Boardman, George Dana, 320

Bocca, Geoffrey: *Life and Death of Sir Harry Oakes,* 252, 255, 257

Bogan, Louise, 224

Boissevain, Eugen, 218–19, 222–23, 225, 226

Bok, Edward, 196, 197, 202, 207, 210; *A Man from Maine,* 196, 198, 207, 210

Bok, Mary Louise Curtis, 198, 202

Bond, Ward, 269

Boston and Maine Railroad, 238

Bowdoin College, 82, 83–84, 88, 89, 90–91, 95, 146, 250

Boyd, Nancy. *See* Millay, Edna St. Vincent.

Bradbury, Bion, 172

Bradbury, James W., 164, 166

Brennan, Joseph, 300, 302, 303

Brewster, Ralph Owen, 240

Briefe Narration (Gorges), 24

Broad Bay. *See* Waldoboro.

Brook, Thomas, 96

Brown, Roza, 253

Browne, Charles Farrar. *See* Ward, Artemus.

Buchanan, James, 165, 166

Buck in the Snow, The (Millay), 225

Buckley, William, 290; *National Review,* 290

Butler Hospital, 102

Butler, Charles, 102, 107

Calais Free Library, 179

Calhoun, Charles: *Longfellow: A Rediscovered Life,* 89

Canadian Pacific Railway, 230

Cap Haitien, Haiti, 313

Cappy Ricks (Kyne), 135–36

Capra, Frank, 273

Carasque, El Salvador, 313–24

Carey, Harry, 264

Carlyle, Thomas, 91, 177; *Life of Schiller,* 91

Caroline, 146

Carson, Johnny, 300

Carson, Rachel, 106–07

Carvalho, Shirley, 309

Centennial Crisis: The Disputed Election of 1876 (Rehnquist), 169

Centro Bom Pastor. *See* Good Shepherd Center.

Challons, Henry, 22, 23

Chamberlain, Joshua, 95

Channing, William Ellery, 94, 103–04, 106; *Slavery,* 103

Chase, Salmon P., 173

Chesebrough, 314

Chitwood, Michael, 287

Chow, Charlie, 254

Christie, Harold, 256

Church, Benjamin, 42

Churchill, William, 257

Citizen Kane (movie), 267

City of Boston, 128

Civil War (American), 111–12, 167, 173, 174, 177, 199

Clarke and Lake Trading Company, 32, 33

Clarke, Thomas, 32

Clay, Henry 162

Clean Clothes campaign, 314

Clemens, Samuel. *See* Twain, Mark.

Cleveland Plain Dealer, 117, 118, 119

Clifford, Hannah Ayer, 160, 163

Clifford, Nathan, 158–69, 170, 171

Clifford, Phillip G., 161

Coburn, Abner, 172

Colby College, 250, 297

Collis P. Huntington (locomotive), 165

Cong, Ireland, 270

Constitution, USS, 66–67, 68, 70, 76
Cooper, Merian C., 267, 270
Coos Bay, Oregon, 138–39
Cornell, Kitty, 219
Crellius, Joseph, 58
Cromwell, William, 232
Crowinshield, Clara, 91, 92
Curtis Hall Arboretum, 209
Curtis Island, Maine, 209
Curtis Publishing Company, 202–03, 207, 208
Curtis, Cyrus H. K., 194–204, 207–10; *Ladies Home Journal,* 202; *People's Ledger,* 201; *Saturday Evening Post,* 202; *Tribune and Farmer,* 202; *Young America,* 200
Curtis, Cyrus Libby, 195–96
Curtis, Kenneth, 311
Curtis, Louisa Knapp, 201, 202, 204, 209
Curtis, Mary Louise. *See* Bok, Mary Louise Curtis.
Czech Legion, 239–40

Davis, Ronald L.: *John Ford: Hollywood's Old Master,* 273
Dawson City, Yukon, 251, 252
de Castin, Baron, 38, 43, 90
de Champlain, Samuel, 31, 38
de Hegemann-Lindencrone, Lillie, 188–89; *The Sunny Side of Diplomatic Life,* 188–89
de Lesseps, Ferdinand, 233
de Lima, Luana Celia Rochelly, 321
de Marigny, Marie Alfred Fouquereaux, 257–58
de Olveira, Joao Fabio, 321
Decatur, James, 73
Decatur, Stephen, 71–72, 73
December 7th (movie), 268
Deering, Dorcas, 67–68

Deering, Mary. *See* Preble, Mary Deering.
Dell, Floyd, 218, 222, 223; *The Angel Intrudes,* 218; *Masses,* 218
Denning, Haley, 316–17. *See also* Safe Passage and *Recycled Lives.*
Devereux, Robert, 21–22.
Dickens, Charles, 93–94, 177
Dix, Dorothea Lynde, 98, 101–13, 115
Dix, Elijah, 99–101
Dix, John, 100
Dix, Joseph, 100–01
Dix, Mary, 101–13
Dixfield, 99–101
Dole, Daniel, 151
Dole, Sanford Ballard, 151
Dome, Zoltan, 188, 189
Dorothea Dix Award, 113
Dorothea Dix Psychiatric Center, 102, 113
Dow, Caroline, 215–16
Dow, Neal, 167, 170
Downing, Major Jack, 116
Drake, Francis, 21
Drew, John, 320
Dudley, Joseph, 42, 43, 44
Dunbar, David, 50–51, 52, 54, 55
Durden, Robert Franklin, 175, 178

Eames, Emma, 188, 189
Earp, Wyatt, 266
East Cambridge jail, 105, 106, 113
Eastman, Max, 218, 219
Ebon, Marshall Islands, 150, 151–52, 153
Edgermet, 42
Edison, Thomas Alva, 246
Edna St. Vincent Millay (Shafter), 225
Edward VIII, King, 257, 258
Elizabeth, 66
Elizabeth, Queen, 21–22, 294
Emerson, Mary Moody, 115

Eminent Mainers (Stover), 320
Emerson, Ralph Waldo, 60, 115, 129
England's Homage to Longfellow
   (Latham), 96
Enterprize, 70
Essex, 67
Essex, Earl of. *See* Devereux, Robert.
Europe's Morning After (Roberts), 206
Every Man a King (Long), 278
Eyman, Scott, 262: *Print the Legend,*
   262, 263, 266, 269, 270

Feeney, Barbara Curran, 261–62
Feeney, Francis "Frank." *See* Ford,
   Frank.
Feeney, John Martin "Jack," Jr. *See*
   Ford, John.
Feeney, John Martin, Sr., 261–62, 272
Fessenden, William Pitt, 82, 88, 89,
   162, 166, 167, 175, 177
Few Figs from Thistles, A (Millay),
   220–21, 222
Ficke, Arthur, 221, 223, 224
Five Kidnapped Indians (Molloy), 19,
   23
Flucker, Lucy, 58
Flucker, Thomas, 58, 59
Fonda, Henry, 269
Ford, Frank, 262, 263, 270
Ford, John, 260–73
Ford, Mary Smith, 265
Forsberg, Randall, 293
Fort Apache (movie), 270
Four Sons (movie), 266
Fox, William, 265. *See also* Twentieth
   Century Fox.
Francis, David, 239
Fuller, Walter D.: *Life and Times of*
   Cyrus H. K. Curtis, 208, 209

Galicich, Anne: *Samantha Smith: A*
   Journey for Real, 301
Gardiner, Sylvester, 100

Gattine, Melissa, 113
Genius in the Family, A (Maxim),
   246
Gift of God, 24
Gilbert, Humphrey, 21, 24
Gilbert, Ralegh, 24, 25
Gillars, Mildred, 276, 289–90
Gilmore, John Patrick, 183–84
Glackins, Ira, 186, 188
Gluskabe, xi, *xii,* 1–10, 13
Go-Getter, The (Kyne), 136
Goddard, Mary, 91, 92
Goethals, George Washington,
   237–38
Good Shepherd Center (Centro
   Bom Pastor), 308, 309
Good Will-Hinckley School, 277
Goodman, Giselle, 287
Goold, Walter, 200
Gorgas, William, 233–34
Gorges, Ferdinando, 21, 22, 24, 25,
   29–30; *Briefe Narration,* 24
Gosnold, Bartholomew, 15–16
Gottingen, Germany, 82, 88–89
Governor Dummer Academy, 64
Gower, Frederick Allan, 186–87
Grapes of Wrath (movie), 267
Great Northern Railway, 229, 230,
   231, 232
Great Portland Fire, 200
Greeley, Horace, 166, 170, 172, 178,
   201
Greene, George W., 87–88
Greylock, SS, 283
Griffin, Owen, 17, 18
Griffith, D. W., 263, 264
Guadalupe Hidalgo Treaty, 164–65
Gulston, Ralph, 51, 53
Gurko, Miriam: *Restless Spirit: The*
   Life of Edna St. Vincent Millay,
   220, 226

Haldeman, George, 299

Hale, Washington, 127
Hall, Donald, 243–44
Hamilton, John, 280
Hamlin, Cyrus, 111, 115, 145
Hamlin, Hannibal, 115, 166, 172
Harp-Weaver and Other Poems, The (Millay), 222
Harrison, William Henry, 164
Harte, Bret, 124
Hawkins, John, 21
Hawthorne, Nathaniel, 82, 129
Hayes, "Bully," 153–54, 155, 156
Hayes, Rutherford B., 168, 169
Haynes, Henry, 186
Heath, Anne, 103
Heckwelder's Account of the History, Manners, and Customs of the Indian Natives..., 83
Hell Bent (movie), 264
Henry, 35
Hepburn, Katherine, 269
"Hiawatha" (Longfellow), 82
Hill, James J., 229, 230–31, 232, 235, 238
Hinckley, George Walter, 277
Hinckley, N. H., 278
Hines, Glenn, 303
Hingston, E. P., 123, 124, 125, 126
History of Old Broad Bay and Waldo-boro (Stahl), 55
Holding, Franklin, 192
Holmantown. *See* Dixfield.
Hoquiam, Washington, 140
Horse Soldiers (movie), 272
How Green Was My Valley (movie), 268
Howe, Julia Ward, 94
Howe, Samuel Gridley, 94, 105, 107
Howells, Anne Molloy (*Five Kidnapped Indians*), 19, 23
Hull, Mary Spencer. *See* Phips, Mary Spencer.
I Wanted to Write (Roberts), 209

Informer, The (movie), 266, 270
Intrepid, 71, 72, 73, 74, 75, 76
Iron Horse, The (movie), 264, 265, 267
Irving, Washington, 86, 87, 90, 96
Isthmian Canal Commission, 233, 234

Jackson, Andrew, 116, 160, 163
James and Mary, 35
James I, King, 22
James II, King, 36–37
Japan Day by Day (Agassiz), 311–12
Jefferson, Thomas, 76
Jersey, 65
Jewell of Artes, The (Waymouth), 15
John Adams, 76
John Ford (Davis), 273
John Ford Festival, 271–72
Johnson, Bradish, 167
Joles, Thomas, 33
Journey to the Soviet Union (Smith), 301

Kamehameha III, King, 146
Kansas-Nebraska Act, 171
Karamanli, Yusuf, 70, 73, 77
Kennedy, John F., 163, 307
Kimball, Richard B., 202
King's Henchman, The (Millay and Taylor), 224, 227
Kirkland Lake, Ontario, 253–54
Klondike gold rush, 251–52
Know Nothings, 171, 289
Knox, Henry, 58, 66
Koischwitz, Max Otto, 290
Koluscap and His People (movie), 4
Konbit Sante, 313
Kosrae, Micronesia, ix, x, 144, 146, 147–57
Kotzschmar, Hermann, 195, 196, 197
Kotzschmar Organ, 197, 209
Kreymbort, Alfred, 219

Krishina, Natasha, 298
Kruse, K. V., 141
Ku Klux Klan, 289
Kurtze Beschreibung derer landschaft Massachusetts Bay in New England, 54
Kyne, Peter B., 135–36, 142, 206: *Cappy Ricks,* 135–36; *The Go-Getter,* 136

Lacey-Baker, Marjorie, 219
Ladies Home Journal, 202, 208, 209
Lady Awakens, The (Segal), ix, x
Laemmle, Carl, 264
Lafayette, General, 85
Laine, Linda Noe, 272
Lake Shore Mines, Ltd., 254
Lake, Thomas, 32, 33
Lane, James, 176
Lansing, Robert, 238
Latham, Edward Connery: *England's Homage to Longfellow,* 96
Lear, Tobias, 69
Leland, Charles G: *The Algonquin Legends of New England,* 3
Leland, Charles Godfrey, 119
Lenora, 155
Lepalik, Awane I "good King George," 146–47, 148–49
Lepalik, Nele, 149
Levasseur, Jamila Levy, 288
Levasseur, Patricia Gros, 287
Levasseur, Raymond Luc, 276, 284–89, 308
Leverett, John, 47
Life and Death of Sir Harry Oakes (Bocca), 252, 255, 257
Life and Times of Cyrus H. K. Curtis (Fuller), 208, 209
Life of Schiller (Thomas), 91
Life of Sir William Phips (Mather), 29, 33–34, 36, 39, 43, 44
Liliuokalani, Queen, 151, 191

Lime Street (TV series), 301, 302
Lincoln, Abraham, 111, 115, 116–17, 121–22, 173, 175, 176, 177, 200
Lively Lady, The (Roberts), 209
Long, Huey, 278; *Every Man a King,* 278
Longfellow, Elizabeth, 86, 89
Longfellow, Fanny Appleton, 92, 93, 95
Longfellow, Henry Wadsworth, 66, 69, 75, 80–97, 129, 164, 177; "Battle of Lovewell's Pond," 82; "Hiawatha," 82; "Morituri Salutamus," 95; "My Lost Youth," 95; *Outre Mer,* 90, 91; "Songo River," 95; *Tales of a Wayside Inn,* 90; "The Village Blacksmith," 266
Longfellow, Mary Potter, 91, 92
Longfellow, Stephen, Jr., 81, 82, 88
Longfellow, Stephen, Sr., 83, 85, 89
Longfellow: A Rediscovered Life (Calhoun), 89
Lorimer, George Horace, 203–04, 205–06, 209, 210
Louisbourg, Fort, 56, 57, 63
Lovejoy, Asa, 133, 134–35
Lowell, James Russell, 96
Lydia Bailey (Roberts), 210

machine gun, 245, 248–49
Madockawando, 38, 42–43, 47
Maine Association of Police Chiefs, 288–89
Maine Roots (Walker), 275
Maine–Rio Grande do Norte partnership, 307, 310–11
Man from Maine, A (Bok), 196, 207, 210
Man Who Shot Liberty Valance, The (movie), 270
Maneddo, 20, 22

Manning, Thomas, 288–89
Marias Pass, 230–31
Martin, Patricia Stone: *Samantha Smith: Young Ambassador,* 301
Mary and John, 24
Mary, Queen of Scots, 22
Mason, John, 30
Massachusetts Bay Colony, 31
Massasoit, 33, 83
Masses, 218
Mather, Cotton, 29, 37, 41–42; *Life of Sir William Phips,* 29, 33–34, 36, 39, 43, 44
Mather, Increase, 34, 37, 40, 41
Mavodones, Nick, 313
Maxim and Welch, 246
Maxim Gas Machine Company, 246
Maxim, Harriet Boston Stevens, 245
Maxim, Hiram Percy, 246–48; *A Genius in the Family: Sir Hiram Stevens Maxim Through a Small Son's Eyes,* 246
Maxim, Hiram Stevens, 242, 243, 244–49, 259
Maxim, Isaac Weston, 245
McCullough, David, 235, 236
McDonald, George, 192
McLeod, Frances, 141
Melba, Nellie, 189, 191
Menken, Adah Isaacs, 120–21, 124
Merriam, 65
Metacom, 33.
Michigone, 138
Milford, Nancy: *Savage Beauty: The Life of Edna St. Vincent Millay,* 217, 220, 221
Milholland, Inez, 219, 223
Millay, Cora Buzzelle, 214, 216, 219–20, 225
Millay, Edna St. Vincent, 212–27; *Aria de Capo.* 220; *The Buck in the Snow,* 225; *A Few Figs from Thistles,* 220–21, 222; *The Harp-Weaver and Other Poems,* 222; *The King's Henchman,* 224, 227; *The Princess Marries the Page,* 217, 220; "Ragged Island," 226; "Renascence," 215, 216
Millay, Henry Tolman, 214, 215
Millay, Norma, 218, 219, 227
Millinocket, SS, 282, 283
Missouri Compromise, 171
Monroe Doctrine, 177
Morey, David (*The Voyage of Archangell*), 19
"Morituri Salutamus" (Longfellow), 95
Morning Star, 153
Morrison, Marion. *See* Wayne, John.
Morse, Edward Sylvester, 311, 312, 320
Moulton, Earl, 277
Mowatt, Henry, 63–64
Mr. Roberts (movie), 270
Muscongus Patent, 47, 48, 49, 50, 99
My Darling Clementine (movie), 266
"My Lost Youth" (Longfellow), 95
Mytilene, Greece, 313

Natal, Rio Grande do Norte, Brazil, 306, 307–10
Native Americans (in Maine), 1–10, 13–26, 33, 38, 42–43, 64
Neptune, Arnie, 4
New York, 70
Newcomen Society, 208
Niagara Falls, Ontario, 255
Nicolar, Joseph, 2
"Nordica." *See* Norton, Lillian Bayard.
North Africa campaign, 68–70, 76, 77, 269
Norton, Amanda Allen, 182, 183, 184, 185, 186, 188

Norton, Edwin, 182, 185
Norton, Ephraim, 181–82
Norton, Lillian Bayard, 180–93, 198, 223
Norton, Wilhemina Kossuth, 182, 183
nuclear freeze, 293
Nuestra Señora de la Conceptión, 34, 35

O'Brien, George, 265
O'Fearna, Sean Aloysius. *See* Ford, John.
O'Hara, Maureen, 268, 279
O'Neill, John, 183
Oak Hall, 258–59
Oakes Garden Theater, 258
Oakes Park, 258
Oakes, Eunice MacIntyre, 255, 257
Oakes, Gertrude, 251, 252, 254, 258
Oakes, Harry, 249–59, 261
Oakes, Louis, 251, 252, 254, 258
Oakes, Nancy, 255, 257
Oakes, Colonel William, 250
Oakes, William Pitt, 250
Ohio Seven, 284, 287
Old Dominion Zeitung, 89
Oliver and Bangs, 237
Opunui, Daniel and Doreka, 147, 149
Order of the Immaculate Heart of Mary. *See* Sisters of the Good Shepherd.
Outre Mer (Longfellow), 90, 91

Paine, John Knowles, 196, 197
Paleo Indians, 1–2
Panama Canal, 232–38
Partners of the Americas, 307, 311
Peace through Interamerican Community Action (PICA), 314
Peninsula, The (Rich), 320–21
People's Ledger, 201

Pepperrell, Andrew, 56, 58
Pepperrell, William, 56, 57, 58, 59, 244
Perkins Institute for the Blind, 94
Pettigrove, Francis W., 133–34
Philadelphia, 71, 72, 75, 77
Philip, King. *See* Metacom.
Phillips, David Graham: *The Treason of the Senate,* 207
Phips, James, 30–31, 32
Phips, Mary Spencer, 32, 36, 42, 44
Phips, Spencer, 44, 47
Phips, William, 28–30, 32–44, 47, 49, 66. 244
Pickering, 67
Pidianske, 43
Pierce, Franklin, 109
Pike, Charlotte Grosvenor, 170
Pike, Elizabeth Ellicott "Lizzie," 173, 176, 177
Pike, Frederick A., 172
Pike, James Shepherd, 158–59, 169–79; *The Prostrate State,* 177–78
Pilgrims, 31, 83
Plymouth Company, 30
Plymouth, England, 21, 29
Polk, James K., 164, 165
Popham Colony, 23–24, 25, 30
Popham, George, 23–24, 25
Popham, John, 21, 22, 25
Port Royal, 38–39
Portland, Oregon, 133–34
Portland Project, 318
Portland Victory Garden Project, 288
Portland–Arkhangelsk partnership, 312, 316
Portland–Cap Haitien partnership, 313
Portland–Mytilene partnership, 313
Portland–Shinagawa-ku partnership, 312
Potter, Mary Storer. *See* Longfellow, Mary Potter.

Pownall, Thomas, 59, 63
Preble, Commodore Edward, 62,
    63–78, 81, 145, 154, 210
Preble, Edward Deering "Ned,"
    81–82, 83, 85, 88–89, 95
Preble, Jedidiah, 62, 154
Preble, Mary Deering, 67–68, 69, 78
Princess and the Page, The (Millay),
    217
Pring, Martin, 15, 22, 23
Print the Legend (Eyman), 262,
    263, 266, 269, 270
Prohibition, 140, 167, 170
Prostrate State, The (Pike), 177–78
Protector, 65
Pullen, John J., 115, 123
Punahou School, Oahu, 171
Puritans, 31–32

Quadratus, 139
Quiet Man, The (movie), 270, 271

Ragged Island, Maine, 226
"Ragged Island" (Millay), 226
Raleigh, Walter, 21, 22
Randolph, Edward, 37, 42
Rathbone, William, 104–05,
    108, 109
Ray, Isaac, 102
Recycled Lives (movie), 317. *See also*
    Denning, Haley, and Safe
    Passage.
Red Star North Bookstore, 296
Rehnquist, William, 169;
    *Centennial Crisis: The Disputed
    Election of 1876,* 169
Reid, John G., 33–34
"Renascence" (Millay), 215, 216
Restless Spirit (Gurko), 220, 226
Rich, Louise Dickinson: *The
    Peninsula,* 320–21
Roberts, Kenneth, 77–78, 81, 195,
    203–06, 209–10, 239; *Europe's*

Morning After, 206; *I Wanted to
    Write,* 209; *The Lively Lady,* 209;
    Lydia Bailey, 210; *Why Europe
    Leaves Home,* 206
Robinson, Edwin Arlington, 224
Rockwell, Doc, 290, 291
Rockwell, George Lincoln, 276
Rockwell, Norman, 207, 290–91
Rogers, Francis, 35–36
Romany Marie's Café, 221
Roosevelt, Franklin Delano, 275, 278,
    283, 290
Roosevelt, Theodore, 191, 232, 233,
    234, 235, 236–37
Root, Elihu, 238, 239
Rose of Algiers, 34–35
Rosier, James, 14–15, 17–20; *A True
    Relation,* 14
Rotary, 309, 310
Roy, Sister Priscille, 306–10, 321
Rusk, Dean, 300
Russian Railway Service Corps, 239,
    240

Safe Passage, 316–17. *See also* Denn-
    ing, Haley, and *Recycled Lives.*
Salem, Massachusetts, 41–42
Salk, Lee, 301
Samantha Smith (Galicich), 301
Samantha Smith (Martin), 301
Sangerville, Maine, 243–45, 248, 249,
    250, 257, 259, 261
Sasanoa, 24
Sassacomoit, 21, 22, 23
Saturday Evening Post, 202, 203, 204,
    206, 207, 209–10
Savage Beauty (Milford), 217, 220,
    221
SCAR, 296
Schuyler, Spencer D., 246
Schwartz, Robert, 288, 289
Scott, Dred, 171
Seafarers International Union, 280–81

Searchers, The (movie), 270
Sebanoa, 24–25
Seeds of Peace Camp, 303–04,
    318–19
Segal, Harvey Gordon: *The Lady
    Awakens,* ix, x
Seitz, Don C., 118
Selznick, David O., 267
Semmes, Ralph, 174–75, 176
Seward, William, 173, 175, 176, 177
Shafter, Toby: *Edna St. Vincent Millay:
    America's Best Loved Poet,* 225
Shariki, Japan, 314
Sherman, William Tecumseh, 123
Shinagawa-ku, Tokyo, 311, 312
Shirley, William, 53, 54, 56, 59
Shonts, Theodore, 234, 236, 237
Shore Acres State Park, 135, 142
Sickles, Daniel, 177
Sigrah, Aaron, 156
Sigrah, John, 156
Sigrah, Rensley, 156
Simmons, E. Romayne, 193
Simpson Lumber Company, 135
Simpson, Andrew, 137
Simpson, Asa Meade, 132, 135–42,
    145, 276
Simpson, Elbridge Gerry, 139
Simpson, Isaiah Hayes, 136–37
Simpson, Lewis Pennell, 136–37
Simpson, Louis Jerome, 135, 139,
    140–41, 142
Simpson, Robert Wyer "Big Bob,"
    139–40
Simpson, Robert Wyer, 137
Simpson, Sophia Smith, 138
Simpson, Thomas, Jr., 136
Simpson, Thomas, Sr., 136
Simpson, Wallis, 257
Simpson, William R. "Little Bob,"
    139
Simpsons of Shore Acres, The
    (Beckham), 135, 141

Sinatra, Frank, 269
Sinlaku, 148
sister cities, 307, 310, 311, 312, 313,
    314, 315, 316
Sisters of the Good Shepherd, 307,
    308
Skicoweros, 20, 23, 24
Skilling, Fred, 156
Skilling, Harry H., 154
Skilling, Harry N., x, 154–56
Skilling, Jenny, 154
Skilling, Samuel, Jr., 154
Slavery (Channing), 103
slavery, 60, 74, 94, 103–04, 161,
    170–71, 175–76, 177–78
Smith, Arthur, 293, 297, 299–300,
    302
Smith, James W., 151
Smith, Jane, 294, 299–300, 304
Smith, Samantha Reed, 292–304;
    Journey to the Soviet Union, 301
Smith, Samuel E., 160
Smith, Seba, 116
Smith, Sophia Dwight. *See* Simpson,
    Sophia Smith.
Sneed, Doug, 288
Snow, Benjamin Galen, ix, x, 145,
    146–54, 157
Snow, Caroline "Carrie," 150, 153
Snow, Frederick Galen, 153
Snow, Lydia Vose Buck, 145,
    146–47, 150, 152, 153
Socialist Workers Party, 282, 283, 287
Soctomah, Donald, 26
Somers, Richard, 74
"Songo River" (Longfellow), 95
Soul Herder, The (movie), 264
Southern Student Organizing
    Committee, 285
Sparhawk, Nathaniel, 56
Spear, Albert, 240
Spencer, Roger, 32
Spokane, Portland, and Seattle

Railway, 238
Squanto, 21, 22, 25
St. John, New Brunswick, 313–14
Stagecoach (movie), 267
Stahl, Jasper Jacob: *History of Old Broad Bay and Waldoboro,* 55
Stanford, Dennis, 4
Stanton, Edwin, 112, 121, 122
Steepletop, 223, 225, 226, 227
Stevens, Harriet T. O'Brien, 232, 238
Stevens, John Frank, 228–41
Stevens, John L., 172
Stover, Arthur Douglas (Doug): *Eminent Mainers,* 320
Stowe, Calvin, 82
Stowe, Harriet Beecher, 82; *Uncle Tom's Cabin,* 82
Stowell, Peter, 100, 101
Straight Shooting (movie), 264
Sulaimen, Moulay, 67
Suslovic, Ed, 312
Sumner, Charles, 105
Sumter, 174, 175
Sunny Side of Diplomatic Life, The (de Hegemann-Lindencrone), 188–89
Surcouf, 67
Sustainable Harvest, 317–18

Taft, William Howard, 190, 233, 234, 237
Tahanedo, 20, 23, 24, 29
Tales of a Wayside Inn (Longfellow), 90
Tasman, 192
Taylor, Deems, 224; *The King's Henchman,* 224
Taylor, Zachary, 167
They Were Expendable (movie), 270
Thursday Island, 192
Ticknor, George, 91
Tilden, Samuel, 168

Tisquantum. *See* Squanto.
Trans-Siberian Railroad, 239
Treason of the Senate, The (Phillips), 207
Trenton Asylum, 107, 112
Tribune and Farmer, 202
Tripoli. *See* North Africa campaign.
Trotsky, Leon, 280, 282, 283
Trotskyists, 280
True Relation, A (Rosier), 14, 19
Tuke, Daniel Hack, 110
Tunisia. *See* North Africa campaign.
Twain, Mark, 124–25, 126, 129–30, 296, 300
Twentieth Century Fox, 265
Tyng, William, 65

Uncle Tom's Cabin (Stowe), 82
Uncommon Life of Louis Jerome Simpson, The (Wagner), 135, 137. 138
Universal Film Company, 263, 264, 265
USM Art Gallery, 288

Van Buren, Martin, 164
Vanity Fair, 119, 220, 221
Vassar College, 215, 216–17
Vickers, Albert, 249
Vickers, Son and Maxim, Ltd., 249
Vietnam Veterans Against War, 296
Virginia, 24
Voyage of Archangell, The (Morey), 19

Wadsworth, Henry, 68–69, 70, 73, 74–75, 77–78, 81, 210
Wadsworth, Peleg, 65, 68, 73, 81
Wagner, Cosima Liszt, 188
Wagner, Richard and Judith: *The Uncommon Life of Louis Jerome Simpson,* 135, 137, 138
Wagner, Robert, 300, 301, 302
Waldenses, 48

Waldman, Pat, 243
Waldo, Cornelius, 48, 49, 53, 55
Waldo, Hannah, 56, 58
Waldo, Jonathan, 48, 49
Waldo, Peter, 48
Waldo, Ralph Gulston, 51, 60
Waldo, Samuel, 46, 47, 48–50, 51,
    52–60, 63, 99
Waldo, Samuel, Jr., 57, 58
Waldoboro, Maine, 55, 60
Walker, Cephas, 276–77, 278–79
Walker, Josephine Williamson, 277
Walker, Malcolm Marcellus. *See*
    Walker, Mark.
Walker, Mark, 274, 275, 276–82,
    287; *Maine Roots: Growing Up
    Poor in the Kennebec Valley,* 275;
    Working for Uptopia, 1937–1953,
    275, 281
Walker, Nina Tucker, 282
Walker, Richard, 275
Walker, Solomon, 275
Wallace, John F., 232, 233
Ward, Artemas, 116
Ward, Artemus, 114–30, 133, 175;
    Artemus Ward, His Book, 121,
    122
Warren, John, 320
Washington, George, 66, 69, 76, 118
Waterford, Maine, 115–16, 127, 129
Watterson, Henry, 128–29
Waymouth, George, 12–20, 22; *The
    Jewell of Artes,* 15
Wayne, John, 266, 267, 269, 270
Welles, Orson, 267
West Indies, 35–36

Westbourne, Bahamas, 256
Westbrook, Thomas, 51, 53, 154
"White Indians," 100
White, John, 31, 32
Whittredge, Eugene, 254
Why Europe Leaves Home (Roberts),
    206
Williamson, Joseph, 48–49
Willows, The, Bar Harbor, 255, 258
Wilson, Edmund, 214, 220, 224
Wilson, Woodrow, 239
Winthrop, 65
witchcraft trials, 41–42
Woodbury Campus Center (USM),
    288, 289
Woolwich, Maine, 31, 32, 38
Working for Utopia (Walker), 275,
    281
Wright, William, 253–54
Wyancote, Pennsylvania, 208, 209
Wyeth, Andrew, 14
Wyeth, Betsy, 14
Wyeth, Jamie, 14
Wyeth, N. C. 14

Yates, Elizabeth Upham, 320
Young America, 200
Young Communist League, 279, 280
Young Mr. Lincoln (movie), 269
Young, George Washington, 190,
    191

Zanuck, Darryl F., 269
Zimbalist, Efrem , Jr., 198
Zorach, William, 219
Zuberbuhler, Sebastian, 54–55, 56